CHRISTOLOGY AT THE CROSSROADS

ORBIS BOOKS
Maryknoll, New York 10545

CHRISTOLOGY AT THE CROSSROADS

A Latin American Approach

JON SOBRINO, S.J.

TRANSLATED BY JOHN DRURY

The Catholic Foreign Mission Society of America (Maryknoll) recruits and trains people for overseas missionary service. Through Orbis Books Maryknoll aims to foster the international dialogue which is essential to mission. The books published, however, reflect the opinions of their authors and are not meant to represent the official position of the Society.

Special thanks are due to Sister Mary Eucharista Coupe, M.M., for her preparation of the Index to this volume.

Second Printing, May, 1978
Third Printing, July, 1979
Fourth Printing, September, 1980

First published in 1976 as *Cristología desde américa latina (esbozo a partir del seguimiento del Jesús histórico)* by Centro de Reflexión Teológica, Río Hondo 1, México 20, D.F.

Library of Congress Cataloging in Publication Data

Sobrino, Jon.
    Christology at the crossroads.

    Translation of Cristología desde América Latina.
    Includes index.
    1. Jesus Christ—Person and offices.
2. Liberation theology. I. Title.
BT202.S6213   232   77-25025
ISBN 0-88344-076-8 pbk.

For
Father Rutilio Grande, S.J.,
and
Father Alfonso Navarro,
martyrs for the kingdom of God
in El Salvador

Imprimatur:

Francisco Estrada, S.J.
Provincial de la viceprovincia centroamericana
April 1976

Imprimatur:

(English translation)
Cesar Jerez, S.J.
Provincial, Society of Jesus
Central America and Panama
April 1978

CONTENTS

Preface to the Spanish Edition   xi

Preface to the English Edition   xv

1. *The Historical Jesus: The Starting Point for Christology*   1

   The Starting Point for Understanding Christ   2
   The Historical Jesus and Liberation Theology   9

2. *The Approach to Christology: Preliminary Remarks*   17

   The Christology of Karl Rahner   22
   The Christology of Wolfhart Pannenberg   25
   The Christology of Jürgen Moltmann   28
   Latin American Christology   33

3. *Jesus in the Service of God's Kingdom*   41

   Import of the Term "Kingdom of God"   42
   The Kingdom of God as Grace   46
   The Reign of God and Sin   50
   Conversion and the Kingdom of God   55
   Excursus I: On the Eschatological Nature of the Kingdom   61
   Excursus II: Reformulating the Problem of Jesus' Own
        Consciousness   67
      Jesus' Consciousness vis-à-vis the Kingdom of God   67
      Jesus' Consciousness vis-à-vis the Father   70

4. *The Faith of Jesus: Its Relevance for Christology and Following
       Jesus*   79

   Preliminary Observations   80
   Jesus' Faith and Christology   87
      The Term "Faith of Jesus" in the New Testament   87
      The History of Jesus' Faith   91
      The Human Condition of Jesus' Faith   95
      The Faith of Jesus and Systematic Christology   103

Jesus' Faith and Fundamental Moral Theology   108
The Meaning of "Fundamental Christian Morality"   108
The Following of Jesus as the Fundamental Moral
    Exigency   115
The Features of Discipleship and Their Consequences for
    Morality   118
The Limits of Fundamental Moral Theology in Terms of the
    History of Jesus Himself   131
The Import of Jesus for Fundamental Christian Morality: A
    Summary   136

5. *The Prayer of Jesus*   146

Jesus' Criticism of Contemporary Prayer   146
The Prayer of Jesus Himself   151
The God of Jesus as the Basis of His Prayer   158

6. *The Death of Jesus and Liberation in History*   179

The Post-Resurrection View of Jesus' Death   182
Jesus' Cross as the Historical Consequence of His Life   201
The Presence of God on Jesus' Cross   217

7. *The Resurrection of Jesus: Hermeneutic Problem*   236

What May I Hope For?   241
    The Horizon of Hope in the New Testament   241
    Systematic Consequences   244
What Can I Know?   246
    A Hermeneutics for Grasping the Historical as Such   246
    Prejudices Surrounding Historicity and the Concept of
        History   248
    History in Terms of Promise and Mission   251
What Should I Do?   253
Conclusion   256

8. *The Resurrection of Jesus: Theological Problem*   259

The Theological Meaning of Jesus' Resurrection   260
The Soteriological Meaning of Jesus' Resurrection   262
The Christological Meaning of Jesus' Resurrection   264

9. *The Historical Jesus and the Christ of Faith: The Tension Between Faith and Religion*   273

The Tension Between Jesus of Nazareth and the Spirit of the
Risen Lord   278
The Tension Between Faith and an Explicative, Metaphysical
Theology   286
The Tension Between Prophetic Political Theology and
Power-Centered Political Theology   292
The Tension Between Cultic Worship and Concrete
Discipleship   299
Conclusion   305

10. *The Christological Dogmas*   311

Preliminary Remarks on the Notion of "Dogma"   312
Historical Development of the Notion of "Dogma"   312
The Problem of the "Interpretation" of Dogma   316
The Positive and Necessary Significance of Dogma   321
The Christological Dogmas   326
The Basic Christological Dogmas   327
Criticism of the "Formulation" of These Dogmas   328
The Dogma of Chalcedon as a Doxological Statement About
Christ   332
Jesus' Personal Oneness with God   335
Jesus as the Way to the Father   338
The Verification of the Truth of Chalcedon's Dogmatic
Formula   340

11. *Theses for a Historical Christology*   346

1. Presuppositions for Christology   346
2. The Starting Point of Christology   351
3. Jesus and the Kingdom of God   353
4. Faith and Discipleship Based on the Historical Jesus   359
5. The Consciousness of Jesus   362
6. The External Conflicts of Jesus   367
7. The Death of Jesus   370
8. The Resurrection of Jesus   374

9. The Tension Between the Historical Jesus and the Christ of
   Faith in Christian Living   381
10. The Dogmatic Formulations of Christology   384
11. General Features of the Christian Life from the Standpoint
   of Christology   388

Appendix: The Christ of the Ignatian Exercises   396

The Explicit and Implicit Theology of the Exercises   397
A Christology of the Historical Jesus   400
   The Life of Jesus   400
   Concrete Features of the Historical Jesus in the Spiritual
      Exercises   402
The Conception of "God" in the Exercises   412
   A Different Socio-Cultural Conception   413
   A Different Theological Conception of God   414
   The Significance of the Initial Meditation on God   416
   The Idea of God in the Ignatian Exercises   417
Conclusions   422

Index   425

Preface to the Spanish Edition

The pervasive and persistent complaint that liberation theology has continued to lack any Christology was first met by
Boff's important book entitled *Jesus Cristo Libertador*
(Petrópolis, Brazil: Vozes, 1972). His book opened the way for
a more systematic historical reading of Jesus Christ from the
horizon of Latin America. It faced up to the uneasiness which
had already been voiced by such major theologians of liberation as Comblin, Gutiérrez, Vidales, Assmann, and Miranda.
They had suggested the first steps toward such a historical
reading, spelling out in primarily negative terms the route to
be followed in elaborating a Latin American Christology.

The findings of these theologians, however, were not the
result of their own private musings. They expressed the experience of various groups of committed Christians. Contact
with populist and university movements enabled them to see
the inoperativeness of traditional Christologies. The classic
texts had been written for the most part to meet the needs of
theological students in Europe. Not only were they becoming
more and more irrelevant for the praxis of Christians; they
were actually impeding the workings of a faith truly involved
in the history of our peoples.

It was among groups of committed Christians that we saw
the dawning of a concrete theology related to daily life and
based on both an analysis of various situations and the light of
the gospel message. This in turn led to pastoral implementa-
tion. As time went on, it became evident that this new practice
of theology needed some frame of reference, some theoretical
scheme in which to situate pastoral praxis and the historical
project it proposed to encourage. This limit-situation, a concrete theology without new grounding standards, was what
allowed for the theological advance on our continent. Chris-

tian praxis now sought to focus on that which had provided it with its initial impetus and enabled it to delineate a motivating utopia. Apart from the more systematic and elaborate work of Gustavo Gutiérrez on the fundamentals, these Christian groups had only the rough outlines of scattered theological essays in Latin America or the more advanced works of contemporary European theologians to work with. The latter, in particular, focused on issues and problems in a way that was wholly inadequate in terms of our historical horizon and situation.

It is generally recognized that the most serious steps taken by Latin American theology so far have been in the area of theological methodology. The two most important conventions so far, in El Escorial (1973) and Mexico City (1975), sought to gather up the fruits of the new movement; and both concentrated on the problem of methodology. This being the case, many have already called for some qualitative advance as the only way to avoid the impasse that now threatens liberation theology. Such an advance cannot stay on the level of methodology; it must take place on the level of strictly theological content having to do with key affirmations of the Christian faith.

So now we are witnessing the first steps of a foundational theology in Latin America. Recognizing the questions and anxieties of the earlier situational theology, it now seeks to go beyond this and structure Christian reality in a more systematic way. There is now room for a theoretical frame of reference grounded in the very roots of Christianity; but the elaboration of that frame of reference will take place from a rather precise and limited horizon, praxis, and utopia.

The work of Jon Sobrino presented here is akin to that of Boff, but it is of a distinctive and penetrating sort. It specifically seeks to contribute to a new theoretical frame of reference. Its focus is Christology, a Christology that is historically positioned and constructed from the Latin American situation of oppression, injustice, and exploitation. It is rooted in the historical Jesus and in the history of a people's pain and sorrow. By virtue of that twofold rootedness, this systematic study is tremendously radical. The radicalism does not lie in the presuppositions of the author himself. It lies in his sensitivity as a man of faith who keeps our desperate Latin American situation before his eyes all the time.

How can we possibly know Jesus of Nazareth, whom the church recognized as the Son of God? It is not a matter of personal whim at all. We do not get to know him personally by reading the witnesses to his words and deeds, or hearing sermons, or taking solid courses. The only way to get to know Jesus is to follow after him in one's own real life; to try to identify oneself with his own historical concerns; and to try to fashion his kingdom in our midst. In other words, only through Christian praxis is it possible for us to draw close to Jesus. Following Jesus is the precondition for knowing Jesus.

This presupposition and some of the core ideas of the author will cause a rupture for many readers, a break with their conceptions, ideas, and practices. A new style of life in a moralizing vein will not suffice, nor will a clear grasp and intellectual understanding of what is said here. What is necessary is a decision to follow Jesus Christ and a praxis based on that following, together with a passionate concern for the kingdom and a resultant yearning to experience the gratuitous historical mystery of Jesus and make our own life an inescapable part of it. It is that mystery that will break down our preconceptions, just as it did those of his contemporaries, and give impetus to a historical process of liberation for the oppressed peoples of the world.

This book is the product of a course in Christology which was given at the San Salvador Center for Theological Reflection in El Salvador (1975). That is why some of the chapters bear a resemblance to class outlines and class notes. The Center for Theological Reflection in Mexico City was glad to take on the task of publication. It fully realizes that this work is particularly significant in the growing maturation of Latin American theological thought.

Several of the chapters were published previously as articles in other sources. Chapter 4 was published in *Christus* (Mexico City, March 1976, no. 484, pp. 15–40). Chapter 6 was published in *Estudios Centroamericanos* (San Salvador, August-September 1975, no. 322–23, pp. 483–512; abbreviated *ECA*). Chapter 11 was published in the same issue of *ECA* (pp. 457–82). Chapter 9 was published in *ECA* (April 1975, no. 318, pp. 201–224) and in *Christus* (December 1975, no. 481, pp. 6–18). The Appendix appeared in *Christus* (July 1975, no. 476, pp. 44–54).

Centro de Reflexion Teologica

Preface to the English Edition

In presenting this book to English-speaking readers, I should like to offer a few observations that may help them to understand its background and its point of view. This particular Christology was written against the backdrop of Latin America. Its direct aim is to give Latin Americans a better understanding of Christ and to point up his historical relevancy for our continent. It is a Christology at the crossroads. Behind it lies a long tradition, part of which it proposes to reject. Before it lies a new and authentically Latin American Christology which does not yet exist, which yet remains to be formulated, and toward which this book points.

Let me begin by pointing out some of the things that we wish to reject. Here in Latin America we can read many of the old, classic treatments of Christology as well as more current ones. When we do, and when we notice their practical repercussions on the life and praxis of Christians, we cannot help but formulate certain suspicions. Basically those suspicions come down to this: For some reason it has been possible for Christians, in the name of Christ, to ignore or even contradict fundamental principles and values that were preached and acted upon by Jesus of Nazareth.

Thus we are led to analyze how it has been possible for christological reflection itself to obscure the figure of Jesus and to examine the dire consequences of such christological reflection. This gives rise to a threefold suspicion. First of all, quite frequently Christ has been reduced to a sublime abstraction. Insofar as he is sublime, he always is seen as something positive. But insofar as he is an abstraction, it is possible to ignore or deny Christ's truth. The bad feature of this abstractness is seen in practice, where a separation is introduced between the total or whole Christ on the one hand and the concrete history of Jesus on the other. This opens the way for the theoretical possibility of an alienating comprehension of Christ. The practical consequences are seen in the existence of all sorts of spiritualism and pentecostalism that invoke the Spirit of Christ but do not look to the concrete Spirit of Jesus for their real-life verification. Here we find the precious alibi used by many to hide and maintain the stirrings of a bad conscience. They keep appealing to some vague spirit that is not the Spirit that served as the driving force behind the concrete history of Jesus.

We cannot get beyond that abstraction by working with some conception of Christ as Love or Christ as Power; for in that case we simply replace the abstraction with formal categories. Considering Christ as Love, for example, Christians maintain an apparent neutrality vis-à-vis the flagrant inequities in our society. Such neutrality is wholly contrary to the partiality that Jesus displayed in favor of the oppressed. By the same token, the notion of Christ as Power has justified the sacralization of power in the political and economic realms, even giving rise to secularized versions of the same idea. So we have the abstract Christ, the impartial Christ, and the power-wielding Christ. These are the religious symbols that those in power need. These are the symbols that they have used, wittingly or unwittingly, to maintain the Latin American continent in its present state.

Suspicion leads to a second observation. This has to do with the affirmation that Christ is the embodiment of universal reconciliation. The statement is true in itself, but it is not given its dialectical thrust. It is an eschatological truth that some seek to pass off as a historical truth pure and simple. Thus they present a pacifist Jesus who does not engage in prophetic denunciations, a Jesus who pronounces blessings but who does not pronounce maledictions, and a Jesus who loves all human beings but who is not clearly partial toward the poor and the oppressed. Even soteriology, as normally employed, has fostered this particular kind of Christology. It affirms that Jesus died on behalf of all people in order to free them from their sins; it tends to ignore the fact that Jesus died as a direct result of historical sins. That still allows the church to preach something about sin, of course. But in a subtle way it prevents the church from uttering its most profound word about sin and its outright condemnation of it.

Sin is that which brought death to the Son of God. Today too, then, sin is that which brings death to the children of God, to human beings; it may be sudden, violent death, or it may be the slow, unremitting death caused by unjust structures. This leads us to a different view of the insistent emphasis on Christ as the embodiment of universal reconciliation, which is ingenuously preached by some and defended by others out of self-interest. Such an emphasis is nothing else but an attempt to exempt Jesus from the conflict-ridden toils of history, to use Christianity as a support for some sort of ideology espousing peace and order and as a weapon against any kind of conflict of subversion. It is an attempt to keep Christians strangers to the sinfulness and conflictual nature of history. When Christians do get involved in the conflicts of history, they can simply be accused of being subversives and phony Christians.

There is room for suspicion in another area as well. Here it has to do with the tendency to absolutize Christ while, once again, neglecting the dialectical side of the matter. This statement may sound radically new and rather shocking to many Christians. In their consciousness, at least on the superficial level, it may seem quite obvious that Christ *is* absolute for the Christian. But the logical and, even more important, the historical consequences of this belief do render it suspect. If Christ is in fact an absolute from every point of view, then we have the theoretical justification we need for any sort of personalist or individualist reduction of the Christian faith. By that I mean the view which sees contact with the "Thou" of Christ as the ultimate and correct correlative for the "I" of the individual Christian. That view also enables Christian faith to justify everything bad or wrong-headed in various strains of popular religiosity. This topic is obviously a complicated one which goes beyond the limits of this Preface and this book.

Here I should simply like to point out that if Christ is the ultimate or the divine pure and simple, then he is functioning as someone who satisfies and fulfills the needs and wants of the oppressed masses on the ideological level while masking their wants and needs on the level of real life. Total absolutization of Christ also introjects a historical conception into the consciousness of Christians. If Christians already possess the absolute, it is not surprising that their interest in the non-absolutes of history would diminish. Thus repeated stress on the importance of history would seem to be a mere matter of words, maintained by a sheer act of will.

In such a context recalling the essential relationality of Christ is not simply a theoretical question to be debated and settled in dogmatic or exegetical terms. If we recall that in the Gospels Jesus did not preach about himself, that the kingdom of God was his pole of reference, and that even after the resurrection the Son is related to the Father who is not yet all in all (1 Cor. 15:28), then we realize that our history has absolute importance and that it is only through history that we can envision and arrive at the absolute. The most obvious practical consequences of this realization are bound up with our essential obligation to seek out, here and now, those historical mediations that most clearly seem to point out the way to what is authentically absolute.

Our situation in Latin America, then, may well be somewhat different from that in the developed world when it comes to applying the "eschatological reservation" to concrete mediations of the kingdom of God. In developed countries the eschatological reservation, grounded on the absoluteness of Christ, may serve to relativize and reduce the importance of any concrete mediation of the kingdom of God. In Latin America the eschatological reservation makes sense only insofar as we undertake the task of seeking out concrete mediations of the kingdom. Of course we must apply the eschatological reservation to them, insisting that they are not the last word. But at the very least we must find concrete mediations that are decent enough to allow for the application of that reservation. As it stands now in most Latin American countries, asserting that the fullness of the kingdom has not yet arrived here is not the problem; that is all too obvious. What we must do now is assert that our situation is the formal *negation* of the fullness of the kingdom, that we must therefore work to create something that resembles it at least a little.

At bottom the concern to maintain the absoluteness of Christ is bound up with a concern to maintain the absoluteness of the system that now prevails in our Latin American countries. Those who hold economic and political power do not want to see Christians affirming the essential relationship of Jesus to the kingdom of God. They would prefer to maintain the seemingly orthodox affirmation of Christ's absoluteness so that the supposed absoluteness of the prevailing capitalist system might not be called into question. They want to see absolute religious symbols that command respect in and of themselves, even though they may be tangential or even contrary to history. Why? Because such symbols will provide a religious justification for such economic and political symbols as the state, democracy, and capitalism. In this way the latter may share in some of the reputed absoluteness of the former.

These, then, are some of the basic suspicions we have about the traditional way of doing Christology. In theory, at least, the same suspicions might be evoked in other places besides Latin America, and to some extent they have been. To this theoretical side our present situation in Latin America adds the weight of clear-cut evidence and the urgent necessity of engaging in some other sort of Christological reflection. At the very least it should get beyond some of the dangers pointed out above and suggest the proper road to take.

It is against that backdrop that the reader should approach this book. In the first two chapters I attempt to consider certain hermeneutic presuppositions that will move us beyond the aforementioned problems toward a sound Christology for Latin America. In the remaining chapters I attempt to describe the concrete direction that Christology should take. Strictly speaking, there is nothing completely new in these chapters. For one thing, much of the conceptual backdrop is drawn from current European Christologies. Moreover, there is a burgeoning interest in Christology in Latin American theology, and this book attempts to follow along the same line. What may strike the reader as novel is the way in which the various data about Jesus are structured, the stress placed on certain aspects rather than others, and the basic intention to give a new direction to Christology.

Here I should like to spell out the basic intention that has guided the elaboration of this book, for that may help people to read and criticize it more fruitfully. The Christology presented in this book is meant to be ecclesial, historical, and trinitarian.

First of all, it is meant to be an ecclesial Christology in the deepest and strictest sense of the term. In the New Testament itself we find not one but several different Christologies. That points up the relationship that has existed between Christology and ecclesiology from the very start. Two points are worth noting in that connection. On the one hand the various Christian communities took over the reality of Christ in different ways and forms; on the other hand they all go back to Jesus to explain themselves, even though they may have adopted somewhat different Christologies. In my opinion it is in this privileged witness of the New Testament that we find the paradigm for the ecclesial sense of Christology. While that sense goes hand in hand with the church's dogmatic pronouncements about Christ, it cannot be reduced or restricted to those pronouncements. It is, on the one hand, the way Christ is conceived on the basis of the concrete life and reality of a given community, and, on the other hand, the meaning of a given community's life and activity as seen from the standpoint of Christ.

My Christology seeks to be ecclesial. First of all, it is ecclesial in that it reflects the life and praxis of many ecclesial communities in Latin America; as a Christology, it also hopes to foster their life and praxis and to give them meaningfulness. To put it concretely, it seeks to provide the christological underpinnings for all that Latin American theology of liberation has to say about the nature of ecclesial theory and activity.

Needless to say, I am not ruling out ecclesial Christology in a second sense, i.e., Christology based on the conciliar and papal magisterium of the church. However, I do view this as a second stage in the ecclesial nature of Christology. To me the first stage in the hermeneutic circle seems more important. We must first reconsider the relationship between our conception of Christology and Christian ecclesial praxis at a given concrete moment in history. In my opinion the existence of a *dogmatic* ecclesial Christology does not nullify or render superfluous the other kind of ecclesial Christology. Even *after* the church has formulated dogmatic statements about Christ, Christian communities are not excused from the task that the first Christian communities had to undertake. They, too, must contemplate and think about Christ in terms of their own situation and praxis. As doxological and limit-statements, dogmas guarantee the truth *about* Christ. But if Christian individuals and Christian communities are to have *real first-hand knowledge of Christ*, if they are to incorporate the real truth of Christ, as formulated in dogma, into their own lives, then they simply must reconsider Christ from the standpoint of their own situation and activity.

Christology offers statements specifically about Christ, not about any object or person whatsoever. For that very reason it must have a history of its own, and it cannot be frozen at one point in that history. To say that Christ ceases to unleash a Christian reality and a Christian history is formally to deny that he is Christ. And if he does continually unleash a new and novel Christian history, then it is absolutely necessary to integrate that new history into our reflection about Christ.

Second, this Christology is meant to be a historical Christology. Here I do not simply mean that it is worked out on the basis of present-day history, as I just explained. I mean that we must be historical in the very process of reflecting on Christ himself and analyzing the content of Christology. This historicity will appear on different levels. It will appear first in the very logic of our reflection on Christ. If the *end* of Christology is to profess that Jesus is the Christ, its *starting point* is the affirmation that this Christ is the Jesus of history. This has an important implication for the logic of christological reflection. It cannot mean reflecting directly on christological dogmas; it must entail going back over the route that allowed for the formulation of those dogmas. Thus the logical procedure of

Christology is nothing else but the proper chronological procedure. This explains the emphasis here on the historical Jesus. Fully aware of the exegetical difficulties involved in trying to go back to that Jesus, I would offer the basic proposition that the content of our profession of Christ as the eternal Son of God must derive from the content of Jesus' own history and destiny—or, at the very least, from the nucleus of that history and destiny that can be discovered in the various New Testament traditions about him. There can be no Christology of Christ apart from the history of Jesus of Nazareth.

The historicity of Christology also appears in the use of historical categories to comprehend Jesus' history. Concretely this means that we will give preference to the praxis of Jesus over his own teaching and over the teaching that the New Testament theologians elaborated concerning his praxis. Thus the New Testament will be viewed primarily as *history* and only secondarily as *doctrine* concerning the real nature of that history. It also means that much importance will be placed on the historical categories of sin and conflict. The history of Jesus will be viewed in terms of conflict rather than in idealistic terms. We shall be studying the person of Jesus, whose awareness did not grow mechanically but in connection with his own real-life praxis and the conflicts it evoked. It also means that we shall stress that there was a process of evolution going on in Jesus himself, not only on the level of normal human development but also on the theological level of his relationship with the Father. Thus we shall be conceiving the historical Jesus as the history of Jesus, and the Son as the history of his filiation.

Finally, the historicity of this christological reflection is apparent in our stress on the relational nature of Jesus. Formally speaking, his relational nature is seen in the fact that he himself is not the central focus of his preaching or his activity. The central focus is the coming kingdom of God, Jesus' unreserved confidence in the Father, and his work for the realization of the kingdom. Now if that is true, and if in fact that kingdom has not yet arrived, then clearly Christology cannot be used to tie ourselves down to the past or cling to it; christological reflection must be oriented toward the future of God and his kingdom. We cannot turn Christ into an "origin myth" of any sort, for he continues to unleash history here and now and move it toward the future. To put it another way, Jesus' past can be recovered in the present only if it pushes us toward the future. The concrete relationship of Jesus to the coming kingdom of God imposes an obligation on all christological reflection. In the name of Jesus himself, it can and must be oriented toward the future of history if our profession of faith in Christ here and now is to be meaningful.

Third, this Christology is meant to be a trinitarian Christology. At first this statement might seem strange. To mention the Trinity would seem to plunge us into the most sophisticated and least useful of theological themes, to scale the heights of abstract speculation that I so vigorously denounced at the outset. It is my belief, however, that Latin American theology of liberation is the very theology that is reinstating trinitarian reflection as a serious theological theme. The reason is not that this theology is speculating *about* the Trinity. It is that theologizing itself is in fact a trinitarian process, even though the term "Trinity" may not appear in its statements.

My point is that liberation theology poses the hermeneutic circle in trinitarian terms, and that is precisely how I should like to present it in Christology. It is not that I am going to analyze the statements that Jesus may have made about the Trinity. I am simply saying that reflection on Jesus can only be carried out in trinitarian terms.

Reflection on Jesus is theo-logical insofar as we cannot think about him except in relation to the ultimate reality represented by the Father and his kingdom. The latter embody the ultimate mystery of history that cannot be comprehended fully or manipulated. The incomprehensibility and unmanipulability do not disappear with Jesus; on the contrary, they reach their fullest expression in him. Maintaining the mystery of the Father is fundamental for Jesus, as is maintaining the view that the Father is the ultimate mystery. Hence it must also be fundamental for all reflection on Jesus. Christology cannot entertain the view that the Father ceases to be a transcendent

God, ever greater than human beings, once Jesus appears on the scene and reveals an unheard-of intimacy with him. Christology must continue to maintain that the Father remains the ultimate horizon of human existence and history.

Reflection on Jesus is christo-logical because it affirms that in Jesus we have the revelation of the Son of God and all that means. The revelation of the Son in the history of Jesus shows us completely and definitively how human beings can correspond to the ultimate mystery of God in the midst of historical existence. Strictly speaking, Jesus is not the sacrament of the Father. He is not the epiphanic revelation of the ultimate mystery. Rather, he is the revelation of the Son, of the proper way to approach and correspond to the Father. Thus in trying to comprehend Jesus christo-logically here, I have preferred to focus on him as the "Son" and the "way" to the Father. Those are the categories used in this Christology.

Reflection on Jesus is pneumato-logical insofar as it affirms that human beings can see him as the Son and draw closer to the Father only if they live a life in accordance with the Spirit of Jesus. We can come to know Jesus as the Christ only insofar as we start a new life, break with the past and undergo conversion, engage in Christian practice and fight for the justice of God's kingdom. That is why I stress the following of the historical Jesus. It is not just that discipleship is one of the fundamental themes of any Christology that seeks to reflect on the life of Jesus. Nor is it just that discipleship is the gospel's way of expressing what is most fundamental in Christian ethics. I stress the following of Jesus here because it is only this that makes christological epistemology possible at all.

When I talk about a trinitarian approach here, then, I do not mean simply that the Trinity is one of the elements that might possibly be introduced into a Christology. Its role is much more fundamental than that. I am suggesting that *we cannot do Christology at all except within the framework of the trinitarian reality of God.* Let me put the same point in positive terms. Christology is possible only if the Father continues to be the ultimate horizon of reality, the Son continues to be the definitive example of how human beings can correspond to the

Father, and life according to the Spirit of Jesus continues to be the authentic Christian way of acting that makes us sons and daughters in and through the Son.

This standpoint, in my opinion, is the most important contribution of liberation theology to theology in general. It has shifted the basic issue from the content of theology to the precondition for doing any Christian theology. When we insist that theology can be done only from within the context of praxis, we are saying that people can understand and appreciate the Jesus who sends the Spirit only if they live a life in accordance with that Spirit. When we stress the full realization of the kingdom of God, we are saying that this mysterious, utopian reality is the ultimate horizon of theology; though it ever remains ahead of us and we are incapable of realizing it fully, it is the deepest source of our life and being because it points us toward our future. When we stress the historical Jesus, we are underlining his importance as the definitive example of sonship. That example has quite enough concrete details: He proclaims the coming utopia; he denounces injustice as the epitome of sin; he shows partiality toward the oppressed; he unmasks alienating religious mechanisms. And he does all this so that his Spirit will not remain vague and that his God the Father will not remain abstract and manipulable. The mutual interaction between an active Christian praxis based on the Spirit of Jesus and firm hope in the utopia of God's kingdom is the Christian expression of the hermeneutic circle required for any theological reflection. In this case it is the Christian version of the hermeneutic circle required for all christological reflection.

These, then, are the underlying intentions of the book presented here. We are trying to attain an understanding of Jesus based on a praxis that follows Jesus in proclaiming the coming of the kingdom, in denouncing injustice, and in realizing that kingdom in real life—even if only partially. That, in turn, will lead to a new round of discipleship. Insofar as we keep that process alive and operative, we effectively express our hope in the mystery of the Father and the coming of his kingdom. We also provide the most radical and thorough verification of the truth of Christology: i.e., that Jesus is the eternal Son of the Father. For we thereby show that through his Spirit he is continually capable of raising up followers and shaping other human beings in his image.

While these are the underlying intentions of this Christology, the author is also well aware of its deficiencies. First of all, it is addressed to a specific group of Christians, to those who have seriously committed themselves to the process of liberation. But while it is addressed to those Christians who have committed themselves to the cause of the masses, to the cause of the majority of Latin Americans, it does not offer an adequate analysis of the problems to be found in the Christology held by the majority of the population. Nor does it provide a clear and direct expression of what the majority think about Jesus. In my opinion, theology does face the urgent task of analyzing, criticizing, and giving direction to the Christologies held by the popular masses; but I do not propose to undertake that task in this book.

Second, the scriptural texts introduced in this book stand in need of more solid exegetical grounding, for this particular Christology purports to be based on the historical Jesus. To be sure, I have tried to take due account of what exegesis has to say about the various passages used here; and I have also tried to use treatises in systematic theology that are grounded solidly on exegesis. But the exegetical analysis needs to be worked out in greater detail.

I should have liked to overcome these limitations, and possibly others, by reworking the whole text and offering a second edition. But there was a pressing demand for this translation, and our land and our church find themselves in an exceptional set of circumstances right now. It was impossible for me to revise the text from beginning to end and to eliminate a certain amount of repetitiveness in the various chapters. Instead I have revised the chapter on the christological dogmas (Chapter 10), written a further chapter on the prayer life of Jesus (Chapter 5), and added this explanatory introduction to the English edition.

JON SOBRINO
January 1978   San Salvador, El Salvador

1.

The Historical Jesus:
The Starting Point for Christology

It is a fact that in recent years Christian existence has entered upon a state of profound crisis. The values that used to shed light on our lives seem to a large extent to have lost the power to give organization to our action and our reflection. This crisis is clearly embodied on the ecclesial level, and particularly in Latin America. Traditional ecclesial praxis, pastoral activity, the relationship of the church to what we call the "world" in all its varied dimensions (social, economic, political, and so forth), the liturgy, the concept of Christian education, and the meaning of the hierarchy, priests, and lay people: All these areas have undergone profound changes.

The theological roots of this crisis, both as a disorienting reality and as a challenge to develop a new and better ecclesial praxis, go deeper than ecclesiology itself. It is certainly understandable that the crisis should show up most clearly on the ecclesial level, since that is where Christian *action* unfolds. On our continent action is something that just cannot be postponed, given the urgent need for transformation and liberation. But if we are to have a Christian interpretation of this crisis and, even more important, some authentic Christian action, it will not do to stop at the ecclesial level. We must move on to that which ultimately gives *Christian* meaning to our ecclesial action. That is nothing else but Jesus Christ and the God who reveals himself in him. We must engage in deep and thoroughgoing reflection on Christ. We must ponder the

1

image of him which we have held in the past and continue to hold in the present, and which wittingly or unwittingly is at work in the activity of the church. If we do not do that, we cannot possibly understand the present crisis, much less channel it in a positive and fruitful direction. As Assmann puts it: "What is surprising is the lack of any sense of crisis about the meaning of Christ in the very midst of an acute crisis about the meaning of the church."[1]

Here I propose to deal with various fundamental motifs in Christology. On the one hand they will show that differing christological interpretations lie behind the current divisions of opinion and practice. On the other hand they will be helpful in trying to organize Christian existence in such a situation as that which now confronts Latin America. Thus my aim is to seek out a valid general frame of reference for a Christology suited to our situation, though my concrete analysis will take off mainly from the history of Jesus himself.

THE STARTING POINT FOR UNDERSTANDING CHRIST

In asking about the starting point of a Christology, we are posing a question that seems to be only theoretical. As we shall see, one might as well be able to conjure up various starting points for reflecting on the total phenomenon of Christ and organizing one's view of the matter. But in practice, as we shall also see, it is of the utmost importance that we be consciously aware of the particular feature of the total phenomenon that guides our reflections. To put it plainly, the starting point becomes one of the hermeneutic principles involved in trying to understand Christ.

In discussing the starting point for Christology here, we are going to concentrate on the objective aspect of the Christ event, not on some subjective aspect involving ourselves.[2] Here we are not interested in finding out what kind of personal experience or praxis can make *real in life* what reflection has pondered and found *in thought*. Later on we shall consider the problem of orthopraxis and its relationship to a correct understanding of Christology.

Choosing a starting point for Christology is not as easy or

obvious a task as it might seem. The basic reason is that in the eyes of Christian faith Jesus claims a universal significance: "All were created through him and for him. He is before all else that is. In him everything continues in being" (Col. 1:16–17; see Eph. 1:10). The Christian, then, professes that Jesus is the one who gives consistency and solidity to every side of reality, both personal and social, natural and historical, present and eschatological. The problem of choosing a starting point becomes the quest for some focus on Christ that will best reveal him in his universality and do so in concrete rather than abstract terms. Needless to say, that is no easy task. It explains why in *historical* fact different starting points have been chosen.

Let me say right here that my starting point is the historical Jesus. It is the person, teaching, attitudes, and deeds of Jesus of Nazareth insofar as they are accessible, in a more or less general way, to historical and exegetical investigation. But before I move on to spell out and explore the concrete history of Jesus, I think we would do well to review other starting points that have been used to develop or elaborate a Christology. Some of them may indeed seem far removed from Christology as an issue here and now, but we would do well to keep them in mind for several reasons. First of all, under differing names and labels they still continue to influence our practical understanding of Christ. Second, only by contrasting our starting point with others will we be able to make clear what we mean exactly by the "historical Jesus" and thus avoid letting this term degenerate into an empty slogan.

In traditional Catholic theology it has been customary to start with the dogmatic formulation of the Council of Chalcedon, which affirms that Christ is a divine person with two natures—a human nature and a divine nature. It is certainly a fundamental affirmation that should be taken into account by any Christian theology; but it hardly seems suitable or adequate as a point of departure. Quite aside from the obvious difficulty of understanding such terms as "person," "nature," and "hypostasis," there are also fundamental theological difficulties.

Some of these objections, though important, are of a more

decidedly formal character. For one thing, it is now a commonplace in theology that the content of dogma cannot go beyond, or say more than, the content of the reality of Christ as it is accessible to us in Scripture.[3] Dogma, in other words, is not only chronologically but logically posterior to the reality presented by the Gospels. Moreover, when we analyze the concepts contained in the formulation of Chalcedon, we find that they are limit-concepts not *directly* accessible to human intuition. Such concepts as "divine person," "hypostatic union," and "Incarnation" are, and ever remain, mysteries. But a limit-concept is comprehensible only in connection with the knowledge that has rendered it possible. This means that the *content* of what is known through the use of a limit-concept can only be grasped in and through the *approach* whereby the knowledge was obtained.[4] Thus our observations on the formal level should dispel any illusion that the mere repetition of some dogma gives us access to the reality of Christ.

Quite apart from the formal difficulties, there are more important objections on the level of theological content. The Chalcedonian formula presupposes a Christology of "descent."[5] It starts off with God and then goes on to affirm how the eternal Son became man. But Scripture tells us that the proper approach should be exactly the opposite. It starts off from the man Jesus and then goes on to reflect upon his divinity. The Chalcedonian formula concentrates on the problem of how God became man, but it gives no indication that both the "God" and the "man" in question are not abstractions. Scripture tells us that God has a concrete name, "Yahweh," and that the man in question has the concrete name, "Jesus of Nazareth."[6] Finally, the Chalcedonian formula was heavily influenced by Greek philosophy in its composition. It presupposes an epiphanic conception of God. The realm of the divine and eternal bursts through into the world of human beings; the realm of the beyond suddenly appears in the here-and-now world. Thus God is presented in terms of epiphany rather than in the biblical terms of *being at work* in the world. The Chalcedonian formula does not make it clear that

God is at work, through his own free choice, in the struggle for justice and the expectations of hope.

So the Chalcedonian formula does not seem to be a suitable starting point for Christology. To be sure, it retains its basic theological value for the church insofar as it makes explicit the limits of any Christian understanding of Christ. Those limits must be accepted and respected. But it expresses the universality of Christ in abstract terms, and such abstraction leaves room for the possibility of manipulating the figure of Christ.

To correct that dogmatic focus, some have sought to provide a biblical focus on Christ. The biblical focus, in this instance, need not necessarily be historical in the sense which we noted above. In one way or another, an effort is made to discover the distinctive character of Christ's person—his divine sonship. One approach is to analyze the various honorary titles attributed to Christ: prophet, Messiah, Son of Man, high priest, Servant of Yahweh, Lord, Son of God, Savior, Logos, and so forth. Another approach starts off from the major events in Jesus' life which are already theologized in the New Testament: resurrection, transfiguration, baptism, virgin birth, pre-existence, and so forth.

The advance of this approach over the preceding dogmatic one lies in the fact that its terminology is somewhat more comprehensible. At least the conceptual world is more authentically Jewish and hence brings us closer to the historical Jesus. Yet the basic problem remains much the same that it was in the preceding instance. The titles and events under examination already embody a later process of theologizing the Jesus event.[7] Chronologically they come after Jesus himself, introducing us to an already developed Christology.

There are other difficulties with this second approach, and they are of a more theological cast. The New Testament presents not *one* but *several different* Christologies, and it is impossible to unify them into one. Admitting the existence of christological pluralism is not the problem here. The problem is finding that which really does unify the various Christologies. To get beyond the pluralism, it seems we are forced to admit that it is the concrete figure of Jesus himself, not some later theological effort of conceptualization, that unifies the various Christologies of the New Testament.

A third possible approach was already evident in the Christian community in Corinth.[8] It starts off from people's experience of Christ as present in cultic worship. The community experiences his presence in the liturgy of word and sacrament. Once one does accept the presence of the living, resurrected Christ, then faith *knows* of the existence of the historical Jesus in and through the liturgical experience.[9]

Without denying that faith acknowledges Jesus' presence in the Christian liturgy, we simply cannot accept that presence as the starting point for Christology. First of all, we have to ask ourselves how we can differentiate that liturgical experience from mere illusion and deceit. We must also take seriously the biblical datum that Jesus was taken away from Christians after his Ascension. Cultic contact cannot replace acquaintance with the concrete Jesus. Moreover, as the history of the church and Christian piety makes abundantly clear, cultic contact is open to all sorts of interpretations; and some of them are directly contrary to the reality of Jesus himself.

Somewhat associated with that approach is a fourth one which begins with the resurrection of Christ. Rather than viewing it in terms of his *here-and-now* presence in cultic worship, this approach views the resurrection as the culminating event in Christ's own earthly life. This position would certainly seem to have the New Testament in its favor.[10] But there is a serious difficulty in taking it as our *starting point*.

As I shall explain in later chapters of this book, Christ's resurrection is an object of our cognition and our faith in a very special and distinctive way. It cannot be known directly; it can only be known from a concrete perspective. Christ's resurrection is also a limit-concept: It is an object of our faith while at the same time an object of our hope and praxis. And the hope in question is of a particular sort noted by the New Testament. Rather than simply being a neutral structural component of a particular anthropology, it is a "hope against hope"; and its point of origin is a certain kind of praxis—the following of the historical Jesus.

This might be put in slightly different terms. Though faith in Christ does arise logically and chronologically with his resurrection, the starting point for comprehending it is his cross and that brings us back to the historical Jesus. Christ's resurrection cannot be the starting point for Christology because of the hermeneutic problems involved. Those problems can only be posed and resolved from the standpoint of the historical Jesus.

A fifth possible approach begins with the Christ of *kerygma*. The first to propound this view was M. Kähler. Disappointed by the futility of efforts to write a biography of Jesus, he maintained that "the real Christ is the Christ preached."[11] In more recent times the implications of that statement have been spelled out most fully by Rudolf Bultmann. The reality of Christ lies in the fact that when his death and resurrection are preached, the hearers are faced with the inescapable necessity of making a choice. Either they must choose to live an authentic life based on faith and given meaning by God; or else they must choose to live an inauthentic life of sin, closed up in their own egos and cut off from the full potential of human existence.

We would not deny the truth in this position. Christ really *does not exist* and *is not understood* unless he poses an alternative in people's lives. Yet this approach is open to much arbitrariness insofar as it does not offer any concrete content to guarantee what is and what is not an authentic existence. It simply makes the general assertion that authenticity is necessarily ex-centricity: i.e., living for someone or something other than oneself. Furthermore, many have pointed out that the philosophy underlying Bultmann's theology is extremely individualistic. It overlooks the fact that the realization and fulfillment of the human person, which Bultmann describes as a shift from a prior sinful sort of understanding to the self-understanding of faith, is mediated anthropologically in and through some understanding of the world as history and society. It also overlooks the fact that Christian praxis is not just the consequence of an interior *metanoia* but also the way in which that metanoia is turned into something *real*, as opposed to something merely felt or pondered in thought.

A sixth possible approach would prefer to focus on the *teaching* of the historical Jesus taken in isolation. This view was developed by liberal European theology in the eighteenth and nineteenth centuries, which saw Jesus as the great model and teacher. He embodied Schleiermacher's notion of religion as an awareness of dependence on God. This Jesus was the model of bourgeois morality and citizenship in the nineteenth century (Harnack).[12]

This view overlooked a typical feature of Jesus that has come into more and more prominence in the twentieth century. His *eschatological* character makes it clear that he does not confirm or bolster religious or bourgeois solidity at all. Rather, he creates a crisis for it all.

Finally, Christology cannot begin with soteriology, with the aspect of Christ as savior. We cannot fashion or refashion Christology by concentrating on his significance for humanity and history at the start. It is certainly true that soteriology is a decisive factor for Christology. In the first place, it is an intrinsic element of faith that Christ does have universal significance, and, in the second, there must be some self-interest involved in our reflection on Christology. But the point here is that a soteriological interest cannot serve as the methodological starting point for Christology.

If our interest in salvation were to serve as the starting point, then Christology would become just one other variable in anthropology. Christ would become a symbol, a value cipher, to be filled with whatever set of interests one might wish. Moreover, as we shall see later, the cross of Jesus quite sharply breaks with the set of interests which drew people to Jesus. Christology cannot be based on human interests. Instead it must try to find out what our real interests should be which comes down to denying and contradicting our normal hierarchy of values.[13]

The brief summary above should indicate in *negative* terms how difficult it is to find some starting point for Christology.

We choose to adopt the historical Jesus as our starting point here for several reasons. Our Christology will thereby avoid abstractionism, and the attendant danger of manipulating the Christ event. The history of the church shows, from its very beginning as we shall see, that any focusing on the Christ of faith will jeopardize the very essence of the Christian faith if it neglects the historical Jesus. Finally, we feel that the historical Jesus is the hermeneutic principle that enables us to draw closer to the totality of Christ both in terms of knowledge and in terms of real-life praxis. It is there that we will find the unity of Christology and soteriology.

THE HISTORICAL JESUS AND LIBERATION THEOLOGY

In European theology, of course, the problem of the historical Jesus arose in the context of historical criticism and was framed in terms of what we might *know or not know* about the historical data concerned with Jesus. Bultmann added his own systematic issues to the whole historical problem and ended up dropping all interest in the historical Jesus. The task seemed to him to be impossible on the historical level and of little interest insofar as faith was concerned. Christ simply is the Christ preached in faith. More recently, however, E. Käsemann and J. Jeremias have been in the vanguard of those showing renewed interest in the historical Jesus. They have tried to show that it is indeed possible to establish the basic traits of Jesus with at least moral certainty.

People have also moved from a *historical* interest in Jesus to a *systematic* interest in him. In other words, they look at the historical Jesus to determine the possibility of a Christian existence (W. Marxsen). At present there is a growing body of studies dealing with the historical Jesus that seem to be motivated by the desire to show wherein lies the authentic universality of Jesus. These studies maintain that his universality cannot be demonstrated or proved on the basis of formulas or symbols that are universal in themselves: e.g., dogmatic formulas, the kerygma as event, the resurrection as a universal symbol of hope, and so forth. The real universality of Jesus shows up only in its concrete embodiment. Paradoxically enough, it is access to the concrete Jesus that brings out his universal potentialities in diverse historical situations. As Kasper puts it:

Hence it is no longer a matter of the rightness or correctness of certain affirmations when judged on the basis of the Bible or dogma. That is viewed as a rather *abstract* problem, and now people are concerned about the *concrete* truth—i.e., that which provides existential motivation and interior conviction. It is now a matter of talking about Jesus Christ in such a way that human beings feel they themselves and their problems are being discussed.[14]

In Latin America liberation theology has focused spontaneously on the historical Jesus for guidance and orientation. Since it arose out of the concrete experience and praxis of faith within a lived commitment to liberation, it soon realized that the universality of Christ amid those circumstances could only be grasped from the standpoint of the concrete Christ of history. The historical Jesus would serve as a satisfactory midway point between two extremes: turning Christ into an abstraction on the one hand, or putting him to direct and immediate ideological uses on the other. Assmann frames the matter in these terms:

On the one hand there is the vague, general Christology *ad usum omnium,* unrelated to any particular situation, and on the other, particular embodiments designed to fit a particular ideological purpose at a particular moment. Somewhere between the two there is a legitimate need for a historically mediating Christology relevant to the basic problems of a given historical situation.[15]

Although Assmann does not mention the historical Jesus specifically, he clearly alludes to him as an indispensable feature of any "historically mediating Christology" when he rejects other kinds of Christology. On the one hand he rejects any Christology that would be nothing more than "identification with specific movements or persons involved in the process of liberation."[16] This would suggest clearly that there is something normative about the historical career of Jesus himself. On the other hand Assmann rejects even more strongly any abstract theological shibboleths that cannot be reconciled with the historical Jesus: e.g., "the presence of the risen Christ in the world," "Christ the alpha and omega," and so forth.[17] Even if such Christology wanted to stress Christ at work in the world, it is still "sketched in the vaguest terms, . . . basically ambiguous in its categories."[18] Gustavo Gutiérrez also expresses displeasure with any unrealistic presentation of Jesus and urges interest in the historical Jesus: "To approach the man Jesus of Nazareth, in whom God was made flesh, to penetrate not only in his teaching, but also in his life, what it is that gives his word an immediate, concrete context, is a task which more and more needs to be undertaken."[19]

Ignacio Ellacuría has posed the problem and importance of the historical Jesus in the most clear-cut and radical terms. His purpose is to point up how much salvation history is bound up with salvation in history.[20] This concern is eminently theological and pastoral, and Ellacuría links it up with a set of problems that are strictly christological: "The limitations of the various New Testament Christologies must be overcome in a subsequent Christology which takes them into account and then reworks them historically in a new reading that is framed historically."[21] His effort is wholly in accord with my effort in this volume:

Our new Christology must give history of the flesh-and-blood Jesus its full weight as revelation. Today it would be absolutely ridiculous to try to fashion a Christology in which the historical realization of Jesus' life did not play a decisive role. The "mysteries of Jesus' life," which once were treated peripherally as part of ascetics, must be given their full import—provided, of course, that we explore exegetically and historically what the life of Jesus really was.[22]

Ellacuría also brings out a systematic reason for choosing this starting point. It is the one I noted earlier: "We must move on to an historical *logos*, without which every other *logos* will remain speculative and idealistic."[23] In other words the content of the *logos* as formulated by dogmatic pronouncements or already theologized biblical statements becomes idealistic in the pejorative sense if it is separated from the *historical* pathway of knowing which led to that formulation. Thus the underlying theological supposition is that "the historical life of Jesus is the fullest revelation of the Christian God."[24]

My brief survey of Latin American theologians should make it clear that they are aware of the need to take the historical Jesus as their starting point.[25] The task has scarcely been carried through in all respects, however. Perhaps it is the theme of Jesus and politics that has received most attention so far. Here one of the *primary* principles for proper political thinking and acting on the part of Christians is now said to be the concrete thinking and acting of Jesus himself. In the past, as we all know, people looked to the church's magisterium or to ethico-philosophical considerations of natural law to find the theological aspects of such issues.

Needless to say, the consensus existing among Latin American authors does not in itself justify choosing the historical Jesus as the starting point for Christology, though that consensus should not be underestimated either. In the last analysis we cannot find some clear and indisputable Archimedean point for starting Christology. Given the historical human condition, such a point is in fact unnecessary and worthless: "An absolute point of view would be equivalent to the absence of a point of view."[26]

However, I would like to conclude with two observations which might show why it makes sense to begin with the historical Jesus in our present situation as Latin Americans. First of all, there is a clearly noticeable resemblance between the situation here in Latin America and that in which Jesus lived. Needless to say, we cannot interpret that resemblance in some ingenuous or anachronistic way. The following of Jesus cannot be any automatic process of imitation which pays no heed at all to our own concrete situation and bypasses political, anthropological, and socio-economic analysis. At bottom the resemblance lies in the fact that in Latin America, as opposed to other historical situations, the present condition is acutely felt and understood to be a sinful situation. Thus the resemblance does not lie solely in the objective conditions of poverty and exploitation that characterize Jesus' situation and ours, as well as many others throughout history. It lies primarily in the cognizance that is taken of the situation. In that respect there is a real historical coincidence between the situation of Jesus and that of our continent today, and it is more marked than in other places. The whole complex of themes that surrounds the historical Jesus coincides greatly with that which now surrounds Latin America.

My second observation is a historical one, dealing with the Christologies of the first Christian communities. They did not possess any fabricated Christology. They simply had the testimony of people who claimed to have seen the risen one and who were "of our company while the Lord Jesus moved among us, from the baptism of John until the day he was taken up from us" (Acts 1:21–22).

The diverse Christologies of the New Testament were elaborated from two poles. Jesus of Nazareth was one pole. The other was the concrete situation of each community. Each had its own cultural backdrop and its own set of problems both within the church and vis-à-vis the outside world. The resurrection of Christ made their *faith* possible, but in the elaboration of a Christology they had to deal with the concrete features of Jesus' life. They would have to select and choose between those elements, rejecting some and accepting others. In today's situation the various churches are confronted with the same task—unless they rest content with reiterating the standing dogmatic formulas. The latter tack, by the way, is more orthodox only on the surface level.

In Latin America Christology is *in fact* being worked out by comparing the present-day situation with the historical Jesus. Latin American faithful see that as the best way to give expression to their Christian faith. That reality must be valued theologically just as we would the development of Christologies in the early Christian communities. Dogma does indeed set clear limits on the direction and development of Christology. But that fact in no way rules out the effort of a given community to make real and concrete the universal significance of Christ which finds expression in dogma.

In the following chapters I propose to point up those traits of Jesus which are most securely guaranteed by exegesis, and which offer us a most trustworthy image of the historical Jesus. We want to see what really happened rather than to ponder the historical Jesus *directly in terms of our own situation* and what he can mean for us. But that does not mean that we will not be looking at the historical Jesus *from the standpoint* of our own situation. Certain traits of his will take on importance precisely because we will be viewing them from the concrete situation of Latin America.

NOTES

1. *Theology for a Nomad Church,* Eng. trans. (Maryknoll, New York: Orbis Books, 1976), p. 103.

2. Raúl Vidales, to cite one example, analyzes the subjective starting point in these terms: "Christology based on a liberation perspective begins with the experience of Christ. But the Word of the totally Other is encountered, accepted, and professed beyond all speech and language. It is encountered only in silence. . . . If the first act of Christology is the experience of Christ in the midst of a politicized . . . and conflict-ridden existence, then at no time can Christ be reduced to some scientific object to which we apply some set of scientific tools" ("¿Cómo hablar de Cristo hoy?" in *Spes,* January 1974, p. 7f.). In claiming to look for a starting point for Christology, we are simply trying to explore the content-materials associated with that experience. No scientific analysis can take the place of that.

3. See K. Rahner, *Escritos de Teología* 4, Madrid, p. 383; German original: *Schriften zur Theologie* (Einsiedeln, Benziger, 1959–); Eng. trans.: *Theological Investigations* 4 (Baltimore: Helicon, 1966).

4. See D. Wiederkehr in *Mysterium Salutis,* 3/1 (Madrid, 1969), p. 558.

5. See K. Rahner, and W. Thüsing, *Christologie—systematisch und exegetisch* (Freiburg: Herder, 1972), p. 55.

6. See W. Pannenberg, *Fundamentos de cristología* (Salamanca, 1973), p. 45; German original: *Grundzüge der Christologie* (Gütersloh: Mohn, 1966); Eng. trans.: *Jesus, God and Man* (Philadelphia: Westminster, 1968).

7. Both form criticism and redaction criticism have brought out this point clearly. For a systematic consideration of this matter see K. Rahner, Eng. trans., *Theological Investigations* 5.

8. The first two approaches have been operative mainly in Catholic theology. For some years now Protestant theology has been exploring possible new approaches, as is evident in what follows.

9. Note this bold assertion by W. Künneth: "Since Jesus, as the risen Lord, effectively manifests himself in faith and faith itself is certain that Jesus the Lord lives, faith consequently knows of the historical existence of Jesus of

Nazareth" *(Glauben an Jesus?* [Hamburg: Wittig, 1962], p. 286).

10. The primitive kerygma (1 Cor. 15:3–5; Acts 2:32; 3:15; 4:2; etc.) certainly proclaims Christ's resurrection. But immediately Christians were faced with the problem of understanding that resurrection in something more than merely apocalyptic terms. That immediately brings the problem of the resurrection back to the historical Jesus. As J. Moltmann puts it: "Between eschatological paschal faith and late Jewish apocalypticism intervened Jesus himself and his cross" *(Der gekreuzigte Gott* [Munich: Kaiser, 1972], p. 153; Eng. trans.: *The Crucified God* [New York: Harper & Row, 1974]).

11. M. Kähler, *Der sogennante historische Jesus und der geschichtliche, biblische Christus,* 1892, p. 22 (cited by W. Pannenberg, *Fundamentos de cristología,* p. 20). In English see *The So-Called Historical Jesus and the Historical Biblical Christ* (Philadelphia: Fortress, 1964).

12. Harnack's Jesus is in the service of an overall conception which H. Zahrnt describes pointedly: *"The Essence of Christianity* . . . was the fullest and loftiest embodiment of bourgeois idealism and its age. Inspired by an optimistic faith in the human spirit and the progress of history, it believed it could almost automatically establish unity and harmony between God and the world, religion and culture, divine justice and the human order, and throne and altar. Thus it could look toward the future with confidence" *(A vueltas con Dios* [Zaragoza, 1972], p. 13).

13. Moltmann has explored this point penetratingly in a Christology based on the cross: "Knowledge of God deriving from Jesus' cross takes seriously the situation of disordered man and his interests. . . . As knowledge of God derived from his suffering in the crucified one, it is destructive for man insofar as the latter is a feelingless monster *(Unmensch).* For all practical purposes, knowledge of God derived from Jesus' cross is crucifying for hybrid man" *(Umkehr zur Zukunft* [Hamburg, 1970], p. 135 f.). In German see *Warten auf Gott* (Stuttgart: Kreuz, 1961).

14. W. Kasper, "Die Sache Jesu," in *Herder Korrespondenz.*

15. Assmann, *Theology for a Nomad Church,* p. 103.

16. Ibid., p. 69.

17. Ibid., p. 103.

18. Ibid., p. 69.

19. G. Gutiérrez, *A Theology of Liberation,* Eng. trans. (Maryknoll, New York: Orbis Books, 1973), p. 226.

20. See I. Ellacuría, *Freedom Made Flesh: The Mission of Christ and His Church,* Eng. trans. (Maryknoll, New York: Orbis Books, 1976), chap. 1, pp. 15–19.

21. Ibid., p. 25.

22. Ibid., p. 26.

23. Ibid., pp. 26–27.

24. Ibid., p. 27.

25. This theme and concern is a constant in the work of Latin American theologians, at least insofar as concretizing the figure of Jesus is concerned.

16   The Historical Jesus

Christ without his concrete history is turned into an icon (J. Comblin, *Teología de la revolución* [Bilbao, 1973], p. 306; French original), or into a vague and remote Christ with ill-defined features (H. Borrat, "Para una cristología de vanguardia," in *Víspera* 17 (1970), pp. 26–31). The same concern can be found in other authors: e.g., R. Vidales, "¿Cómo hablar de Cristo hoy?" in *Spes*, p. 7; R. Alves, *¿Cristianismo, opio o liberación?* (Salamanca, 1973), pp. 187–91, the Spanish version of his English work entitled *A Theology of Human Hope* (Washington, D.C.: Corpus, 1969), pp. 119–22. Leonardo Boff has sought to provide a more systematic Christology based on the historical Jesus: *Jesus Cristo Libertador. Ensaio de Cristologia Crítica para o Nosso tempo* (Petropolis, Brazil: Vozes, 1972); "Salvation in Jesus Christ and the Process of Liberation," in *Concilium* 96, 1974, pp. 78–91; "Christ's Liberation via Oppression," in *Frontiers of Theology in Latin America* (Maryknoll, New York: Orbis, 1979). From a pastoral standpoint see Segundo Galilea and Raúl Vidales, *Cristología y pastoral popular* (Bogota: Paulinas, 1974), pp. 24–43. From an exegetical standpoint see J.P. Miranda, *El ser y el mesías* (Salamanca: Sígueme, 1973); Eng. trans.: Being and the Messiah (Maryknoll, New York: Orbis Books, 1977). His prologue spells out the rationale behind his particular focus: "No authority can decree that everything is permitted, for justice and exploitation are not so indistinguishable. And Christ died so that we might know that not everything is permitted. But not any Christ. The Christ who cannot be co-opted by accommodationists and opportunists is the historical Jesus" (ibid., p. 9).

26. J. Moltmann, *Der gekreuzigte Gott*, p. 15.

2.

The Approach to Christology: Preliminary Remarks

As we begin the study of Christology, we do well to take cognizance of the kind of problems involved and the complexity of the whole issue we are going to consider. We should not assume immediately that we know exactly the issue with which we are dealing, the proper way to approach it, and the interest that should guide our inquiry. On the other hand it is obvious that we cannot begin without having some sort of prior understanding and interest. The purpose of these preliminary remarks is to explore some of the problematic factors involved in any approach to the study of Christology. We might well begin, therefore, with the following basic observations before we move on to consider several sample Christologies.

1. A given Christology cannot be comprehended apart from its presuppositions. The only instance in which that would not apply to our subject would be the case where the study of Christology is viewed as nothing more than a mere compilation of data (from Denzinger, Scripture, or wherever) which speaks for itself. Even in that case, however, one might well ask why certain items of data are chosen and others rejected.

2. This means that if we are to understand a given Christology, we must take conscious note of the generic interest which is at work in an author or a theological movement in the process of organizing and elaborating data to formulate a Christology.

3. Investigating the presuppositions underlying a Christology is not justified solely by the general anthropological principle enunciated in no. 1 above: i.e., that any given body of content is clarified and comprehended with the help of its underlying presuppositions. In our present case such investigation is justified as well by the very object of Christology itself. In Christology we attempt to deal with Jesus specifically as the Christ, as someone with universal significance. We must bring out some sort of universality in the concrete reality of Jesus. That being our intent, then the object of Christology itself requires us to clarify the relationship between the Christologist and the object. If Christ is the foundation of all (see Col. 1:16f.; Eph. 1:10), then any study of Christ must undertake to explain first what that "all" signifies. In short, it must offer some understanding of the world, the person, history, sin, liberation, and so forth; or, at the very least, it must spell out at the start how it focuses on that "all." Of course christological study will in turn explain, retouch, or perhaps even radically alter our way of focusing on the "all."

The purpose of this chapter, then, is to help people expand their horizon of understanding, questioning, and problem-solving, so that the study of Christology may probe more deeply. The horizon in question might be expanded and clarified in various ways, but I have chosen a particular approach. Here we shall explore the complexity of the whole christological issue by examining several Christologies that have been worked out to some extent. We want to see the relationship existing between the content of a given Christology and its underlying presuppositions, and we shall do this by considering several concrete examples of Christology. This tack is not meant to prejudice our own study of Christology in this volume. It simply may provide us with certain clues as to how we can frame our own Christology more correctly and thus get more meaning out of it. The following five points should provide us with some clues:[1]

1. *The theological milieu of the author.* This point is necessarily broad and extensive. Basically we want to determine the theological juncture at which given authors stand in the pro-

cess of working out their Christologies. How do they see the whole problem-complex of theology? How do they view the relationship between theology on the one hand and philosophy, culture, social reality, and politics on the other? How do they view their profession as theologians? Those are some of the questions pertinent under this heading.

2. *Attitude toward the phenomenon known as the Enlightenment.* The Enlightenment was liberative in intent. Its presupposition was that humankind had been brought under submission and subjected to alienation. Historically speaking, however, we find that the Enlightenment has been understood in various ways. Some have seen it as espousing the autonomy of reason vis-à-vis any imposition from the outside (the movement which began with Kant). Others have seen it as espousing the autonomy of the whole person vis-à-vis alienating structures (the movement which began with Marx). Christology will incorporate the challenge of the Enlightenment differently, depending on the way it interprets or sees the challenge. One author may seek to make clear the truth of Christology in the light of universal reason, and then subsequently in the light of historical reason. Another author may feel that the challenge is to verify the truth of Christology in the light of an obligation to transform alienating structures. Authors' understanding of the Enlightenment and its essential nature will profoundly influence their Christologies.

3. *The kind of hermeneutics used by an author.* Hermeneutics poses more than one question to the theologian. It is not simply a matter of determining the truth or falsity of historical affirmations (in this case, affirmations made by Scripture, christological dogmas, and their successive formulations). Hermeneutics includes the problem of how we are to understand and interpret those affirmations. The hermeneutic problem arises when the present-day reader of Scripture and dogma, as well as one who hears Christ preached, can no longer readily identify with the horizon of understanding in which the biblical books or the preaching based on them were composed. It entails asking whether it is indeed possible to overcome the historical distance that separates the Christ

event from the present-day Christian's understanding of it.

There are different kinds of hermeneutics in use: existential, transcendental, historical, revolutionary, practical, and so forth. The important point for us here is to note to what extent a given hermeneutic outlook has an impact on the concrete elaboration of a given Christology. Even more important is whether a given hermeneutics actually does justice to Christ himself. To put it in the form of a question: What kind of hermeneutics seems to be the one that will indeed do justice to our present object of study: i.e., Christ?

4. *The way in which the fundamental metaphysical quandary is posed.* Assuming that human thought and reflection really do move forward, we find they go deeper and find themselves in the presence of some fundamental quandary to be resolved. It is by tackling that quandary that they progress further and gain insight into reality. In philosophy this fundamental quandary has been expressed in terms of reconciling such things as the one and the many, subject and object, essence and manifest appearance, transcendence and history, present and future, and so forth. In theology it has generally been formulated in terms of the possible reconciliation between God and what is not God. However, the various theological formulations have assumed two fundamentally different standpoints as their starting point. One basic approach seeks to reconcile God and the world on the basis of *what is positive* in the world; this is the basic model of every natural theology. The other basic approach seeks to reconcile God and the world on the basis of *what is negative* in the world; this is the basic model of any theodicy.

Let us note what this means in practice. The first approach ponders the difficulty of trying to reconcile God with some seemingly positive feature of the world. Sartre, for example, finds it hard to reconcile God with human freedom. The second approach ponders the difficulty of reconciling God with the negative features of the world, with sinfulness and injustice, for example. So Marx found it impossible to reconcile God with the alienation in past and present history. In either case the way in which that fundamental quandary is approached will determine the way in which Christology is seen. One's viewpoint may be basically noetic and explicative on the one hand or centered around praxis and performance on the other.

5. *The density of an author's christological concentration.* I use the term "christological concentration" here to refer to the role that authors give to Christology within the framework of their theology as a whole. To what extent is their theology concentrated in Christology? To what extent is Christology truly the key to all of their theology? It is not a matter of authors saying that Christology is or should be the key to theology; it is a matter of that actually being the case in their own presentations. Concretely this means we must see whether such key concepts as "God," "liberation," and "sin" are christological or have basically been derived from elsewhere in an author's work: e.g., from philosophy, religion, structural analyses, or what have you. Now of course there is a mutual interaction between those concepts as christological on the one hand and as logically derived from some independent source on the other. When I talk about "christological concentration" here, I mean the extent to which Christology does or does not serve to provide the ultimate and fundamental concretion of those basic realities or concepts.

If we want to see how these five basic points operate as underlying presuppositions in Christology, we must have at hand some Christology that has been worked out enough to serve as a sample case. That is why I have chosen to present three European Christologies of the present day, those of K. Rahner, W. Pannenberg, and J. Moltmann. A more comprehensive work would have to deal with many more, even if it restricted its attention to systematic Christologies of this century. It would have to include the dialectical Christology of K. Barth, the existentialist Christology of P. Tillich, and the consistently secularized Christology of P. Van Buren, which prescinds methodologically from God.

Quite aside from the formal advantages involved, there are also material advantages in the works of the three authors chosen. K. Rahner is the great Catholic theologian who consciously broke with an older tradition of positive Christology that had restricted itself to stating and interpreting conciliar and papal texts concerning Christ. Rahner has sought to integrate Christology within the most comprehensive horizon possible, relating it to his overall understanding of the world, humankind, and history. W. Pannenberg is of particular interest here because he has attempted to build up a systematic Christology on the basis of the concrete history of Jesus. Moreover, his consistent eschatologization of all theological concepts has had a real impact on Latin American theologians.[2] J. Moltmann has stressed the role of the historical Jesus, the importance of sin (including structural sin) for understanding him, and a hermeneutics based on praxis.

After reviewing the work of these three theologians, we shall also consider some of the general suppositions underlying Latin American sketches of Christology. In that way we will be in a position to offer at least an indirect evaluation of the European efforts, to judge how useful or unsatisfactory they might be in a Latin American context. We will also be able to make explicit the presuppositions of our own Christology, thus avoiding any hint of phony universalism—so often evident in classical Christologies.

THE CHRISTOLOGY OF KARL RAHNER[3]

Insofar as Rahner's theological standpoint is concerned, we can distinguish three major periods. Rahner began as a Catholic dogmatic theologian anxious to interpret the dogma of Chalcedon. Feeling ill at ease with the ontic and metaphysical concepts used by traditional theologians, he began with a transcendental consideration of man and his nature as unconditionally open to God. He thus translated ontic categories into ontological categories—i.e., into categories which by definition include the subject. This enabled him to get beyond a mythological conception of Christ's divinity in which his humanity would be nothing more than an outer garment or cloak. Rahner asserted that there is a relationship between man as open to God and God as capable of being shown in history, in the human realm specifically. The formula of

Chalcedon thus becomes the key to comprehending what could also be elaborated from the starting point of a transcendental anthropology. Anxious to progress beyond a merely positivist study of dogmatic formulas, Rahner sought out another perspective that would enable him not only to affirm but to shed light on the incarnation of the Son. The transcendental approach provided what he needed. At that stage in his own thinking Rahner was obviously influenced by Kant's formulation of the issues. But he was also influenced by Hegel in his explanation of the dialectics of the Son's becoming, and in more general terms by existentialism.

At a second stage of his thinking, Rahner was influenced by Teilhard de Chardin. He asserted that humanity is waiting and hoping for some Omega Point that will take all history into itself and that even now gives it meaning and direction. This Omega Point is the incarnation of Christ, which recapitulates all history. The reality of Christ is given a new formulation, and Christ himself is seen as "the absolute bearer of salvation."[4]

In the third and latest stage of his thinking, Rahner has been deeply influenced by the eschatological line of thought, which analyzes past and present reality in terms of the future. As a result Rahner no longer places the main emphasis on Christ's incarnation, but rather on Christ's resurrection where the great eschatological event is embodied.[5] Christ already lives in the end of time, and so the openness of man is now considered mainly in terms of hope.[6]

Rahner clearly was very conscious of the challenge of the Enlightenment. This is all the more noteworthy insofar as the theology of the time sounded very much like superstition and myth, arguing its case in positivist and authoritative terms on the basis of traditional dogma. Rahner accepted Kant's challenge and sought to de-positivize theology, though not to de-dogmatize it. By the same token, however, Rahner has not shown as much interest in dealing with the second phase of the Enlightenment, that of such people as Marx. He does not deal with that issue explicitly, although he does affirm in principle that theology must have social relevance and he has explored the notion that love for God is one with love for neighbor.[7]

At bottom it seems clear that Rahner's hermeneutics is eclectic.[8] He does not want any specific methodology to place obstacles in the way of the theological object we are trying to comprehend. But within this basically eclectical approach Rahner shows a preference for a transcendental hermeneutics. Understanding something basically comes down to looking into the subject to find the conditions that make understanding possible at all. The ultimate import of this conception for Christology is that Christology must be *pastoral*. Christology cannot be a mere recital of truths. It must show how such truths can be understood. If something cannot in fact be understood by the believer, it is not worth affirming in the first place. Insofar as it is transcendental, then, this hermeneutics has profound theological repercussions. It suggests that all theology must be salvific; that theology cannot say who or what Christ is *in himself* but only who or what he is *for us*.[9]

The ultimate presupposition here is the radical historicity of divine revelation. There is no direct access to the eternal Son of God. Our only access is to the Son as historicized in Jesus. Another implication has to do with the subjective principle of theological knowledge: i.e., grace. Needless to say, matters are not clarified very much if we leave grace in all its formal abstractness. But we can get much further if we try to translate the basic affirmation about grace into truly historical formulations. To take one example, we can say that human beings can come to know the *risen* Christ only if they are already *living as resurrected human beings*. That brings us to the whole problem of what might go into the historical life and existence of already resurrected human beings. Rahner specifically maintains that access to Christ is possible through unconditional love for human beings.

We would be going too far and forcing his thought if we sought to integrate Rahner's position into a political hermeneutics. But we would not be going far enough if we failed to see that it does in principle assert the need for some general praxis—love of others—if we wish to understand Christ.

The basic metaphysical quandary presented by Rahner is the relationship between transcendence and history. How can God in himself become a God for us? Rahner seeks to answer this question with the concept of a "real-life symbol." Every "spiritual" reality comes to be insofar as it is expressed in the historical realm.[10] In his more systematic writings Rahner ignores the quandary of theodicy. This means that in his Christology he has tended to concentrate on Jesus' incarnation and resurrection rather than on his cross. At times, however, he does consider the omnipotence of God in terms of Jesus' impotence; and in his more existential writings Rahner does stress the role of Christ's cross in Christian existence.

Insofar as the christological concentration of his theology is concerned, Rahner is quite clear. He states unequivocally that the one and only mystery of theology, the mystery of God, finds its ultimate concentration in the mystery of Christ's incarnation,[11] and derivatively in the mystery of grace. Theology, then, is christologically concentrated in the problem of human access to Christ. While Rahner begins with a more generic anthropological concentration (i.e., man as an openness to God), he then proceeds to explore various points of access. The varied multiplicity of these access-points is meant to match the *whole range* of problems that people face. They include hope as an eschatological dimension not only of the person but of history; openness to death as a crisis for history and hence for the individual as well; and openness to radical love for other human beings and society. Christ thus becomes the key for interpreting and solving in principle the problems of human existence. He is the key to the sense and senselessness of history, providing positive access to it through love.

THE CHRISTOLOGY OF WOLFHART PANNENBERG

Pannenberg's basic theological standpoint can be viewed as a reaction to existentialist theology and the theology of the word that once dominated the theological landscape. He states his own theological manifesto in reaction against Bultmann's subjectivity and Barth's recourse to suprahistory: "History is the most all-embracing horizon of Christian theology. Theological questioning and response make sense only within the history that God shares with humanity and, through humanity, with all creation. That history moves toward a future which still lies hidden to the world but which is already revealed in Jesus Christ."[12] The implications for his Christology are clear enough. Insofar as method is concerned, only a historical methodology can lay hold of history. Insofar as the focus of his Christology is concerned, it must be from below; it must be based on the history of Jesus rather than on some action of God from above. Insofar as his treatment of Christ himself is concerned, it is Christ who solves the enigma of history. The end result of history is anticipated in the resurrection of Jesus, which ensures that history itself is a meaningful reality.

Pannenberg's philosophical bent is also part of his basic theological standpoint. He comes to theology as an inheritor of classical European philosophy.[13] Thus even though he maintains that Christology is the key to philosophy itself, he approaches Christ with what are clearly philosophical presuppositions. Two of these presuppositions are of particular importance, one being anthropological and the other theological. The former sees man as a being who is radically open to the future.[14] The latter sees God as the power over everything.[15] These presuppositions affect Pannenberg's Christology more than he himself might be willing to admit. It is evident in the fact that he gives almost no role at all to Christ's cross within systematic Christology.

The challenge that the Enlightenment poses to theology is, for Pannenberg, the challenge posed by Kant. Theology must undertake the basic task of de-positivizing itself. Rather than arguing its case on the basis of some authority (Scripture, inspiration, the church's magisterium, or whatever), theology must base itself solely on reason itself.[16] Theology must also take due account of historical reason: "The object of faith cannot remain untouched by the results of critical historical investigation."[17] Thus "the theologian is not in any position to tell us what is really the case in facts and events which remain obscure to the historian."[18]

The important point here is not to debate those affirmations but to note what he means by liberative Enlightenment. For Pannenberg it means our ability to know on our own, on the basis of human historical reasoning and its nature. It is somewhat curious, then, to see Pannenberg ignoring the challenge of the second phase of the Enlightenment almost completely. Marx is ignored for all practical purposes in all of Pannenberg's works. This is even true in his monumental work on the theory of science and theology (*Wissenschaftstheorie und Theologie*), in which he explicitly explores the status of theology as a science, its methodology, and related questions. While he discusses a number of different philosophers in that work, he mentions Marx only once in a footnote. Marx's own set of problems and his formulations are ignored as such. Pannenberg views them simply as an economic elaboration of Feuerbach's psychological criticism of religion.[19]

Hence Pannenberg's own hermeneutics is basically explicative, not transformational. He works out a novel historical hermeneutics, but it is designed to explain history rather than to transform it. Theology in turn is meant to be the true philosophy, but it is an explicative philosophy. Theological truth is verified insofar as it is capable of offering a better explanation of reality. Statements about divine reality and divine action are useful insofar as we can examine their implications for the *understanding* of "finite reality."[20] The same applies to Christology: "To the extent that all reality becomes much more *comprehensible* with the help of Jesus, to that extent we are confirmed in our conviction that the origin of all things has been revealed in him."[21] Pannenberg's hermeneutic focus, then, is to *understand* Christ in his divinity so that one may better understand the whole of reality. In the actual working out, of course, the two aspects interact with each other.

Thus Pannenberg poses the basic metaphysical quandary in the positive terms of natural theology. His problem is that of

Sartre: i.e., reconciling God as absolute power with human freedom. The problem of sin, injustice, and evil is not viewed as the basic problem. The basic crisis facing us today is a crisis of meaningfulness, according to Pannenberg; it is not a crisis of guilt or misery. This standpoint leads Pannenberg to formulate strikingly innovative notions about God as the power of the future rather than as the provident and omniscient God of the beginnings; but it also induces him to ignore completely the possibly revelatory role of Jesus' cross. Christ's resurrection is the paradigm of liberation standing above and beyond present human misery, but not directly in contradiction to that misery.

Pannenberg is clearly the theologian who has tried most systematically to concentrate theology in Christology. The meaning of history and the possibility of truth really do depend on Christ in his view.[22] But the christological concentration of his theology is reduplicative: everything depends on Christ, and his truth depends solely on the resurrection viewed as a one-time happening or atomistic point in time. Thus the historical life of Jesus is essentially anticipatory, pointing toward the resurrection. Without the resurrection it would have no meaning even as history. Indeed his death on the cross made his life not only anticipatory but ambiguous. In themselves, then, both the life and death of Jesus reveal nothing about Christ.

With this sort of christological concentration on the resurrection, it is not surprising to find that Pannenberg makes no use of such traditions as the Servant of Yahweh to understand Jesus. He makes use only of apocalyptic traditions, explaining them only insofar as the resurrection of Jesus reveals the anticipated end of history. Since those traditions did not look forward to the resurrection of only "one" human being, they make sense only on the basis of hope in the resurrection of all.[23]

THE CHRISTOLOGY OF JÜRGEN MOLTMANN

We can distinguish two distinct stages in Moltmann's basic approach. The first stage is embodied in his "theology of hope," the second in his work on "the crucified God." In the first stage the philosophy of Ernst Bloch played a dominant role. The themes of hope and the future dominated his thinking, as he reacted against any Greek theology centered around origins and already constituted reality. In Christology Moltmann concentrated on the resurrection of Jesus, which points toward the future, rather than on the incarnation, which points toward the past and can be turned into a new genesis myth.

It is characteristic of Moltmann, however, that he would be very open to changing his point of view and would reject any "absolute viewpoint."[24] So without going back on any of the positive elements of the theology of hope, he moved beyond it at a later stage because he felt it was too abstract. It was too abstract not because of its concepts as such but because it bore too little relationship with praxis. The Frankfurt School now became his chief philosophical mentor, replacing Ernst Bloch in that role. His thinking now came to center on the crucified God, and specifically on the cross of Jesus insofar as Christology was concerned. Moltmann moved from the God of the future to the crucified God, from anticipatory recollection of Christ's resurrection to the perilous memory of the crucified Jesus, from hope in Christ's future to the following of the historical Jesus.[25] His Christology now focused on the history of Jesus, but in a manner diametrically opposed to that of Pannenberg. For Moltmann the following of Jesus is not simply a theme in Christology; it is the very way to elaborate Christology, that which makes it possible for us to understand the concepts of Christology and work them out. Says Moltmann: "Christian existence is a practice. It is the following of the crucified one that transforms man himself and his situation. In that sense the theology of the cross is a practical theology."[26] Showing signs of his Barthian heritage, Moltmann talks about "the scandal of the qualitative difference." But it is no longer located in the hereafter of Christian hope; now it is located "in the cross of his life here below."[27]

Moltmann sees the Enlightenment as a process of liberation that must be incorporated into theology. He approves Bacon's criticism of tradition, Kant's criticism of dogmatism,

Feuerbach's criticism of religious projection, and Freud's criticism of psychology. He not only approves of the first stage of Enlightenment but goes on to note that Marx introduced a new feature into the picture. From him we learn that religious alienation is at the root of social alienation; and such alienation can only be overcome by thinking centered around praxis.

Moltmann makes a clear distinction between the two phases of the Enlightenment, seeing the first stage embodied in Feuerbach and the second stage embodied in Marx. The former criticized the *essence* of Christianity while the latter criticized the *history* of Christianity. Moltmann is led to conclude: "If theology wishes to be truly responsible today, then it must consider the psychic and political implications of its words, images, and symbols. . . . In all its talk about God it must consider whether it is offering a religious opiate or a real leaven of liberty. . . . Hence it should not ask itself what linguistic sense there is in talking about God [the problem of the first stage of the Enlightenment] but rather what public repercussions will ensue in a given situation when it talks about God or keeps silent [the problem of the second stage of the Enlightenment]."[28]

As Moltmann's own thought has evolved, so has his view of Marx. At the start it was fairly traditional. He felt that Marx's atheism was not real atheism because in it man took on the features of divinity. Marx's "total man" was a replacement for the "new man" of Christianity. Marx failed to appreciate the eschatological aspect of Christianity, and his utopia could not assimilate absolute nothingness. As time went on, however, Moltmann came to accept fully Marx's way of formulating his critique of religion—though he still continued to criticize Marx's lack of the eschatological reserve. Modern criticism of religion no longer focuses on the question of the "true religion" as earlier writers did, and as Pannenberg has continued to do. Such criticism now focuses on "political power-relationships and man's spiritual frustration, to which religion gives God's blessing and surrounds with an aura of holiness."[29]

As we might expect from his focus on Enlightenment as

praxis, Moltmann offers a hermeneutics of praxis. Theology is not basically explicative as Pannenberg would have it, though explication is not ruled out. Theological hermeneutics is abstract if it is not a theory of praxis, and sterile if it does not provide access to future truth. Moltmann goes on to label this praxis "political," maintaining that theology has always been political. So the real problem is to make sure that this political praxis is really Christian.

This conception of hermeneutics has several corollaries. First of all, theological thinking must always take due account of its implications for praxis. Second, any "orthodoxy" is radically insufficient, whether it means correctly reiterating the statements of the magisterium or, more profoundly, reducing the task of theology to one of understanding. In a strikingly novel way Moltmann points up the inadequacy of orthodoxy by appealing to a conception of God as one who criticizes man and his ways of thinking. In this respect Moltmann reveals his dependence on Barth. He is thus led to reformulate the basic methodology or approach of Christology. It no longer moves in the circle between initiative from "above" or "below," as it does in the thought of Pannenberg. Instead it moves in the circle between initiative from "inside" and initiative from "outside." The indispensable critical element can only come "from outside."[30]

Thus the fundamental task of theology is not "depositivizing" or "demythologizing" but "deidolatrizing." And it is power that must be stripped of its idolatrous worship. Theology, then, is a political theology of the cross. For while authoritarianism and myth can be overcome within the confines of orthodoxy, power cannot.

Moltmann clearly formulates the basic metaphysical quandary in terms of theodicy. We must reconcile God with evil, sin, injustice, and death. Even for Christians "suffering ever continues to be a cry without possible response."[31] The great quandary is "the impotence of love,"[32] and the only serious atheism is the atheism of protest. The problem of theodicy can be summed up in the comment of M. Horkheimer that "the executioner not triumph over his victim."[33]

This formulation of the basic quandary again leads to a hermeneutics of praxis. God cannot be justified by mere thought. He can only be justified insofar as he facilitates a liberative praxis. On the epistemological level it is suffering and pain which now become the motivating force for knowledge.[34] In principle it is impossible to "ponder" God in a world of misery. Moltmann emphasizes this point by showing how any ethics that is merely thought out cannot go anywhere when it is confronted with the problem of love and violence. Ethics thus becomes "transmoral," not because Moltmann disdains the moral criteria worked out by human thought but because real-life misery does not allow for any adequate synthesis in the mind so long as it continues to exist.[35]

Finally, Moltmann's theology is christologically concentrated in the cross: "Either Jesus abandoned by God is the end of all theology or else he is the beginning of a specifically Christian life and theology that is both critical and liberative."[36] But this christological concentration on the cross is not atomistic; it does not concentrate on the cross as an isolated point in time unconnected with the rest of Jesus' life. It takes in both his life leading up to the cross and his resurrection, the latter being the point where Jesus' course was turned into the definitive promise for us.

The key concept which structures Moltmann's whole theology is the cross of the risen one. The cross forces him to redefine God as the crucified God; sin as that which brings death to the Son; faith as a faith against incredulity; hope as a hope against hope; and love as a love against alienation. At the same time, however, the cross does not operate in Moltmann's theology as the resurrection does in Pannenberg's theology. The cross does not allow for a "theory" of Christianity or for a true philosophy. The first thing it does here is to criticize human interest in constructing any theory. Moltmann does not assert emphatically that one can construct a Christology and a theology on the basis of Jesus' cross. He is only willing to go this far: "If faith does arise from the cross . . . then we will get a christological theology that is a critical theory of God."[37]

In the last three sections I have not sought to provide a full description of the three Christologies discussed. I simply wanted to illustrate some of the presuppositions and conditioning factors at work in any Christology so that the reader might approach the following chapters with a clearer idea of what is involved. It may help us to be aware of the standpoint which typifies the various christological sketches now being worked out in Latin America.

LATIN AMERICAN CHRISTOLOGY

For the most part Latin Americans have not worked out systematic Christologies and full presentations of Christ. The only outstanding exception in this regard is Leonardo Boff's work on Jesus Christ as Liberator. But we still can say something about the basic orientation of christological writing in Latin America in terms of the five criteria discussed earlier in this chapter.

The theology of liberation serves as the general frame of reference for Latin American Christology. Unlike European brands of theology, liberation theology does not see itself situated in a broader history of Latin American theology since the latter is of very recent vintage. So rather than engaging in dialogue with other theologies, philosophies, or cultural movements, liberation theology has faced up to the basic Latin American reality of underdevelopment and oppression: "Liberation is then seen as a setting in motion of a process which will lead to freedom."[38]

This facing up to reality itself rather than to mediating factors engaged in pondering reality has taken place in the midst of real-life commitment to the cause of liberation. Thus liberation theology has not arisen primarily as an effort to *justify* real-life involvement. Instead it has arisen as a by-product of a concrete faith that is pondered and lived out in terms of the questions raised by involvement in the praxis of liberation. Its aim is to make that involvement "more critical-minded and creative."[39]

Pondering the real-life situation only after it has been experienced in concrete terms, Latin Americans have been prompted to see Christ in very new and different terms. As Boff puts it: "Each generation brings a new *parousia* of Christ because in each age he is given a new image, the result of the difficult synthesis between life and faith. . . . Today, in the experience of faith of many Christians in Latin America, he is seen and loved as the liberator."[40] So the basic locus of Christology is the place where faith and life meet.

It is not the first stage of the Enlightenment that seems to pose the real challenge today. It is not such movements as liberalism, freemasonry, and theosophy that raise questions for Latin American theology today. It is the whole problem of *reality* and concrete life itself, of the second stage of the Enlightenment, that now holds center stage. The problem of the believing *subject*, who may now find it hard to see the import or truth of faith, has taken a back seat. And the sinfulness of the situation is not something just to be explained; it must be concretely transformed. That is why Latin America is not much interested in clarifying people's understanding of such traditional theological problems as transubstantiation, the hypostatic union in Christ, and the relationship between divine and human knowledge in Christ.

Such problems are ignored, I believe, for two basic reasons that have nothing to do with disdain. First of all, theological clarification of that sort does not seem to have any direct repercussions on the social sphere. Second, and more important, to dally over such questions is to play the game of traditional theology, which is seen to be alienating and totally uninvolved with real issues. We are hiding from real problems and serving the interests of ideology if we focus on the traditional theological problems of transubstantiation and the hypostatic union while such issues as underdevelopment and its implications go unexplored.[41]

So Latin American theology aims to be critical and operative, taking life as a whole rather than the individual Christian as its point of departure. From the horizon of liberation, good theologizing means real service.[42]

The impact of the second stage of the Enlightenment is readily seen in the use which is made of Marx's social, religious, and political analyses, though Latin Americans claim to use them with a critical eye. It is even more evident in the fact that Marx's epistemological revolution plays a great role. We come to know reality really only insofar as we come to realize the necessity of transforming it. The second stage of the Enlightenment also exerts an influence on Christology, however sketchy that Christology still may be. Emphasis is placed on those christological elements that serve to constitute a paradigm of liberation (e.g., the resurrection as utopia and the kingdom of God) or to highlight practical ways of understanding and realizing it (e.g., the socio-political activity of Jesus and the obligation to follow in his footsteps).

So hermeneutics becomes a hermeneutics of praxis, and the implications for Christology are clear: "It is not enough simply to read about the figure of Jesus purely in the light of his *ipsissima vox et facta* and within the apocalyptic framework and the sociological background of his time. Exegetes, using more and more sophisticated methods, have done this and their work is very valuable, but it is not a science in itself. . . . The elements that give permanent validity to this message, above the pressures of history, can only be adequately grasped in a hermeneutic approach. From this, the *ipsissima intentio* of Jesus emerges."[43] And the aim of studying Jesus' intention is to pave the way for "effective collaboration" with him.[44] The course that Jesus took is to be investigated scientifically, not just to aid in the quest for truth but also in the fight for truth that will make people free.[45]

The basic quandary that inspires Latin American theology is summed up in the term "liberation." It is embodied concretely in the coexistence of two fundamental and contradictory experiences: the felt need for liberation as an absolute necessity on the one hand, and the impossibility of achieving it in history on the other. The resulting situation is experienced as one of bondage or captivity, where hope for liberation goes hand in hand with concrete experience of unjust oppression.[46]

In theological terms, then, we are dealing with a question of theodicy rather than a question of natural theology. We must try to reconcile the kingdom of God with a situation of bondage. Yet Latin American theodicy has peculiar features of its own insofar as liberation theology arose out of active praxis rather than static contemplation. Faced with a pervasive situation of misery, it does not take the classic tack to be found in the Book of Job, in the work of Dostoyevsky, and more recently in Rabbi Rubinstein's query as to how Jews can believe in God after Auschwitz. It is not concerned with finding some way to contemplate God and captivity in a meaningful relationship. Instead it is concerned with the practical problem of building up and realizing the kingdom of God in the face of captivity.

The quandary is very much lived as such because there is no evident way out of the dilemma. But it is inspired and sustained by the conviction that the real problem is not to justify God but rather to turn the justification of human beings into a reality. The question of justifying God seems to be all too theoretical in the face of the real-life need to make people just. It is reality that must be reconciled with the kingdom of God, and the quandary of theodicy must be resolved in praxis rather than in theory.

What, then, are we to say about the christological concentration of Latin American theology? It is my firm belief that this is one of the most delicate issues in liberation theology. The basic question is, of course, whether the main interest of liberation theology is Christ or liberation. Needless to say, this alternative is not posed as such, either in theory or in praxis, but it will help us to bring the whole matter of christological concentration out into the open. Only the future course of liberation theology will provide an answer to the problem, but even now some observations can be made.

First, it is worth realizing that certain things which seem to be real alternatives for the mind can be united in lived experience. An example from Paul's theology might help us here. In theory we might well ask whether his theology is concentrated on Christology or on justification; in practice we feel sure that the two were joined together in his own experience. We might begin with his christological experience on the road to Damascus in order to comprehend his experience of being justified.

Or, on the other hand, we might begin with his personal experience of the need to be justified and the impossibility of ever attaining it, and then see how the problem was resolved in his experience of Christ. Something similar seems to be the case with liberation theology. I think that liberation theology as "theology" is profoundly christological; and insofar as it is concerned with "liberation," its most all-embracing theological concept is "the kingdom of God."

We can see this tension in the practice of liberation theology itself. On the one hand the notion of the kingdom of God polarizes the anthropological and historical presuppositions of theology and becomes a hermeneutic principle for the study of Christology: "The Kingdom of God expresses man's utopian longing for liberation from everything that alienates him, factors such as anguish, pain, hunger, injustice and death, and not only man but all creation."[47] On the other hand, the kingdom of God is not "a mere organic extension of this world, as it is encountered in history. The Kingdom does not evolve, but breaks in."[48] It is here, then, that Christology begins to operate. Not only must we try to understand Jesus in terms of the kingdom; we must also try to understand the kingdom in terms of Jesus. Without the kingdom Jesus would be little more than an abstract object of study; without Jesus, however, the kingdom would be only a partial reality.

Hence the christological concentration of liberation theology is dialectical in nature. It does not try to deduce everything from Christology but, on the other hand, this "everything" is not real or truly understood without Christology. Within Christology itself emphasis is placed on the resurrection of Jesus as a paradigm of liberation; but even more insistent is the stress placed on the historical Jesus as the pathway to liberation. It is the historical Jesus who enlightens us with regard to the basic meaning of the task as well as his personal way of carrying it out. Liberation theology is concentrated in Christology insofar as it reflects on Jesus himself as the way to liberation.

NOTES

1. A fuller treatment of these topics can be found in my article entitled "El conocimiento teológico en la teología europea y latinoamericana," in *Estudios Centroamericanos* (San Salvador, 1975), pp. 322–23.

2. In his book *A Theology of Liberation* (Eng. trans., Maryknoll, New York: Orbis Books, 1973), G. Gutiérrez approvingly adopts various generic concepts that were pointed out or deepened by Pannenberg: e.g., the God of the historical future; history as the locus of revelation; the categories of eschatology, promise, and hope; the conception of universal history; and the importance of such concepts for political life. Insofar as the formulation of *generic* theological concepts is concerned, there can be no doubt about the influence of Pannenberg and Moltmann. The contrasts and differences, with Pannenberg in particular, show up when it comes to making those concepts *more concrete* or placing them in the context of a given Latin American author. This will become evident as we proceed.

3. See his christological essays in the first five volumes of his *Escritos de teología* (Madrid). The original German title of the series is *Schriften zur Theologie*, translated into English under the title *Theological Investigations*; see chap. 1 note 3 in this volume.

4. "Every movement of this history draws life from the goal at which it seeks to arrive, from its culminating point where irreversibility of the process takes on reality. It draws life, in short, from the one whom we would call the bearer of salvation' " (Karl Rahner, *Escritos de teología*, 5:200).

5. K. Rahner, *Christologie—systematisch und exegetisch* (Freiburg: Herder, 1972), p. 38f.

6. K. Rahner, "Zur Theologie der Hoffnung," in *Schriften zur Theologie*, 8:561–79; see note 3.

7. See his article on the oneness and unity of love for God and neighbor in *Escritos de teología*, 6:271–92. For his stress on love of neighbor as the concrete access to Christology, see K. Rahner, *Ich glaube an Jesus Christus* (Einsiedeln, 1968), pp. 58–65; *Christologie—systematisch und exegetisch*, p. 61.

8. "Theology is . . . eclectic theology, and it has always been so" (*Schriften zur Theologie*, 8:99).

9. Ibid., p. 52.

10. "A concrete being is of itself necessarily symbolic because it must 'express' itself in order to find its own being" (*Escritos de teología*, 5:292). Thus one can see the history of Jesus as the "expression" of the eternal Logos.

11. *Escritos de teología*, 4:89f.

12. W. Pannenberg, *Grundfragen systematischer Theologie* (Göttingen: Vandenhoeck, 1967), p. 22; Eng. Trans., *Basic Questions in Theology*, 2 vols. (Philadelphia: Fortress Press, 1970–71).

13. I agree with the view expressed by James M. Robinson: "Pannenberg's personal approach to Christianity was primarily by way of rational reflection" ("Offenbarung als Wort und als Geschichte," in *Offenbarung als Geschichte*, edited by Pannenberg [Zurich, 1967], p. 22, footnote 26; Eng trans.: *Revelation as History* [New York: Macmillan, 1968]).

14. His anthropological supposition was spelled out clearly in his very first philosophico-theological work, *Was ist der Mensch?* (Göttingen, 1962), pp. 5–40; Eng. trans.: *What Is Man?* (Philadelphia: Fortress, 1970). He returns to it often in his later writings.

15. See ibid., p. 33f.; *Grundfragen systematischer Theologie*, pp. 252–398; *Teología y reino de Dios*, Spanish trans. (Salamanca, 1974), pp. 11–39; Eng. trans.: *Theology and the Kingdom of God* (Philadelphia: Westminster, 1969).

16. See *Grundfragen systematischer Theologie*, pp. 11–21; 223–51.

17. Ibid., p. 57.

18. Ibid., p. 54.

19. See Pannenberg, *Wissenschaftstheorie und Theologie* (Frankfurt: Suhrkamp, 1973), p. 411, note 768; Eng. trans.: *Theology and the Philosophy of Science* (Philadelphia: Westminster, 1976). In dealing with the basic types of modern atheism, Pannenburg does not treat Marx either. He prefers to focus on Feuerbach and Nietzsche. See his *Grundfragen systematischer Theologie*, pp. 347–60.

20. Pannenberg, "Zur Theologie des Rechtes," *Zeitschrift für Evangelische Ethik* 7 (1963), p. 8f.

21. "Die Offenbarung Gottes in Jesus von Nazareth," in *Offenbarung als Geschichte*, p. 169.

22. "The unity of truth is established solely through God's prophetic revelation in Jesus Christ" (*Grundfragen systematischer Theologie*, p. 222).

23. Even in European theological circles the sharpest criticism of Pannenberg's Christology is that he systematically overlooks Jesus' cross. Without going into detail on the point, we can summarize the criticism under three heads: (1) The cross is viewed solely as a fact, but not in theological terms as something that might reveal something about God; (2) there is a failure to explore sin in theological terms, to see it as a reality which affects God insofar as it is capable of causing real death to the Son and other people; (3) Pannenberg's anthropology is one-sided because it is grounded solely on apocalyptic traditions, overlooking such things as the Servant of Yahweh theme, for example.

24. J. Moltmann, *Der gekreuzigte Gott*, p. 15; see note 10, chap. 1 above.

25. Ibid., p. 10.

26. Ibid., p. 30.

27. See "Crítica teológica de la religión política," in *Ilustración y teoría teológica* (Salamanca, 1973), p. 18.

28. Ibid., p. 16, my brackets.

29. *Umkehr zur Zukunft* (Hamburg: Siebenstern, 1970), p. 169.

30. See *El hombre*, Spanish trans. (Salamanca, 1973), pp. 143–46; Eng. trans.: *Man: Christian Anthropology in the Conflicts of the Present* (Philadelphia: Fortress, 1974).

31. *Teología de la esperanza*, Spanish trans. (Salamanca, 1972), p. 24; Eng. trans.: *Theology of Hope* (New York: Harper & Row, 1967).

40   The Approach to Christology

32. *Der gekreuzigte Gott,* p. 240.

33. *Die Sehnsucht nach dem ganz Anderen* (Hamburg, 1970), p. 62.

34. *Esperanza y planificación del futuro,* Spanish trans. (Salamanca, 1971), p. 69; German original: *Perspektiven der Theologie;* Eng. trans.: *Hope and Planning* (New York: Harper & Row, 1971).

35. *Umkehr zur Zukunft,* p. 54.

36. *Der gekreuzigte Gott,* p. 9f.

37. Ibid., p. 71.

38. L. Boff, "Salvation in Jesus Christ and the Process of Liberation," in *Concilium* 96 (New York: Herder and Herder/Seaburg, 1974), p. 78.

39. G. Gutiérrez, "Movimientos de liberación y teología," in *Concilium* 93, 1974, p. 451; Eng. trans.: "Liberation Movements and Theology" (New York: Herder and Herder/Seabury 1974).

40. L. Boff, "Salvation in Jesus Christ and the Process of Liberation," p. 78.

41. The point is made forcefully in, for example, H. Assmann, *Theology for a Nomad Church* (Maryknoll, New York: Orbis Books, 1976).

42. "The *verum* of the Bible is not a *factum* already given but a *faciendum* ("something to be done"). That is why any theological reflection based upon a historical *logos* is not content to define reality and the import of what has already been done. On the basis of that determination it also seeks to move in the direction of what remains to be done; to verify, to make real and true in actuality what is already true in principle" (I. Ellacuría, "Tesis sobre posibilidad, necesidad y sentido de una teología latinoamericana," in *Teología y mundo contemporáneo* [Madrid, 1975], p. 346; also in *Christus,* Mexico City, February–March, 1975).

43. L. Boff, "Salvation in Jesus Christ and the Process of Liberation," p. 79.

44. R. Vidales, "¿Cómo hablar de Cristo hoy?" in *Spes* 22–23 (1974), p. 10.

45. Ibid.

46. See L. Boff, "Libertação de Jesus Cristo," in *Teología y mundo contemporáneo,* p. 267f.

47. L. Boff, "Salvation in Jesus Christ and the Process of Liberation," pp. 80–81.

48. Ibid., p. 82.

3.

Jesus in the Service of God's Kingdom

The most certain historical datum about Jesus' life is that the concept which dominated his preaching, the reality which gave meaningfulness to all his activity, was "the kingdom of God." This fact and its implications are of fundamental importance. It provides us with two essential keys to understanding Jesus. First, Jesus is not the central focus of his own preaching; this fact is commonly admitted. As Rahner puts it, "Jesus preached the kingdom of God, not himself."[1] The second implication is not given adequate consideration often enough, and it is the root of many misunderstandings about Christianity. It is the fact that Jesus did not talk simply about "God" but about "the kingdom of God."[2] We shall come back to that important distinction in a moment.

Right now the point is that in historical terms we can only come to know the historical Jesus in and through the notion of God's kingdom. By the same token we can only come to understand what is meant by the kingdom of God in and through Jesus.

Dividing Jesus' public life into two basic phases, we can say that the first phase extends to the crisis in Galilee. It is characterized by Jesus' basic attitude and relationship to the kingdom of God. Mark summarizes it near the start of his Gospel: "After John's arrest, Jesus appeared in Galilee proclaiming the good news of God: 'This is the time of fulfillment. The reign of God is at hand! Reform your lives and believe in the gospel' " (Mark 1:14–15).

41

I shall try to explore the content of this summary statement by examining four aspects of it: the import of the term "kingdom of God"; its reality as good news or grace; its opponent embodied in sin; and the radical change or conversion that the kingdom demands of the believer.

IMPORT OF THE TERM "KINGDOM OF GOD"

There is nothing completely novel in the preaching of Jesus. Jesus assumes that his audience knows about the kingdom of God and is waiting for its coming. The distinctive characteristic of Jesus' proclamation is that he radicalizes these presuppositions: "In Jesus the traditional expectation of God's coming kingdom is transformed into the one and only decisive point of view."[3] Thus the first thing we must do in trying to understand Jesus is to see him as a religious reformer preaching the best traditions of Israel.[4] And so we must have some idea of the hopes and expectations which Israel placed in the term "kingdom of God."

We do not know for sure when the appellation "king" was applied to Yahweh for the first time, but its import is clear from the very start. On the basis of the saving events that Israel experienced and attributed to Yahweh, that nation came to see Yahweh as the one who had *dominion* or lordship over it and its history. Following the lead of other religions outside Israel, the Hebrews were led to apply the term "king" to Yahweh analogously. It expressed his dominion over the Israelite nation. Later reflection would expand his dominion to cover all peoples (see Jer. 10:7). This basically historical reflection later found cultic expression in the Psalms, particularly those which are said to deal with the enthronement of Yahweh.[5]

The content of the terms "king" and "kingdom" is more important than their origin. One observation of a more formal character is of importance here because it will very much help us to understand Jesus' relationship to this kingdom. Indirectly it will also shed some light on the notion of God. Our term "kingdom of God" may tend to support a static situation which has no place in the original Hebrew expression (*malkuth*

Yahweh). The latter suggests two basic notions: (1) God reigns with acts of power, (2) in order to establish or modify the order of things. The real emphasis is on the first verb, and so we would do better to talk about the sovereign "reign" of God rather than about his "kingdom." The dynamic element should predominate over any static overtones.

Now to appreciate the content of the term "reign of God" we must go back to the roots of Israel's experience. As a nation it suffered from great catastrophes: the destruction of the northern and southern kingdoms, the Babylonian captivity, the arduous work of reconstruction during the period of Persian dominance, and the failure to achieve national self-determination for all that. This series of negative experiences, pondered in the light of Israel's faith in Yahweh, gave rise to the conviction that it could not be the last word about Israel. There had to be some other possibility because it certainly was not the ultimate that Yahweh could do. There arose the eschatological hope of a complete change in Israel's situation. The Hebrew people began to look forward to some authentic liberation and to a Messiah who would fulfill their hopes.

The articulation of such hopes was part of the work of the prophets. Besides denouncing the existing situation and issuing diatribes against earthly nations, the prophets also sketched the outlines of a future that would be both a judgment and a liberation. Here we have the utopia that nourished the lives of the Israelites as they pondered their notion of God and faced up to the sinfulness exteriorized in real life and the world.[6] Two citations from Isaiah epitomize this utopian view: "They shall beat their swords into plowshares and their spears into pruning hooks; one nation shall not raise the sword against another, nor shall they train for war again" (Isa. 2:4); "he will destroy death forever; the Lord God will wipe away the tears from all faces" (Isa. 25:8).

It is Second Isaiah who actually proclaims the coming of the kingdom. The Lord is on his way as king and shepherd, but as savior rather than as a judge (Isa. 45:21). This salvation is viewed as radically new. "Lo, I am about to create new heavens and a new earth; the things of the past shall not be remembered or come to mind. Instead there shall always be rejoicing and happiness in what I create" (Isa. 65:17).

Jesus shared that prophetic vision and understood his task of proclaiming the kingdom in that context. As Boff puts it: "Jesus makes a radical statement about human existence, its principle of hope and its utopian dimension. He promises that it will no longer be *utopia,* the object of anxious expectation (cf. Luke 3:15) but *topia,* the object of happiness for all the people (cf. Luke 2:9)."[7]

Alongside this political backdrop, however, another factor was at work in Jesus' day: i.e., the apocalyptic formulation of Jewish expectations. It too expressed hope in a total transformation of reality, formulating that hope in the daring expression "the resurrection of the dead." What distinguishes its view from that of the prophets is the fact that it sees the definitive establishment of God's kingdom as the end of history. At present the kingdom is hidden. But human beings can calculate when it will manifest itself and even hasten its coming, even though it remains the exclusive work of God. It will come after a time when confusion and desolation have reached their culmination.[8]

Jesus steps on the scene amid this background of thinking, and he talks about the definitive reign of God that people are awaiting. His message is that God's reign is at hand and already dawning, though it has not yet reached its culmination. It is not merely an extension of human potentialities; it breaks in as grace. Neither is it merely a transformation of the inner person.[9] It is also a restructuring of the visible, tangible relationships existing between human beings. It is authentic liberation at every level of human existence.

Now these brief remarks will help us to make some basic observations about the systematic value of the fact that Jesus preached not merely "God" but "the kingdom of God." Jesus adopts as his own the Old Testament conception of God, which contrasts with that of Greek thought. The Old Testament view is that God acts in history in a specific way, and that his action cannot be separated or isolated from his basic reality.[10] Though we do find both historical and epiphanic conceptions of God in the Old Testament, particularly in its earlier pages,[11] the notion of the kingdom of God stresses that God does not make himself known directly as he is; instead he reveals himself in some situation. "God exists" means that God "acts" or "reigns." The "reign" of God is part of his very reality.

Second, the prophetic and apocalyptic formulations indicate that this active reign of God entails a total renovation of reality. "God exists" means that he "creates fellowship and community among human beings." Apocalyptic pessimism stresses the difficulty of achieving human reconciliation and liberation, thereby focusing on its eschatological character. It is "eschatological" in both senses of the term: "final" because it is of ultimate and decisive importance—the aspect stressed almost exclusively by most existential interpretations; and "final" in the temporal sense.

Whatever sense we may give to "final," it is clear that the Old Testament conception of God sees two aspects in God's reign, which is part of his very essence. First, human beings are to orient themselves toward God vertically: i.e., the grandeur of divine filiation. Second, there is to be fellowship and reconciliation between human beings: i.e., brotherhood. And since God is inseparable from his "reign," both aspects are indissolubly linked as primary realities embodying our relationship to God and God's relationship to us.

Both aspects are of a theological character from the start. They belong to God himself as such. Brotherhood is not merely an ethical exigency that follows from our dogmatic understanding of God. Brotherhood without filiation can indeed end up in atheism; but filiation without brotherhood can end up in mere theism, not in the God contemplated by Jesus. The essence of God as embodied in the notion of God's reign does not allow us to choose between the two aspects; both are of equal and primary importance.

Hence we can now glimpse the inner logic in the preaching and activity of the historical Jesus. The mere verbal proclamation of God without action to achieve his reign is not enough,[12] and orthopraxis must take priority over orthodoxy. The point worth noting is that Jesus' attitude is not simply the product of his ethical consciousness or his enlightened common sense. It wells up from the inmost depths of his being, from the reality of the one he calls Father. And how can he be Father if he does not create a community of brothers and sisters? That is the ultimate theological reason why Jesus equates "proclaiming God" with "realizing God's reign in practice."

THE KINGDOM OF GOD AS GRACE

Other contemporary eschatological preachers, John the Baptist for example, proclaimed the imminence of God's judgment. Unlike them Jesus proclaims the nearness of the kingdom as good news ("gospel"). Here we have the core of what is meant by "grace."

Jesus views the kingdom as grace in two senses. First of all, it is due to God's initiative. The old world, the world of tribulations described by prophecy and apocalypticism, has already come to an end in principle. That fact, however, is not due to any initiative on our part. It cannot be hastened by strict fulfillment of the law as the Pharisees think, or by driving out the Roman conquerors with arms as the Zealots think; nor can its coming be gauged by external signs, as apocalypticism envisions. Jesus simply tells people that the kingdom of God is already on hand, already breaking through. That is how we should interpret his remark in Luke's Gospel: "Blest are the eyes that see what you see. I tell you, many prophets and kings wished to see what you see but did not see it, and to hear what you hear but did not hear it" (Luke 10:23–24; see Luke 6:20f.).

Like Second Isaiah, Jesus proclaims that the arrival of the kingdom is salvation and that the kingdom (as we shall see) has the decisive connotation of liberation. But this salvation and liberation is not expressed solely in words (sermons and parables); it is also expressed in *deeds*. The need to preach the good news in deeds flows of necessity from the reality of God as described above. God is insofar as he acts, insofar as he alters reality; and we must view the *actions* of Jesus in that light. His actions are not simply accompaniments to his words, nor are they primarily designed to illustrate his own person. Their primary value is theo-logical: They are meant to demonstrate the kingdom of God.

The deeds of Jesus are basically signs of the coming of the kingdom, as he himself states in his reply to the emissaries of John the Baptist: "The blind recover their sight, cripples walk, lepers are cured, the deaf hear, dead men are raised to life, and the poor have the good news preached to them" (Matt. 11:5). This reply, lifted out of Isaiah, makes very clear what the coming of the kingdom means to Jesus. It presupposes that the kingdom is the transformation of a bad situation, of an oppressive situation, and that God's activity can only be envisioned as the *overcoming* of a negative situation. God's action does not simply affirm the positive aspect of human existence. Rather, it affirms it through *negation*—which is to say, through a liberation. Thus Jesus does not simply affirm the infinite possibilities of God and then go on to affirm human possibilities. Instead his aim is to act in such a way that human possibilities might be realized concretely in oppressive situations.

That is why the Gospels place Jesus in the midst of situations embodying divisiveness and oppression, where the good news and salvation can only be understood as being in total discontinuity with them. The freedom that Jesus preaches and effects in practice cannot help but take the form of liberation. Jesus appears in the very midst of those who are positively despised by society and segregated from its life. It is to such people that he addresses his proclamation of the coming kingdom: to the sick, who are helpless in themselves and dominated by a stronger force; to the lepers, who are cultically separated from the rest of society; to the Samaritan woman, who is regarded as a schismatic; to the Roman centurion, who is a foreigner; and to others of this sort. Jesus allows women to follow in his company and tend to his needs, though women were allowed only a marginal role in society. He eats meals—a clear sign of the eschatological reality—not only with his friends but also with sinners. He goes out to meet those possessed by demons, which embodied the division existing within people.

All these situations exemplify and help us to understand the signs of the kingdom that Jesus gave in line with his own conception of it. They suggest that the figure of Jesus can be laid hold of only by viewing him in relation to the kingdom; it cannot be grasped directly in itself. Unfortunately the emphasis has been misplaced by traditional interpretation of two features of Jesus' activity, namely, his miracles and his pardoning of sins. Mainly in the interest of apologetics, both have been considered directly in terms of Jesus' own person; his relationship to the kingdom has been slighted. But the curious fact is that when we try to gain direct access to Jesus' divinity through his miracles and his forgiveness of sins, we then pare down the theo-logical dimension of Jesus, his relationship with Yahweh. *Both his miracles and his forgiveness of sins are primarily signs of the arrival of the kingdom of God. They are signs of liberation, and only in that context can they help to shed light on the person of Jesus.*

In western culture the traditional conception of a miracle is something that breaks with the known laws of nature. Since the assumption is that only the deity can have power over nature, a miracle would bear direct witness to the divinity of Jesus. Thus we gain direct access to the personhood of the historical Jesus quite independently of the kingdom of God. The Gospels, however, do not present miracles in those terms. They do not focus on the exercise of power over nature, nor do they suggest that the enigma of Jesus can be solved directly on the basis of his miracles. To begin with, the biblical conception of a miracle is quite different from our western one. The Jews did not picture nature as a closed system. Miracles were not important because of their disconcerting or astonishing aspects but because they bore witness to God's saving action. The New Testament commonly uses the term *teras* to describe the wondrous aspect of a miraculous work. Yet curiously enough it never uses that term to describe Jesus' miracles. For the latter it uses such terms as *dynamis* ("act of power"), *ergon* ("work"), and *semeion* ("sign"). We would do better to refer to them as "signs" rather than "miracles," and to interpret them as being related to the kingdom of God (see Luke 11:20; Mark 3:22f.; Matt 1:21f.). They are preaching about the kingdom in deeds, in which the nearness of God is made concrete and visible. This is particularly true of the exorcisms that break the lordship of Satan. The dominant overtone in the miracles, as opposed to Jesus' other signs, is the evident power being exerted by the coming kingdom. But their basic impact is substantially the same as that of Jesus' other activities. In all of them he is positing signs of liberation.[13]

Neither can Jesus' pardoning activity be understood directly in terms of his own person. It too is a consequence of the approaching kingdom of God.[14] The forgiveness of sins exemplifies the same liberative activity of the kingdom that is embodied in Jesus' other signs. It is important to note that most of the accounts of Jesus' forgiving sins have to do with sinners who are not only alienated from God but also socially ostracized. Jesus seeks to liberate the sinners from their own egotism and sinfulness, but the social and religious backdrop is always one in which the sinners seem to have no possibilities left to them. His forgiveness is seen as the authentic liberation provided by God as opposed to the false liberation promoted by those who see sinners as people without hope or any possibilities at all.

"Sinners" are the prototypes of human beings who cannot have any hope of salvation if God judges them according to their works. By preaching the approach of God in grace, Jesus opens up to sinners the only future left open to them. If they are willing to accept the idea that God is really approaching in grace, Jesus pardons their sins. That is why Jesus chooses to address his proclamation to sinful publicans, drunkards, prostitutes, and the like. They all are people whose present social and religious situation allows them no hope of liberation. The other kind of sinner, the Pharisees, who put their trust in the works prescribed by the Mosaic law, are not pardoned by Jesus. They see liberation as lying in continuity with their present situation; as a reward for their works. By contrast the present situation of the ostracized sinners is precarious and absurd if measured by social or religious standards. If they are to have a future at all, it can only come from God. So if they accept the fact that nothing in their present life is an obstacle for the God who is coming, then they have done the best that they can do. They have accepted the fact that God is drawing near in grace to give them hope and a future.

This, then, is the first and foremost liberative aspect of Jesus' work of forgiveness. The underlying logic is not that Jesus is coming with power to do justice to people according to their works; it is rather that the kingdom of God is approaching as liberation. The type of sinner pardoned by Jesus is the person who is living under oppression, the person who is despised by those who are just in society according to the law and who is condemned to a life with no future by the law itself.

Thus Jesus' whole activity, including his miracles and his pardoning of sins, must be viewed primarily in terms of the kingdom of God drawing near to liberate people. Of course his deeds also shed some indirect light on the figure of the historical Jesus himself. But it would be a serious mistake, fraught with baneful hermeneutic consequences, to use Jesus' activity in order to prove his divinity in apologetics. The whole gospel account suggests something quite the contrary: i.e., that Jesus must be understood in terms of something quite distinct from himself (the kingdom of God). In that framework he is seen as someone who is essentially "in the service of" something else. His person is essentially relational, not absolute in itself.

That brings us to a conclusion which we shall explore in detail later but which I will mention here. Our relationship to Jesus must embody this same relational character. Contact with Jesus is rendered possible only when our attitude is one of service to the kingdom of God. To put it in straightforward but pointed terms, we can say that Jesus' intrinsic relationship to the kingdom means that our contact with him will not come primarily through cultic acclamation or adoration but through following Jesus in the service of God's kingdom.

THE REIGN OF GOD AND SIN

Jesus' attitude toward sin is of fundamental importance if we wish to understand the relationship between the historical Jesus and the kingdom of God. First of all, his preaching of the good news takes place in the context of a sinful world. Structurally speaking then, the good news must be viewed not simply as liberty but as liberation. Second, Jesus views sin in strictly theological terms, not simply in ethical terms; and the point worth noting is that sin is not seen simply as saying no to God but as saying no to the kingdom of God. Sin strikes at the very heart of human reality, both personal and social. Overcoming sin becomes the criterion for verifying whether one has accepted the good news or not. Sin is not just something that must be *pardoned*. It must be *taken away*, eradicated. So true is this that the following of Jesus can be verified as real only to the extent that sinning against the kingdom is taken away completely.

Taking away sin is what gives seriousness and single-mindedness to one's acceptance in faith of the coming of the kingdom. It is the indispensable negative moment in the dialectics of faith, expressing the fact that faith is a victory precisely over those things which seem invincible: i.e., evil, sin, and oppression. That is why there is a deep underlying parallelism between Johannine statements on faith as a victory over the world (1 John 5:4) and on the life of Jesus himself as taking away the sin of the world (John 1:29). Jesus' denunciation of sin has two main features, in which the two aspects are closely related. For Jesus sin is the rejection of God's kingdom which is drawing near in grace; and the anthropological essence of sin is people's self-affirmation which leads them to assert their own power in two negative ways. On the one hand they use it to secure themselves against God; on the other hand they use it to oppress others.

Following the prophetic tradition, Jesus stresses the personal character of sin as coming from the human heart —though we should not equate personal with an "individualistic" emphasis. Jesus does not view sin in legalistic terms as a transgression of the law. He interiorizes the reality of sin, stressing that it is already inside people in their twisted intent long before it shows up in their exterior conduct. Sin denies our filial relationship with God, which is historically rediscovered in the message of Jesus himself. In the context of Jesus' own historical situation, where the presence of God's approach in grace is keenly felt, the essence of sin is seen to be a refusal to accept that coming. People close their hearts to the future of this coming God by concentrating on the present and relying on works that are regarded as just by the law.

Sin, then, means, a willingness to offer anything and everything to God (ritual services, tithes, ascetic practices, and so forth) except one's own security. The God who is coming soon is rejected precisely because he is coming as a future that we cannot control, because God therefore calls into question the only thing that real sinners are not disposed to give up—their own security; and the real sinner is typified by the Pharisee and the person with power.[15] Paradoxically enough, Jesus sees the sinful attitude epitomized in those who are waiting for Yahweh to come as a just judge rather than as Father.

The other major thrust of prophetic denunciation is also shared by Jesus: i.e., denunciation of the public, social, and structural aspect of sin. The inherent logic of his attitude is readily evident if we recall our basic thesis about the historical Jesus. With an essential relationship to the kingdom of God, Jesus cannot help but denounce certain features of social life that are inconsistent not only with the definitive kingdom but also with an anticipatory stage of it.

Jesus was not familiar with our modern formulation of the Christian quandary concerning the relationship between the ultimate transcendent realization of the kingdom and our cooperation in its building. To some extent it is akin to the tension evident between apocalyptic emphasis on the end of time and prophetic emphasis on the quest for justice here and now. Both dimensions, however, were equally evident to Jesus.[16] He could not proclaim the ideal state of the kingdom and the eschatological banquet without simultaneously denouncing any form of sin that made human reconciliation impossible in the brief interim that would remain, so he expected, between the breaking-in of the kingdom and its transcendent fulfillment.

Sin, therefore, has two dimensions for Jesus. The personal dimension was a refusal to accept the future of the God who was approaching in grace. The social dimension was a refusal to anticipate that future reality in our here-and-now life. The twofold commandment of loving God and neighbor is clearly grounded in the logic of the kingdom. Sin is no longer seen as directed against God but rather against the kingdom of God. Divine filiation is broken because human brotherhood is broken.

It is important to note that both aspects of sin are found in the authentic sinner, the person who is a sinner almost by definition. The real sinners are the persons with power who use it both to secure themselves against God and to oppress others. This leads them to deny both the future ordained by God and anticipatory embodiments of his coming reign.

Sinners are frequently described as hypocrites by Jesus, and their hypocrisy is verified in their sin against the kingdom. Jesus hurls anathemas at the Pharisees because they pay no attention to justice; at the legal experts because they impose intolerable burdens on people and have expropriated the keys to knowledge for their own use; at the rich because they refuse to share their wealth with the poor; at the priests because they impose restrictions on people's freedom; and at the rulers of the world because they govern despotically.

The first thing to note about these anathemas is that they are almost always *collective*. Rather than being directed against individual egotism, they are directed against group manifestations of such egotism. This crystallization of egotism in groups creates a sinful atmosphere wholly contrary to that which describes the kingdom. The second noteworthy feature about the anathemas is that they are directed against *use of power*, be it religious, intellectual, economic, or political. Jesus did not speculate about the nature of power; he condemned its improper use in the concrete. Improper or evil use of power produces a clear-cut division between those who hold power (the oppressors) and those who suffer from its use (the oppressed). Though Jesus did not think in terms of present-day structures and social classes, he certainly saw the relationship existing between use of power and a situation of oppression. Religious oppression exists *because* the Pharisees impose intolerable burdens on people. Ignorance exists *because* the levites have expropriated the keys to knowledge. Poverty exists *because* the rich will not share their wealth.

Jesus does not see the juxtaposition of oppressors and oppressed as some necessary or eternal law. It is not that the situation, however lamentable, is inevitable. The situation is rather the historical consequence of collective sin. It should also be noted that there is often a harsh accusation of hypocrisy attached to Jesus' condemnation of collective wrongdoing. He implies that groups seek to justify some sort of inhuman or antihuman conduct by appealing to religion. Thus we see how Jesus looks at the relationship between sinning against God and sinning against the kingdom in historical terms. Because people's attitude toward the God coming in grace is radically false, their use of power turns into sinful oppression that is destructive of the kingdom. And the same holds true if we start from the other direction. Oppressive use of power proves one's false relationship to the God who is coming in grace.

Now let me make some final observations about sin and the kingdom of God as viewed by the historical Jesus. First of all, Jesus is aware of the fact that every human being can be an oppressor, and that traits of oppressor and oppressed can be found in all. This shows up more clearly in the highly theologized accounts of the passion, where it is *the whole people* that rejects Jesus. Paul and John will also affirm that every human being is a sinner. In Jesus, however, this universal theological truth is framed in historical terms. In other words, Jesus does not invoke this universal theological truth to avoid spelling out clearly who is oppressor and who is oppressed in a given concrete situation. The transcendent dimension of the kingdom and its fulfillment does not prevent him from analyzing what sin against the kingdom means concretely and what it means to anticipate the kingdom in history. Quite the contrary is true. The personal dimension of sin can be tangibly verified in the oppression to which it gives rise. And this is the criterion that Jesus uses to denounce sin, even insofar as its personal dimension is concerned.

Second, Jesus relates the essence of sin to the essence of

power. Only one kind of power is proper if one seeks to anticipate the kingdom. It is the power of love, of sacrifice, of service, of truth. Every other kind of power, far from being even neutral, is historically sinful. To the extent that it is not power dedicated to service, it is sin. [17] This view of sin as power is intimately bound up with his conception of God. The political religions of Jesus' day, which we shall consider in a later chapter, shared the notion that power is by very definition the mediation of the deity. That the Roman emperor was considered a god was not outlandish, therefore. Jesus sought to undermine the traditional conception of the deity and power as its mediating influence. Power and its use is viewed entirely differently by Jesus. As a basic human experience, power is the mediation of God only insofar as it is love and service; otherwise it turns into sin. Rather than mediating God, it will then express what is most directly opposed to the reality of God; it will be sin.

Finally, if the reign of God is the "verfication" of God, if it is making the reality of God true in fact, then sin against the kingdom is the "verification" of sin against God; it is making sin true in fact against God. Personal sin is not so personal that it does not have visible repercussions. Though Jesus does not speculate on the essence of sin in exactly these terms, his view of the person with power as the prototype of the sinner clearly suggests that human self-assertion always has two dimensions. On the one hand it is assertiveness against God, grounded in one's own works; on the other hand it is assertiveness against others grounded in the use of one's own power.

CONVERSION AND THE KINGDOM OF GOD

Jesus' basic proclamation of the kingdom ends with an exhortation: "Reform your lives and believe in the gospel" (Mark 1:15). There is a trace of intimidation in it. Faced with the existing situation here and now, people must make a choice. The alternatives are presented in different ways in the Gospels (God or money, Jesus or one's own family, and so forth), but the central idea is clear enough. Now is the time to make a decision, and it will entail a conversion. The kingdom of God presupposes a radical change in one's form of existence; it cannot be attained by living on the inertia of one's old way of acting.

The novelty of the new lifestyle is spelled out programmatically in the Sermon on the Mount. There the wellsprings of external behavior are internalized and the basic exigencies are radicalized. The kernel of the Sermon on the Mount is the assertion that love, service, and truth constitute the only kind of power capable of anticipating the kingdom. Seen in this light, the command to love one's enemies expresses the complete radicalness of Jesus' demand. Jesus' own attitude makes it clear that it has nothing to do with pacifism, as pietistic interpretations would have it. Rather, love of one's enemy is what verifies one's conversion, for the enemy is the most extreme and acute embodiment of other people.

The problem of conversion becomes the whole problem of how we are to participate in the kingdom of God, how we are to cooperate in its fulfillment. It is the problem of the tension existing between transcendent fulfillment and historical effort, between grace and works and also, to a certain extent, between orthodoxy and orthopraxis. Here we shall consider the matter as it was posed to the historical Jesus. This is not directly applicable to the postpaschal situation because the delay of the parousia altered the formulation of the whole issue to some extent.

Jesus himself shares the apocalyptic conviction that the breaking-in of the kingdom is God's work alone. No one knows the day or the hour (Mark 13:33). It is God who gives the kingdom (Luke 12:32). All human beings can do is plead for its coming (Matt. 6:10) because the kingdom, like a seed, grows in secret on its own (Mark 4:26, 29). Jesus' descriptions of the final catastrophe, his parables on the crisis, and his warnings to stay alert make clear the sudden and unexpected nature of God's day and his sovereignty over the end of time.

Corresponding to this work of God, however, is a human

attitude that is usually designated with the Greek word *metanoia*. Its meaning is described and exemplified in terms of two complementary attitudes. The first attitude is that of the "poor" or "lowly" persons who are exploited and alienated from society, who find no trace of dignity in their present situation and no hope for the future. These people are living proof of the absence of God's reign, and the first thing asked of such people is faith. They must believe that their present situation is not the last possibility open to them because it is not the last possibility open to God. They must believe in a God who is drawing nigh in grace rather than in justice. They must believe that God is infinitely greater than the God preached by priests and rabbis.

This type of person serves as the inspiration and model for all that is correct in the existentialist interpretation of the kingdom. In some sense every human being is a human being who is not really such, who is leading an unworthy, sinful life. What people bring to the kingdom, in this sense, is faith Systematic reflection may then go on to see that faith, understood in this sense, is not an arbitrary demand imposed by Jesus; that it is rather the essential mediating factor for any access to God, the element of utopian hope that renders present as totally "other" the God who is not merely in continuity with our own potentialities.

In the Gospels, however, we find another type of human being to whom the exigencies of the kingdom are presented in a very different form. These people are presented with the demand to follow Jesus. Not only must they have faith in the sense just described; they must also cooperate actively in preaching the kingdom and turning it into a full reality. As we noted above in the case of Jesus' miracles and his forgiveness of sins, this obligation to follow Jesus has usually been explained in apologetic terms. It has been used to point up the unique distinctiveness of Jesus' person, and the following of Jesus has been distinguished from all other kinds of discipleship (e.g., that connected with John the Baptist or the Jewish rabbis). Undoubtedly the following of Jesus does have christological import and can tell us something about the person of Jesus. Aside from that fact, however, the discipleship demanded by Jesus must be understood first and foremost as an exigency of the kingdom of God.[18]

To begin with, even the choice of twelve apostles (Mark 3:14–19) has a symbolic character with respect to the kingdom. It symbolizes the eschatological revitalization of the twelve tribes of Israel. The twelve are sent out to preach the kingdom. They are given power over unclean spirits (Mark 6:7f.), i.e., power to work signs that attest to the presence of the kingdom. In the second half of Mark's Gospel, however, the following of Jesus is given a new and definitive form. As we noted earlier, Jesus proclaimed the kingdom in line with the logic of Jewish traditions. But after his failure with the masses and his fights with those in power, his life came into jeopardy and the work of implanting the kingdom took on the features of the work attributed to the suffering Servant of Yahweh. As a result of this shift, the following of Jesus also took on a new dimension. Instead of being sent out with power, his followers would now have to follow the suffering-laden pathway of Christ himself, with all the perilous social, personal, and political implications involved. The terse phrase in Mark's Gospel sums it up: "If a man wishes to come after me, he must deny his very self, take up his cross, and follow in my steps" (Mark 8:34).

Here we see the start of what we might call an epistemological "break" both in Jesus and in his followers. It is no longer a matter of following someone who is proclaiming a kingdom of which his followers have a more or less accurate idea in their minds already. It is no longer a matter of cooperating in a project that stands in continuity with their own legitimate aspirations as human beings and Jews. Rather than following something pretty much in line with Jewish orthodoxy, they must follow something which will call that very orthodoxy into question. Their discipleship is now typified by Jesus in all his historical concreteness.

At the start they were summoned to place themselves at the disposal of the kingdom. Though Jesus served as the catalyst for their discipleship, the basic criteria governing it were independent of him. Now the figure of the historical Jesus himself becomes normative, becomes the one and only criterion. Though he himself is distinct from the thing they hope for, his person and course is the only way to enter the kingdom. No longer is Jesus simply the one who proclaims and anticipates the kingdom. Now he is also the new, unknown, and painful way—the only way—in which one can come to understand that God is drawing near to human beings and how he is doing it.

The concrete implications of following Jesus will be brought out when we consider the attitudes of Jesus specifically. Right now, however, two points must be stressed. First, the historical Jesus sees people's relationship to the kingdom exemplified in two types: the "poor" or "lowly" person on the one hand and the "follower of Jesus" on the other. Faith and hope is demanded of the first, practical service to the kingdom and behavior akin to that of Jesus is demanded of the second. Now while the Gospels exemplify these attitudes in two different types of people, as we noted above, they really should coexist within every Christian. Hope in God gives expression to the gratuitous nature of the kingdom. Following the praxis of Jesus gives expression to the concrete obligation to fight for love and justice among human beings. These two attitudes or dimensions are not chosen arbitrarily by Jesus. They are the concrete means that tie in with the kind of God that Jesus reveals. Because his God is the God who opens up a meaningful future for people living an oppressed life, one must have hope (a "hope against hope," as we shall see later). Because his God exists only insofar as he "reigns," thereby liberating people and creating human fellowship, access to God is only possible in a liberative praxis based on following Jesus.

Second, we must consider the relationship between orthodoxy and orthopraxis that flows from Jesus' conception of faith and discipleship. It is worth noting that the Jewish religion was a religion of orthodoxy. It had its creeds and its orthodox hopes of various sorts concerning the coming of God's kingdom. At the start of Jesus' public life, his followers did not have any special problem with Jewish orthodoxy. It was the concrete course of the historical Jesus that brought their orthodoxy into question, as one passage in Mark's Gospel brings out clearly (Mark 8:27–38). In what seem to be very orthodox terms, Peter answers Jesus about his person (verse 29). In reality a scandalous lack of faith lies buried in his response (verse 33). Jesus offers a little catechetical lesson to explain what authentic orthodoxy is, but it does not take the form of a theoretical explanation. It simply states the obligation to follow him by taking up one's cross (verse 34).

In the eyes of the historical Jesus the reality of God and the kingdom, and indirectly the reality of his own person, are not directly accessible to mere orthodoxy. It is not just for the elementary philosophical reason that limit-concepts such as God and transcendence are not directly accessible to human insight. The deeper, underlying reason is that only in the *praxis* of following him do we glimpse the mental categories that will enable us to understand the real nature of the kingdom of God and formulate it in a meaningful way.

To summarize this chapter briefly, we can say that any initial attempt to approach the historical Jesus must be done from the standpoint of the kingdom of God. This is our first basic thesis about Jesus: He did not preach about himself, or even simply about God, but rather about the kingdom of God. This thesis enables us to properly appreciate the activity of Jesus as liberation. It enables us to see the original unity of the horizontal and vertical dimensions in Christian faith, as well as the relationship of sin to it. It enables us to adopt the following of Jesus, understood as a praxis rather than as a theory, as the basic hermeneutic principle for comprehending who God is and, as we shall see later, who the Christ of faith is.

The temptation we hope to avoid with this thesis is the mistake of trying to broach the problem of Christ's divinity *directly*. Such an approach would imply that we already knew enough about the nature of divinity and could apply that knowledge to Jesus himself. Instead we propose to adopt a *relational* conception of Christ's divinity. We choose to view him as the Son, as the one who is the way to the Father. And the obvious implication, which is of fundamental importance nevertheless, is that Jesus *qua* "way" is accessible to others insofar as they are willing to follow the same course. In short, we are seeking to avoid any sort of Christology that starts right off by saying that access to God and his Christ is possible through mere orthodoxy, cultic worship, or some sort of cultic relationship rather than through the concrete following of the historical Jesus.

EXCURSUS I
On the Eschatological Nature of the Kingdom

Modern exegesis discovered that the kingdom of God does possess an eschatological character. The first point to be considered by us here is the theoretical and practical import of that discovery within the theological milieu which made it.

A. Harnack, the last great representative of nineteenth-century theology, drew a famous portrait of Jesus in his book on the essence of Christianity.[19] He pictured Jesus as one who preached the fatherly goodness of God, love for humankind, and the infinite value of the human soul. His description was meant to provide a harmonious blend of the ideals that dominated German-speaking society in the nineteenth century. He sought to reconcile divine justice and human order, altar and secular throne, religion and culture. His Jesus, who fulfilled all basic human yearnings, was nothing other than the ideal bourgeois citizen of the nineteenth century with faith in progress. Jesus thus stood in a direct line of continuity with human realities, confirming and perhaps ennobling them but certainly not criticizing them.

Given this portrait, we can readily understand and appreciate the shocking impact of the views expressed by J. Weiss and A. Schweitzer. They discovered the "eschatological" character of the kingdom of God that was preached by Jesus. In their view Jesus was not someone whose preaching supported human dreams and ideals. Even though his message was "good news," it spoke about something that forced people and their world into a crisis. This crisis affected a centuries-old brand of Christian existence that included the Constantinian view of church-state relationships, the Holy Roman Empire, the Christian culture of Western Europe, temporal power invested in the popes, and so forth. The critical problem was that Jesus no longer stood in continuity with the yearnings of bourgeois Christians. In proclaiming the imminent coming of the kingdom, Jesus was saying that things could not go on as they are, and that the inertial thrust of inner evolution alone would not bring about any real improvement.

In its literal sense, "eschatology" means a set of doctrines about the last or final things. The *eschaton*, as the last and ultimate reality, creates a crisis for people and history. It reveals what is of ultimate and definitive relevance. The first thing we must do now is explore the precise meaning of this "ultimate" reality, because on it will depend any systematic interpretation of Jesus' proclamation concerning the kingdom of God.

In the history of systematic and exegetical theology we find a host of answers to this question, but they divide into two basic groups. One set of answers interprets "ultimate" or "final" *in a temporal sense*; the other set interprets it *in an existential sense*. Christology has tried to combine what is best in both interpretations.

A. Schweitzer is one of the outstanding representatives of the temporal or chronological interpretation of eschatology.[20] At the start Jesus believed that the kingdom would come during his own lifetime (see Matt. 10:23); later he thought that its coming would be hastened by his own death (see Matt. 26:24). It was the later Christian community, disappointed by the failure of the kingdom to arrive, that shifted the coming of the kingdom to the end of time (see Mark 13:32). Thus the New Testament stresses a consistently future eschatology.

C.H. Dodd thinks that the eschatological passages of the Gospels refer to temporal events rather than to ethico-existential requirements.[21] The kingdom is not still to come; it has already been realized in the figure and activity of Jesus himself. Thus the New Testament is talking about a realized eschatology. The "future-directed" eschatology is a clear addition of the early Christian community.

Cullmann coined the now famous notion of "already and not yet."[22] The end of time has begun with the coming of Jesus. Satan and sin have already been overcome in principle. The day of judgment will reveal and make clear what Christ already is.

The problem faced by such temporal interpretations is what to make of history after Jesus. Either the import of history is already given fully with him, or it will only show up at the end of time, or there is a tension existing in some meaningfulness that is already breaking through but has not yet been fully realized.

The classic proponent of existential eschatology is R. Bultmann.[23] In this view "the ultimate" is what affects people in some ultimate and unconditional way. The preaching of Jesus himself (and later proclamation of the resurrected Christ) is eschatological because it confronts people here and now with the ultimate reality and meaning of their lives. Faced with this proclamation, people are compelled to make a critical choice. Either they will continue as sinners, furnishing their own meaning for their existence; or else they will choose to believe, letting God furnish the meaning of their lives. What are we to say, then, of the New Testament language that seems to suggest a temporal eschatology—signs and wonders at the end of time, the angels appearing, the solemn final judgment, and so forth? It is a literary device using mythical language to point up the depth and seriousness of life here and now. The same holds true for the *spatial* language of the New Testament that places people between heaven and hell. It is simply another device for pointing up the basic choice that people must face in this life. Insofar as the import of history is concerned, every concrete historical situation is equally near to, or far from, the kingdom of God. It is people's decisions, not objective social conditions, that fashion the kingdom of God right now or keep it a reality still to come.

At present we find various systematic theologians trying to

reconcile the temporal futurity of the kingdom with the aspect of personal involvement here and now. Pannenberg accepts Cullmann's basic notion of a tension, but he reworks it substantially.[24] The tension does not lie between "already and not yet"; it lies in seeing the kingdom as already present precisely because it continues to be in the future. By proclaiming that the kingdom is not yet present, that it is still to come though very close, Jesus lets God be the God of the future, unable to be controlled or manipulated by people. The proper and basic attitude for human beings, then, is unconditional trust in this God of the future and a refusal to rely on anything in the present. Paradoxically enough, the "not yet" of the kingdom (i.e., its temporal dimension as future) is the condition which makes it possible for people to live solely on the basis of trust in God (the present realization of the kingdom). Thus the kingdom can be present now (through unconditional trust in God) precisely because God has not yet arrived (God as future).

Moltmann maintains that the kingdom has not yet arrived though it does exist now in the form of a definitive promise.[25] It can also be rendered present in a concrete way of life, not through simple trust or existential ideas, but through the concrete praxis of following Jesus. If the paradigm of the kingdom is "universal resurrection," then the kingdom is rendered present to the extent that people here and now live as resurrected beings with history. Since history is filled with conflict and offers no guarantee that the fullness of the kingdom will be realized within it, the presence of the kingdom is made real by people's decision to fashion the definitive kingdom on the level of their personal and societal life. Thus the full reality of the kingdom is "in the future"; it is a "promise." But the life of a person who seeks to fashion the kingdom is a life that corresponds to the life of the definitive kingdom within the conditions of history. For it is a life based on love and self-surrender to God and other people.

Boff's position is very reminiscent of Moltmann's but he stresses partial historical realizations of the kingdom more than he stresses a basic intent to live the life of that kingdom.[26]

The kingdom of God as a totality is a utopia realized in the risen Jesus but not in world history. Insofar as it is simply pondered in thought, it can only be an "ideology." Indeed "idea" would be a better word here, so that we might avoid the pejorative connotations of the term "ideology." But this idea, which becomes fully real only in the future, is rendered present insofar as it serves as a wellspring for functional ideologies. Subjectively the presence of the kingdom shows up in the liberative existence of the Christian based on Jesus himself: "With this in mind, the Christian must not be afraid to make a concrete decision and risk failure. This decision may well be a historical mediation for the coming of the kingdom"[27]

The typical notion shared by these views is that the kingdom of God is rendered present insofar as people allow it to remain a personal and social utopia: i.e., a future reality. The real problem is how we are to live this utopia in a way that will really correspond with the coming kingdom. Do we live it by maintaining an attitude of unconditional trust and confidence? Or do we live it through a concrete praxis that follows in the footsteps of Jesus himself, opening ourselves to discipleship and to functional ideologies that may help us to fashion approximations of the kingdom in history?

As I see it, we can derive the following systematic consequences from the eschatological character of the kingdom. First of all, eschatology means "crisis," even though it has to do with proclaiming the "good news." God's kingdom does not confirm the present reality of humankind and its history; rather, it passes judgment on that reality in order to re-create it. This crisis may be interpreted in many different categories: temporal, existential, situational, or practical. They all share the notion that people and history cannot go on as before in the face of this proclamation of the kingdom. No longer permitted to follow the old routine, people and history must change. Hence the concept of "eschatology" is wholly consistent with Jesus' fundamental demand for a conversion *(metanoia)*.

Second, Jesus' eschatology has a historico-temporal character. Jesus believes in a temporal fulfillment of the world which, strictly speaking, is not the work of people insofar as it is a fulfillment. It is the work of the God who comes. His coming cannot be hastened in any strict sense by Pharisaic observance of the law or by a theocratic revolution in arms as the Zealots would want; nor can it be discovered by analyzing the signs of the time in apocalyptic terms.

Third, Jesus' eschatology also has a present aspect. It does so negatively because no type of present existence really "corresponds" to the kingdom. It does so positively because it unveils another kind of existence that does "correspond" to the kingdom. For us that form of existence is the following of Jesus. Subjectively that means we must be open to living a life like that of Jesus. Objectively it means that we must be open to the work of transforming reality. Jesus' own attitude, which seems somewhat inconsistent at first glance, points up both aspects. On the one hand he seems to wait passively in hope for the coming of the kingdom; on the other hand he actively propounds and displays a way of life in accord with the kingdom on both the personal and social level.

Fourth, on the basis of eschatology we can reformulate the traditional quandaries of theology in a novel and truly operational way. Consider the matter of the relationship between God and human beings, which has been traditionally presented in terms of a relationship between liberty and grace, or works and faith. In my opinion the most suitable and relevant way to pose that quandary today is in terms of a tension between fashioning the kingdom on the one hand and asserting that God is drawing near in grace on the other. On the basis of Jesus' own eschatology we can say that both aspects are real and important, even when they cannot be reconciled by thought. However, the quandary can be reconciled in and through concrete praxis insofar as the individual or some larger group undertakes the work of partially fashioning the kingdom and experiences that effort as a gratuitous gift or grace. We may not experience it as such subjectively because it goes against all our normal inclinations. We may not experience it as such objectively because many times the reaction to this effort will not lead to the establishment of greater justice but to the very opposite. But if we experience our following of

Jesus as grace, if we find ourselves actually trying to fashion the kingdom, then we can resolve the quandary between grace and action which does not allow of a theoretical solution.

Fifth, eschatology presents the problem of God in a new light, pointing up his relationship to the future as a mode of his own being.[28] Insofar as temporal comments on God are concerned, the emphasis must be shifted from the genesis of time to the future. The definitive revelation of God will take place at the end of time, and thus the whole temporal process is important in the revelation of God. This we shall see more clearly in discussing the cross of Jesus.

EXCURSUS II
Reformulating the Problem of Jesus' Own Consciousness

The problem of Jesus' consciousness is much debated in both exegesis and systematic theology. I do not propose here to explore the issue exegetically and spell out exactly what Jesus thought about himself. In the next chapter I shall try to sum up the most important and profound depths of his own awareness by considering his operative faith. My aim here, on the other hand, is to consider how that whole problem can be posed correctly on the basis of Jesus' own history. To do that, I shall offer a few methodological principles and concrete examples.

Jesus' Consciousness vis-à-vis the Kingdom of God

Traditional theology started off from the *dogmatic* supposition of Jesus' personal union with the eternal Logos. This union had to be an object of awareness in the human condition of Jesus, and so the man Jesus was aware that he was the Son of God in the strict, metaphysical sense of the term. Various citations from Scripture were used to support this dogmatic assertion, such as passages of John's Gospel (John 10:30, 36, 38) and the so-called Johannine logion in Matthew's Gospel: "No one knows the Son but the Father, and no one knows the Father but the Son" (Matt. 11:27).

Even back in the days of D.F. Strauss, however, those

passages were viewed as not coming from Jesus. A new approach arose, focusing on the titles and epithets applied to Jesus in the Gospels which pointed to his own messianic consciousness. Further exegetical exploration has raised serious questions about that approach. It is not unlikely that Jesus did come to view the nature of himself and his work on the basis of certain figures and types in the Old Testament. After his Galilean crisis in particular, he may have come to see himself in close relationship to the prophets and the suffering Servant of Yahweh. But exegetically we have a hard time confirming that Jesus assumed certain titles and applied them to himself unequivocally, except perhaps for the epithet "Son of Man."[29]

Confronted with these exegetical difficulties, our new way of looking at Jesus' own consciousness is not based on deducing directly what Jesus might have thought about himself. Instead we now try to deduce the nature of his own distinctive consciousness from his general attitudes and actions.

Jesus is aware of the fact that in and through his own person the kingdom of God is drawing near. And the term "kingdom" refers to an assertion of power that will bring about salvation. Jesus does not simply preach the approach of the kingdom. He also works signs indicating its approach: "If it is by the finger of God that I cast out devils, then the reign of God is upon you" (Luke 11:20). Exegesis makes it quite certain that Jesus did forgive sins (Mark 2:1–12) and did sit down to eat with sinners at table (Mark 2:15–17). These actions were so novel and scandalous that Jesus must have been conscious of his own distinctive relationship with the kingdom of God.

The same awareness is evident in his parables about the kingdom. He realizes that the kingdom has arrived in some incipient, hidden way but that it will reveal its full power soon enough (see the parable of the mustard seed in Mark 4:30f.). In this interim period when it is just breaking through, people are blest if they lay hold of the kingdom in the person of the "lowly" Jesus and are not scandalized (Matt. 11:6). Here we see the difference between the earlier prophetic proclamation of salvation and that of Jesus. The earlier prophets proclaimed a future salvation; Jesus proclaims that with himself salvation has already commenced.

This same awareness also is apparent in *a comparison of Jesus with the great figures of the Old Testament*. In discussing the indissolubility of marriage, Jesus is bold enough to interpret the law in a new and more original way than Moses did (see Mark 10:4f.). This whole attitude is quite evident in the Sermon on the Mount when Jesus contrasts what was said of old with what he himself says (Matt. 5:22, 28, 32, 34, 39, 44).

When Jesus talks that way, he goes far beyond the preaching of the prophets. They sought to legitimate their preaching by saying that it was the word of Yahweh. Jesus, by contrast, starts off many of his comments with a phrase such as: "Of this much I assure you . . ." (see Matt. 5:18; 6:2, 5, 16; 8:10). Ordinarily the term "Amen" was only used at the end of a discourse to express hopeful confirmation of what had been said. Jesus uses it at the start to assert that that is the way things really are.

Jesus is bold enough to assert that eschatological salvation is determined by the stance a person adopts toward Jesus' own person. He says: "If anyone in this faithless and corrupt age is ashamed of me and my doctrine, the Son of Man will be ashamed of him when he comes with the holy angels in his Father's glory" (Mark 8:38). In this passage Jesus seems to make a clear distinction between his own person and that of the coming Son of Man. This tends to verify the historicity of the saying; and the same distinction is made in Luke 12:8f., though the thought is there formulated in positive terms. In Matt. 10:32f., by contrast, Jesus is identified with the Son of Man because the distinction no longer was meaningful after the resurrection.

Let us be clear as to what is important for our purpose here. The point is not that Jesus was aware that he himself was the Son of Man who would come as a judge to establish the kingdom at the end of time. The point is that Jesus is quite conscious of the fact that people's ultimate salvation or condemnation is functionally related to his own person.

The phenomenon of discipleship itself was not new in Jesus' day. The rabbis had disciples and envoys. The Zealots demanded total dedication to their cause, even if it meant death. *The novel feature in Jesus' teaching is the salvific function of discipleship.* It means service to the kingdom, but it is associated with *his own concrete person* (Mark 8:34f.), particularly in the second phase of his public life. He calls for unconditional following of himself (Matt. 8:19–22) and the renunciation of everything closest to a person: possessions, family, and one's own self.

All these aspects of Jesus' life combine to point up his self-awareness *indirectly.* We do not know what Jesus thought explicitly about himself. We do not know for sure whether he saw himself as the Messiah or the Son of Man. The *absolute* self-awareness of Jesus can scarcely be derived directly from the data provided by the New Testament. All we can get at is his *relational* self-awareness: i.e., what he thought about himself in relation to the kingdom, and the decisive importance of his own person in its arrival.

However, that does enable us to draw a very important conclusion: "The prepaschal Jesus is of the opinion that this new approach of the kingdom is taking place *in and through* his proclamation of its nearness."[30] It is the concrete person of Jesus that determines what the kingdom is and how one draws closer to it. Earlier we considered the figure of Jesus in terms of the traditions concerning the kingdom of God. Now we see that what the kingdom is exactly will depend on Jesus himself. I put the statement in rather general terms here. What it means more precisely will be seen when we study the death and resurrection of Jesus in later chapters. The point here is one made by Rahner: "God's approach in victorious salvation cannot be viewed as given once for all in exactly the same way in Jesus' awareness. It is not a perduring, unchanging existential situation which at worst can only be forgotten or restricted, so that it must be preached ever anew. In Jesus and his preaching the nearness of God's kingdom shows up in a novel, unique, and insuperable way."[31]

Jesus' Consciousness vis-à-vis the Father

The Gospels make clear that Jesus was not only conscious of

a mission on behalf of the kingdom but also aware of a relationship to the Father. Here again we cannot rely on *explicit* statements by Jesus about his sonship. It shows up indirectly, particularly in two respects: his unconditional trust in the Father and his unconditional obedience to the Father's will.

Jesus' *trust* in the Father is seen in his use of the word "Abba" to address Yahweh, and this fact is not disputed by modern exegesis.[32] It was not frequently applied as such to God himself (see Mark 14:36). It indicated an *exclusive* relationship of Jesus to the Father in two senses. First, Jesus lives his life wholly in and through the Father: "Let it be as you would have it, not as I" (Mark 14:36). Second, Jesus' relationship with the Father is wholly different from that of other human beings. In the Gospels Jesus constantly makes a distinction between "my Father" and "your Father." The expression "our Father" appears only in Matt. 6:9, when Jesus is teaching his disciples to pray as a group. Thus the gospel passages in which Jesus talks about himself as the Son should not be interpreted in a dogmatic sense but in the sense just indicated. They express Jesus' confidence in the Father, which gives substance and consistency to his whole way of life (see Matt. 11:27; Mark 12:1–19; 13:32).

Confidence in God as Father is not exclusive to Jesus. It can be found in the Old Testament and in other religions. What characterizes Jesus is the way his whole life is concentrated in this confidence that the Father is near to him. Because God is not hidden at a remote distance, this familiarity and exclusivity is both possible and legitimate. Moreover, it heightens and brings out the whole drama of the cross, where Jesus is abandoned by the Father in whom he has placed all his trust.

The prayer of Jesus must be interpreted in this light. Jesus prayed like a pious Israelite, and he followed the prescriptions of the Jewish cult. But the fulfillment of those religious obligations is not what typifies the prayer of Jesus. What typifies it is his complete abandonment and submission to the Father, which gives expression to his complete theological poverty. Jesus is fully conscious of the fact that he is not the Father, that his life is rooted in Another.

It is also important to note that Jesus' prayer, expressing confidence in the Father, is bound up with, rather than detached from, the fundamental moments of his historical activity. His prayer is in no way mechanical. It is closely bound up with life. That is what gives reality to his confidence in the Father and to the temptation to give up that confidence. Besides mentioning prayer of a more regular sort (e.g., saying grace before meals; Mark 14:19; 15:36; 26:26f.), the Gospels also indicate that Jesus prayed at crucial points in his life: at his baptism, at the start of his public ministry (Luke 3:21), before choosing his disciples (Luke 6:12), before teaching the Our Father (Luke 11:1), when Peter made his profession at Caesarea (Luke 9:18), and at the transfiguration (Luke 9:28 f.).

It is clearly Luke who reflected most on the prayer of Jesus, but the basic pattern of Jesus' prayer is brought out by Mark when he talks about the agony in the garden. The important point is that Jesus' prayer expresses his felt sense of dependence on the Father and trust in him *in the face of* important concrete events affecting himself and his disciples.

Alongside this movement of Jesus toward the Father in total trust and confidence is Jesus' awareness of the Father's movement toward him. The Father has given him a mission, and Jesus' response is one of total *obedience*. His awareness of a mission from the Father is so patent that the Synoptic Gospels do not talk about it explicitly even though it pervades every page. Jesus' life makes sense only in terms of his awareness of this mission. Later on, Paul's theology will describe Jesus as the *one sent* by the Father (Rom. 8:3; Gal. 4:4), and the Johannine writings will say the same thing (John 3:16; 1 John 4:9 f.). The Letter to the Hebrews will describe it in terms of the Son's obedience (Heb. 5:8).

So we can deduce what Jesus' awareness vis-à-vis the Father was in terms of these two traits. Trusting in the Father, he lived his whole life accordingly. Obedient to the Father, he lived his whole life to carry out the Father's will. Here again we do not touch the *absolute* awareness or consciousness of Jesus about himself. Again we get a *relational* awareness. Who Jesus is and what he thought about himself is to be deduced from his awareness of a relationship with the Father.

Now normally people are not satisfied with this explanation and so they try to uncover the direct awareness of Jesus. This is due to an underlying philosophical supposition which should be mentioned here. It has to do with a specific notion of "person." This particular· notion seeks to define "person" in terms of *self-awareness,* and it ultimately goes back to Greek philosophy and its conception of the human being as a *rational* animal. That conception has made its way through the Enlightenment to the modern philosophy of subjectivity: To be a person is to have possession of one's self. The point of it here is that according to this view we are more of a person when we understand ourselves more and better. By the same token, we "know" who Jesus was insofar as we know what Jesus "thought" about himself.

But there is another conception of "person" that has its roots in discussions of the Trinity (in Augustine's works and others). According to this view, it is the *relational nature* of the person, not any absoluteness in itself, that is the typifying characteristic of "person." Thus Richard of Saint Victor (d. 1173) says that personhood is ex-istence, a type of being that gets its consistency from another outside. In Scotus's famous description, a "person" realizes its existence either in dependence on God or in opposition to him. This line of thought culminates in Hegel's definition: "The essence of person is to surrender oneself to the other and find fulfillment precisely in the other."

These two different lines of thought provide two different ways of focusing on Jesus' self-awareness. If we adopt the first line of thought on what a person is, then knowing who Jesus is will mean trying to find out exactly what Jesus himself thought explicitly about himself. If we adopt the second line of thought, then knowing who Jesus is will mean finding out to whom Jesus surrendered himself and how he did it.

Here I have chosen the second approach for two reasons. One is historical: The Gospels simply do not provide us with enough data to figure out what Jesus thought about himself exactly. The other is systematic: It is my belief that it is by observing the relational character of a person that we plumb the depths of that person; and the same holds true for the person of Jesus.

On the basis of these considerations we can try to explain the usual theological statements made about the consciousness and knowledge of Jesus. In traditional tracts it is customary to say that Jesus had divine knowledge because he was united to the divine person of the Logos; and that he also had three kinds of human knowledge—the kind of knowledge acquired normally, infused knowledge, and the beatific vision.

Now the Gospels give no reason to allow for infused knowledge and the beatific vision. So we must ask ourselves *why*, in spite of that, such knowledge is attributed to Jesus. And the answer, once again, is to be found in the underlying conception of what "person" is. If "person" and knowledge are self-possession, and if Jesus is a person—or possesses a *perfect* human nature, to use the language of dogmatic theology —then he must possess perfect knowledge. And so we get the principle of *perfectionism:* If Jesus is perfect, then we must attribute to him everything that is presumed to go along with human perfection. If it is a matter of knowledge, for example, then he must possess every possible sort of human knowledge to the hilt. So that includes normally acquired knowledge, infused knowledge, and the knowledge that human beings enjoy in the beatific vision.

What has happened is that a particular philosophical conception about the nature of person and its perfection in the area of knowledge has been enlisted in the service of a theological conception: i.e., that Jesus was really human, and a perfect human being. But the two conceptions certainly can be separated, in principle at least. The interpretation proposed here is, I think, far more biblical. In the New Testament it is the relationship of Jesus to the Father in trust and obedience that typifies his person. It is also far more in accord with the present-day conception of the person insofar as its use for systematic theology is concerned. For today we see "person" more in terms of surrender or dedication to another.

NOTES

1. K. Rahner, *Christologie—systematisch und exegetisch* (Freiburg: Herder, 1972), p. 29.

2. This point is of major importance. A detailed treatment of it would require us to point up the various aspects of the Jewish conception of God based on the various strands of tradition in the Old Testament. I do not mean to suggest at all that Jesus was not fully aware of the prophetic, sapiential, and apocalyptic traditions about God. The point here is that Jesus, in his person and his activity, seems to have woven all those traditions into a unified conception in which God was viewed from the standpoint of, and closely bound up with, the "kingdom of God."

This point has been brought out by many writers: F. Hahn, *Christologische Hoheitstitel* (Göttingen: Vandenhoeck, 1963), p. 27; U. Wilckens, *Das Offenbarungsverstandnis in der Geschichte*, 1965, 3rd edition, p. 56, footnote 35; W. Pannenberg, *Fundamentos de cristología*, pp. 284–88, see note 6 of chap. 1 in this volume. J.P. Miranda sums up the Old Testament conception of God as one based on justice. To know God, then, is to do justice, particularly in defense of those who have been wronged. Though our term "kingdom of God" may seem at variance with his emphasis on "justice," his focus corresponds to our particular concentration on the kingdom here. See J.P. Miranda, *Marx y la Biblia* (Salamanca: Sigueme, 1972); Eng. trans.: *Marx and the Bible: A Critique of the Philosophy of Oppression* (Maryknoll, New York: Orbis Books, 1974), especially chaps. 2–4.

3. W. Pannenberg, "Die Offenbarung Gottes in Jesus von Nazareth," in *Offenbarung als Geschichte*, p. 143; see note 13 in chap. 2 of this volume. Here I do not propose to provide an exhaustive analysis of the notion "kingdom of God." I simply want to provide the minimum amount of data needed to provide a historical and systematic understanding of the historical Jesus.

4. In his concrete activity it is certain that Jesus was a "liberal" with respect to traditional notions: E. Käsemann, *La llamada de la libertad*, Spanish trans. (Salamanca, 1974), pp. 22–55; German original: *Der Ruf der Freiheit* (Tübingen: Mohr, 1968); Eng. trans.: *Jesus Means Freedom* (Philadelphia: Fortress Press, 1970). He was also a "nonconformist": J. Ernst, *Anfange der Christologie* (Stuttgart, 1972), pp. 145–58. But while his liberalism and nonconformism really did bring him to the cross, both must be understood in terms of his basic and primary identification with his own people.

5. See R. Schnackenburg, *Reino y reinado de Dios*, Spanish trans. (Madrid, 1967), pp. 15–20; German original: *Gottes Herrschaft und Reich* (Freiburg: Herder, 1963); Eng. trans.: *God's Rule and Kingdom* (New York: Herder & Herder, 1963).

6. See L. Boff, "Salvation in Jesus Christ and the Process of Liberation," p. 80f.; see note 38, chap. 2 in this volume.

7. Ibid., p. 81.

8. There are various interpretations of the apocalyptic thrust. J. Moltmann has stressed the point that while apocalypticism does entail a historicization of the world and embody a final hope, its deepest underlying thrust is the

expectation of God's justice: "Only superficially is world history a historico-universal problem, the solution of which would provide a horizon of meaning for the whole of existence. At bottom the inquiry into world history is an inquiring quest for justice" (*Der gekreuzigte Gott*, p. 162; see note 10 in chap. 1 of this volume).

9. See L. Boff, *Jesucristo el liberador*, Spanish trans. (Buenos Aires, 1974), p. 70f.; Portuguese original, *Jesus Cristo Libertador. Ensaio de cristologia crítica para o nosso tempo* (Petrópolis, Brazil: Vozes, 1972); English trans. by Orbis Books forthcoming. As is now recognized, the term "kingdom of God" does not signify "kingdom of heaven" (Boff, ibid., p. 67) or "church" (see *Mysterium Salutis*, 4/1 (Madrid, 1973), pp. 58, 108–12).

10. This formulation is certainly at variance with customary ontological thought, which is also reflected in the dogmatic statements about God issued by Vatican I (DS 3001f.). But it is at the very heart of the biblical conception of God. This is evident in the earliest creeds of the Old Testament (Deut. 26:5–9), where God's reality is defined on the basis of his actions in history. It is also evident in the New Testament, where the eschatological dimension of God's reality is radicalized on the basis of his activity at the end of time (1 Cor. 15:24–28). Vatican II rehabilitated and accepted that historicized conception of God, in principle at least (see *Dei Verbum*, nos. 2f.).

11. W. Pannenberg, "Dogmatische Thesen zur Lehre von der Offenbarung," in *Offenbarung als Geschichte*, p. 91f.; J. Moltmann, *Teología de la esperanza*, pp. 124–33, see note 31 of chap. 2 in this volume.

12. Acts 1:1 already mentions this twofold activity of Jesus in terms of "doing" and "teaching." The point is picked up by Vatican II in *Dei Verbum* (nos. 2–4). Here we are saying something more, however: that it is absolutely essential and necessary that this word or message be turned into action. The "word" of Jesus about the kingdom is the first and initial phase of a needed proclamation. But if that kingdom is to even be understood in terms of its real nature, the word cannot merely be proclaimed. Since it has to do with justice and love, it must be *done*. That, I think, is the logic that pervades John's Gospel, where Jesus is the word of the Father precisely because he makes historically real the Father's essence: i.e., love.

13. My feeling is that the whole issue of the miracles, which is under consideration again today, should not be viewed in terms of some possible violation of the laws of nature. That is a rationalist approach to the issue, and in principle it has been overcome by biblical theology itself. Current theology, and liberation theology in particular, would do better to view it in terms of the whole problem of power and its use. Jesus' miraculous activity was a predominant feature of the first stage of his ministry; it diminished almost to the point of disappearance in the second stage of his ministry. That fact raises the whole question as to what sort of power really does make present the kingdom of God, what ultimately is the message and activity of Jesus which sets him off from the message and activity of other people. His miraculous activity, for example, might well be good but not the ultimate thing. In the next chapter we shall consider the importance of such reflections for Christian ethics today.

14. "Trusting in the arrival of God's reign is the one and only condition for participating in it. Hence carrying out the traditional law is no longer decisive insofar as justice is concerned. Jesus automatically pardons the sins of people

who had this attitude because they were in tune with the God drawing near"
(W. Pannenberg, "Zur Theologie des Rechtes," *Zeitschrift für Evangelische
Ethik* 7 (1963), p. 29). The important thing to note in this citation is not the
concrete way in which Pannenberg relates the pardoning of sins to the kingdom of God; it is that Pannenberg sees the pardoning of sins as related to the
kingdom of God, not as a personal demonstration on Jesus' part.

15. This is the aspect rightly stressed by the existential interpretation. Faith
is risking the loss of one's security: "The person whom God's action seeks to
vivify anew is first destroyed by that very action" (R. Bultmann, *Glauben und
Verstehen* [Tübingen: Mohr, 1968 edition], 2:119; Eng. trans.: *Faith and Understanding* [New York: Harper & Row, 1969]).

16. It is important to note that Jesus does not allow social injustice, not even
in the brief space of time which he thought remained before the imminent
coming of the kingdom. See O. Cullmann, *Jesús y los revolucionarios de su
tiempo,* Spanish trans. (Madrid, 1973), p. 37f.; Eng. trans.: *Jesus and the Re-
volutionaries* (New York: Harper & Row, 1970).

17. The need for a theology of power is recognized by all. My statements
here relate to the situation of Jesus as he expectantly waited for the imminent
arrival of the kingdom. The complexity of the problem will be brought out in
the next chapter. A sample attempt to tackle and solve the issue can be found
in I. Ellacuría, *Freedom Made Flesh* (Maryknoll, New York: Orbis Books, 1976),
chaps. 6–8.

18. See R. Schnackenburg, *Existencia cristiana según el Nuevo Testamento,*
Spanish trans. (Estella, 1973), pp. 95–106; German original: *Christliche Existenz
nach dem Neuen Testament* (Munich: Kösel, 1967); Eng. trans.: *Christian Existence
in the New Testament* (University of Notre Dame Press, 1968). His study is too
"psychologizing," in my opinion. Only in passing does Schnackenburg mention what typifies the following of Jesus, particularly in the first stage of Jesus'
public life: "Those called are to become fishers of men, abandoning their
previous calling as fishermen" (p. 98). This "change of profession" is not just
another exigency of Jesus, however; it is the one which explains and motivates
all the other exigencies.

19. See *Das Wesen des Christentums* (Munich: Siebenstern, 1964), p. 42.

20. See *Geschichte der Leben-Jesu Forschung,* Band 2 (Munich, 1966), pp.
402–50; Eng. trans.: *The Quest of the Historical Jesus* (New York: Macmillan, 1968
reprint).

21. See *The Parables of the Kingdom* (New York: Scribner's, 1961), p. 146f.

22. See *La historia de salvación,* Spanish trans. (Barcelona, 1967), pp. 217–26;
German original: *Heil als Geschichte* (Tübingen: Mohr, 1965); Eng. trans.:
Salvation in History (New York: Harper & Row, 1967).

23. See *Jesus* (Munich: Siebenstern, 1967), p. 38f.; *Geschichte und Eschatologie,* 2nd ed. (Tübingen: Mohr, 1964), p. 180, Eng. trans.: *The Presence of
Eternity: History and Eschatology* (New York: Harper & Row, 1957): "The New
Testament announces Jesus Christ as the eschatological happening, as the
action of God in which he puts an end to the old world. In announcement and
proclamation the eschatological happening is rendered present time and
again; every time it thus becomes a happening in faith. For the believer, the old
world has come to its end. It is now a 'new creation in Christ.' The old world

has come to an end for him because the life of the old man has come to an end for him; he has been turned into a new, free man."

24. See *Fundamentos de cristología*, pp. 280–91, see note 6, chap. 1, in this volume; *Teología y reino de Dios*, pp. 11–39, see note 15, chap. 2, in this volume.

25. Moltmann's conception can be gathered, not so much from any particular section of his work, but from its overall thrust and content. See, for example, his works entitled *Theology of Hope* (see note 31, chap. 2, in this volume) and *The Crucified God* (see note 10, chap. 2, in this volume).

26. *Jesucristo el liberador*, pp. 65–77, see note 9 in this chapter; "Salvation in Jesus Christ and the Process of Liberation," pp. 78–91, see note 38, chap. 2, in this volume.

27. Ibid., p. 90.

28. See Pannenberg, *Grundfragen systematischer Theologie*, pp. 361–98, see note 12, chap. 2, in this volume. Posing the problem of God in those terms does not seem radically Christian enough, in my opinion. To consider God's mode of being, one must look at not only the future but also suffering, as we shall see when we analyze the death of Jesus in chap. 5. Both aspects, the future and suffering, are hardly the focal point of classical theology.

29. Needless to say, there are many conflicting exegetical opinions on this question insofar as it is a historical issue. By way of comparison the reader might want to consult these two works for a start: O. Cullmann, *Dei Christologie des Neuen Testaments* (Tübingen: Mohr, 1957); Eng. trans.:*The Christology of the New Testament*, rev. ed. (Philadelphia: Westminster Press, 1963); and F. Hahn, *Christologische Hoheitstitel* (Göttingen: Vandenhoeck, 1963); Eng. trans.: *The Titles of Jesus in Christology* (London: Lutterworth, 1969). The point I would like to stress here is that one cannot focus systematically on the person of Jesus by starting out from the titles attributed to him, even though he himself may have really identified himself with one or more of them. One must start out from his *real life*.

30. K. Rahner, *Christologie—systematisch und exegetisch* (Freiburg: Herder, 1972), p. 31.

31. Ibid., p. 29.

32. See the now classic exposition of J. Jeremias, "Kennzeichen der *ipsissima vox* Jesu," in *Synoptische Studien* (Munich, 1955), pp. 86–93.

4.

The Faith of Jesus: Its Relevance
for Christology and Following Jesus

Liberation theology has rehabilitated the figure of the historical Jesus within theology. On the one hand it seeks to overcome a highly abstract conception of Christ that is readily open
to manipulation. On the other hand it seeks positively to
ground Christian existence on the following of this historical
Jesus.

The aim is not just to overcome the aura of mythology that
surrounds Christology and thus indirectly get at the real Christian morality of Jesus. It also is looking for a focus that will
historicize the figure of Jesus in an authentic and truly operative way. As Ellacuría puts it: "We must move on to a historical
logos, without which every other *logos* will remain speculative
and idealistic."[1] The supposition is that in and through a real
historicization of Jesus we will discover the most profound
dimension of his existence as the Son, and hence the most
profound dimension of those whom "he is not ashamed to
call . . . brothers" (Heb. 2:11).

In my opinion, one concrete and effective way of recovering
the real historicity of Jesus is to reflect on something that has
generally been overlooked yet represents one of the deepest
aspects of Jesus' person: i.e., his faith. As Boff puts it: "Jesus
was an extraordinary believer and had faith. Faith was his very
mode of existence."[2] Now obviously we are not trying to
introduce some new concept, faith in this case, in order to

historicize Jesus in a purely nominalist way. Our aim here is to picture the historical Jesus in terms of "the history of Jesus" or, more specifically, in terms of "the history of Jesus' faith."

PRELIMINARY OBSERVATIONS

To point up the significance of describing the historical Jesus in terms of his faith, I shall offer some preliminary observations.

The notion of "Jesus' faith," even formulated explicitly, does have roots in the New Testament and in the history of modern theology.[3] For all that, it still strikes us as a novel and even shocking formulation. It is a polemical formulation. It is precisely because it is polemical that it can be effective in breaking the inertia of more mythical thinking about Jesus or a train of thought that abstractly avows the "humanity" of Jesus without getting at the roots of his existence as a human being and as the Son.

The polemical nature of the formulation is clear enough when we consider Thomas Aquinas's classic rejection of the idea that Jesus had faith. His view, in fact, is still very much alive in our own day. Aquinas says: "The object of faith is divine reality that is hidden from sight. . . . Now a virtue, like any other habit, takes its image from its object. Hence when divine reality is not hidden from sight, there is no point in faith. From the first moment of his conception Christ had full vision of God in his essence. . . . Therefore he could not have had faith."[4]

This view of Aquinas has had a continuing impact on theology and on the subsequent history of normal Christian faith. The polemical feature is the certainty and sureness with which St. Thomas affirms that Jesus could not have had faith. It is a statement of principle, not just of fact, constituting an ultimate horizon in any attempt to understand Jesus. And it is all the more dangerous in that there is no deeper reflection on it.

The notion of "Jesus' faith" is polemical mainly because it touches on the very dimension where his radical difference from all other human beings is presumed to lie: i.e., the theological dimension. Reflection on Jesus in recent years has certainly done a great deal to recover the humanity of Jesus, but it has also stopped short of considering the theological dimension of his humanity with respect to God and the kingdom of God. While much effort has been made to consider the humanity of Jesus in its individual, social, and even political dimensions that bespeak solidarity with all human beings, there has been little or no reflection on his solidarity with us in the theological dimension of his faith. People have unthinkingly reiterated the teachings of Chalcedon concerning the coexistence of divine and human natures of Jesus. Talk about the "faith of Jesus" seems to be alien to that schema of coexisting humanity and divinity. The fact is, however, that divinity and faith do not rule each other out at all. Indeed it is the faith of Jesus that provides us with the key to understanding what constitutes his divinity in the concrete.

The term "Jesus' faith" is meant to shed light on the subject, not just to be polemical. It seeks to sum up the whole thrust of Christology in recent years, a thrust more evident in Catholic than in Protestant theology. We can describe the shift in terms of several basic stages.

First, there was a dogmatic Christology based primarily on the teaching of Chalcedon. That teaching was considered the last word in reflection on Christ, though it might need successive reinterpretations. Despite the possible need for such reinterpretation, the basic focus of Christology would not change so long as the Chalcedonian formula was presumed to have spoken the last and most profound word about Jesus.[5]

This way of doing Christology ran into a crisis for two basic kinds of reasons. One set of reasons had to do with methodology, the other with content. In methodology people came to notice the one-sidedness of the concepts expressed in the Chalcedonian teaching. They all derived from *one* philosophy: Greek philosophy. A more serious methodological difficulty lay in the fact that Chalcedon had expressed the reality of Jesus in limit-concepts such as divinity, humanity, and the union of two natures in one person. Such concepts, however, cannot be intuited in themselves; they can only be grasped in conjunction with the approach by which one arrives at them.[6] Now in this case our approach has its roots in Scripture, and so our dogmatic focus calls for a return to Scripture. To put it another way: the Chalcedonian formula marks an advance in Christology only insofar as it is read and interpreted as a hearkening back to its historical 'source.[7]

To these methodological reasons we must add reasons having to do with substantive content. Basically they come down to two. One is the fact that the Chalcedonian formula presupposes certain concepts that in fact cannot be presupposed when it comes to Jesus. They assume we know who and what God is and who and what human beings are. But we cannot explain the figure of Jesus by presupposing such concepts because Jesus himself calls into question people's very understanding of God and human beings. We may use "divinity" and "humanity" as nominal definitions to somehow break the hermeneutic circle, but we cannot use them as real definitions, already known, in order to understand Jesus. Our approach should start from the other end. The second reason related to content is a most important one as we shall see, though at first glance it might seem to be highly theoretical. In the Chalcedonian formula we find Jesus identified with the Logos, but we do not find the essential feature of Jesus as described by Scripture: i.e., his relational nature to the Father.[8]

The second stage in the gradual shift of Christology saw a reaction of various sorts to this situation. In general people sought to go back to the data of Scripture. This focus too, however, had its problems. The various biblical Christologies centered around Christ's various titles are at bottom dogmatic Christologies. That is to say, they try to comprehend Christ in terms of explanatory concepts of a universal kind: e.g., logos, lord, Son of God, and so forth.[9] The various Christologies dealing with "the teaching of Jesus" isolate his words from his own history.[10] The various Christologies of the resurrection separate the final stage of Jesus' life from his overall historical process; the fundamental fact becomes the fact that Christ rose from the dead, but it is not exactly clear who this "Christ" is.[11] The various existential Christologies talk about Jesus as a proclamation-event which forces people into a decision-making situation; but aside from incurring a dangerous concentration on individualism, they also interpret his whole concrete history in terms of the eschatological events of his cross and his resurrection.

All these Christologies share a common feature: They ignore or partialize the history of Jesus. There is clearly a movement from dogmatic Christology to a more biblical Christology that takes more account of Jesus' life, but so far the movement is not carried through to the end.

We can understand why this should lead some people on to a third stage: i.e., toward a Christology of the historical Jesus. In principle such a Christology rejects any abstract, idealistic *logos* and any merely doctrinal or personalist *logos*. It seeks to affirm a truly historical *logos*, and that is what is being done by current Christologies based on the historical Jesus. History is felt to be more all-embracing than some idea or some merely personal experience, and hence our focus on Jesus should be a historical one.

Now this focus clearly represents an advance over the earlier ones, but it can stop half way in two respects. First of all, it can again turn into an epiphanic rather than a historical conception of Jesus. Jesus may well be viewed as a revelation in and through a historical action rather than as the revelation of some abstract idea. But this historical action may be taken in isolation and separated from the total historical movement that serves as revelation. The whole history of Jesus may be summed up under some formal or abstract aspect, however rooted in history it may be. Thus Jesus may be viewed as a prophet or man of prayer—both true enough—without any attempt being made to examine the concrete history of his prayer life or prophetic life.

The second danger here is selectivity.[12] Instead of organizing the story of Jesus in terms of his own real history, we may organize it in terms of some preconceived idea which we then find reflected in his history. We organize the historical data that are of interest to us, and there is a real danger that we will destroy the concrete history of which the data is a part. Let me give two examples of different sorts. First of all, we might consider Jesus' history in terms of all the historical data concerned with "liberation." This would lead us to emphasize such things as the following: his proclamation of the coming kingdom, his prophetic denunciations, his affinity with the Zealot movement, his condemnation of alienating cultic or legalistic practices, his resurrection as a utopian paradigm of liberation, and so forth. Or we might organize the history of Jesus around his "prayer," his proclamation of God's goodness and provident compassion, and his total trust in God. Now the data used in both cases could certainly be verified in the life of the historical Jesus. Our selectivity would not necessarily falsify the data as real elements in the life of Jesus. But one question would still remain: Is our selective way of organizing the data really reproducing the history of Jesus?

A point-by-point consideration of the historical facts relating to Jesus may bring out historical features without necessarily recapturing his real-life history. A few examples might make this clearer to the reader. Jesus mentions God from the start of his public life (Mark 1:14) to its end (Mark 15:34). The question is whether Jesus understood the term "God" in exactly the same way at the end of his life as he did at the beginning. My point is that the important thing is not just to verify historically that Jesus held a certain conception of God at a given moment but also to ascertain the concrete history of that conception of God. The very same point applies to other historical features of Jesus: his view of his liberative activity (see Luke 4:16–19 for the start of his public life, and Mark 14:24 for the end of his life); and his demands regarding discipleship (see Mark 6:7–11 and Mark 8:34). The problem is not so much to juxtapose or harmonize the various texts but to relate them to each other in a historical way. We want to see Jesus in the historical process of change and development.

We get an atomistic study of Jesus' history if we use a partializing or epiphanic or selective approach. What we want to recover is the totality of the historical Jesus. That is not simply the sum total of his historical actions and attitudes but the latter organized in his life history. Thus the "historical Jesus" is nothing else but "the history of Jesus."

If we want to see and understand the history of Jesus as the revelation of the historical Jesus, we must have certain guidelines to help us. I would suggest the following as useful in this effort:

1. Every human action in history, insofar as it is positive, is guided by certain values accepted as basically good at the start: e.g., love, justice, brotherhood, trust in God, and so forth. But insofar as they unfold in a given situation, they must be concretized in some way. If they remain in their general and initial form, they can lose all power or even turn into the very opposite. Hence the historical course of a person must entail the concretion of those values which triggered that course.

2. Change and conflict are part of every movement in history. Historical concretion, then, is a dialectical process carried out in the presence of opposing, negative factors that must be overcome. That is why change and conversion are incumbent on any historical subject or agent.

3. In the historical process we find a dialectical interplay between fashioning reality and fashioning oneself as an active subject.

4. On the basis of the above remarks we can now see what it means to study "the faith of Jesus." Basically we are not going to study just another datum connected with the historical Jesus. Instead we are going to try to recover his totality in history in theological terms. We are going to try to recapture the history of Jesus in terms of that which is most profoundly his: his faith. For it is the point of convergence for the factors described above. Now in a sense we could do the same thing by focusing on his hope or his love. My choice of faith is not meant to suggest any opposition to those other two realities. I choose faith because it is the key Old Testament concept in terms of which Jesus understood himself.

Let me make one final set of observations that may help to explain the interest underlying this attempt to analyze the history of Jesus' faith. It is one thing to ascertain that Jesus had faith; the standpoint from which we ascertain that fact is something else again. If we want to appreciate the basic Latin American standpoint for which the faith of Jesus has relevance, we might do well to compare it with other possible standpoints.

Hans Urs von Balthasar certainly deserves a great deal of credit for breaking the silence in Catholic circles and calling attention to the whole theme of Jesus' own faith. The theme is important because it points up Jesus' relational character to God. His whole existence finds its fulfillment in that relationship: "The Son of Man offers total fidelity to the Father. It is given once and for all, yet fleshed out anew at every moment in time. He shows an absolute preference for the Father—the Father's nature, love, will, and commands—over his own desires and inclinations. He sticks doggedly to that will, come what may. Above all, he lets the Father arrange and direct everything. He has no desire to know anything ahead of time, to anticipate the Father's hour."[13]

Not long ago W. Thüsing reincorporated the faith of Jesus into Christology as a systematic and fundamental datum. The systematic import of this central theme lies in the fact that "the orientation of the *risen* one toward God, which is so decisive in soteriological terms, . . . is grounded in the earthly life of Jesus."[14] It also has implications for ecclesiology insofar as the church is made up of the "faith" of believers in union with the unique believer; and for eschatology insofar as Jesus is the model for the line of ascent toward God. The notion of Jesus' faith serves to organize all the themes of theology.[15]

These authors place novel stress on the relationship of Jesus to the Father as the formal constituent of his faith; but they generally ignore Jesus' relationship to the kingdom of the Father and the concrete history of this relationship. In other words, they ignore the history of his faith.

With its interest in the faith of Jesus, Latin American theology cannot ignore these new approaches; but I do think that its formal way of focusing on those same aspects is different.[16] First, it is not too much interested in the faith of Jesus as opposed to some sort of potential unbelief; rather it is interested in the history of his faith because it sees a real parallel with the concrete situation of the believer here and now. The problem in Latin America is not the typically European problem of choosing between faith and unbelief. Instead it is the problem of moving on from an inherited faith that is rather abstract to a new concrete faith that is truly liberative. Second, it focuses on the conflict-ridden nature of Jesus' faith on the basis of real-life experience of conflict, regarding this as a fundamental datum of historical experience. The victory of faith is not given for good once and for all, nor is it a question of "persevering in the faith." Instead it is a matter of recovering faith in the presence of something that calls it into deep question: i.e., a pervasive situation of sinfulness. Finally, the relational aspect of Jesus' faith is not viewed in terms of a relationship to God but rather in terms of a relationship to the kingdom of God. Thus the history of Jesus' faith is not simply the history of his own subjectivity, but rather the history of his subjectivity framed in the context of a sinful world which must be transformed. Analysis of the concrete situation becomes basic for any attempt to understand the faith of Jesus. It is not simply a matter of trying to figure out how Jesus fashions himself in his subjectivity. It is rather a matter of the relationship between his fashioning of self and his fashioning of the kingdom.

JESUS' FAITH AND CHRISTOLOGY

The Term "Faith of Jesus" in the New Testament

Insofar as language is concerned, we do not generally find any such term as "the faith of Jesus" used in the New Testament. It does not talk about Jesus' faith as such, or about Jesus as a person of faith. One of the reasons would seem to be that it does use such terms as "faith" to describe the existence of the average Christian. Thus it would be hard to bring out the fullness of Jesus' own life by using the same terms that are applied to the partial and unfulfilled lives of his Christian followers. Another more basic reason is the fact that the faith of the average believer already includes Jesus himself as part of its content. In a sense Jesus takes on an absolute character to which the believer can only respond with faith. Hence the New Testament generally talks about faith *in* Jesus rather than the faith *of* Jesus himself.

However, there are two passages in the New Testament that talk explicitly of Jesus' faith. The first is in Mark's Gospel, where the father of a possessed boy asks Jesus to cure him if it is possible. Jesus replies: "If it is possible! Everything is possible to one who has faith" (Mark 9:23). The other passage is the Letter to the Hebrews: "Let us not lose sight of Jesus, who leads us in our faith and brings it to perfection" (Heb. 12:2).

The Marcan passage is usually interpreted in christological terms—i.e., as referring to Jesus himself.[17] It is he himself who lives a life of unlimited faith. The first point to be noted is that Jesus himself, or the author of the Gospel, had no difficulty in attributing faith to Jesus. Here faith is seen to be a way of life vis-à-vis God, quite in line with the Old Testament view. Faith is trust in God, a way of life grounded in Another who gives security and meaning to one's own existence. Thus although the term "faith" is not applied to Jesus explicitly in the Synoptics as a general rule, those Gospels clearly indicate that he led a life of faith. This shows up most clearly when they talk about the prayer of Jesus and his familiar conversation with God under the name of "Abba" ("Father").

Faith also is seen in his life in terms of his fidelity. Jesus' faith is embodied in a persevering trust. Jesus' life in relationship to God is not pictured in idealistic terms. He is faced with the obligation of persevering in faith, as his prayer in the garden of Gethsemane makes quite clear.[18]

In reality it is Mark's whole gospel account that makes explicit what is affirmed *terminologically* in the passage under consideration here. We obviously cannot explore that whole matter here, though we shall indeed return to the real-life history of Jesus later on. The point I want to make here is that I do not propose to deduce the "faith" of Jesus from an analysis of one or another isolated gospel verse. To do that would be to fall into the trap to which I alluded earlier: i.e., an atomistic consideration of Jesus' history. It would also be a subtle way of ignoring what truly goes to make up the faith of Jesus.

The second text, in the Letter to the Hebrews, is a programmatic rather than an analytic view of Jesus' faith, but it offers us more light in our attempt to comprehend the problem of Jesus' faith in all its complexity and historicity. The aspect that it points up specifically is the history of Jesus' faith.

To begin with, we must realize that the epistle is addressed to Christians who are aware that the parousia has not taken place. They are conscious of their situation being framed within history; and it is a conflict-ridden situation because persecution has arisen. They can no longer live on the inertia of the faith they once acquired; their faith must now be recaptured anew. Loyalty to their faith is no longer obvious or taken for granted. So this particular community of Christians, as a wayfaring Church, is becoming much more aware of the historicity of their faith.

It is in this context that the text asserts that Jesus is the one who initiates their faith and brings it to perfection. One reason for the assertion is obviously to offer inspiration and consolation to the believing community (Heb. 12:3). Yet the statement about Jesus' faith is independent of any trials that his followers may have to endure. Jesus is not simply an example to be imitated in faith. Of prime importance is the fact that he himself was the one who first lived a life of faith in all its fullness. In that sense Jesus is not just an exemplar, a meritorious cause, or an object of our faith; rather, he himself is the first and foremost of believers.[19]

This view parallels Paul's conception of Christ as the firstborn. But whereas Paul views Christ as the first of the resurrected ones and our elder brother in glory, the Letter to the Hebrews views him as the first of the wayfarers and the first of believers. In other words, he is the first to have lived as a resurrected one in history because he fully lived a life of faith.

The content of this faith—what exactly Jesus does in full measure—can be found if we focus on the notion of faith in the

Old Testament, which Jesus affirms, and on Jesus' rejection of the Old Testament priesthood. Faith means trust in God, as it did in the Old Testament (Heb. 11); but it is an active faith, a victorious struggle against the difficulties posed by one's situation in real life. It has nothing to do with a victorious struggle against doubts about the faith; it is instead a victorious struggle against the conflicts to be found in real-life existence. So faith becomes fidelity (Heb. 3:2; 2:13), not an idealistic fidelity but a fidelity lived in and through suffering (Heb. 2:10, 18; 12:2).

This faith is not simply a fidelity to God. It is a fidelity to his mission. In the Synoptic Gospels it is presented in terms of a mission to proclaim and make present the kingdom of God; here, in the Letter to the Hebrews, the mission is presented in terms of Jesus' priesthood. His mission on behalf of the kingdom is translated into a priestly mission on behalf of human beings (Heb. 5:1) that takes place in history. The old cult and priesthood, which are of a more symbolic and intentional nature, are now abolished. They are to be replaced by the real, historical, and secular love of Jesus.

Finally, the faith of Jesus is viewed in its historicity. Though it is dealt with in only a programmatic way, the treatment goes beyond anything to be found in other writings of the New Testament. Jesus' history is presented unequivocally, though it is more in terms of what happens to Jesus than in terms of what Jesus himself does. Jesus had to be perfected (Heb. 2:10) through trials (Heb. 2:18). He "learned obedience from what he suffered" (Heb. 5:8). He thus became a guide to salvation for his brothers (Heb. 2:10). Jesus, then, is the first to live out the process of faith to the full. He is "a priest forever" (Heb. 5:6), but that "forever" has a history. He is the Son forever (Heb. 1:5; 5:5), but he had to offer up loud cries and tears (Heb. 5:7) in order to attain perfection (Heb. 5:9).

So the Letter to the Hebrews asserts that faith is the very mode of Jesus' existence and that it has a history. His trusting fidelity to the Father and his priestly mediation on people's behalf are not given once for all time. They have a history of their own precisely because they are situated within history. In this history Jesus is akin to other human beings and in fellowship with them (Heb. 2:1); he is not ashamed to call them his brothers (Heb. 2:11). Hence he is the first-born, not only of the resurrected but also of believers.

The History of Jesus' Faith

As we have just seen, the Letter to the Hebrews offers a theological reading of the history of Jesus and his faith, seeing it as one of trust in God and fidelity to his mission. What that epistle describes programmatically is described historically in the Gospels, though the Gospels do not describe that history in terms of the *concept* of faith.

In this section I should like to focus briefly on the life of Jesus precisely as history, as something subject to change and conflict. We shall consider two basic stages in Jesus' life, the dividing line between them being the crisis in Galilee [20]

At the start of his public life Jesus appears as an orthodox Jew following the best religious traditions of his people. He does not introduce anything basically new that could not have been known by his listeners. [21] His relational view of his person and activity is certainly part of his initial orthodoxy. Jesus does not preach about himself. Another exists who gives meaning to his existence. This essentially relational aspect is the first characteristic of Jesus' faith.

The "Other" in question, the referential pole of Jesus' life, is not simply "God" but the "kingdom of God." [22] Thus Jesus' original experience of faith entails trust in the Father and confidence in the Father's activity; it also entails hope in God's future and that of God's kingdom. To put it a bit differently, it entails hope in people's filiation with the Father and in brotherhood between human beings.

Jesus also believes that God's coming and his kingdom are imminent in time. His faith in the futurity of God is qualified historically, and his expectation of the imminent arrival of the kingdom has practical repercussions on his faith.

Jesus' relational nature to God and the kingdom of God finds expression in his prayer and his mission. He views his mission in operational terms. Despite the gratuitous nature of the approaching kingdom, Jesus performs acts and gestures indicative of the kingdom's presence or dawning approach. His most fundamental gesture is taking sides with human beings in a concrete situation where the existing politico-religious structure has dehumanized people. It has turned those with power into brutes, while alienating and oppressing everyone else. Jesus does all he can to concretize and make present real love as the quintessence of the kingdom. He puts all he has at the disposal of the kingdom: his time, his clear-sightedness, his personal gifts of persuasion, and that special power which is embodied in what are called "miracles," whatever its essential nature may be.

On the basis of this conception of the kingdom, Jesus comes down hard on all sinfulness that goes against God's kingdom. His maledictions are not just ethical conclusions. They well up from the very depths of Jesus' faith. Structural injustice is the formal negation of everything for which Jesus lives. Those who put their faith in the Father are blessed. Those who put their faith in anything else are cursed. For the clear and verifiable fact is that such infidelity to the Father is the root of all sin against the kingdom.

Inspired by this same initial faith, Jesus calls for faith and hope on the part of the ostracized and oppressed to whom he draws near. He also calls disciples who are to carry out his very own task. They, too, are to preach the nearness of the kingdom, and so they are invested with Jesus' own power.

Summing up this first stage of Jesus' public life, then, we can say that Jesus lived the faith of earlier Jewish tradition in its purest form. His orthodoxy and his praxis are wholly consistent with this basic personal experience of faith. Whatever his own distinctive consciousness may have been, and we are not going to consider that point here, the thrust of Jesus' faith is that of an inherited faith in a God who is drawing near to establish universal fellowship. People must fix their gaze on that God and obey him. In his name people must perform effective signs of human reconciliation.

All the Gospels clearly indicate that this first stage of Jesus' public life did come to an end. The faith of Jesus as the guiding principle of his life did enter a new stage that was not an inertial continuation of the first stage, though it was not necessarily in direct opposition to that first stage either. The end of the first stage comes with what is called the "crisis in Galilee." It is given that geographical label because Jesus abandons the heart of Galilee, heading first to Caesarea Philippi and then toward the ten towns of the Decapolis on the borders of Syria and Phoenicia. This geographical break in Jesus' activity expresses an even deeper break in the person of Jesus himself. Jesus comes to realize that he has failed in his mission as he had previously understood it. The crowds are abandoning him, the religious leaders of the Jewish people will not accept him, and God is not getting any closer with power to renovate reality. So there is a real break in both the internal awareness and external activity of Jesus. It finds expression in chapter 8 of Mark's Gospel. The Pharisees keep asking for a sign because they have not understood him, and Jesus leaves them (v. 13). His disciples do not understand him (v. 21), and neither does Peter in his profession of faith (v. 33). Jesus begins to talk about his coming passion (Mark 8:31, 9:30; 10:32) and about following him in self-sacrificing discipleship (Mark 8:34).

In Matthew's Gospel the break comes in chapter 13. Jesus stops talking to the crowds and concentrates his activity on his own disciples: "To you has been given a knowledge of the mysteries of the reign of God, but it has not been given to the others" (Matt. 13:11). Luke follows the same basic scheme as Matthew. It is perhaps John who details the change in situation most vividly. After Jesus' discourse on the bread of life (John 6:22–59), the masses abandon him: "From this time on, many of his disciples broke away and would not remain in his company any longer" (John 6:66). He is left with the twelve. There are two attempts to stone him (John 8:59; 10:31,39). One takes place in the temple, suggesting that Jesus has been excommunicated from his people. Shortly afterward, Jesus retires to the other side of the Jordan (John 10:40) and, at the risk of his life, goes to visit his friends Lazarus, Martha, and Mary (John 11:8,16).

Thus all the Gospels talk about a crisis in Jesus' life, each portraying it in line with its own distinctive theological interests. There is some rupture in his inner consciousness and his outer activity, suggesting a rupture in his faith. Jesus comes to see clearly that his historical way of living out his trust in the Father and his obedience to his mission cannot proceed according to its old logic. He is tempted to withdraw into seclusion, to picture his mission more in terms of some restricted sect. That is why the Gospels talk about him withdrawing from his usual geographical haunts and heading to more distant regions. This geographic retreat symbolizes the temptation to close his heart to his mission. Jesus does overcome that temptation, but it will entail a radical change in his understanding of himself and his mission.

The second stage of Jesus' life runs from the Galilean crisis to his death on the cross. Jesus overcomes the crisis, but it has thoroughly reshaped his faith. He now sees it in a novel way that he had never suspected before. Comparing his faith in this second stage with that of the first stage, we can discern the following features.

The referential pole of his life continues to be the Father. He continues to have confidence in him, but now that confidence finds nothing in which to root. It becomes a confidence or trust against trust. Jesus' prayer in the garden of Gethsemane does not presuppose the same conception of God that Jesus had at the start of his life. Fidelity to the Father now stands in the presence, not of the Father's imminent coming, but of Jesus' imminent death. And Jesus sees his death as the death of his cause. Letting God remain God now lacks any verification; it is done in the absence of any verification at all.

Insofar as the kingdom of God is concerned, Jesus no longer sees its imminent arrival. He also realizes that people have rejected it as an ideal. His work in favor of the kingdom no longer means placing all that he has at its disposal but rather placing all that he himself is at its disposal. He must surrender his ideas and his person, accepting death. The power which he displayed at the start of his public life, and which was concretely embodied in his miracles, has now proved to be ineffective. All that is left is the power of love in suffering.

His attitude toward sin is no longer embodied in the analysis and prophetic denunciation of a sinful situation. Jesus must now shoulder the very burden of sin. Sin is no longer simply the absence of fellowship; it is something that has real power and that will lead him to the cross if he shoulders it. So the demand of discipleship is no longer simply an invitation to preach the kingdom and perform deeds of power that will attest to its breakthrough into history. Discipleship is now a summons to take up the cross as Jesus himself did.

Thus in the second stage of Jesus' life we find the same basic elements in his faith, but now their concrete embodiment is very different. The faith of Jesus has had a concrete history that has made him different. It has not been an abstract history, however, a history of ideas that has been giving shape to a different conception of God, the kingdom of God, sin, justice, love, and power. Instead it has been a real history. The history of Jesus' faith has been mediated historically through the history of his praxis in the midst of a conflict-ridden situation.

The Human Condition of Jesus' Faith

The evolution of Jesus' faith was not an idealistic one. It went hand in hand with his concrete history. Jesus typically finds himself in a given concrete situation that he does not ponder ideologically but rather accepts as it is. It is this immersion in history that will call his faith into question repeatedly: both in the sense that the given situation can be a temptation to his faith and in the sense that faith is something worth pondering in the light of a given concrete situation.

Here I should like to provide a brief overview of the human condition of Jesus' faith from two standpoints. I should like to consider it in terms of the temptation faced by Jesus and in terms of Jesus' ignorance. I am not motivated by an a priori interest in demonstrating the human quality of Jesus. It is simply that we can ascertain his human character from what is clearly seen in his history. Furthermore, these two dimensions are not embodiments of human limitation but rather of the perfection of one's faith. Faith does not signify possession of

God and his kingdom but rather an ongoing search for them. And paradoxically enough, temptation and ignorance are part and parcel of the historical completion and perfection of this search.

It is noteworthy that in the Synoptics we find the scene of the temptations. It is clearly an anachronism that they are placed at the start of Jesus' public life. Even from the viewpoint of style, it is clear that the passages dealing with them are an interpolation. They are the fruit of theological reflection rather than a historical description of what happened at the start of Jesus' public life.

But the placing of the temptation scenes is of great importance in itself. They come right after the scene of Jesus' baptism, where Jesus becomes aware of his mission and his sonship. The setting of the temptations clearly suggests what will be typical in Jesus' life. Temptation will not center around the general reality of his life as a human being; it will not be due to the simple fact that he is a human being. Instead temptation will center around what is most typical in Jesus' life, outlook, and history: i.e., his relationship with the Father and his mission of service to the kingdom. In that sense his temptations will not take place on the level of concrete ethics but rather on the level of faith as that which most profoundly defines his personality and activity.

Having made that clear, we must now realize that the scene of the temptations refers directly to the person of Jesus; it is not directly meant to be something of an edifying nature. In the texts as we have them, we can certainly see some concern to solve certain problems in the primitive Christian communities, to point out that Christians too live in the midst of temptation even after Jesus' triumph and that they too are aided by the Holy Spirit as he was.

But the main and original concern is christological. It is not a morality tale nor a pious lesson against the backdrop of an essentially Docetist Christology. The idea is not that Jesus endured temptation simply to give us an example. This can be concluded from the fact that in Mark's version it is the Spirit who drives Jesus into the desert (Mark 1:12). That idea could not have originated in the community where the temptation scene was redacted, because in the eyes of the Christian community it was precisely the Spirit who helped Christians to overcome temptation. There is also the passage in Luke's Gospel: "You are the ones who have stood loyally by me in my *temptations*" (Luke 22:28). That text belongs to the oldest stratum of tradition, and it rules out any moralistic interpretation. So there can be no doubt that the temptation in question affects the person of Jesus himself. He himself "is threatened with critical crises of self-identity."[23]

The temptations offer us a key to understanding the faith of Jesus in its two main aspects: as trust in the Father and as obedience to the mission of the kingdom. In systematic terms we can say that Jesus, too, was faced with the choice of becoming a person through surrender to God or rejection of him; he, too, could fashion his person as a believer or an unbeliever.[24] If we choose to describe the content of Jesus' typical personality in terms of "messianism"—though in all likelihood Jesus never thought of himself explicitly as the Messiah—then the temptation faced by him had to do with the essence of authentic messianism. Jesus was faced with the task of choosing between true and false messianism in trying to fashion his concrete personality as a human being. This choice constituted a real problem for Jesus throughout his life.[25] It was not confined to the beginning or end of his public ministry. It was the atmosphere[26] surrounding the whole historical unfolding of his life of faith, though it crystallized in such acute moments as the Galilean crisis and the passion.

A literary and conceptual device is used to bring out the radical nature and seriousness of the temptations. They are associated with Satan, who plays the role of tempter. In the accounts of Mark and Luke there is an explicit dialogue between him and Jesus. The introduction of Satan into the picture, which is quite understandable in terms of the Jewish mentality, is merely designed to point up graphically the elements of struggle and choice in Jesus' own person. It has nothing to do with satisfying Satan's curiosity about the real personality of Jesus. It is Jesus himself who must be convinced about his own reality, about the import of his life and mission. Strictly speaking, the dialogue does not take place between Jesus and Satan but between Jesus and the Father.[27] The numerous citations from the Old Testament in the Matthaean and Lukan accounts make it clear that the authentic backdrop of the temptations is Jesus' conception of God and God's kingdom. In functional terms the temptation has to do with the concrete way in which Jesus will carry out his mission.

The concrete content of the temptation is Jesus' use of power in exercising his mission.[28] In Luke's account particularly we see Satan's conception of power and of the kingdoms of this world. Herein lies the alluring and tempting aspect of Satan's proposal. At the same time, however, the temptation does not center around effective use of tactics and means in order to proclaim the kingdom and make it present. Rather, it has a profoundly theological dimension; it has to do with one's conception of the true nature of God. The question at stake here is: What sort of power truly mediates God and hence brings his reign nearer? Is it the sort of power that controls history from outside or the sort that immerses itself in history? Is it the kind of power that exercises command and control over human beings or the kind that gives itself in self-surrender to them?

All the Gospel accounts say that Jesus overcame the temptation, but they make the point in different ways. In Mark's account Jesus looks like a winner from the start, and there is no report of how the whole process unfolded. The significance of the victory is brought out clearly a bit later (Mark 3:22–30). Jesus wins out over Satan because he is the stronger: "No one can enter a strong man's house and despoil his property unless he has first put him under restraint. Only then can he plunder his house" (Mark 3:27). In the accounts of Matthew and Luke the devil withdraws in defeat, but Luke adds a phrase that is worth noting: "When the devil had finished all the tempting he left him, *to await another opportunity*" (Luke 4:13).

That last phrase points up two things. First, temptation will crop up throughout the life of Jesus, not just at the start of his public ministry. Second, the overcoming of temptation is not an idealistic process based merely on Jesus' inner intention, as the isolated scene in the desert might suggest at first. Rather, Jesus will overcome temptation in his concrete history and in his clash with the historical forces of sin.

Both of these dimensions are clearly brought out in the temptation scene of Gethsemane. First of all, it is framed historically rather than in terms of Jesus' subjective life alone. After the Galilean crisis we see the growing intensification of Jesus' conflicts. He has serious disputes with the priests, and he drives the merchants out of the temple. Jesus realizes that his life is in great jeopardy, and his disciples are now armed. It is in this concrete context that he agonizes over the use of power and feels the full weight of the temptation in that direction. It truly seems that only the use of force can save him. The agony in the garden is poles apart from any serene perplexity. It is the total, absolute crisis of the logic of the kingdom with which Jesus commenced his public life. Overcoming this temptation no longer means some intentional overcoming of the power of Satan as it did at the start of his public life; now it means succumbing to Satan's power. Luke puts it in a bold phrase: "This is your hour—the triumph of darkness!" (Luke 22:53). The temptation cannot be overcome by fleeing from the conflictive situation and the public gaze, by going off and forming some isolated sect. It can only be overcome by immersing oneself in it and allowing oneself to be affected by the power of sin.

It is in the passion that temptation takes on its most pointed theological overtones. The God approaching in grace has abandoned Jesus (Mark 15:34). Jesus' faith now faces a radical temptation: Who is this God who has withdrawn and who now demands Jesus' total abandonment of self in total obscurity and darkness? It is the same *formal* concept of old that enables Jesus to overcome the temptation: "Let it be as you would have it, not as I" (Mark 14:36); but now the content of God's will can no longer be checked or verified by Jesus. That faith should mean total self-surrender and that liberative love should mean a love fraught with suffering is entirely new to Jesus. He accepts that novel reality and thereby overcomes the temptation.[29]

Thus temptation, as the pervasive atmosphere and culminating reality of his life, is the historical condition for the historicization of his faith. The concrete actualizing of the basic sonship which he experiences at the start (Mark 1:11) takes place through the overcoming of temptation in history. It is this process that gives him a new concrete sonship (Mark 14:37). The faith of Jesus is fashioned through his history.

The matter of Jesus' ignorance is much debated for exegetical and dogmatic reasons, and challenged by the Hellenic supposition that ignorance is an imperfection in a person. I am not going to tackle all those issues here. I simply want to spell out the positive features of Jesus' ignorance as they appear in the Gospels.[30]

First of all, we must note that Jesus was ignorant of certain things as is normally true of human beings. His likeness to human beings extended to the process of intellectual growth, which always presumes some sort of ignorance. That is the meaning of the phrase: "Jesus, for his part, progressed steadily in wisdom . . . " (Luke 2:52). Here we have in principle the possibility of ignorance and error in Jesus as an *anthropological* dimension; and in principle that does not stand in opposition to the perfection of a person's total being. On the anthropological level, then, there is no reason to be surprised about some possible ignorance or error on Jesus' part. As Rahner puts it: "Thus making mistakes is better for the historical person, and hence for Jesus too, than knowing everything always."[31]

A theological treatment of Jesus' ignorance should not stop with the fact that on the anthropological level Jesus was in fellowship with other human beings in this respect. The theological import of Jesus' ignorance comes through when we examine its specific content. Of what was Jesus ignorant? The Gospels certainly do not say a great deal on the matter, but they do provide enough information for us to analyze his ignorance to some extent.

Let us consider Mark 9:1: "I assure you, among those standing here there are some who will not taste death until they see the reign of God established in power" (see Mark 13:30; Matt. 10:23). This text makes it clear that Jesus' ignorance is not merely in matters of incidental detail. It goes right to the core of his own person and his mission. Jesus views his mission in terms of the kingdom and its realization. He did not envision the existence of a "church" as it appeared after his resurrection—though that does not mean there was no continuity between Jesus and the later church. Jesus himself, however, was concerned with the concrete realization of God's kingdom. The single reference to the church in the Synoptic Gospels pales in comparison with the plethora of references to the kingdom of God. It was in terms of the kingdom that Jesus pictured his mission.

Jesus was also mistaken about the day or time when the kingdom would arrive. Later that mistaken idea was replaced with mere ignorance of the time (Mark 13:22) Jesus trusts fully in the Father, but he is mistaken or ignorant as to "when" the revelation of the Father will take place. The mistake is not simply quantitative, it is qualitative. It is not simply a matter of mistaking the number of months or years involved; it is not knowing, or being in error about, the basic fact as to whether the kingdom will arrive in the near future or at some wholly unknown and unforeseen date.

Viewed in terms of the Hellenic conception of the human beings this ignorance or mistake about God and his kingdom might seem to be the height of imperfection. In terms of biblical faith, however, such ignorance and error are part of the perfection of faith. It is of the essence of faith to let God be God. That is part of what the Old Testament views as the transcendence or holiness of God. The future character of God's revelation and the prohibition of divine images give concrete expression to the holy, transcendent, and non-manipulable reality of God. In Jesus we find an absolute familiarity with God and a total surrender to the Father, but all this is framed in the basic context of letting God be God. This shows up existentially in carrying out the Father's will, as we saw in our consideration of the agony in the garden. The noetic counterpart of the same attitude is Jesus' ignorance concerning the day of Yahweh. This ultimate secret is God's alone. Jesus, mistaken at first about it, ultimately chooses not to force the issue. To put it into systematic language, we might say that Jesus respects God's transcendence, and hence his ignorance about the day of Yahweh is not an imperfection at all; rather, it is an expression of his filial creatureliness and of a messianism that takes its life from the Father rather than from one's own initiative.

So there is no imperfection in the fact that Jesus could not synthesize his belief in God's imminent coming within his historical consciousness and did not know when it would happen. This fact expresses his solidarity with the human condition, and hence it can point up his real condition as Son, as the firstborn in faith. The limitation on his knowledge is the historical condition that makes real his trusting surrender to the Father and his solidarity with humankind. As Pannenberg puts it: "No omniscience or infallible prescience is necessarily linked up with Jesus' submission to his mission and to the Father who has sent him. The limitation on Jesus' knowledge, even where his own relationship to God is concerned . . . belongs rather to the perfect completion and fulfillment of his personal surrender to God's future."[32]

Systemic Christology says certain things about the submission of the eternal Son to the Father. In an historical Christology we must use historical categories to express that submission. Jesus' faith is made up of his trust in God and his obedience to his mission. In a historical Christology those traits stand in need of such historical categories as conflict, temptation, and ignorance. Letting God be God is not an idealistic intention; it is a historical attitude made possible by history, called into question by history, and ultimately realized concretely in history. Thus in "not knowing" the day of Yahweh, Jesus "knew" the Father precisely because he let the Father be the Father—i.e., the absolute mystery of history.

The Faith of Jesus and Systematic Christology

Here I should like to briefly summarize what we have learned from our analysis of the history of Jesus' faith so that we may then reformulate certain fundamental principles of Christology. Those principles will obviously need further elaboration and more detailed comparison with other classical Christologies. The point is not to supplant the latter, but to make them more concrete on the basis of Jesus' history.

Understood in the biblical sense expounded in the Old Testament, the term "faith" sums up the most fundamental reality of a person. In concrete terms the faith of Jesus can be summed up in his attitude of exclusive confidence in the Father (vertical relationship) and his total obedience to his mission of proclaiming and making present the kingdom (horizontal relationship). This twofold attitude makes explicit the unique faith of Jesus.

Perseverance is another intrinsic feature of faith according to the Old Testament. Faith, in short, implies "fidelity." However, this fidelity cannot be comprehended in abstract terms. It must be viewed in terms of a concrete historical situation. The motive force underlying Jesus' faith is the conflict-ridden historical situation in which it is framed. Jesus had no theoretical doubts about his faith; it did not represent a problem to him because the underlying concepts were somehow meaningless. Rather it was existence itself that raised questions about his faith and forced the issue of fidelity upon him. More concretely, it was a specific praxis carried out in the framework of certain specific expectations and leading to certain specific consequences—to the triumph of injustice over love in Jesus' case.

In Jesus' case fidelity and the overcoming of conflict does not end up in mere perseverance in his old faith or certain minor alterations in it; it leads to a new faith. There is certainly continuity between his first faith and his later faith. On the formal level Jesus continues to trust in the Father and to remain loyal to his mission on behalf of the kingdom. But the concretion of that formal faith is very different. Real history, a history which in his case proves to be antagonistic to God and his kingdom, forced Jesus to immerse himself much more deeply in the absolute dimension of faith rather than stopping half way. If the Father is to be the absolute, it cannot simply be a matter of intent. The Father can only be the absolute for Jesus through affirmations and negations in concrete history. If the kingdom of God—with its love, justice, and brotherhood—is to be the ultimate truth of history, it can only come to be so in the dialectical interaction between effective love and hope on the one hand and their apparent inefficacy in life on the other. The concretion of all this is not a matter for mere contemplation; it is something that must be done. Hence the history of Jesus' faith is not the history of his ideas; it is simply his history.

Jesus' faith is what it turned out to be in fact. Viewed theologically, Jesus' life is the shift from his initial faith to his final, definitive faith. Thus the historical Jesus is not one aspect or moment of the history of Jesus nor the sum of those aspects or moments; it is what Jesus will eventually turn out to be. His faith, as trust and obedience, cannot be understood without narrating its history.

On the basis of the history of Jesus' faith we can reformulate the fundamental problems of Christology, though here we may do it only by way of suggestion. As we noted earlier, there has been a shift of perspective in Christology's point of departure insofar as it seeks to be reflection on the totality of Christ. While Christology may still begin with the divine sonship of Jesus, it has moved from the dogmatic formula of Chalcedon and the biblico-dogmatic formulations of the New Testament to the reality of Jesus of Nazareth. Thus instead of starting "from above," it now starts "from below." Let us now consider what the totality of Christ might mean if we take as our point of departure the history of Jesus as it is concretized in the history of his faith.

First of all, this new focus enables us to reformulate what goes to make up the "divinity" of Jesus as it appears in the faith of the Church. In classical Christology his divinity is presented in terms of his divine nature and the union of Jesus' human nature with the divine person of the Logos. This formulation seeks to directly identify Jesus with the eternal Logos, though it is pointed out that the human and divine elements in Jesus are ever indivisible and unconfusedly united.

From the standpoint of the history of Jesus' faith, however, the first evident thing is that it is the Father, not the eternal Logos, that is directly correlated with Jesus. It is his *relationship* to the Father that constitutes the essence of his person.[33] Thus the category of relationship is important in trying to describe the total reality of Christ, and it may serve as a better basis for trying to understand what goes to make up his divinity. Here we propose to reformulate in relational categories what Chalcedon affirmed in ontic categories. The divinity of Jesus consists of his concrete relationship to the Father. This unique, peculiar, and unrepeatable way of being in relationship with the Father is what constitutes his concrete way of participating in divinity.

While this assertion may seem to be very abstract and theoretical, I believe it has important consequences for our understanding of Jesus and for Christian existence. First of all, the category of "relationship" allows for a dynamic and evolutionary conception of Jesus' sonship which is not apparent, at least theoretically, in the category of "divine nature." As we saw earlier, Jesus' relation to the Father is the history of that relation. Thus we can say that Jesus *becomes* the Son of God rather than that he simply *is* the Son of God.

Second, it should be noted that Jesus, strictly speaking, does not reveal the Father. In that sense it is incorrect to refer to Jesus as the "sacrament" of the Father as both classical and modern Christologies tend to do. They suggest that Jesus makes visible in history the ultimate mystery of existence and history, the older Christologies talking about a God without beginning and the more modern Christologies talking about God as the absolute future. Strictly speaking, however, Jesus reveals the Son. And if we view Jesus in terms of his concrete history, we can say that what Jesus reveals to us is the way of the Son, the way one becomes Son of God. Jesus does not, then, reveal the absolute mystery. He reveals how one may respond to that absolute mystery through trust and obedience to the mission of the kingdom.

These considerations do not give us any intuitive or direct comprehension of what goes to make up the divinity of Jesus, but neither does the formula of Chalcedon. Their aim is to provide a meaningful reformulation of Jesus' divinity that is based on the history of Jesus. Instead of using ontic categories, we here choose to use relational ones. They include the *personal* category of a person's submission to God and the *practical* category of obedience to a mission.

On that basis we must rehabilitate a neglected New Testament category: The designation of Jesus as the "firstborn," the elder brother, the first of the believers. "Firstborn" signifies "son" to begin with, thereby suggesting Jesus' relationship with the Father; but it also signifies "brother," thereby suggesting his relationship with other human beings. This means that the feature of "brotherliness" is part of Jesus' divinity. Shocking as that idea might appear, I think it is a fundamental statement. Bound up with the divinity of Jesus is the work of pointing out the way to the Father, facilitating it, and making sure that it can be traversed by others.

A citation from Karl Rahner might help to clarify what I am trying to say here:

If Jesus' resurrection is the valid perpetuity of his person and his cause, and if this person and cause signify the victoriousness of his claims rather than merely the vague perpetuity of any man whatsoever and his history, then *faith* in his resurrection is a feature intrinsic to the resurrection itself. It is not simply taking cognizance of an event which in and of itself could just as well go unnoticed. If Jesus' resurrection is to be the eschatological victory of God's grace in the world, then it definitely cannot be envisioned without the accompanying faith in it, a faith given *de facto* though freely. It is in that faith that the very essence of the resurrection attains its fullness.[34]

Here Rahner states flatly that if there had not been faith in the resurrection, then Jesus would not have been resurrected;

for a resurrection that is meant to be revelation on the one hand but that is not recognized as such on the other is a contradiction in terms. I am trying to say much the same thing here, only in operational language. The path of Jesus is the revelation of the Son's path. If it were incapable of incorporating others into it, then Jesus would not be the Son. Hence being the "firstborn" is part and parcel of Jesus' divinity. He traverses the way to God and makes it possible for his brothers and sisters to do the same.

That brings us to the eternal theoretical question as to the difference between Jesus and all other Christians. The classic formulation is that Jesus possesses something by his very essence which belongs to other human beings only by grace. If we start off from the history of Jesus, we can reformulate the difference in historical categories. They may seem to be less incisive, but I think they are far more significant. The fundamental difference is that Jesus is the one who has lived faith in all its pristine fullness, who has opened up the pathway of faith and traversed it to the very end. We might also say that he is the one who has lived hope absolutely, precisely insofar as he experienced the Father's total abandonment on the cross, whereas in the case of the Christian we find that the kingdom has become something definitive, at least as a promise.

The importance of such considerations lies in the fact that they pose the issue of Jesus' difference from us in historical terms. Even more importantly, they pose the issue in terms of the essential communion between the firstborn and the rest of his brothers and sisters. So long as history continues, the fundamental problem will continue to be: What is the sense of history (the problem of God); and how is history fashioned (the problem of the kingdom of God)?

The divinity of Jesus can have no meaning so long as we assume that those questions have already been answered right at the very start. It can have no meaning so long as we withdraw it from history and formulate it in terms of nature. The fact is that for the Christian the divinity of Jesus unfolds historically in the experience of fashioning history together

with Jesus. To put it briefly, we can say that we only know that
Jesus is the Son in brotherly communion with him, in following the path of his faith.

These statements may seem too modest and minimalist. Yet
it might well be asked whether other formulations, which at
first glance seem to be more radical and incisive, really say
more or are more operational. Our affirmation here is that it is
in joining Jesus on the road which fashions the kingdom and
leads toward the future of God that we come to "understand"
what constitutes his divine sonship and, at the same time, his
difference from us.

What, then, is the meaning of the New Testament declara-
tion about faith *in* Jesus? Obviously it has nothing to do with a
merely nominalist orthodoxy that now includes Jesus in the
pantheon of deities. Faith is always directed to the absolute of
God and his kingdom. Faith in Jesus means accepting the fact
that in him there has been revealed the Son—which is to say,
the way to God. That can be done in orthodox confessions and
in cultic acclamations. But faith in Jesus attains its maximum
radicality when we accept his path as normative and traverse
it. The most radical and most orthodox affirmation of *faith in
Jesus* is affirming that the *faith of Jesus* is the correct way to draw
nearer to God and realize his kingdom, and then acting accordingly.

JESUS' FAITH AND FUNDAMENTAL MORAL THEOLOGY

The Meaning of "Fundamental Christian Morality"

Here we want to explore the import of a Christology—based
on the history of Jesus' own faith—for the moral life of the
Christian. Once we experience the fact that Jesus is the one
who lived faith in all its pristine fullness, how do we translate
that into moral terms?

It is apparent that moral theology is more complicated than
Christology for reasons we shall explore here. But right at the
start I want to state one basic principle that underlies my

treatment. Adopting what I regard as a historical option, I envision moral theology here precisely insofar as it is *Christian*.[35] It is the adjective "Christian" that is normative here. Thus I am not alluding to the morality which Christians have in fact elaborated in the course of history. I am referring to that which finds in Christ, meaning here the Jesus of history, its criterion for formulating the principles and tasks of morality.

In negative terms this means that we are not going to consider moral theology directly as a theology based on some natural ethics—more specifically, on one or another of the ethics that have appeared as philosophical ethics in the course of history and then have been referred to Jesus for confirmation, completion, alteration, or rejection. We are not going to baptize any natural ethics. Instead we are going to try to find the ethical strand in the fundamental Christian experience.

Neither am I concerned here with exploring a theoretical question that is much debated and discussed: i.e., whether the morality that goes back to Jesus involves something radically novel vis-à-vis natural ethics. I do not mean to prejudice the whole question as to whether Jesus did offer something new to ethics. I simply mean that the criterion for determining the Christian nature of ethics does not necessarily come down to the matter of innovation. It is not as if the moral life of the Christian were a combination of natural elements and additional Christian elements of a novel sort.

Neither am I interested in another issue that follows from the preceding. If one agrees that Jesus does offer something new to ethics, one might then wonder whether it is novel merely in time or also in terms of human logic. In other words, is it of such a nature that people could not have figured it out and hence stand in absolute need of Jesus' contribution, or is it something that people could have figured out in natural ethics but did not before Jesus arrived on the scene?[36] Those questions shall not concern us here.

Neither am I directly concerned here with exploring the various moral theologies that can be found in the New Testament: i.e., the concrete embodiments and moral practices of the various Christian communities in the early church. I do not mean to suggest that this is not an important matter for moral theology. In the last analysis, what a Christian community must do today is formally the same thing that the early communities did: make Christian morality concrete in time and place, in specific historical situations. In this process of concretion we glimpse the need to relate historically the fundamental Christian exigency with various historical mediations: Judaism, Stoicism, and so forth. In the moral theologies of the New Testament we see attempts to integrate the core of Christian morality into different concrete historical situations; and so we have different moral theologies there.

All of these problems are important for Christian moral theology. But in dealing with them here I shall go behind them. In other words, I shall tackle those problems by exploring the original nucleus of the Christian moral experience insofar as it is grounded in Jesus. Here, then, the adjective "Christian" means "going back to Jesus." Needless to say, I realize that any attempt to lay hold of that nucleus takes place within the hermeneutic circle which runs between "Jesus" and "the understanding of Jesus in subsequent history."

When I refer to *fundamental* morality (or moral theology) here, I mean that our interest is not to determine the ultimate concrete embodiments of what the Christian is supposed to do. The concrete embodiment of moral theology cannot in principle be deduced without further ado from Jesus precisely because action is concrete and historical by very definition. We must take due account of the hermeneutic circle. By "fundamental," then, I mean that which founds Christian morality and gives it a Christian sense.

Here I should like to use this standpoint to reflect on the "ought" of Christian morality in terms of its object, leaving its subject for treatment later on. In analyzing the aspect of "ought" or obligation in fundamental Christian morality, we are looking for the original experience from which it arises. Hence it is not a matter of studying the moral subject as someone who by very nature is under an obligation to do a certain thing. Rather, we want to see the meaning of this obligation in terms of Jesus.

In the framework of the Christology sketched above, the obligatory aspect of morality is not to be deduced directly from the demands that Jesus imposes on people but rather from a broader experience with a more comprehensive meaning: i.e., in Jesus there appears the authentic way. This basic experience has two characteristic notes: a note of *urgency* and a note of *gratuitousness*. The urgency is grounded in the theological nature of the resurrection-experience, in the fact that the history of Jesus reveals truth and love to the fullest. Christians did not grasp this revelation as seers might have. They laid hold of it as witnesses, as people who were to give an account of that truth in both their proclamation and their concrete lifestyle. Hence the obligatory quality of the experience was not something imposed on them from the outside nor was it even imposed on them simply by the words of Jesus himself. It resulted from an inner experience in which they came to realize that the ultimate meaning of history and their own person would come from being like Jesus. What "ought" to be showed up clearly and fully in the light of what had actually been realized in Jesus.[37]

The urgency to be like Jesus also was framed in historical terms. It was not historically clear and obvious that in Jesus truth and love had made their appearance, that he was the one who had lived faith in all its fullness. On the contrary, this fact was mediated through the normal Jewish expectations. Thus the urgency to be like Jesus was framed and experienced in terms of an urgency to be grateful. This was true in at least two senses. First, Christians could sense the gratuitous nature of the Jesus-event itself (John 1:17), which did not stand in any direct continuity with history (John 1:13). It was not a straightforward human possibility but something given to us as a gift. Thus the urgency of this morality took on the nature of a grateful response to a proffered possibility that had not been contemplated previously.

There was another important historical tinge to this gratitude. Jesus' course was not only in discontinuity with other ways but actually in contradiction to them; and his death was a by-product of the contradiction. In the resurrection-experience, which is typified by the apparitions, Jesus does not turn against those who failed to recognize him and put him to death; instead he offers them pardon and invites them to follow his own path. Hence the urgency to be like Jesus is grasped in the experience of one's own sinfulness.[38] One now realizes that one's own sinfulness is no perduring obstacle to finding meaning in life and fleshing it out in reality.

So when we try to seek out the exact nature of the "ought" in Christian morality, we must realize that it is essentially grounded on the urgent need to be like Jesus and its attendant note of gratitude. It is the total reality of Jesus, not merely his verbal demands, that makes Christian morality obligatory. The verbal demands are taken into account also, to be sure, but only within the framework of the more comprehensive reality and the Christian's experience of it. It is basically the experience that Paul succinctly states: "The love of Christ impels us" (2 Cor. 5:14).

Now it might seem strange to the reader that I have appealed to the historical Jesus as the basis of Christology and then gone on to explain the obligatory note in Christian morality in terms of the resurrection-experience. But the reason is simple enough. Jesus' life prior to his death was not yet complete; it was not yet the whole history of Jesus. For this reason his history up to that point could not be turned into some absolute moral exigency; it could only be partial at best. Moreover, this moral exigency was not in fact grasped by his followers during Jesus' life, as we shall see further on. His followers had not yet experienced the fact that the historical life of Jesus is in fact the definitive way, though they had chosen in some way to follow it themselves. Finally and most important, there is the experience of the resurrection and its importance. Though we do find certain pointers in other directions within the New Testament, the fact remains that the resurrection-experience constitutes the experience of Jesus' history precisely as true and authentic. It is the experience in which the historical Jesus, not some Christ pondered in abstract terms, is transformed into an urgent moral exigency for his followers.

The obligatory quality of Christian morality, then, is to be found in the impact that the history of Jesus actually had on Christians. That is our supposition here; and we further suppose that it will continue to have such an impact, as was noted earlier. Now if that is the case, then the object of moral theology, precisely as *fundamental* moral theology, is nothing else but the task of historically reproducing Jesus' own history.

To get the point of this assertion, let us first consider what is not meant by it. A fundamental moral theology understood in these terms does not seek to determine *directly* what is good and what is evil, to establish some hierarchy of moral values, or to ask directly what makes the moral subject a good person. All those questions must obviously be given some consideration by fundamental moral theology. But its formal object should be something else: i.e., What does it mean to reproduce the life of Jesus and how is that task carried out? The problems noted above are to be subsumed under that basic task.[39]

On the basis of that methodological criterion we can say that the object of moral theology is concretized through the ethical experience of Jesus himself, which was the proclamation of the "kingdom of God" and the effort to make it real and present. What does that mean for moral theology? First of all, it means that moral theology should clarify the meaning of that particular task. It must focus directly on the question: *What must be done* in order to establish the kingdom of God in history? The direct focus, then, is on the kind of action that correctly fashions the kingdom. And while that will really involve consideration of moral subjects and their goodness, it will do so only indirectly.

The basic reason for all this is to be found in the relational character of Jesus' own life. It finds fulfillment insofar as its pole of reference, the kingdom of God, is brought to real fulfillment. Moral theology's focus on its object is not "egocentric," in the neutral sense of being concerned with how the moral subject attains perfection. It is practical, in the sense of focusing on how the kingdom of God is fashioned in life. Of course the two aspects are not mutually exclusive, as we shall see. But our formulation of the matter here seeks to rule out at the start a formulation on the basis of subjective intention, a formulation that implies that the *typical* feature of Christian morality is somehow polarized in the subjects so that they can be good even when reality remains completely untouched and unchanged.

Once that fundamental point has been clarified, then moral theology does have to consider what exactly makes the moral subject good as well. But here again it must consider the question in terms of Jesus. We have already seen that Jesus becomes the Son through his work of bringing about the kingdom. In that sense it is clear that the object of morality includes and requires a personal morality, but it does so in a characteristic way insofar as it is a Christian morality. It is not a matter of considering whether and how the Christian, as an individual, is a good person. That question is equivalent to the age-old question as to what one must do to be saved, a question to be found in any ethics. The specific question of Christian morality is how individuals become Christians through their efforts to fashion the kingdom into a reality.

The point of this last distinction is that the goodness of the moral subject cannot be studied solely from the standpoint of certain values that purportedly are an essential part of his personhood. It is not a matter of saying that the virtue of justice makes a person just, for example. That is certainly true, of course, but the focus must be on the real, concrete embodiment by which one actually does justice to the benefit of the kingdom. In this sense Jesus becomes normative for personal morality as well, not by proclaiming the validity of certain universal values but rather by historicizing them. And that historicization is nothing else but the fashioning of the kingdom.

In this way we recover and rehabilitate personal morality within our scheme. But we do so, not in terms of the subject "being good," but rather in terms of the subject becoming good through bringing about the kingdom. The fundamental ethical question is viewed formally as the whole issue of making history good, which includes the question of how the moral subject becomes good. If we adopt that approach then, in principle at least, we avoid the trap of a morality based on good intentions on the one hand and that of an idealistic morality on the other. We avoid the former by asserting that it is the historical concretion that really proves whether one's will or intention was good. We avoid the latter because the conflict-ridden nature of history prevents us from picturing morality as based on certain absolute but wholly abstract values.

The Following of Jesus as the Fundamental Moral Exigency

So far we have seen that a global or general moral exigency arises out of the fundamental experience connected with Jesus. In this section I propose to describe what this exigency consists of. In his historical life Jesus posed many concrete demands to human beings; but the most comprehensive one was the general demand to reproduce his own way of life in oneself and one's life. During his own lifetime, this demand of discipleship met with failure for the most part. His disciples did not in fact follow him. Later on, however, they recalled this demand of his and realized that it was the great moral demand of Jesus.

Before we consider the following of Jesus as he himself understood it, we would do well to resolve one difficulty that might seem to arise from Jesus' own life. The Synoptic Gospels often report that Jesus approached certain types of people —including the poor, the sick, and the public sinners—and imposed on them the fundamental demand that they have faith in the approaching God. He asked them to accept the belief that their present situation of poverty and social ostracism was not the last word on their life because it was not the ultimate that God could do. What he demands of them, then, is faith and hope in God along with certain moral exigencies, summed up in his phrase: "Go and sin no more." He does not ask them to follow him in any strict sense, though the Sermon on the Mount is addressed to every human being and certainly outlines a new way of life based on his own.

If we want to explain why we do not find an explicit summons to follow Jesus in such passages, we must realize that the Synoptic writers chose to typologize different exigencies in different situations. The kingdom of God has to be seen, not only in terms of the activity that would flesh it out in reality (i.e., the following of Jesus), but also in terms of its results (i.e., liberation). The faith achieved by those ostracized from society is already a kind of liberation, at least in germ. Through this faith and hope in the approaching God, the ostracized persons recovered the dignity that society had stripped away from them. Thus the kingdom of God was realized in at least a germinal way, though this does not mean that Jesus might not pose some further demand to the person involved. The silence of the Synoptics with regard to Jesus' imposing the demand of discipleship on those people does not affect our position here. It does not mean that we are wrong in saying that discipleship is the most comprehensive demand made by Jesus, for Jesus' relationship to those people is examined from a different standpoint. In their case the Gospels focus on the moment when liberation becomes possible for them and describe what Jesus demands of them at that point.

We must also realize that there is an ongoing development in Jesus' own view, as we shall see further on. At first Jesus believes that the arrival of the kingdom is near, and he restricts the summons to discipleship to only a few. The majority of people need simply accept its coming and undergo conversion, which does not strictly mean following Jesus. At a later stage in his life, when Jesus no longer feels that the arrival of the kingdom is near, the moral demand of discipleship is made basic and universal.[40]

We must consider the whole history of Jesus as the font of Christian morality rather than focusing on isolated phases of his life, however important these may be. If we do that, then we cannot reduce his fundamental demand to a passive one of faith and hope as opposed to the active one of discipleship. Neither eliminates the other, but the demand for faith and hope must be integrated into the demand to follow him. In other words, we do not get to the roots of the faith and hope demanded by Jesus if we see them only as external impositions. Instead we must view them as the lifestyle of Jesus himself.

To fully appreciate what following Jesus means in Jesus' own terms, we must realize that his idea of it grew and developed even as his faith did. Hence it is not a vague, abstract idea but the historical embodiment of attitude.[41]

Restricting our considerations to Mark's Gospel, we can pinpoint two basic stages or moments in Jesus' view of this particular discipleship. In the first stage it centers on the band of chosen disciples. They are called and chosen on the initiative of Jesus alone (Mark 1:16–20; 3:14–19). The content of this call is a summons to carry out a task as Jesus envisioned it at that point. They are sent out to proclaim the kingdom (6:12), to preach conversion (6:12), to cure the sick and drive out demons (6:12), and to exercise power over unclean spirits (6:7). The personal attitude of these envoys is to be that of Jesus himself. They are not to take anything with them for the trip—neither food, nor knapsack, nor money (6:8).

This conception of the kingdom entails an active demand, a demand to work for the kingdom of God. Here the figure of Jesus is important insofar as it is he who freely chooses to call people without any word of explanation. But we are dealing with a messianic conception of discipleship rather than a christological conception in the strict sense. Though it is Jesus who calls the disciples and their service to the kingdom is in imitation of his work, the task of bringing about the kingdom of God can be interpreted in orthodox Jewish terms at this point. It is not yet riddled with problems, and its exigencies, though harsh, are not scandalous. We could say that at this point in his life Jesus demands an enthusiastic embracing of discipleship that could be inspired by the intrinsic grandeur of the cause he represents.

In the second phase of his public life we find a shift in Jesus' understanding of discipleship paralleling the shift in his own self-understanding and work. Following Jesus now means following him in a situation where his relationship to the kingdom no longer corresponds in any obvious way with the expectations of Jewish orthodoxy, the disciples, or even Jesus himself.

This shows up clearly in Mark's Gospel (Mark 8:27–35). There has been a change in Jesus' consciousness concerning reality, the future, and the way to inaugurate the kingdom. It is no longer work and active deeds of power that are demanded of him for the kingdom's sake. Now he must display a love frought with suffering (v.31). His service to the kingdom can no longer follow the old logic, and hence he severely rebukes Peter (v. 33). Discipleship no longer means following a messiah in his messianic function. It now means following his own person in all its scandalous concreteness: following him even to the cross (v. 34).

Thus we get a real change in perspective concerning the following of Jesus. The general horizon continues to be God and concrete praxis for the kingdom, but now all that is concretized in the person of Jesus himself. This shift in perspective is basic for any understanding of Christian morality because it indicates a shift from a line of action based on the universality of certain values (those of the kingdom) to a line of action based on a specific and particular reality (Jesus' own line of action). We also get a deep concentration on discipleship at this new stage: "If a man wishes to come after me . . . " (Mark 8:34). The demand for discipleship is no longer restricted to those disciples who are to preach the kingdom; it is now proposed to all as a way of life. Discipleship now takes in all the attitudes and activities of a person, giving meaning to the other facets of life such as orthodoxy, for example (compare Mark 8:29 with 8:33).

The Features of Discipleship and Their Consequences for Morality

I have already remarked that Jesus is his history, and that the moral values embodied by him must therefore be understood in terms of his concrete realization of them. But we must also consciously realize what those fundamental values are, how they are fleshed out, and how radical they are.

When Jesus calls his disciples to go out and proclaim the "kingdom of God," they understand him. The phrase "kingdom of God" is a utopian symbol for a wholly new and definitive way of living and being. It presupposes renewal in many areas: in the heart of the human person, in societal relationships, and in the cosmos at large. Today we ignore the last dimension because it clearly is bound up with cultural conceptions of Jesus' own age. It simply indicates how total the renewal is to be. The utopian import of the kingdom is a summary way of saying that things should be different than they are—better, of course.

Viewed in terms of its end result, the final goal is one of universal *reconciliation.* People must work for that end, and the morality of specific actions depends on whether they do or do not point in that desired direction. By its very nature, however, the reconciliation stands in opposition to existing reality. To effect reconciliation is to do *justice,* and we can say that the basic general value of Jesus is that of doing justice. But here we should not understand it as retributive or vindictive justice designed to give all persons and situations what is due to them by virtue of what they are. Justice here is meant in the Old Testament sense. It is the liberation of Israel. Yahweh is just, not because he gives all their due, but because he tries to re-create human beings and situations, to "save" them. Thus the justice of God is "the essentially salvific activity of God whereby the people of Israel [in the New Testament, the whole human race] obtain the restoration of the good things promised by God."[42]

Here the question arises as to whether this justice is directed to the individual or to society, and whether people become just as individuals or in structural terms. These modern ways of framing the question are obviously quite alien to Jesus' explicit way of viewing the recipient and subject of justice. Hence we cannot come down apodictically in favor of one side or the other. My belief is that in Jesus we find a dialectical conception embracing both sides, particularly if we consider what Jesus himself does as well as what he says.

Insofar as the first question noted in the last paragraph is concerned, it is quite apparent that Jesus repeatedly addresses himself to the individual in terms of re-creation. When he approaches the poor, the oppressed, and the sinner, he does not simply offer consolation; he offers justice. In other words, he does not propose to leave people as they are and simply console them in their plight; he proposes to re-create their present situation and thus do "justice" to them. This is the quintessence of Jesus' understanding of the kingdom.

But when Jesus addresses himself to oppressed persons the fact is that he is not simply addressing wretched individuals who stand in need of justice. Historically speaking these individuals are in a state of misery because they have been ostracized by society and deprived of status. In approaching these individuals, Jesus is not only doing them justice but also clearing away the barriers of class that have made them not only individuals in misery but also persons ostracized by society. The justice of Jesus, then, points toward some new form of social coexistence where class differences have been abolished, at least in principle.

This shows up even more clearly when Jesus condemns sin, the basic anti-value. Strikingly enough, his harshest condemnations are not directed against the individual sinner who does not fulfill the law out of frailty; they are directed against the collective sins that create a situation contrary to the kingdom. From the de facto evil use of collective power there arises a situation that is the negation of brotherhood and of reconciliation. The resultant sin covers the religious sphere, the economic sphere, the cultural sphere, and the political sphere. There is poverty because the rich do not share their wealth. There is religious oppression because the priests impose intolerable burdens on people. There is ignorance because the Levites have carried off the keys to knowledge. There is political oppression because the rulers rule despotically. In short, the sinfulness of these people is not something that affects only the subjective life of the individual; it is visibly crystallized in the social realm. Jesus' condemnations against these various groups of sinners clearly suggest a desire to re-create the social situation, not just the concrete individual sinner.

The second question is something else again. How did Jesus view the practical realization of the kingdom and its ideals? Was it to come about through personal conversion of the individual or through structural changes? What relationship, if any, did he see between the two? Now it is quite apparent that Jesus wanted to see both come about, that he did not believe in structural change without a personal change in the individual. In that sense I think it is anachronistic to force the data dealing with the historical Jesus in such a way that he is presented as someone who thought that structural change would solve the problem of personal change in the individual. Jesus sees the de facto evil use of power rooted in the will to power—specifically in the power that tries to manipulate God. Insofar as human beings do not let God be God, they themselves cease to be human. And when these nonhumans hold power, they use it against the kingdom. This facet obviously applies to groups with power, not directly to those groups of people who are ostracized by society.

Now we cannot simplify the whole issue by concluding that Jesus was interested in the individual rather than in structures. Even if we were to reduce the problem of conversion to that of individual conversion, we are still left with the problem of relating personal conversion to structural justice. If we take due note of Jesus' demand to bring about the kingdom, and even more of his own personal example, then we are forced to conclude that personal conversion must always be associated with social praxis. Speaking in terms of justice, we are forced to conclude that Jesus sees people becoming just only insofar as they do the work of justice. In systematic terms people become "children" of God by doing the work of "brotherhood." So even the aspect of personal justice is inseparably bound up with some form of social justice.

In analyzing the moral subject as subject, Jesus stresses the danger of a particular temptation. One must make sure that one's yearning for justice does not turn into an affirmation of one's own ego rather than that of others. The human heart must be pure. Jesus poses the limit-case of relations to one's enemy. The good of one's enemy must be sought rather than a vengeful affirmation of the moral subject. That is why Jesus talks about love for one's enemies.

As the history of Jesus makes clear, that has nothing to do with pacifism. Jesus was the first to utter harsh condemnations of the unjust enemy. But this concentration on the moral subject cannot be used as an expression of disinterest in the work of bringing about the kingdom, in the social and structural aspect. His analysis of the moral subject is designed to make sure that in doing justice people really do precisely that, that they do not let themselves be guided by a retributive or vindictive notion of justice rather than a truly re-creative notion. Moral subjects must renounce the will to power, not because that alone will make them just, but because it is through such renunciation that their justice will really be the justice of God and his kingdom.

To sum up, then, we can say that the basic moral value proclaimed and exemplified by Jesus was re-creative justice. That is the value that his followers must realize in the concrete. He does not summon them directly to become just as individuals; he summons them to do justice. Precisely because his interest is in the justice of God as understood by the Old Testament rather than in some substitute form of justice of a retributive or vindictive nature, Jesus analyzes the moral subject in terms of will to power. So long as the moral subject does not renounce that will to power, then in theological terms that person has not yet converted to God. And Jesus doubts that such a person is capable of doing the work of justice proper to God's kingdom.

But if we look at the history of Jesus, we find that the relationship between renouncing one's will to power and doing justice is a dialectical one—as we shall see. It is an oversimplification to say that one must first undergo a personal conversion and then go about the task of bringing about the kingdom. For even personal conversion as such is not given once and for all. It is verified in the concrete history of realizing the kingdom, and that history calls for ever new conversions.

So now we see that the fundamental moral value for the follower of Jesus is bringing about the kingdom of God, which means doing the work of re-creative justice and achieving brotherhood. It is through this effort that the follower of Jesus simultaneously becomes a just person and a child of God. But as we noted earlier, Jesus does not constitute the moral standard for his disciples because he incarnates vague or generic moral values, however lofty they might be. Jesus serves as the moral standard through the concrete history whereby he turns those values into reality.[43] Thus reflection on the historicity of moral values and on the historical unfolding of discipleship must be part of any fundamental moral theology purporting to be Christian.

According to a traditional view in fundamental moral theology, the first obligation of conscience is the obligation to form one's conscience. What I propose to deal with here is the Christian view as to how we do form our conscience in historical terms. My concern, then, is with the fundamental principles required to historicize generic values.

On the basis of Jesus' own history we can say that the first principle governing the concretion of moral values is *the situation itself*. In Jesus' case it was a society divided into classes who were in conflict with one another. The first step in concretizing the basic value of justice is to be found in the basic outlook from which Jesus views the essence and necessity of justice. Does he focus on the situation as a totality or does he view it from a specific position within society? Now Jesus clearly had some notion of the situation as a totality, for that is what is suggested in the term "kingdom of God." But he concretizes his morality by immersing himself in the situation on the basis of a class outlook rather than by disregarding or evading the dualism in society.

The term "class outlook" is meant to be somewhat ambiguous because in Jesus' case its meaning is not crystal-clear. Yet there are certain elements that help us to see what his under-standing of justice from a "class outlook" means. First, the poor are the people who understand the meaning of the king-dom best, even though their knowledge and understanding comes by way of contrariety. Second, Jesus reinforces his experience of the necessity for justice through his contact with the poor. Third, Jesus' service to the totality is concretized directly in his service to the poor. Fourth, in his own personal life he experiences poverty. At the very least it is a relative poverty that somehow includes him in the ranks of the poor. Fifth, Jesus undergoes the experience of class-identity, and specifically the consequences of his fellowship with the group known as the poor. The power wielded by the other major group in society is directed against him.

It would be anachronistic to look to Jesus for an analysis of classes such as we find in the work of present-day sociology. Yet his general attitude makes it clear that in trying to under-stand justice Jesus adopts a stance that is rooted in the poor and is meant to benefit them. Justice as a universal ideal cannot be understood or rendered operational unless one somehow does that through concrete experience of injustice. In that sense the first principle for concretizing moral values is noth-ing else but the first principle of Christology itself: i.e., incar-nation. One must deliberately adopt some partial stance in order to comprehend the totality. To look for some stand that will give us the totality directly is to do the very opposite of incarnation.

A second principle or feature underlying Jesus' concretion of moral values is *the element of conflict.* If social groups do not merely coexist alongside each other, if there is tension be-tween them, then we necessarily have conflict. There is a complete contradiction between the ideal of justice and the reality of injustice. This contradiction reaches its maximum concretion not insofar as it is pondered in the abstract but insofar as it is experienced in real life. The pointed edge of conflict is not to be found solely in passively suffering the consequences of injustice, as we noted earlier. It also includes one's experience of the fact that justice can be realized in history only through an active struggle against injustice, a struggle that often ends in defeat.

The element of dynamic conflict in a given historical situation means that our concrete realization of basic moral values must be a fight as well. The realization of justice must necessarily entail a fight against injustice, for injustice will not disappear simply because one has a positive intention to establish justice as Jesus did. Not only the avoidance of evil but also the fight against evil is part of morality by virtue of its historical nature. Bringing about the kingdom is necessarily bound up with fighting against injustice.[44]

This way of posing the whole issue puts an end to any merely idealistic formulation of moral theology. However, the fact that struggle is an intrinsic part of the effort to embody moral values in reality is not something that need only be thought about to be realized. On the contrary, the realization comes only through the historical realization of moral values. To take an example from the life of Jesus that is pertinent here, we can certainly say that his "love" for people was universal in intent. But that love was translated into different concrete forms when he sought to make it a reality in the context of a historical situation riddled with conflict. In Jesus' case, his universal love was translated into a decision to be "with" the oppressed and to be "against" the oppressors, precisely so that his love could be "for" all of them.

So the concretion of the basic ideal of justice entails not only proclaiming and doing it but also fighting against injustice. This means that a moral way of life in accordance with that of the historical Jesus must be dialectical. If we want to formulate the basic moral exigency in a phrase, we cannot say that it comes down to "doing good and avoiding evil." Rather, it comes down to "doing good and fighting evil to wipe it out."

A third feature in the historicization of Christian fundamental morality has to do with *the "conversion" of the subject.* The following of Jesus does not mean reproducing the historical traits or acts of Jesus; rather, it means reproducing the whole process in which he was involved. This conception of the following has important consequences for what goes by the name of conversion. Discipleship entails some sort of initial break and also a process in conversion itself. Conversion is not something given once and for all, nor can we choose to stop wherever we are with it when the historical situation requires us to take a further step in the conversion process.

The initial break is implied in one's election of certain fundamental moral values. As Jesus sees it, we give up an egocentric conception of existence and focus on the reign of God. Given the historicity of the task involved in bringing about the kingdom and the conflictive nature of the real situation, this first step in conversion will soon call for a second step. In the first stage we are asked to make a fundamental change in our interests and our moral values, to put our possessions in the service of the kingdom. In the second stage of conversion we are asked to give up our ideas and our very lives.

An example might help to clarify this point. The first stage in conversion certainly demands that we choose love as the supreme value in life. Since this love seeks to be effective, to really establish the kingdom, it makes use of the power at its disposal to achieve that end. Insofar as we use power for the sake of love, we thereby become good ourselves. Now when the sinfulness of the real-life situation deprives us of our power, the mediation of love takes another form: i.e., suffering. Now it is our very persons, not things or possessions, that are demanded of us. Thus the basic ideal of love passes through distinct historical stages making different historical demands. They cannot be envisioned and planned for in advance; they can only be discovered in the historical process itself. Becoming a good human being in the process of discipleship means not only bringing about the kingdom but also staying open to the need to do this in ever new ways.

How this concrete embodiment of discipleship will work out in any given concrete case is another problem. We cannot determine ahead of time whether our discipleship will follow the same *chronological* steps and phases that were verified in Jesus' process of concretizing love. The only point I want to stress here is that in the following of Jesus conversion is not some thing given once and for all. To opt for certain moral values is to opt for them in all their historicity and for the concrete embodiments that they will require.

A fundamental moral theology must also concern itself with the *absolute* character of the moral exigency. In one sense we alluded to that absolute character earlier when we noted what happened to the early Christians after Jesus' resurrection. It was then that they experienced the absolute character of his whole life, realizing that the definitive way to the Father had been revealed in Jesus' own history. What I want to do here is explore that absolute character from the standpoint of Jesus' whole history. To put it briefly, we can say that the demand to follow Jesus is a *radical* one. Its radicalness can be considered from several different but complementary standpoints, and that is what I shall do now.

First, we may consider the radicalness of the demand for discipleship in terms of the alternative that the kingdom of God poses to the present world. Insofar as it is eschatological, the proclamation of Jesus presents people with a moral demand that places them in crisis and offers them a choice between two alternatives: A person cannot serve two masters. The alternatives can be described in theological terms (God or wealth), christological terms ("He who is not with me is against me"), or anthropological terms ("Whoever would preserve his life will lose it, but whoever loses his life for my sake and the gospel's will preserve it"). The important point here, however, is the structural nature of this basic choice. The alternatives are not presented as complementary, as if it were possible to effect some partial reconciliation between the kingdom of God and the present situation. Nor are they presented as dialectical alternatives, as if to say that the present situation is supposed to be negated and then incorporated into the kingdom of God in some sublimated form. The basic choice is between two mutually exclusive alternatives: either the present world or the kingdom of God.

This has an important consequence for the moral conception of how subjects fashion themselves. Moral activity is not aimed at turning a person into the *whole* person, the person whose potentialities as such are fulfilled. Instead moral activity is aimed at turning a person into the *new* person, who stands in discontinuity with, and even opposition to, the old person. That is why the New Testament describes the person's process of self-becoming as running counter to what one already is. To put it in programmatic terms, we can say that the basic categories that have been used traditionally to describe the self-becoming of the Christian human being are categories of opposition and contradiction. Faith is a faith against unbelief, a faith that must overcome the world in order to come into being. Hope is a hope against hope. And love is a love against alienation in a situation where sin holds power.[45]

Second, we may see the radicalness of the demand for discipleship in Jesus' insistence to carry a certain moral attitude through to the very end. This insistence is voiced in temporal terms when Jesus says that we must not look back. It is viewed in utopian terms when Jesus tells us to be perfect as our heavenly Father is perfect. And it is viewed in existential terms when Jesus suggests that we must be ready to give up anything that might be an obstacle to the kingdom: our eyes, our family, and so forth.

Jesus is well aware that it is not easy to see a radical demand through to the end. He frequently unmasks a lack of radical commitment in people, and their attempted substitutes for it. Not everyone who says "Lord" will enter the kingdom: Mere verbal conversion is not enough. Interior conversion to God is not enough if it is not accompanied by concrete effective conversion to the kingdom, hence his diatribes against the priests and Pharisees and his parable on the Good Samaritan. A false sense of security may also prevent someone from seeing the radical nature of the demands he imposes, as the parable of the Pharisee and the Publican praying in the temple suggests. And his dialogue with the rich young man indicates that good intentions are not enough.

The whole underlying supposition here is that radical conversion is very different. According to Jesus, it is all the less evident as one makes progress in the moral process. The moral subject will tend to use any excuse to foreshorten and delay the process.

Third, the radicalness of Jesus' demand of discipleship is brought out by his insistent stress on the need for discernment. The moral demand imposed by Jesus basically has to do with a way of acting. In history, however, it is not clear-cut or readily self-evident. Hence there is a need for discernment. To see in what sense discernment implies that there is something radical involved in morality, we must make a distinction between Jesus' discernment and that of his disciples during his own lifetime. In the case of his immediate disciples, the problem was solved in principle because discipleship simply meant imitating Jesus, who shared the same basic historical situation they did.[46] For his disciple today, the problem of discernment is much the same as it was for Jesus himself, as opposed to the problem faced by his own immediate followers in his own time. The disciple living today, however, does possess one ultimate criterion for correct discernment: i.e., Jesus himself.

The whole problem of discernment shows up quite clearly in the temptations of Jesus. It implies, first of all, some form of ignorance or not-knowing. The radical nature of this ignorance becomes clear if we view the temptations, not in terms of a possible choice between God and Satan, but as a questioning search for the authentic reality of God. If it were simply a matter of choosing between God and Satan, then in theory one could know the difference between the two. In this case, however, discernment must operate against the backdrop of God's infiniteness. The process of overcoming ignorance, of trying to find out and know the authentic reality of God, becomes an unending quest that does not rest content with any historical mediation of God. Thus the process of discernment is not basically concerned with determining what is good and what is evil, though the obvious assumption is that God's will is good. Rather, it has to do with discerning what the will of God is. Hence the radical nature of Jesus' experience of God is matched by an equally radical effort to discern God's will. And since God's will is historical rather than eternal or universal, the whole context of the moral subject becomes very complex, going far beyond any straightforward search for what is obviously good and what is obviously evil.

So there are two stages in Christian discernment. The first is preliminary to any specifically Christian discernment, and it has to do with a general determination of what is good and what is evil. The second and specifically Christian stage of discernment is concerned with the problem of the essential nature of the good that one is obliged to do. We see this in Jesus, when he is tempted with regard to something that is positively good: i.e., bringing about the kingdom. The temptation he faces in this connection is not designed to draw him away from this task in its abstract goodness. The discernment he must exercise here has to do with the concrete way in which he is to perform this task rightly and well. It is not a choice between a life of service and a life based on egotism. Rather, Jesus must try to discern how to live a life of service that will authentically correspond with the concrete will of God.[47]

Discernment, then, is not a later step which follows upon the discovery of moral values (or antivalues). Instead it is the specifically Christian way of finding out what is truly and authentically good. To cite an example from fundamental moral theology as it was traditionally presented, the choice between marriage and celibacy is not posed as a Christian problem when one asks if one or the other is good or bad, or when one asks whether one is superior to the other. It becomes a Christian problem when one asks which a person is to choose in the concrete. That problem, however, does not lie above and beyond the whole basic problem of morality insofar as it is Christian. Traditional language wrongly gives that impression when it talks about "counsels" and "commandments," and when it makes distinctions between what is commanded, what is recommended, and what is permitted. Such language is based on a conception of moral knowledge that is content to make a distinction between what is good and what is evil.

In that sense Christian discernment is radical. Goodness is not simply the avoidance of evil. (Note that most of the formulations in the various Old Testament decalogues are negative in form.) Goodness is the positive concretion of what one must do, the choice between various possible goods. It is true that certain passages in the Gospels give the impression that Jesus, too, made a distinction between what is merely good and what is especially recommended, as classic moral theology is wont to do. In his dialogue with the rich young man (Matt. 19:16–22), for example, Jesus makes a distinction between being good and being perfect. Even there, however, we must also note that in the final redaction of that scene we find the famous *logion* asserting how difficult it is for the rich, who presumably keep the commandments, to enter the kingdom of heaven (Matt. 19:23–26).[48]

Be that as it may, however, the concrete exigencies that Jesus laid down at a given moment are not the guiding criterion in trying to prove the need for radical discernment in Christian morality. It is the moral life of Jesus himself, not any specific demands that he may have voiced, which points up the need for such radical discernment.

The Limits of Fundamental Moral Theology in Terms of the History of Jesus Himself

So far we have been trying to discover the fundamental features of a Christian moral theology on the basis of Jesus' own historical process rather than in terms of any specific moral teachings of his. Now it is time to go back over the same theme from a somewhat different standpoint. The pathway of Jesus himself is *one* path. Of course Christian faith believes that in the path of this particular individual we find the model for what every Christian path ought to be. If Jesus is the one who lived the faith in some original and pristine way, then there must be something original and creative in his way that should be incorporated into any way which purports to be Christian. That is the point I have tried to deal with above. On the other hand, his course was a historical one. That being the case, it was not absolute in the sense that in it the absolute concretion of the proper moral path was given once and for all. Jesus' path led him to the kingdom of God, which is the absolute. Speaking in historical terms, however, we can say that Jesus showed us the absolute dimensions of a historical path but that he did not show us any path as being absolute in itself.

Here I propose to push our reflections further along and to distinguish between the absolute and the relative in Jesus' own path. I am well aware of the difficulties entailed in any such effort. In trying to make such a determination, we are influenced by our hermeneutic horizons. Indeed outside of those horizons we cannot comprehend what is allegedly absolute or what is allegedly relative in Jesus' course. Still such a determination must be made if the path of Jesus is not to be absolutized in every respect on the one hand or totally relativized on the other. Total absolutization is impossible, quite aside from the fact that it would go against the intention of Jesus himself. Total relativization would mean the end of Christian faith, and hence of Christian morality.

Having already delineated some of the normal and meaningful features of Christian morality which seem to me to be "absolute," I should now like to examine some of the limitations in Jesus' own history insofar as Christian moral life and theology are concerned.

The following of Jesus does not come down to the mere imitation of Jesus. First of all, it is in fact impossible to do exactly what he himself did. Second and even more important, the Christian should not "imitate" Jesus precisely because an intrinsic and essential feature of Jesus' own moral course is its localization in history. As Jesus himself sees it, there is no moral life that is not localized in history. Precisely because of this historical localization, a person's moral life is unrepeatable. Christians must accept the moral responsibility of determining how to situate themselves concretely in history. If they shirk that responsibility and appeal to the allegedly eternal example of Jesus, then they are going against the deepest thrust of Jesus' own morality, though it is certainly true that he has left us certain basic criteria, discussed above, which will make sure that our localization of morality is really Christian. If we wish to operate in the name of the historical Jesus, then, we must accept the *historicity* of his concrete morality and the obligation to *historicize* every later concrete morality.

Discipleship is not imitation, therefore; and neither is it a reproduction of certain historical traits of Jesus. Being open to discipleship means being open to the work of reproducing the fundamental thrust of Jesus' effort to concretize certain generic values. But we must be open to doing this *in a different historical context,* and we cannot say beforehand how the process will work out exactly.

Because Jesus' morality is historically situated, concrete moral evaluations will depend essentially on the historical situation. It is not the proper task of fundamental moral theology to determine concretely what values and actions ought to be realized in the concrete. What is the proper task of fundamental moral theology is the work of reflecting on the relationship between some concrete moral value and the whole process that led us to formulate it.

Certain types of analysis are proper in the process of elaborating these concrete values, but they do not derive from any sort of ethical evaluation. In Jesus' own case, then, we must distinguish between the ethical values he proclaims and the various analyses wherewith he concretizes certain values. Take marital morality and social morality, for example. Here it is obvious that Jesus concretizes the supreme values of love and re-creative justice on the basis of more or less implicit analyses which depend on the Jewish cultural world around him and the traditions of his people as they have concretized certain moral values. Jesus does indeed reject some of these concretions and qualify others, but the horizon from which he makes his evaluation ever remains a concrete analytical horizon that cannot be universal.

This has important implications for any fundamental moral theology purporting to be based on the following of Jesus. Though such a theology ever remains within the hermeneutic circle, it must make a clear distinction between the absolute moral values of Jesus and the various analyses underlying his concrete moral applications. It should not absolutize Jesus' own sociological, economic, and political analyses as such. What it should absolutize instead is the necessity of concretizing absolute moral values through the mediation of such analyses.

A third limitation derives from Jesus' own historical situation in its theological dimension. As we saw early in this book, Jesus looked for the imminent arrival of the kingdom of God, particularly at the start of his ministry. This historical datum defines both his own concrete moral life and the way it differs from those in later situations. The difference does not lie so much in his understanding of God as future; rather, it lies in the implications for any effort to concretize absolute moral values.

Once we take due account of this historical datum, we can understand why Jesus stressed the basic need for faith and hope among the poor and outcast and demanded active participation in the work of the kingdom of a relatively small group of followers. This he certainly did in the early stage of his public life. But it would be wrong to conclude from that fact that here and now today, when the parousia does not seem imminent, the most correct ethical attitude is one of passive waiting for the kingdom. Here I am leaving aside the whole sociological issue as to whether huge masses can be actively mobilized or whether they tend to remain passive by comparison with the leaders of minority groups.

Using the same example, we can try to see what is absolute in Jesus' demand for faith and hope and in its various possible historical concretions in diverse historical situations. Jesus repeatedly asserts that people must "ask for" the coming of the kingdom, even though he and his immediate followers are actively working on its behalf. If we analyze this attitude of "petition" in depth, then we come upon something which, in my opinion, is "absolute" for all Christian morality. It is the *experience of gratuitousness*, the experience that I chose earlier as the basis for the note of obligatoriness in Christian morality. The question then becomes: What is the best way to express this experience in a situation where the parousia has not taken place? Is there a better way of expressing it than merely pleading passively for its coming? In our present-day situation, for example, it can be expressed in positive action on behalf of the kingdom and, in my opinion, it should be so expressed. Hope enters the picture here insofar as our partial efforts to establish the kingdom fail to establish it in all its fullness or even are met with outright rejection. Our experience of gratuitousness in this new historical situation, where the parousia has not yet taken place, is better expressed by not giving up than by merely reciting prayers of petition. And the same would seem. to be the case in the second stage of Jesus' own public life.

This point is of singular importance in the present-day situation. The urgent obligation to bring about the kingdom remains a problem of fundamental morality; but its whole tint is different because our historical situation is different from that of Jesus. History moves on. Today the masses are taking cognizance of their misery and poverty in a new and different way; and we possess new technological possibilities for eliminating certain types of inhumanity. So the fundamental ethical urgency is posed to us in a different form. Speaking concretely, we are faced with two problems.

The first problem has to do with the matter of "eschatological reserve," that is, the realization that we cannot possibly realize the kingdom in all its fullness because it is a gift. In Jesus' day people were looking for its imminent arrival, and the early Christian communities expected Jesus' imminent return. So their eschatological reserve might well lead them to relativize every concrete historical embodiment of the kingdom that was partial and incomplete. It cannot prompt us to do the same today, however. The non-arrival of the kingdom does not call for the moral relativization of every partial historical configuration of it. It calls for the very opposite. We are faced with the urgent obligation of drawing up and carrying out concrete projections of the kingdom, however partial and incomplete they may be.

The second problem is related to the first, and it has to do with the new form that love should take today. In the history of Jesus himself we find love taking the form of effective action at first and then the form of accepted suffering. Jesus even says that in a sinful world, a world fighting against love, no love can really be effective without the note of gratuitousness that finds expression in love embodied in suffering. In Jesus' own life, the two forms of love seem to follow in chronological order. Jesus moves from a love embodied in effective action to a love embodied in suffering.

Today I think both aspects of love should be present in every moral effort that purports to be Christian. We must be open to love as effective action and love as suffering even unto death. But the relationship between the two can be very different because history presents us with the urgent task of rendering the kingdom of God present in at least partial form. Moral casuistry, in the good sense of that term, is a much more complicated matter today than it was in Jesus' day—precisely insofar as we take his demand to bring about the kingdom with absolute seriousness. The relationship between love and power is becoming ever more complex. Followers of Jesus know that if the sinful world has not robbed them of power, to some extent at least their love has not been like that of Jesus. But because they also seek to effectively establish the kingdom in some partial form at least for the sake of the majority, they will not view impotence as an ideal either. The chronological course of love in Jesus' life may turn out to be the concrete course of today's Christian also, but it need not be. Instead the two phases of love (as effective action and as accepted suffering) may coexist simultaneously, so that Christians continually seek effective power on behalf of human beings while being open to the realization that it may be snatched from them.

My feeling is that this is the most crucial and ticklish point in any Christian morality, the point where discernment becomes absolutely necessary. The motive force behind this discernment is well expressed by Paul: "The love of Christ impels us" (2 Cor. 5:14). The Christian must not leave the world abandoned to its misery, but he must also be willing to accept the world's rejection of his effort.[49]

The Import of Jesus for Fundamental Christian Morality: A Summary

The points I have just made in this section might seem to suggest that Christian moral life and theology end up being a formal morality without any hard content insofar as it appeals to Jesus himself. It would seem to suggest that Jesus does not teach us any concrete content having to do with morality; that basically he teaches us how to learn what a moral way of life is in different historical situations and then how to realize such a life.

Such a view is partly true and partly false, in my opinion. It is false because there is content that remains valid in all the differing situations of history: i.e., Christian morality is bringing about the kingdom, fighting for a justice that will re-create humankind and its situation from the viewpoint of the poor. Openness to love as effective action and love as suffering is also a historical constant in any morality based on Jesus. So is the principle of letting oneself and one's viewpoint be shaped by the poor. It is not simply a translation of the abstract moral principle that one must do good; it is a Christian concretion of that basic principle.

Yet there is some truth in the view noted above. It is true in the sense that Christian morality does not make Jesus into a "law"; rather, he serves as its "spirit." Here again, however, we must understand the point aright. When we say that Jesus is not a "law," we mean that his moral summons is not a moralizing indoctrination. Jesus does not give us certain moral norms that are to be accepted as good because he voices them, whether or not their goodness can be seen in real existence. That is why my methodological starting point here was his own concrete history rather than an analysis of the demands he voiced. The foundation of Christian morality is not some sort of indoctrination in what Jesus said we must do; rather, it is the experienced meaningfulness of the fact that he lived the life of faith in all its pristine fullness. This experience invites us to re-create the process of living the faith, and it is in that process that various moral demands take on meaning; it has nothing to do with indoctrination. When I chose the following of Jesus as the basic criterion of Christian morality, I did not choose it as one possible exigency among many offered by Jesus. I chose it because it is the one that points us toward reproducing the overall experience of Jesus.

In a real sense, then, the criterion of moral living is the Spirit of Jesus. It has nothing to do with any sort of spiritualism focusing on the private sector or the isolated individual; nor

does it have anything to do with a pentecostalism that prescinds from history in theory or practice. Instead it is the
fundamental experience that appears in the New Testament
after the resurrection of Jesus. The Spirit of Jesus is the one
who paradoxically prompts a re-creation of Jesus' human history. Yet this Spirit is not some abstract cipher or some inven-
tion without content and verification that might be used to
justify any innovation or fixation in history. Prescinding here
from the problem viewed in terms of the Trinity, we can say
that the Spirit of Jesus is the same Jesus who has unleashed a
history and set it in motion.

When we appeal to Jesus as spirit rather than as law, then,
we are trying to say two things. First of all, the obligation to
historicize morality derives from Jesus himself. It is the basic
experience of which Paul spoke in many different ways: moving forward under the impetus of Christ's charity, filling up
the sufferings that were lacking in Christ's passion, heeding
the groans of all salvation, and so forth. To truly lay hold of the
history of Jesus is to lay hold of it in terms of its summons to
historicization. Second, we are making the most profound
profession of faith in Jesus when we appeal to him as spirit, for
we are professing his universality in truly operational terms.
Instead of focusing on some abstract notion of his universal
meaning, we are concentrating on the concrete, historical embodiment of it. We are saying that Jesus, as the firstborn Son, is
capable of making people his brothers and sisters in every
historical situation; that he is capable of finding followers to
historicize his own universality in every time and place.

To speak of Jesus as "spirit" rather than as "law," then, is to
say that the most profound reality of the historical Jesus is his
ability to open up a wholly new history through his followers.
The objective of that history will always remain the same: to
bring about the kingdom of God as Jesus did. So long as
domination and protest have not been overcome completely,
so long as sinfulness and conflict perdure in history, Jesus will
ever remain present as a "dangerous" memory and a point of
crisis. He will remain to call our own path into question on the
basis of his own historical path. But the innermost core of his

history will be turned into reality only insofar as his followers re-create his path rather than merely retrace it. In this way the history of Jesus as history will serve as spirit, standing in need of flesh to concretize itself. As Boff puts it: "Christian faith does not prescribe a specific concrete programme but demands a specific attitude which must be present in any practical action or any position taken."[50] We learn that "attitude" by seeing how *Jesus* lived his history. Then, in that spirit, we learn how to live, not *his* history, but *our own*.

NOTES

1. I.Ellacuría, *Freedom Made Flesh*, Eng. trans. (Maryknoll, New York: Orbis Books, 1976), pp. 26–27.

2. L. Boff, *Jesucristo el liberador*, p. 124; see note 9 of chap. 3, in this volume.

3. Among present-day Protestant theologians see E. Fuchs, "Jesus und der Glaube, " in *Zur Frage nach dem historischen Jesus* (Tübingen: Mohr, 1960), pp, 238–57; G. Ebeling, "Jesus und Glaube," in *Wort und Glaube* (Tübingen: Mohr, 1960), pp. 203–54; J. Moltmann, *Teología de la esperanza*, see note 31, chap. 2, in this volume; J. Moltmann, *Der gekreuzigte Gott*, see note 10, chap. 1, in this volume; W. Pannenberg, *Fundamentos de cristología*, pp. 403–33, see note 6, chap. 1, in this volume.
   Among present-day Catholic theologians see P. Schoonenberg, *Un Dios de los hombres*, Spanish trans. (Barcelona, 1973), pp. 168–74; Eng. trans.: *The Christ: A Study of the God-Man Relationship in the Whole Creation and in Jesus Christ* (New York: Herder & Herder, 1971); C. Duquoc, article on the hope of Jesus in *Concilium* 59, 1970; W. Thüsing, in *Christologie—systematisch und exegetisch* (Freiburg: Herder, 1972). pp. 211–26; D. Wiederkehr, "Esbozo de cristología sistemática," in *Mysterium Salutis*, III/1 (Madrid, 1969), pp. 649–52; H. Urs von Balthasar, "Fides Christi," in *Ensayos Teológicos*, II, Spanish trans. (Madrid: Sponsa Verbi, 1964), pp. 51–96; both volumes translated into English, *Word and Revelation: Essays in Theology I*, and *Word and Redemption: Essays in Theology II* (New York: Herder & Herder, 1964–65).

4. *Summa Theologiae*, III, q. 7, a. 3.

5. P. Schoonenberg, p. 70; D. Wiederkehr, pp. 511–26; W. Pannenberg, pp. 351–63; see note 3 of this chapter for these entries.

6. D. Wiederkehr, p. 560; W. Pannenberg, p. 229; see note 3 above.

7. K. Rahner, *Escritos de Teología*, 4: 383; see note 3, chap. 2 above.

8. D. Wiederkehr, p. 519; W. Pannenberg, pp. 420–28; see note 3 above.

9. H. Assmann rejects any abstract Christology, even a biblical one, which describes Jesus as "the presence of the risen Christ in the world" (p. 103) or as "something completely ethereal" (p. 69): *Theology for a Nomad Church*, see note 1, chap. 1 above.

10. "To approach the man Jesus of Nazareth, in whom God was made flesh,

to penetrate not only in his teaching, but also in his life, what it is that gives his word an immediate, concrete context, is a task which more and more needs to be undertaken" (G. Gutiérrez, *A Theology of Liberation*, Eng. trans. [Maryknoll, New York: Orbis Books, 1973], p. 226).

11. J. Moltmann has underlined this fundamental problem in debating the view of W. Pannenberg. The latter may be regarded as the chief contemporary exponent of a resurrection Christology. Moltmann's complaint about such a Christology is this: "Jesus' claim and the destiny which befalls him in the resurrection are too readily converted into nothing more than an example of some anthropological and historico-universal idea which is completely independent of the history of Jesus himself" *(Der gekreuzigte Gott*, p. 164, see note 10, chap. 1 above).

12. "A temptation which is common to Christians is the tendency to justify their praxis with a gospel text or an action of Jesus. They appeal to violence because Jesus made use of it (cf. John 2:15–17). Nonviolent action is acclaimed because Jesus preached it and lived it (cf. Matt. 26:52; 5:39)" (L. Boff, "Salvation in Jesus Christ and the Process of Liberation," p. 89, see note 25, chap. 1 above.

13. H. Urs von Balthasar, p. 67, see note 3 above.

14. W. Thüsing, p. 223, see note 3 above.

15. Ibid.

16. H. Assmann remarks: "The result is that we still do not possess anything that might be called a satisfactory *analysis historica fidei:* understanding 'historical' in the sense of referring to what is implied in the concept of liberative historical praxis: the accumulation of data concerning the main challenges facing the process of liberation, alternative courses of action, ideological and political options, and so on" *(Theology for a Nomad Church*, p. 82). He goes on to say: "The 'truth' of faith, its verification, its 'becoming true' in history, all comprise the living totality of practice. The aspect of 'what concerns faith' cannot be separated from the rest" (ibid., p. 83).

The reader might wish to compare those remarks with Rahner's description of the historicity of faith in "La fe del sacerdote hoy," *Orientierung*, 19–20 (1962), pp. 215–19, 227–31. The important thing to note about Rahner's article is that he stresses the historicity of the faith. It must take on a new visage with changing times, places, and persons. It would be anachronistic to fault a 1962 article for failing to touch upon the specifically political and practical dimensions of such a historical faith. But it is evident that the article is written from a different perspective than the one we propose today. Rahner is talking about the historicity of faith as its inevitable changeableness over time. We are talking now about its changeableness deriving from concrete action in history.

17. See W. Thüsing, p. 213, cited in note 3 above.

18. Ibid., p. 214f.

19. Ibid., p. 212.

20. A more complete study of the history of Jesus would obviously be desirable. But as a first step it is enough to divide that history into two major stages, thereby indicating the beginning and end of the whole process.

21. Jesus presumes his listeners know about the coming of the kingdom and are expecting it. What typifies Jesus specifically is that he *radicalizes* these presuppositions. "In Jesus, the basically traditional expectation of God's kingdom is turned into the one decisive perspective" (W. Pannenberg, "Die Offenbarung Gottes in Jesus von Nazareth," in *Offenbarung als Geschichte,* p. 143; see note 13, chap. 2 above).

22. In Jesus we find crystallized various conceptions of God deriving from various Old Testament theologies: e.g., those of the prophets, the wisdom literature, and the apocalyptic tradition. I am not saying that Jesus did not talk about "God," as he evidently did in passages of a sapiential cast. The point is that he preferred to integrate his conception of God into the notion of the kingdom of God. This is evident in Mark's programmatic description of his task (Mark 1:14f.). An attempt to subsume the sapiential conception of God under the prophetic and apocalyptic conceptions can be found in W. Pannenberg, *Fundamentos de cristología,* pp. 284–88.

23. K. Rahner, *Christologie—systematisch und exegetisch* p. 28; C. Duquoc, *Cristología, Ensayo dogmático sobre Jesús de Nazaret,* Spanish trans. (Salamanca, 1974), pp. 64–72; French original: *Christologie: Essai dogmatique sur l'homme Jésus* (Paris: Ed. du Cerf, 1968).

24. This systematic conception of "person" is not based on the notion of self-possession but on that of "relationship," as suggested by Scotus and further deepened by Hegel: "In friendship and love I renounce my abstract personality and thereby obtain a concrete personality. The authentic reality of the person, then, consists in submerging oneself ontologically in the other" (*Vorlesungen über die Philosophie der Religion,* III, posthumous edition, vol. 16, 239).

25. I. Ellacuría, *Freedom Made Flesh,* p. 56.

26. See C. Schütz, "Los misterios de la vida y actividad pública de Jesús," in *Mysterium Salutis,* III/11, p. 92; L. Boff, "Salvation in Jesus Christ and the Process of Liberation," p. 82.

27. See Schütz, "Los misterios de la vida," p. 96.

28. Boff describes it as a temptation to "regionalize" the kingdom ("Salvation in Jesus Christ and the Process of Liberation," p. 82). I. Ellacuría (*Freedom Made Flesh,* p. 60) puts it this way: "These three temptations indicate that the purely political dimension was never far from Jesus' mind. He got beyond it, but it was the great temptation of his life. However, he did not go to the other extreme. He never gave up the political 'bite' of his salvation message. If he had given it up, what finally happened would probably not have happened."

29. On the meaning of Jesus' death, see chap. 6.

30. For a dogmatic analysis of the problem see: K. Rahner, "Dogmatic Reflections on the Knowledge and Self-Consciousness of Christ," *Theological Investigations,* 5:193–215; W. Pannenberg, *Fundamentos de Cristología,* pp. 405–15. A compendium of various explanations of this issue can be found in H. Riedlinger, *Geschichtlichkeit und Vollendung des Wissens Christi,* Quaestiones Disputatae 32 (Freiburg: Herder, 1966).

31. K. Rahner, *Christologie—systematisch und exegetisch,* p. 28. The reason

why any trace of ignorance or error in Jesus strikes us as suspicious is not due to any biblical exigency demanding perfect knowledge of him; it is due to the prejudice generated by Hellenic philosophy and its conception of the essential nature of knowledge insofar as a person is concerned.

32. W. Pannenberg, *Fundamentos de Cristología*, p. 414.

33. This point has been fully developed by W. Pannenberg (ibid., pp. 415–19) and D. Wiederkehr (p. 578f., see note 3 of this chapter). Pannenberg (p. 415) puts it this way: "Thus the sonship of Jesus can be adequately understood only in terms of his relationship with God the Father. In that sense we can say that the whole issue of the union of the man Jesus with the eternal Son of God cannot be broached or solved directly. . . . That oneness can only be inferred *circuitously*. . . . We must go by way of Jesus' relationship with the 'Father', i.e., with the God of Israel whom Jesus called his Father. Only the personal communion of Jesus with the Father proves that he is one and the same as the Son of that Father."

34. K. Rahner, *Christologie—systematisch und exegetisch*, p. 38.

35. In asserting that moral theology must be Christian, I am doing so in a historical context. Many manuals of moral theology have been based on Aristotelian ethics. They do not even deal descriptively with such themes as the Beatitudes or the following of Jesus. They were designed to be a helpmate for confessors rather than a clarification of Christian life as an ethical endeavor. Obviously much progress has been made on that front, though some treatments do not go far enough. We might well ask whether B. Haring's famous work, *The Law of Christ*, really gets beyond the traditional schemas. It might indeed be the case that its organizational criteria represent no change whatsoever.

36. B. Schüller poses the problem this way: "What commandments cannot be understood in and of themselves, so that the mediation of divine revelation is needed? Love of neighbor? Love for one's enemies? The need for humility? The indissolubility of marriage? It is one thing to demonstrate that Jesus of Nazareth was the first in history to speak of them; it is something very different to show that these commandments are not intelligible in themselves. In other words, *pedagogic* (or maieutic) mediation is one thing, logical mediation is something else again. It might well be that Jesus of Nazareth was the first to speak of love as the quintessence of the law. But in that case he would still have been acting simply as a pedagogue if human beings on their own could see intrinsically why love of God and neighbor is the plenitude of the law" ("Naturrecht und Offenbarung," in *Die pedagogische Provinz*, February 1968, pp. 103–13; reproduced in *Selecciones de Teología* 28, 1968, p. 312).

I cite Schüller here to point up the difference between his view and our interest in dealing with Christian morality here. First of all, here we are not considering divine revelation insofar as it poses concrete demands that might be comparable with other demands known or knowable through the use of logic. We are interested in revelation insofar as Jesus reveals an overall pathway that is to be taken. Thus our direct interest is not whether this pathway is novel, but whether it is the true pathway. Second, we do not share the underlying metaphysical presupposition that is evident in Schüller's view. I would not assert that the historical appearance of something that is knowable through logic deserves to be downgraded as something merely "pedagogical." History is not the lucky realization of eternal ideas which might well have gone on without ever being historicized. History is what history itself gives; in that sense the "pedagogy" is as essential as the idea.

37. This is what R. Schnackenburg points out in the Introduction to his work entitled *El testimonio moral del Nuevo Testamento*, Spanish trans. (Madrid, 1965); Eng. trans.: *The Moral Teaching of the New Testament* (New York: Herder & Herder, 1965). He says: "Christianity essentially builds upon the foundation of Jesus' moral teachings. But there is a shift in theological motivation and stress in the Christian community after the Resurrection. The message that Jesus proclaims now becomes the message of Jesus already made manifest" (p.7). Even if we would say that Jesus "carries out" certain ethical demands rather than "proclaiming" them, it is important that we keep one fact in mind. The note of moral obligatoriness in the various strata of the New Testament arises out of a more all-encompassing experience than any merely external demand posed by Jesus. It is the concrete experience that Jesus himself manifested clearly that what he was proclaiming was true.

38. That is the experience of Paul: "The love of Christ impels us who have reached the conviction that since one died for all, all died. He died for all so that those who live might live no longer for themselves, but for him who for their sakes died and was raised up" (2 Cor. 5:14–15). It is also the experience of Ignatius of Loyola: "Imagine Christ our Lord present before you upon the cross, and begin to speak with him, asking how it is that though He is the Creator, He has stooped to become man, and to pass from eternal life to death here in time, that there He might die for our sins. I shall also reflect upon myself and ask: 'What have I done for Christ? What am I doing for Christ? What ought I to do for Christ?' " (no. 53, *The Spiritual Exercises of St. Ignatius*, see note 1, Appendix in this volume).

The important thing in these two citations is not the concrete language used. It is the clear relationship between gratitude and impelling exigency as the components of Christian obligatoriness.

39. This formulation of the real thrust of moral theology and its subsequent translation into what we are obliged to do for the kingdom today is meant to provide a christological concentration of moral theology at its most fundamental level. Its implications will become clearer if we compare it with the following description of moral theology in the *Lexicon für Theologie und Kirche*, 7:613: "How ought we behave as Christians? Assuming that dogmatic theology has already managed to make clear the truth of revelation, moral theology deals with the statements of revelation that have to do with carrying out and fulfilling a Christian way of life (P. Hadrossek). It presents them as an organized whole, highlighting especially their normative character and spotlighting the 'fatal line of sin' (R. Egenter)."

Our differences with such a viewpoint will be brought out gradually throughout this book. Here, however, we might note three points in which our view differs: a different way of integrating moral theology with dogmatic theology, the priority of the moral subject over the action to be carried out, and our way of formulating what is "good" as opposed to what is "sin."

40. This statement should be elaborated in more exegetical detail. In Matthew 16:24 Jesus addresses himself to his disciples, in Mark 8:34 to the crowd along with his disciples, and in Luke 9:23 to all explicitly. "As these remarks have been transmitted, the boundary line between demands imposed

on the disciples and demands addressed to people in general is vague and indistinct" (R. Schnackenburg, *El testimonio moral del Nuevo Testamento*, p. 36, see note 37 in this chapter). What is clear, however, is that in the second stage of his public life Jesus universalized his demands more on the basis of following him than on the basis of merely having faith and hope.

41. It has not been common practice to consider the historical unfolding of the demand to follow Jesus in terms of his own life. Usually elements from the two stages of his public life are intermingled freely. Thus there is a danger that one may overlook or completely disregard that historicity precisely insofar as it is a norm for Christian morality. Our concern here is not to see the "exigencies" involved in following Jesus but rather the historicity of those exigencies.

42. S. Lyonnet, *La historia de la salvación en la carta a los romanos*, Spanish trans. (Salamanca, 1967), p. 50; see his Latin works, *Quaestiones in Epistulam ad Romanos*, 2 vols., and *Exegesis Epistulae ad Romanos*, 2 vols. (Rome: Pontifical Biblical Institute).

43. This point is of the utmost importance, in my opinion. By way of contrast, here is what Schnackenburg says: "Jesus proclaims a religious message. On it are based the moral demands that he imposes. Any attempt to interpret this message in some other way—e.g., as cultural criticism or as a revolutionary social program—entails a radical misunderstanding. There is an indissoluble unity between the religious and the moral throughout the New Testament" *(El testimonio moral del Nuevo Testamento*, p. 7).

Quite apart from the question whether the content of his statement is correct, there is a methodological difficulty with Schnackenburg's view here. It assumes that the history of Jesus can be subsumed under some generic concept such as "religious message," "cultural criticism," or "revolutionary social program." If one does conceive the history of Jesus thus, it is hard to see how anyone can say that Jesus does not put forward moral demands that have to do with cultural criticism and a revolutionary social program. In fact Jesus was condemned and executed as a political malefactor. The view that this was due to a misunderstanding, which Bultmann maintains, is a wholly gratuitous one that is rejected by other exegetes (E. Käsemann and O. Cullmann, for example).

The important point is that whatever generic attitude Jesus may have had at the start of his mission, we must pay heed to the historicization of that generic attitude. It is wholly gratuitous to maintain that the history of Jesus did not modify his initial ideas, intentions, and values. If we do not consider Jesus' life history, then it really makes no difference for moral reflection whether we present him as "religious," "political," "ascetic," or whatever. If we do not consider his concrete historicization of the values expressed by those adjectives, then the adjectives themselves simply do not express the reality of Jesus himself.

44. To J.P. Miranda goes the credit for pointing out that the justice of Yahweh in the Old Testament is also dialectical. That Yahweh is "judge" means that he is the warrior who defends the wronged from oppression *(Marx and the Bible*, p. 123; see note 2, chap. 3 in this volume). The justice of Yahweh means that he not only re-creates a situation but also indignantly fights against injustice. The same pattern is reproduced in the life of Jesus.

45. J. Moltmann, *Esperanza y planificación del futuro*, pp. 88–97, see note 34, chap. 2 in this volume; *El hombre*, pp. 143–147, see note 30, chap. 2 in this volume.

46. The problem of discernment, its import and need in the postpaschal communities has been dealt with by G. Therrien, *Le discernement dans les écrits pauliniens* (Paris: Gabalda, 1973).

47. Rahner has reappraised discernment as the most Christian way of knowing the will of God in the *Spiritual Exercises* of Ignatius of Loyola (nos. 169–88). Rahner says: "The *Exercises* are an orientation, a set of guidelines, an indication of what is to be done in this specific case" (*Lo dinámico en la Iglesia*, [Barcelona, 1968], p. 99; Eng. trans.: *The Dynamic Element in the Church*, Quaestiones Disputatae [New York: Herder, 1964]). Discovering this concrete will of God is essentially the task of an "existential logic" (ibid., p. 93). The importance of Rahner's reappraisal of St. Ignatius is that in it he poses anew the fundamental problem of moral knowledge as a specifically Christian reality.

48. In contrast to more traditional lines of exegesis, Schnackenburg interprets this passage as a clear demand imposed on the rich young man: "Hence he is not offering him two paths or courses, one the normal path of obedience to the ten commandments, the other the extraordinary path of renouncing worldly goods completely" (*Existencia cristiana según el Nuevo Testamento*, p. 105; see note 18, chap. 3 in this volume). Schnackenburg also uses this passage as an example of the need for discernment. Jesus "gives us all a criterion in obliging the rich young man to ponder what Jesus is asking of him personally insofar as following Jesus is concerned" (ibid., p. 106).

49. A problem which we have not broached, and which derives from the limitations on Jesus' own course and career, is this: Who really is the subject of morality insofar as this subject is specifically Christian? Jesus preached the kingdom of God, but after his resurrection we get the church. The question, then, is whether it is the individual as such or the church as a collective body that is the subject of Christian morality. Even if it is the latter, needless to say, individuals *qua* Christians would still have the responsibility of reproducing in their own lives the whole movement of following Jesus. But if the church is a body, then such problems as the charisms, laws, and their institutionalization are not just dogmatic or pastoral problems but *moral* ones as well. Suppose that I do not ask what I am supposed to do as an individual to establish the kingdom of God in history. Suppose that instead we ask what *we all* are supposed to do, not as a collection of individuals, but precisely as church. Thus formulated, the question gets no clear answer from the historical Jesus. I do not propose to answer that question here. I simply want to formulate it and pose it on the level of fundamental moral theology.

50. L. Boff, "Salvation in Jesus Christ and the Process of Liberation," p. 89, see note 25, chap. 1 in this volume.

5.

The Prayer of Jesus

This chapter does not purport to be anything more than a brief overview of themes that are treated more extensively in the literature of this subject.[1] It is important, however, if we want to isolate the fundamental criteria that tell us what Christian prayer ought to be. Here I shall focus on the Synoptic Gospels for the most part, but the reader should realize that each of these Gospels presents the prayer of Jesus in terms of its own literary makeup and specific theological interests. The fundamental datum is clear enough in any case: Jesus did pray, and both the content and context of his prayer is certain enough on historical grounds.

JESUS' CRITICISM OF CONTEMPORARY PRAYER

Jesus was a Jew who knew and practiced the traditional prayer of his own people. In principle, then, Jesus had a favorable attitude toward prayer and toward the concrete forms it took among his people. But if we want to find out what typified Jesus' own prayer, we must probe more deeply into Jesus' attitude toward the concrete prayer life of his people. We must consider his demystification of prayer as well as the dangers historically inherent in prayer which he noted and denounced.

We shall begin, therefore, with a dialectical approach, considering what Jesus condemned or criticized in the concrete prayer life of his contemporaries. This will make it clear that

Jesus did not have a naive attitude toward prayer. He did not pray simply as a matter of routine or tradition. He did not think that the prayer life of his people was a completely isolated and autonomous aspect of their faith that could not be manipulated. Indeed at times we get the impression that the term "prayer" was as useless to Jesus in trying to understand and explain the deeper reality involved as it is to many people today.

I shall proceed in systematic fashion here, offering sample texts of Jesus' attitude toward prayer. They will point up the dangers that Jesus saw in a particular conception of prayer and also the ways in which prayer had been vitiated by some of his contemporaries.

"The Pharisee with head unbowed prayed in this fashion: 'I give you thanks, O God, that I am not like the rest of men—grasping, crooked, adulterous—or even like this tax collector' " (Luke 18:11).

Here we find what might be called the basic anthropology of Christian prayer expressed in terms of its opposite. Jesus condemns the prayer of the Pharisees because it is the self-assertion of an egotistical "I" and hence vitiated at its very core. Missing in that kind of prayer is the necessary "other-directedness" [alteridad] required to initiate the process of prayer. The pole of reference in the Pharisee's prayer is not God but the man who thinks he is praying. The Pharisee is even less oriented toward other human beings. He holds them in contempt (see verse 9), and he thanks God that he is not like them (verse 11).

Here prayer is merely a mechanism for narcissism and self-gratification. It is an exercise in self-deception. Jesus unmasks this stratagem, addressing a parable to "those who believed in their own self-righteousness while holding everyone else in contempt" (verse 9). In short, the basic attitude of "other-directedness" is missing. The Pharisee does not realize that we can pray only insofar as we focus on someone or something other than ourselves. He does not focus on God and he positively despises his fellows.

"When you are praying, do not behave like the hypocrites who love to stand and pray in synagogues or on street corners in order to be noticed" (Matt. 6:5).

Jesus condemns this kind of prayer because real prayer presupposes an attitude of theological poverty before God. People who pray in order to be noticed by others are trying to vaunt their own grandeur. They are displaying hypocrisy precisely in that area where they should be willing to be completely humble.

The whole context of the Synoptic Gospels points up the basic mistake of all hypocrites. They assume that they will get the reputation of being just through public religious acts of this sort. But such is not the case, according to the Synoptic Gospels. Religion can give people a good reputation only when it embodies and finds expression in works of justice and charity.

"In your prayer do not rattle on like the pagans. They think they will win a hearing by the sheer multiplication of words. Do not imitate them. Your Father knows what you need before you ask him" (Matt. 6:7–8).

In the first part of this remark Jesus criticizes the mechanical, magical form of prayer used by people who think that they can reach God by multiplying words or simply repeating certain formulas. Matthew's pericope seemed to be directed against the pagan idea of wearing God down under a barrage of words. The error of such an approach to God is that it seeks to substitute wordiness for self-commitment and self-revelation in one's approach to God. It also attributes some sort of isolated autonomy to prayer itself, enshrining it in fixed formulas. It seems to suggest a lack of confidence in God, but such confidence is an indispensable prerequisite for all authentic prayer.

In the second part of this passage Jesus alludes to the prayer of petition. Now there is no doubt that Jesus often refers to this type of prayer in laudatory terms (see Luke 5:8f.; 11:9f.). We cannot tell for sure, however, what Jesus actually thinks about asking for concrete things from God in prayer or receiving them from him. The positive feature in the prayer of petition and the way one engages in it seems to lie in the fact that it embodies and expresses our theological poverty before God. Above we noted that "other-directedness" was a basic prerequisite for true prayer. Here we see that in prayer we must adopt an attitude of "poverty" before God.[2]

The positive feature of the prayer of petition is the fact that it reveals our discernment of God's will, and of God himself as someone who ever remains greater than us. It is not a matter of looking for something that we want, of an egocentric search for some satisfaction. Our Father "knows what you need before you ask him." In our prayer of petition we try to discover something that our Father knows already. That is what we ask him to reveal and grant. Human psychology being what it is, it is obvious that this basic petition will find expression in the concrete petitions and desires of the person who is praying. But there can be only one basic petition: "Your will be done" (Matt. 6:10). The wordy prayer of pagans is condemned, not because their words express legitimate desires but because they do not contain the one basic petition.

"None of those who cry out, 'Lord, Lord', will enter the kingdom of God but only the one who does the will of my Father in heaven" *(Matt. 7:21).*

Following the footsteps of the great Hebrew prophets, Jesus here criticizes an alienating type of prayer. Here anthropology is not simply a matter of the correct attitude; it also has to do with praxis. Mere appeals to God are useless; they must embody and go hand in hand with real-life practice. In this particular passage we find that praxis is given primacy, for it is directly associated with entrance into the kingdom of God—i.e., with salvation. Matthew's text stresses the ultimate importance of praxis; without it, prayer cannot express anything that is of ultimate importance.

In systematic terms we can say that this passage tells us clearly that ultimate meaningfulness is to be found in actually doing the will of God. Prayer without action is useless, indeed literally impossible. Without praxis there is no concrete material around which a Christian experience of meaningfulness could be structured; and hence there is no concrete material around which prayer might be structured.

"Be on guard against the scribes. . . . These men devour the savings of widows and recite long prayers for appearance' sake" (Mark 12:38, 40).

Here Jesus is attacking prayer insofar as it is turned into an item of commerce and used to exploit others. Widows serve as a biblical symbol for the defenseless and the oppressed, and here Jesus says that they are being oppressed by the scribes. Such oppression takes on an extreme cast when it uses prayer as its tool, for prayer is meant to provide us with access to God. Whereas the previous passage attacked the dissociation of prayer and praxis, this passage attacks prayer insofar as it is used as a concrete way to oppress people. Both the oppression itself and prayer as a tool of oppression are condemned by Jesus.

Jesus vehemently attacked the commercialization of prayer when he expelled the merchants from the temple. They had turned the house of prayer into a den of thieves. We are reminded of Hosea's savage anger against the priests of his day. They, too, had perverted the temple, turning it into a place for profit-making (Hos. 4:6). Enjoying the benefit of the victims offered by people for their sins, the priests "feed on the sin of my people and are greedy for their guilt" (Hos. 4:8). It is the same perversion of worship that Jesus condemned in this gospel passage. Under the pretext of reciting long prayers, the scribes eat up the life savings of widows.

"When all the people were baptized, and Jesus was at prayer after likewise being baptized, the skies opened and the Holy Spirit descended on him in visible form like a dove" (Luke 3:21–22).

"While he was praying, his face changed in appearance and his clothes became dazzlingly white" (Luke 9:29).

These passages do not quote the words of Jesus. They clearly reflect the work of Luke. I cite them here because they show Luke's concern to demythologize prayer. Or, to put it better, they show Luke's concern to demythologize the figure of Jesus precisely in terms of prayer. Consider the various narratives of Jesus' baptism (Matt. 3:13–17; Mark 1:9–11; Luke 3:21–22) and his transfiguration (Matt. 17:1–9; Mark 9:2–10; Luke 9:28–36). In them we find miraculous phenomena adorning the essential elements of the given scene: i.e., Jesus being anointed by the Spirit, his consciousness of his mission, and his unique sonship with God. Only Luke adds the remark that these miraculous phenomena took place while Jesus was "at prayer." He wants people to disregard the miraculous elements and to concentrate on the essential features of a scene. And he does this by mentioning something as commonplace and normal as prayer.

All the passages cited above lead us to a clear conclusion. Jesus himself, and even more surely the earliest Christian communities who pondered the example of Jesus, had a clear awareness of the typical ways in which prayer could be counterfeited and vitiated: e.g., by spiritual narcissism, hypocrisy, wordiness, alienating and oppressive misuse of prayer, and sensationalism. The point is that Jesus did not have a naive outlook on prayer. He did not think that prayer was some autonomous mechanism that automatically guaranteed salvation. Indeed he felt quite the contrary. It is on the basis of his denial on one level that we can now move on to consider the positive aspects of Jesus' own prayer.

THE PRAYER OF JESUS HIMSELF

Here again we shall restrict our attention to what the Synoptic Gospels have to say. In John's Gospel, to be sure, we find the prayer of Jesus elaborated in depth and at great length; but there the text is even more obviously influenced by the theology of the gospel author.

From the Synoptics we learn that Jesus did pray, and that prayer was of major importance in his life. But the importance of Jesus' prayer lay in its own intrinsic quality, not in any external conditioning factors (e.g., time, place, or form).

The Synoptic Gospels present the prayer of Jesus in two

different ways. Some passages talk *about* Jesus at prayer; other passages, fewer in number, tell us what the prayer of Jesus was. In the first case it is important to realize that the Synoptic Gospels make a clear distinction between Jesus' activity of analysis and reflection on the one hand, and what might properly be called his prayer on the other, though of course the two are interrelated. As for the actual prayer of Jesus, three levels can be distinguished: the kind of prayer typical of pious Jews, the kind of prayer voiced by Jesus when making important historical decisions, and the kind of prayer in which Jesus concentrated the innermost depths of his life.

The first level of typically Jewish prayer seems evident in Jesus' life. He blessed food at mealtime (Matt. 14:19; 15:36; 26:26), observed the Sabbath worship, and joined with the community at prayer (Luke 4:16). From a close analysis of the texts Jeremias concludes that Jesus was quite familiar with the three occasions for prayer each day: "It is highly probable that a day did not go by that Jesus did not observe these three times for prayer; that he never ate a meal without saying grace before and after."[3] While this assertion might be regarded as an exaggeration, there can be no doubt about what the Synoptics tell us: Jesus not only denounced all forms of false prayer but also participated in the prayer life of his people. But important as this first level is, it does not show what is most typical of Jesus' own prayer.

Further light is shed on this matter when we examine the second level mentioned above: i.e., the times when Jesus prayed in connection with some important historical event or decision. This is the level of personal prayer as opposed to prayer that was prescribed by the Jewish religion.

According to the Synoptics, Jesus' whole life unfolded in an atmosphere of prayer. His public life began with prayer at his baptism (Luke 3:21; Matt. 3:13–17; Mark 1:9–11). This is interpreted as Jesus' taking cognizance of his mission, of that which would serve as the focus for his whole life. Jesus' life also ends with prayer (Matt. 27:46; Mark 15:34; Luke 23:46). Whether it is described as a prayer of anguish or as one of hope, it clearly implies an explicit relationship between Jesus and the Father.

The Synoptics allude to prayer in the life of Jesus from beginning to end. In moments of important historical decisions he is seen praying: e.g., when choosing the twelve (Luke 6:12f.), when teaching the Our Father (Luke 11:1), and before curing the epileptic boy (Mark 9:29). Jesus prays for concrete individuals such as Peter (Luke 22:32) and his executioners (Luke 23:34). He alludes to prayer on important occasions, linking it up with faith (Mark 11:23f.) or asserting that it is indispensable for casting out certain kinds of demons (Mark 9:29).

Even when it is associated with historical happenings, Jesus' prayer sometimes seems to mark a withdrawal from public activity. As the whole context of the Gospels makes clear, this does not imply the sacralization of particular places, much less the separation of prayer from real-life praxis and action and its transformation into an autonomous entity. At different times Jesus withdraws to a mountainside, a garden, or a desert area (Mark 1:35; 6:46; 14:32; Luke 6:12; etc.). Thus prayer was a habitual activity of Jesus. Luke brings this out clearly in a passage that seems to sum up much of Jesus' activity: "His reputation spread more and more, and great crowds gathered to hear him and to be cured of their maladies. He often retired to deserted places and prayed" (Luke 5:15–16).

It is obviously difficult to determine what exactly was the prayer of Jesus on the basis of these Synoptic passages. From the standpoint of his own theology, for example, Luke was mainly interested in showing Jesus at prayer. But the overall picture of Jesus that emerges from these passages is clear enough. Prayer was something that he habitually engaged in. He not only participated in the cultic prayer of his people but also prayed in concrete situations of major importance.

The third level mentioned above is not noted too frequently in the Gospels, but there are a few important passages that discuss the content of Jesus' prayer. They are of singular importance because they have to do with critical moments in his life when Jesus attempts to grasp the ultimate sense and meaning of his person, activity, and destiny in the Father's eyes. The two fundamental passages are the one in which he gives praise and thanks to the Father and the one in which he prays to the Father in the Garden of Olives. We shall consider these two passages in detail.

"On one occasion Jesus spoke thus: 'Father, Lord of heaven and earth, to you I offer praise; for what you have hidden from the learned and the clever you have revealed to the merest children" (Matt. 11:25; Luke 10:21).[4]

This is a prayer of praise and thanksgiving. We can better appreciate the way it is formulated if we view it against the apocalyptic backdrop presented in the Book of Daniel. There it has to do with the communication of a revelation (Dan. 2:20–23), the content of which pertains to the reign of God (Dan. 2:44).

We cannot determine when exactly Jesus uttered this prayer; but it is clear that he had already engaged in a fair amount of public activity and that this prayer was uttered at some critical juncture in that activity. Thus it is set in a historical context: "Behind this prayer lies the fact that Jesus has experienced: Broad segments of the Jewish people, and especially those who were influential leaders, had proved unwilling to accept his message on faith. Indeed they contradicted it and maliciously opposed him."[5] In this historical context Jesus thanks the Father because it is the unlettered who have understood his message while the wise and the learned remain blind. Jesus' exultation goes hand in hand with his public activity in history, and he makes no reference to the synergistic aspect of the problem. He simply rejoices that the reign of God is being realized among the lowly.

This act of thanksgiving appears in a dialectical and polemical context. The impossible seems to have happened. Those seemingly incapable of understanding his message have in fact understood it while those seemingly capable of understanding have not. Injected into Jesus' prayer here is the element of scandal that is constantly brought up in the Gospels. This element of scandal cannot be neglected or avoided if one wants to gain access to the Father of Jesus specifically rather than to some deity in the abstract.

Finally, in this prayer it is evident that the Father is the ultimate horizon of Jesus' person and activity. However, this transcendental horizon (the Father) is described in a very definite way rather than in abstract terms. This God is "partial" to the little people. He is certainly not a deity equally near to, or far away from, all human beings. He is also a God with a definite will that is to be searched out and fulfilled: "Father, it is true. You have graciously willed it so" (Matt. 11:26).

It is in this overall and specific context that Jesus formulates a prayer that sums up his experience and its meaningfulness. Conscious of the divisiveness that his mission has caused, Jesus gives thanks to the Father because something marvelous and unexpected has happened. Giving thanks is one fundamental experience of meaningfulness, for it means that we know we are somehow related to someone to whom we can give thanks. It is not the mechanical repetition of some formula of thanksgiving; instead it embodies a profound experience of meaningfulness. It is the Father who is at work in history, and he works through human beings. He discloses his will in unexpected ways, carrying it out in ways that are a source of scandal to the world. With this realization Jesus turns to the Father and offers him thanks.

"He advanced a little and fell to the ground, praying that if it were possible this hour might pass him by. He kept saying, 'Abba, O Father, you have the power to do all things. Take this cup away from me. But let it be as you would have it, not as I' " (Mark 14:35–36; Matt. 26:39; Luke 22:41f.). [6]

This passage, as presented to us by Mark, is clearly a work of composition. [7] However, it seems that we can be fairly sure that the core of this scene and of Jesus' prayer is historical: "The christological scandal raised by this pericope makes it difficult for us to assume that it was made up on the whim of the author alone." [8]

The content of this prayer shows Jesus facing a severe crisis. The whole meaning of his life seems to be in jeopardy. When that threat confronts him, Jesus goes off to pray. The same point was presented in the account of his temptations in the desert, though in a much more stylized form. It will show up again in Jesus' prayer on the cross, where he recites Psalm 22 according to Matthew and Mark, or Psalm 31 according to Luke. The important thing to note is that Jesus puts himself before the Father and prays when the meaningfulness of his life is placed in jeopardy.

This prayer, too, is historically situated. It is preceded by a long history and it leads to a historical decision. The "cup" that Jesus would like to see taken away is nothing else but his own imminent death. It is not simply death as such that Jesus wants to elude, however. It is the death that will be a direct historical consequence of his life. This is not the place to detail Jesus' prophetic activity in unmasking the self-interested and unjust actions of those in power. What is clear is that his activity provoked a hostile reaction in the latter, and that they wanted to put him to death. Early in Mark's Gospel we read that "when the Pharisees went outside, they immediately began to plot with the Herodians how they might destroy him" (Mark 3:6). When John's Gospel describes the work of Jesus, it constantly alludes to the fact that his life is in danger (John 2:24; 5:16–18; 7:1; 7:19; 7:25; 7:30; 7:32–35; 8:20, 59; 10:30, 39; 11:8, 53, 57). In all these passages it seems clear that Jesus is aware of the fact that his unmasking activity is bound to end in his own death, and that this realization gradually dawns on his disciples. Thus his prayer in the garden crystallizes a crisis faced by Jesus throughout his life. It is a prayer that sums up and recapitulates his own life.

By the same token it also leads to a historical action: i.e., Jesus' decision to be faithful to his Father's will to the very end. Though he does ask the Father "to usher in the kingdom without prior suffering,"[9] he also submits in the end to the Father's will. Even knowing that fact, we still cannot help but be surprised by Jesus' submission when we consider it in the light of his whole life. The "I" that Jesus entrusts here to the Father's will is the same "I" that appears earlier in the Gospels as a font of supreme authority vis-à-vis the law (Matt. 5:17), as one that sends the disciples out on a mission (Matt. 10:16), and as one that cures people (Mark 9:25). Praying in the garden,

Jesus is still fully conscious of who he is, of the "I" that has resounded so authoritatively through the earlier stages of his life. Yet, in this particular prayer, he surrenders that "I" to the Father and sacrifices it to the Father's will. It is a moment of profound significance and meaningfulness, bearing witness to the essential relationality of Jesus' person and life.

Finally, in this prayer we hear the word "Abba," the word that Jesus addressed to the Father with unusual confidence. His trust in the Father would remain alive in the very depths of his passion even though he did not want the Father's will to take the form of the cross, and even though he did not know for sure who this Father was that would demand his death and later abandon him on the cross. Non-knowing is an essential feature of Jesus' prayer at this moment of supreme crisis; it becomes part of a deeper knowledge of the Father.

Thus Jesus' prayer in the garden is a typical prayer of his. It is voiced in a specific historical context that is in continuity with the past and the future. It also contains features essential to true prayer: i.e., seeking the Father's will and maintaining trust in him. Even in such a moment the Father is the ultimate pole of reference and meaningfulness. Just as in the earlier prayer Jesus summed up his whole life with a word of thanks, so here he does the same thing by asking that God's will be done.

At bottom, then, the prayer of Jesus is a way of approaching the Father that is not simply analytic or reflective on the one hand nor identical with his historical activity on the other. His prayer embodies and expresses that something "more" which continually surfaces in his history. It appears in his seeking out the Father's will, in his joy at the approach of the kingdom, in his unconditional confidence in the Father, and in his acceptance of the Father's will down to the very end. For Jesus, to pray is to express himself fully and totally. It is not something merely intentional because it draws its life from his own concrete history. By the same token, however, it is in this prayerful expression that Jesus finds the full and deeper meaning of his own history.

Jesus' prayer implies that the meaning of his life cannot be complete without reference to Someone else, even though Jesus himself is gradually fashioning the meaning of his life. It is this Someone else who brings completion and fulfillment to what appears as partial and incomplete in history. Thus Jesus' prayer is what it is because it arises out of a very definite understanding of who that Someone else is. For Jesus, prayer is not simply "contact with God." It is placing oneself before a very definite and specific God. In the last analysis it is the reality of that God which will explain the prayer of Jesus. That is the point we shall explore in the next section.

THE GOD OF JESUS AS THE BASIS OF HIS PRAYER

So far we have briefly considered the prayer of Jesus and what seems to typify it. Here we shall not simply consider *what* his prayer was like but *why* it was that rather than something else. The answer is simple enough: Jesus prayed a certain way because he had a specific conception and personal experience of God. "Prayer" and "God" are correlative. Whatever problem we find in connection with prayer is simply a reflection of the problem connected with the reality of God. That holds true for Jesus, for Christians today, and for human beings in general. So we shall briefly try to explore the notion of God that Jesus had, for that will explain his prayer. [10]

We shall begin by making some systematic observations that will shed light on the subject and help us to integrate the data dealing with Jesus' relationship to God. This should make it easier to discuss Jesus' notion of God afterwards.

Prayer differs from merely analytic discourse insofar as it is a historical attempt to bring together the total sum of meaningfulness and the meaning of the totality. The fact that prayer takes place *historically* means that even this experience of totality is made possible and conditioned by concrete history; but if prayer *does take place,* then the totality will appear in it in some way or other.

Prayer presupposes the reality of some referential pole of meaningfulness that can be fulfilling and all-embracing. If it is to be that, however, two conditions must be met. On the formal level the pole of meaningfulness must be radically "other" insofar as the praying subject is concerned; otherwise totality is reduced to one's own subjectivity. This means that at no time should it be satisfactorily comprehensible to, or controllable by, the praying subject. On the content level the referential pole of meaningfulness must be ever capable of unleashing a history within which the praying subject can find meaning.

Expressed in traditional language, this means that the God to whom one prays is formally *transcendent,* and that the content of his reality is *love.* Obviously this point must be analyzed and explained in greater detail, but it can serve as a starting point for analyzing Jesus' notion of God. We must also ask whether the relationship between transcendence and love is accidental, or whether transcendence is of the very essence of love. If the latter is the case, then we start off with an initial view of the essential nature of Jesus' prayer. We can see it as a continuing quest for the will of a God who ever remains greater and whose nature as such is revealed insofar as it demands and equips people for a line of action in history which is at bottom love.

A second preliminary observation is that the reality of God, as the reference pole of total meaningfulness, influences Jesus on two different levels: (1) on the level of analytic discourse and concrete strategies; and (2) on the level of prayer and its overall strategy. I make this distinction so that we may be able to pinpoint Jesus' prayer to the Father a bit more specifically.

If Jesus' external activity can shed light on what was going on inside his own conscience, then it is worth noting that both of the two levels just mentioned are evident there. On the level of the ministry of the word Jesus makes a distinction between the fundamental proclamation and its analytic explanations. This distinction is evident in the vocabulary used when the Gospels distinguish between *kerygma* and *didache,* proclamation and teaching. *Kerygma* refers to what is fundamental and all-embracing, to that which commands respect on its own authority and which cannot be grounded on something even more basic. *Didache* refers to analysis of and reflection on the kerygma. The kerygma includes the proclamation of the kingdom of God and its imminent arrival as that which confers meaning on everything else; and it also includes the commandment of love as the ultimate way of life. This kind of proclamation is assumed to be ultimate, justified in and of itself, and a formalized way of expressing the totality of meaning and the meaning of the totality. Didache takes in all kinds of explanation in parables, hortatory discourses, and apocalyptic utterances.

The same distinction could be made in connection with Jesus' activities. For example, the temptations in the desert call into question his mission as a whole and his journey to Jerusalem represents a decision to confront the totality. Alongside such basic actions we find concrete reflections, tactics, and strategies. Will he reveal himself to the public or not? Will he speak to the crowd or to his disciples? Will he work in Galilee or elsewhere?[11]

The point here is that if these two different levels can be detected in Jesus' external reflection and activity, then we can surmise that they also exist in his own "inner life." And even though we may not be able to make a neat distinction between them on the historical level, they can and should be considered separately. Thus we find the level of concrete, specific reflection and what might be called day-to-day prayer on one hand, and on the other the level of all-embracing reflection and what might be called simply prayer.

It is the latter level that is of interest to us here in considering the God of Jesus. We want to find out to what sort of God Jesus prayed in those critical moments that summed up and embraced his existence as a whole.

Moving on now to Jesus' notion of God, we must first realize that Jesus was a member of the Jewish people, and that *different* traditions about God existed in their religion. Without claiming to deal with the matter exhaustively, we can examine the life and preaching of Jesus to see which of those traditions really did exert an influence on Jesus.

First of all, Jesus did make use of the *prophetic* tradition. There God is seen as one who is partial to the poor and the defenseless. He is clearly opposed to the historical sinfulness that creates a situation of injustice. He wants to establish justice on the earth. This God also wants the inner, personal conversion of the individual. He is responsible for the vocation of the prophet, from whom he demands everything—perhaps even his life. He is a God of conflict precisely because he is partial to the oppressed.

Jesus also made use of the *apocalyptic* tradition. It stresses the renewal of reality by God at the end of time. It is a gratuitous act on his part, which is carried out by his power and which will be preceded by a worldwide cataclysm.

Jesus also made use of the *sapiential* tradition. There the emphasis is on a creating, provident God who allows both the just and the unjust to grow up together in history. Only at the final judgment will he impart justice. He is a kind and good God in whom we should trust, for his providence extends even to our daily needs.

Finally, toward the end of Jesus' life in particular, we find another tradition about God at work. According to this tradition, we are faced with the silence and seeming absence of God, as Jesus was in the garden and on the cross. We find earlier strains of this tradition in some of the Psalms, in the book of Lamentations, and in the book of Ecclesiastes.

All of these traditions, with their somewhat different conceptions of God, had some influence on Jesus' life. On the conceptual level, at the very least, they reveal a certain amount of tension. God is glimpsed in day-to-day life, in the natural rhythm of living; but he is also seen as eschatological, as one who will reveal himself at the end of history. God seems to impose an obligation on us, to call for clear-cut action on behalf of the oppressed; but he also seems to be something or someone who is wholly gratuitous in his approach to us because he lies at the absolute beginning and in the final future of the kingdom. God seems to be someone near who can be called "Father"; but he also seems to be an impenetrable mystery who must ever remain God for us. Toward the end of Jesus' life God seems to be both a presence and an absence, both power and impotence.

From of old there has been a problem in any attempt to reconcile *conceptually* the various traditions about God in which Jesus grew up and of which he made use. Any attempt at such conceptual reconciliation involves selecting one of those traditions as the one that can tie all the others together.

For some people such conceptual reconciliation is simply impossible: "On the one hand we find an allusion to God's dominion over the world. He brings sunshine and rain to the just and the unjust, caring for the flowers of the field and the birds of the air. On the other hand we find an allusion to the imminent end of a world rooted in evil."[12]

For others such reconciliation is possible; it is grounded on the near approach of the kingdom announced by Jesus: "As Jesus sees it, surrendering oneself to the day-by-day care of God and straining hopefully toward the kingdom of God are one and the same. . . . The immediacy vis-à-vis God, which grounds both ideological aspects, is based on the basic eschatological conception of Jesus—i.e., on his conviction that the reign of God is near."[13]

This attempt at a solution is not satisfactory. Insofar as content is concerned, it attempts to reconcile the sapiential viewpoint and the apocalyptic viewpoint; but it ignores the prophetic tradition.[14] It attempts a conceptual reconciliation, but not a historical one. My feeling is that we must adopt a different approach in trying to resolve the question of Jesus' notion of God. Any attempt at a solution must be based on the history of Jesus himself. We should not start off assuming that Jesus held some notion of God from the very start. Instead we should assume that in his concrete history he gradually wove together strands from the various traditions about God in order to form his own fabric. The originality of Jesus lies precisely in the concrete synthesis that he was fashioning his whole life long.

This historical synthesis points toward something that I have already mentioned briefly. Its conclusion seems to be that God ever remains greater than human beings, and that his innermost reality is love. It is this view that will explain the prayer of Jesus.

In Jesus we do not find any systematic concept of "transcendence" or of God being "greater" than human beings. But such a concept can be gleaned from his teaching and his own attitudes. Here I shall simply enumerate a few basic points.

The idea of God as creator occurs seldom in the sayings of Jesus, though it is not absent altogether (see Mark 10:6; 13:19). The idea of God's sovereignty is far more operative in his words, and it occurs in many different ways. God is incomprehensible (see Matt. 11:25f.). He has power over life and death (Matt. 18:23–25). He can cause body and soul to perish in hell (Matt. 10:28). His name must be respected; we must not swear by it (Matt. 5:33–37; 23:16–22). People stand before God as his servants (Luke 17:7–10) or slaves (Matt. 6:24; Luke 16:13).

Thus Jesus recognizes the sovereignty of God: "Jesus' life is instinctively immersed in that thought. We can see this in the many varied circumlocutions he uses to designate God. . . . Jesus elaborates his own distinctive mode of expression, and the circumlocution he uses with great frequency is the use of the passive voice to talk about God (*passivum divinum*)."[15]

But talk about the transcendence of God, his sovereignty, and the corresponding attitude of reverence and respect is not what is most typical of Jesus. We get much closer to his notion of God when we realize that for him God is grace. This point is made in parable after parable: the parable of the importunate friend (Luke 11:5–8); the identification of God with a human father, who would not give his child a stone instead of bread; and so forth. At this level the gratuitous goodness of God is presented in terms of criteria that are normal and comprehensible to human beings. However, Jesus is simply preparing people to realize that the grace of God is something absolutely unimaginable. That point is brought out in the parable of the prodigal son, for example (Luke 15:11–24). Here the transcendence of God is depicted as the realization and execution of what seems impossible. When Jesus is asked if rich people can be saved, since he has already noted how difficult it is, he replies: "For man it is impossible but not for God. With God all things are possible" (Mark 10:27).

Realization of the impossible, then, is an expression of the transcendence of God. But here the realization is not presented in the classical religious context of miracles or prodigies. Here it is presented in a new and unexpected context: i.e., as a grace that renews and revitalizes human beings, even lost human beings. "Here the impossible is not depicted as supernatural events coming from a world beyond and producing weird consequences in this world. Instead it appears in the fact that the poor, the impious, and the wicked can unexpectedly go back to calling themselves human beings once again."[16] This realization of the impossible by grace is the way that God's transcendence is mediated in the eyes of Jesus.

Jesus also points up this divine transcendence in his debates with the Pharisees. Here I shall consider the discussion that takes place in Mark 7:1–17. In verses 8–13 Jesus accuses the Pharisees of trying to manipulate God through the use of merely human traditions. The sharpness of his accusation and his defense of God's transcendence is all the more noteworthy in that here he is referring to human *religious* traditions. Through these *religious* traditions the Pharisees "nullify God's word" (verse 13), and Jesus denounces this manipulation of God.

He then goes on to make an even more radical pronouncement about God's transcendence: "Hear me, all of you, and try to understand. Nothing that enters a man from outside can make him impure; that which comes out of him, and only that, constitutes impurity" (verses 14–15). The context is an ethical one, and the conclusion is clear. Nothing outside people can be automatically impure, even if it is covered by the law. In positive terms Jesus is saying that God is above and beyond any space created by people in order to define him.

Finally, it is the transcendence of God that explains Jesus' own history. In the previous chapter I tried to show that the historical Jesus is the history of Jesus, that the faith of Jesus is the history of his faith. The unfolding pageant of his life is not a lineal development, with the end implicit in the beginning. When Jesus uses the word "God" at the start of his public life (Mark 1:15), his conception of God is different from that which he has when he pronounces that same word on the cross

(Mark 15:34). Jesus' life went through different stages, stages that are distinct not only on the external, descriptive level but also on the level of his interior life. His conception of God changes, and the transition from one stage to the next does not take place without temptations, crises, and areas of ignorance being involved. That is the concrete way in which Jesus allows God to be God in his life. The reality of a transcendent God, of a God who remains ever greater than human beings and even than Jesus' own reflections on him, is what explains the life of Jesus with its transitions and ruptures.

The transcendence of God, his holy and unmanipulable mysteriousness, is the underlying presupposition of Jesus' preaching, of his reverent attitude, and of his polemical debates with those who thought they had God neatly boxed in their traditions. It underlies the whole trajectory of his life, which remained ever open to the sovereign will of God.

If the formal side of Jesus' God lies in the fact that God remains ever greater, the content of this divine reality lies in the fact that God is love. But we must understand exactly what this means according to the Gospels, so we shall proceed step by step.

"Respect for God as absolute Lord is an essential element of the gospel message, but not its core. . . . At its core we find something else. For the disciple of Jesus, God is the Father."[17] Here I do not intend to consider in detail what "Abba" signified in the life of Jesus. It is enough to say that Jesus used this term to express his most intimate relationship with God. It is an expression of love-filled trust and confidence.

The application of the word "father" to God is obviously an anthropomorphism, but it does indicate who or what God is for Jesus.[18] To put it anthropomorphically, it seems that for Jesus the ultimate experience of meaningfulness lies in love. Love is the ultimate reality that gives meaning to everything else, without which nothing else can attain full meaningfulness. It seems almost self-evident to us that Jesus should address God as "Father." But that is not so self-evident at all if we consider the matter historically or logically. Jesus could have used some other expression to signify what he considered to be the ultimate in meaningfulness, though that too would be anthropomorphic. He might have chosen to refer to God as "King" or "Lord," thus picturing the ultimate reality in terms of power rather than in terms of love.

Hence the term "Father" addressed to God by Jesus tells us right away how he pictured the ultimate ground of reality. It was not to be viewed in terms of beauty or power but in terms of love. That is why he chose to address God as "Father."

This God whose essence is revealed as love is not an abstract, intemporal love, however. God is a love that expresses itself in history and amid the conditioning factors of history. From the very start, then, it is a partisan love. It is not directed to those who hold power and who assume that God is power; instead it is addressed to those without power. Luke's Gospel puts the words of Isaiah on Jesus' own lips, for those words express the partisan nature of God's love: "He has sent me to bring glad tidings to the poor, to proclaim liberty to captives, recovery of sight to the blind and release to prisoners; to announce a year of favor from the Lord" (Luke 4:18–19).

The partisan nature of God's love is also brought out in Jesus' remarks concerning those who are blest and those who are not. The poor and the powerless are blest (Matt. 5:1–11; Luke 6:20–22); but there are maledictions for all those who have set their heart on something less than love (Luke 6:23–26), and for all those who use their power to dominate and oppress other human beings (Matt. 23:13–32; Luke 11:37–53). These denunciations do not well up solely from Jesus' ethical awareness. They also stem from his theo-logical awareness, from his conception of God. Because God is love, he cannot tolerate the oppression of the lowly.

The reality of God is love, and God is the partisan of human beings. Love for human beings, then, is the privileged way for gaining access to God. This is pointed up clearly in the Gospels, particularly in those passages where it seems that love for human beings would clash with God's rights. As Jesus sees it, God does not choose to claim any right for himself outside of real and effective love for human beings. Let us now consider this point in what Jesus has to say about worship, the Sabbath, and the twofold great commandment.

Cultic worship functions as the realm of the sacred. It is presumed to be completely autonomous, the realm of "God's rights." The point here is that Jesus completely desacralizes that sphere. It is not that he nullifies it or that he has a secular conception of God. He desacralizes the cultic sphere precisely because of the notion of God that is his. If God is indeed love, then it is strictly and literally impossible for any kind of cultic worship to exist that is not itself a manifestation of love. If such a cultic worship could exist, then there would be an outright contradiction between the medium used for access to God and the innermost reality of the God we sought to approach.

When the Pharisees are scandalized by the fact that Jesus breaks the cultic rules by eating with sinners and not observing the Sabbath, Jesus quotes Hosea to them: "It is mercy I desire and not sacrifice" (Hos. 6:6; see Matt. 9:13; 12:7). To those who are angry with their fellows he says: "If you bring your gift to the altar and there recall that your brother has anything against you, leave your gift at the altar, go first to be reconciled with your brother, and then come and offer your gift" (Matt. 5:23–24). To anyone who would pray he says: "When you stand to pray, forgive anyone against whom you have a grievance so that your heavenly Father may in turn forgive you your faults" (Mark 11:25–26).

Worship, cult, and religion in general have no absolute autonomy of their own for Jesus. His God is not an egocentric being. He is a being for others, not a being for himself alone. Cultic worship is not only hypocritical but absolutely meaningless if it is not accompanied by love for other people; for in such a case it cannot possibly be a way of corresponding to God.

Jesus' conception of God is admirably brought out in the well-known passage where he spells out the correct relationship between people and the Sabbath (Mark 2:23–28; Matt. 12:1–8; Luke 6:1–5). This text is the fourth of the five debates between Jesus and the Pharisees as depicted in Mark's and Luke's Gospels. The real-life context behind the final redaction of this passage may have been an attempt to humanize the observance of the Sabbath by Jewish Christians. In the final redaction we also find a clear-cut christological motive. The writer wants to bring out the fact that the Son of Man, Jesus, is also Lord of the Sabbath.

Mark and Matthew, however, also present the theological backdrop of the controversy. To put it simply, we find a comparison between the "rights of God" and the "rights of human beings." And the solution is clear. Nothing at all can be set over in opposition to right relationships between human beings. In his narrative Matthew includes the text of Hosea cited above. Mark adds the famous phrase: "The sabbath was made for man, not man for the sabbath" (Mark 2:27).

It is a radical statement, and it presupposes a certain experience of God on Jesus' part. To understand and appreciate it fully, we should recall something pointed out by Braun: "As the Jews pictured it, God himself celebrated the Sabbath in heaven with all his angels. The chosen people of Israel were permitted to participate in that celebration. Thus the commandment to worship on the Sabbath spelled out and stressed the correct way to worship God. . . . Here God is viewed as a reality *in se* in the most eminent sense. Man is ushered into the service of that reality. Man is made for the Sabbath, for God. Jesus' statement is a terrifying reversal of that whole picture."[19]

This shift of emphasis from the Sabbath to human beings, to put it more crudely, from God to human beings might sound like blasphemy if one has not understood Jesus' experience of God. God continues to be the ultimate reality for Jesus. But God is love, not an end in himself. Hence we cannot gain proper access to this God if we do not correspond with this reality of love. If God is for human beings, we cannot have worship of God or a Sabbath without being for human beings. This is the theological revolution for which the ground was prepared in the Old Testament and which Jesus proclaimed openly. As Braun puts it:

God is no longer someone who is served through cultic worship and observance of the Sabbath. Service is no longer addressed to God as if he were some reality *in se*. Proper service to God is service to man, to human beings in their need. That is the correct observance of the Sabbath. That is authentic worship of God. According to Jesus, correct service to God is not something that simply *can* be service to man; it *must* be service to man.[20]

Finally, let us consider the passage in which he talks about the commandments of loving God and one's neighbor (Mark 12:28–34; Matt. 22:34–40; Luke 10:25–27). This passage is of the utmost importance for understanding Jesus' personal experience of God and his theological revolution.

It must be noted, first of all, that in all three Synoptic Gospels we find an assertion that is far from evident to Jesus' listeners. It is not that the whole passage is completely novel, for we find it in hellenistic Judaism. But Jesus asserts that love of God and love of neighbor are to be compared as equals. In the final redaction of each Synoptic Gospel we note that the writer has found some way to evoke the surprise of the reader over this comparison. In Mark's Gospel we have a scribe asking him about a disputed question: Which is the first of all the commandments? Jesus replies by quoting the book of Deuteronomy (6:4ff.): "You shall love the Lord your God with all your heart, with all your soul, with all your mind, and with all your strength." The element of surprise enters in when Jesus, without being asked, adds something from the book of Leviticus (Lev. 19:18) as the second commandment: "You shall love your neighbor as yourself." The response of Jesus in Matthew's account is the same, except that the second commandment is introduced with the phrase: "The second is *like* it" (Matt. 22:39). Luke's Gospel puts the basic answer in the mouth of a lawyer. He states the two commandments and is praised by Jesus. But then Jesus goes on to tell the parable of the good Samaritan, which is centered around the Samaritan's good deed for his neighbor (the second commandment). The priest and the levite, professionals in the exercise of the first great commandment, avoid the wounded man, do not fulfill the second great commandment, and are implicitly condemned by Jesus.

It may seem scandalous enough that Jesus seems to correlate and equate love of God with love of neighbor. What is even more scandalous is the possibility that love of God as the chief commandment may not have been in the original version of Mark's Gospel at all! This view is regarded as highly probable by some scholars. Boismard, for example, offers the following reconstruction of the text in its most primitive form:[21]

And one of the scribes said to him, "Well, Master," and asked him: "Which is the greatest commandment of all?" Jesus replied: "It is this: You shall love your neighbor as yourself; there is no greater commandment." And no one dared to ask him anything further.

This reconstruction of the original text is consistent with other passages in the Synoptic Gospels and with theological reflection. Insofar as scriptural analysis is concerned, the expression "love of God" only appears in the texts just cited and in Luke 11:42. The latter text says: "Woe to you Pharisees! You pay tithes on mint and rue and all the garden plants, while neglecting justice and the love of God." The dearth of texts on "love of God" is food for thought. This is all the more true when one realizes that the Lucan text is a later version of a Matthaean text in which the love of God is not mentioned at all: "Woe to you scribes and Pharisees, you frauds! You pay tithes on mint and herbs and seeds while neglecting the weightier matters of the law, justice and mercy and good faith" (Matt. 23:23).

Another passage worthy of attention is the scene where the rich young man approaches Jesus and asks him what he must do to attain eternal life (Mark 10:17–22; Matt. 19:16–22; Luke 18:18–23). Jesus replies by citing those commandments of the decalogue that talk about our obligations to others; he says nothing about the first three commandments that deal with our obligations toward God. Two other sections of Matthew's Gospel are also noteworthy in this respect. Matt. 5:21–48 and Matt. 6 and 7 present a catechesis on the root Christian way of doing things. In them we find much about the proper way to deal with other people, and relatively little about duties of a religious nature such as prayer and fasting. This raises a suspicion voiced by Braun: "The juxtaposition of love of God and love of neighbor, as preached in Mark 12:28–34, is only a superficial juxtaposition."[22]

Even when we leave the context of the Synoptic Gospels, we find similar hints. Consider what Paul says when he is talking about the fullness of the law and the one great commandment. He tells us that the whole law has found its fulfillment in one saying: "You shall love your neighbor as yourself" (Gal. 5:14). He also tells us that those who love their neighbor have fulfilled the law: "The commandments, 'You shall not commit adultery, you shall not murder, you shall not steal, you shall not covet,' and any other commandment there may be are all summed up in this, 'You shall love your neighbor as yourself' "(Rom. 13:8–9).

This brief exegetical study may be shocking to some, but only to those who have not grasped the novel attitude of Jesus towards God. "Needless to say, the surprising novelty of this situation does not lie in the fact that Jesus or the tradition stemming from him has simply chosen to ignore or disregard God. The notion of the kingdom of God is certainly a central conception in the preaching of Jesus."[23] The paucity of references to love of God in the gospel narratives does not mean that love is not the correct way for human beings to relate to God. It simply means that this relationship of love is going to be quite distinctive in the Christian faith because the reality of God is quite distinctive in this case.

To appreciate that fact, let us do a bit of reflecting. This particular line of reflection may well be expressed more systematically in the Johannine writings than in any other part of the New Testament. The Johannine writer makes this basic statement: "Beloved, if God has loved us so, we must have the same love for one another" (1 John 4:11). The premises are clear enough: God is love; he loved us first; he has demonstrated this love by sending his Son into history (see John 3:16; 1 John 4:8–10). It is the conclusion that is surprising: we correspond to that divine love when we love others in turn (John 15:12–17). We certainly cannot accuse the Johannine writer of not reflecting on the mystery and reality of God. But in the process of doing that reflection in Christian terms, he arrives at a seemingly paradoxical conclusion: responding to God means corresponding to God. In other words, the correct way to make contact with God is to act like God, to share in God's very own reality. If we know that we are loved by God and want to correspond to that love, then we must do what God does: love human beings.[24]

When we talk about "loving God" in Christian terms, we are using the expression in a totally novel and complicated way. "Love of God" is a doxological expression. It asserts that the ultimate human reality and the ultimate experience of meaningfulness is to be found in the practice of love. The complexity arises when we try to figure out the historical ways in which this doxological expression is to be mediated. Christian faith maintains that it is impossible to "love God" directly, that this love must be mediated through a historical love.

When Christians talk about love of God, then, they are talking *materially* about real, historical love for human beings. It is the *formal* nature of this love of neighbor that determines whether it can also be called love of God. If that love is displayed unreservedly and unconditionally, if it is done in the conviction that those who love to the utmost have lived life in all its fullness no matter what happens, then the historical experience of love for neighbor is formally meaningful as love for God.

It is not that there are two distinct objects of love on which one may choose to focus: God or our neighbor. The praxis of love constitutes one unique experience. Materially it is love of neighbor. Formally, when that love is given without reservations, it is also an experience of God and hence can be formulated as love for God.

But "love of neighbor" is not simply a prerequisite if the doxological formulation of "love of God" is to be meaningful. It is also the precondition for experiencing God as transcendent, as the God who is ever greater than human beings. If there is any historical reality at all that can mediate the transcendence of the Christian God, it is the historical reality of love. On the one hand love is the reality that brings out most clearly the extra something, the "more" of reality and meaningfulness. On the other hand the historical praxis of love is the place where one experiences the fundamental quandary of existence. The person who loves truly is persecuted. Those who set their feet on the pathway of love feel all the weight of sin upon themselves. It is here that we encounter the formal Christian structure of transcendence as a vis-à-vis, as one thing over "against" another. Christian acceptance of transcendence is not any naive identification with the existence of some Absolute; it entails corresponding to some Absolute *in spite of the fact* that the latter is called into question by history. To use Paul's traditional phrase, it means hoping against hope.

It is in the praxis of love for neighbor that we experience the transcendence of the Christian God. Its content is love; its surrounding aura is the added "more" that all love expresses and unleashes; its result is that hope that refuses to die in spite of all the power that sin unleashes against it. Thus historical love is the Christian embodiment of the basic principles that I enunciated at the start in more abstract terms: i.e., that the experience of God has love for its content and the God who ever remains greater as its formal principle.

Objectively, then, Jesus' experience of God can be summed up in the tradition concerned with the "kingdom" or "reign" of God. This kingdom of God represents the ultimate other-directedness of Jesus. Insofar as it is a "kingdom," it points toward real-life, historical love as a way of being. It is a love that is found in the communion of the individual with all other human beings, and of the latter with their origin and future, God. Insofar as it is the kingdom of "God," it points toward the ultimate inner depths of that kingdom.

Jesus' experience of God can be understood only against the backdrop of the kingdom of God and the history of Jesus' relationship with it. God continues to appear in two ways —as "love" and as a God who ever remains "greater." For Jesus, God is undeniably a God on the side of human beings. But this partisanship also has a history that keeps unfolding and growing more concrete. It implies a salvation that brings fulfillment and liberation from historical sin. It means that

God works justice, not in vindictive but in creative terms. It means that God is partisan, positively favoring those who have no one else on their side. It means that the salvation of the powerful can be effected only insofar as they are converted to the oppressed. That God is love is something which Jesus will also make concrete in his own person, through the vicissitudes of his history with all its conflict. For Jesus personally, God is his loving Father. He confidently calls him "Abba." That confidence reaches its culminating point in the agony in the garden. Poles apart from some ideologized optimism, it becomes a confidence that has been thoroughly tried and tested.

That God ever remains "greater" for Jesus can be seen in his respect and reverence for him as creator and provider. But this aspect is concretized, not in nature, but in his personal experience of ethics and actual practice. He experiences it as a vocation and a mission, to which there is no limit. He may even have to give up his own life for the sake of this "greater" God. Corresponding to a God who is truly "greater" than human beings means responding to the demands laid down by love. It is in and through the historical unfolding of those demands that the reality of God as someone "greater" is made concrete horizontally in history. There is no limit to the ethical demand when it has to do with love. Neither conflict, nor failure, nor rejection, nor death itself can set limits on God's demand. This is the way in which the greatness of God is brought out in history and respected to the very end. At no point in his history can Jesus get a "fix" on God once and for all.

In this final section, then, I have sought to bring out the basic substratum underlying the prayer of Jesus. Of course Jesus was a concrete human being. As such, he had a psychology of his own. He had his own needs and distinctive features that are reflected in his concrete prayer life, in the times and places and modes in which he prayed. But the basic character of his prayer was determined by his conception of who God, his Father, really was. It is that which made his prayer what it was.

In summary we can say that for Jesus the Father was the God of the kingdom. The "other" required for all true prayer was not merely some abstract deity, nor even a "personal" deity with whom one could dialogue. For Jesus it was a person whose reality could not be divorced from the kingdom he was fashioning. The relationality evident in Jesus' life from the start and expressed in his prayer necessarily took in the horizon of the kingdom as well.

This means that the prayer of Jesus had, in principle, a privileged locale. Of course Jesus prayed in many places: in the temple, in the desert, and on hillsides. But the basic locale for his prayer was the place where the kingdom was being fashioned into reality. That place was to be found in the praxis of hearing the word of God and in the praxis of love. The God of Jesus is a greater God, with a concrete will for his kingdom. Hence Jesus' prayer is a quest for his will and submissiveness to it. That is the concrete way in which he allows himself to be overtaken by God's transcendence. The God of Jesus is also a God of love. Hence the locale of Jesus' prayer is the praxis of love. On the one hand this praxis is a result of the word that Jesus has heard; on the other hand it is the cause of the words that Jesus will enunciate in his own prayer. Hence the locale of Jesus' prayer is not some vague contemplative attitude, nor some vague subjective intention to make contact with God. Instead it is the place where one objectively encounters God by hearing his will and then doing it.

It is this locale that makes room for the basic action of Jesus: his *self-surrender*. In a moment fraught with meaningfulness prayer will affirm doxologically the self-surrender that is fleshed out in the real everyday life of Jesus. In prayer the sacrifice of his ego is expressed in different ways: as confident trust or as acceptance of the will of God, for example. But that is not some sacrifice in the realm of intention alone. It merely expresses the authentic sacrifice of his self in real life.

The innermost *content* of Jesus' prayer is very simple. It seeks to show his acceptance of God's will for the kingdom and his own person, and to express his joy and thanks at the fact that the kingdom is spreading. This content expresses Jesus' ultimate experience of meaningfulness: i.e., that God is making himself present in history through love.

This brief summary of the prayer of Jesus may seem overly simple. It may not seem to shed too much light on the complicated problem of prayer in day-to-day life. But in my opinion it does point up what is fundamental. Christian prayer is not addressed to just any deity; it is addressed to the Father of Jesus. A correct relationship with the latter is possible only if we participate in his very reality. We must be love as God is, and do works of love as God does. Here we find the privileged locale that enables us to engage in prayer. Nowhere else can we find such a locale. Nor can we make up for it by simply having the abstract intention of trying to make contact with God.

In this activity of love we also find the positive "more" that is both imbedded in history and questioned by it. Hence it is also the proper locale for ensuring that the Christian at prayer will confront a God who ever remains greater rather than some deity modelled after our own image and likeness. When and if people experience God in the praxis of love, then they can formulate that experience doxologically and say thanks as Jesus did. They can also re-read the Psalms and call God "good," "provident," and "Father." But without the praxis of love people cannot experience the God of Jesus, and hence they cannot pray to the God of Jesus.

NOTES

1. On the prayer of Jesus and his teaching about prayer see: J. Jeremias, *Teología del Nuevo Testamento*, Spanish trans., 1974, pp. 218–38; Eng. trans.: *New Testament Theology* (New York: Scribner's, 1971); in Eng. see also *The Prayers of Jesus* (Naperville, Ill.: Allenson, 1967); G. Bornkamm, *Jesús de Nazaret*, 1975, pp. 139–44; Eng. trans.: *Jesus of Nazareth* (New York: Harper, 1960), J. Gnilka, "Jesus und das Gebet," *Bibel und Leben*, Heft 2 (Düsseldorf: Patmos, 1965), pp. 79–91; K. Rahner, W. Thüsing, *Christologie—systematisch und exegetisch*, pp. 187f., 211–17; P. Beauchamp, "Prière," *Vocabulaire de Théologie Biblique* (Paris: Cerf, 1970); Eng. trans.: "Prayer," in *Dictionary of Biblical Theology* (New York: Desclée, 1967); F. Wulf, "Oración," *Conceptos fundamentales de teología*, 1966, 3:236–39.

2. "For modern man, praying is envisioned as the activity of someone who is not looking for anything more because he has already found it. He no longer has to knock on the door from outside because he has already entered a life in which there is an uninterrupted interchange between the one who prays and God. For Jesus, on the other hand, that is not the situation of a human being at prayer" (Bornkamm, *Jesús de Nazaret*, p. 140).

3. Jeremias, *Teología del Nuevo Testamento*, p. 222.

4. Ibid., pp. 220–24. See P. Benoit and M.E. Boismard, *Synopse des Quatre Evangiles* (Paris: Cerf, 1965), p. 169f.

5. Gnilka, "Jesus und das Gebet," p. 82f.

6. See Benoit and Boismard, *Synopse*, pp. 390–94. For more detailed studies see G. Schneider, *Die Passion Jesu nach den drei älteren Evangelien* (Munich: Kösel, 1973), pp. 43–54; L. Schenke, *Der gekruzigte Christus* (Stuttgart: KBW, 1974) pp. 111–34; J. Jeremias, *Teología del Nuevo Testamento*, pp. 166, 296f.

7. According to Benoit and Boismard *(Synopse)*, the present account in Mark's Gospel on Jesus' prayer in the garden was elaborated in three stages. In the first stage the text would be: "The hour is on us. You will see that the Son of Man is to be handed over to the clutches of evil men" (14:41b); "My heart is filled with sorrow to the point of death" (14:34a); "He . . . praying that if it were possible this hour might pass him by" (14:35b). In the second stage of elaboration the text stresses Jesus' acceptance of God's will: "But let it be as you would have it, not as I" (14:35c). It also adds the appeal to the Father (14:35b). In the third stage the whole scene is expanded and the appeal to Peter is added: "Asleep, Simon? You could not stay awake for even an hour?" (14:37b).

8. Jeremias, *Teología del Nuevo Testamento*, p. 166.

9. Ibid., p. 167.

10. In talking here about Jesus' notion and experience of God, I am obviously referring to the impact of the Father on the *human* consciousness of Jesus. I am not going into the eternal relationship between the Father and the Son within the Trinity. If we want to analyze the figure of the historical Jesus, and especially if we want to view his prayer as a model for that of the Christian, we cannot evade the task of analyzing who or what God was for Jesus. On Jesus' notion of God see the following: Jeremias, *Teología del Nuevo Testamento*, pp. 80–87, 211–20; Bornkamm, *Jesús de Nazaret*, pp. 101–49; H. Braun,

Jesus (Stuttgart: Kreuz, 1969), pp. 159–70; N. Perrin, *Rediscovering the Teaching of Jesus* (New York: Harper & Row, 1967); K. Niederwimmer, *Jesus* (Göttingen: Vandenhoeck, 1968), pp. 53–70; Pannenberg, *Fundamentos de cristología*, pp. 280–91, see note 6, chap. 1 in this volume; Moltmann, *Der gekreuzigte Gott*, pp. 119–46, see note 10, chap. 1 in this volume; K. Rahner, W. Thüssing, *Christologie—systematisch und exegetisch*, pp. 28–33, 185f., 210f.; L. Boff, *La experiencia de Dios*, Spanish edition, 1975, pp. 54–68.

11. The value of F. Belo's book *(Lecture matérialiste de l'évangile de Marc* [Paris: Cerf, 1974]; to be published in English by Orbis Books) lies in the fact that it analyzes the activity of Jesus in terms of his concrete tactics and strategy.

12. Pannenberg, *Fundamentos de cristología*, p. 285.

13. Ibid., p. 286.

14. For a critique of Pannenberg see Moltmann, *Der gekreuzigte Gott*, pp. 153–66.

15. Jeremias, *Teología del Nuevo Testamento*, p. 211; see also pp. 21f. and 120.

16. Braun, *Jesus*, p. 167.

17. Jeremias, *Teología del Nuevo Testamento*, p. 212.

18. See W. Pannenberg, "Wie kann heute glaubwürdig von Gott geredet werden?" in *Die Gottesfrage heute* (Donauworth: Auer, 1969), pp. 51–64.

19. Braun, *Jesus*, p. 161.

20. Ibid., p. 162.

21. See Benoit and Boismard, *Synopse*, p. 350f.

22. Braun, *Jesus*, p. 164.

23. Ibid., p. 163.

24. The distinction here between "responding" and "corresponding" is meant to point up the fact that we must ultimately not just respond to God as an Other but correspond to God by becoming like God. Obviously enough God ever remains an Other. But Christians integrate the otherness of God into their lives by becoming like that Other. This is the classic theme of the divinization of human beings. Taken in all its radical import and stripped of its atemporal and ahistorical connotations, it expresses the innermost depth of Christian reality. It is what H. Bergson glimpsed when he said that in creation God undertook to create creators (see the *Two Sources of Morality and Religion* [New York: Holt, 1949], p. 243).

6.

The Death of Jesus and Liberation in History

At the very center of Christian faith lies the assertion that Jesus of Nazareth, the Son of God, died by crucifixion. This is a central datum of the Christian faith, and right from the start it marked off the difference between the new faith in Christ and the various religious conceptions current in the world of the time. Paul was fully aware of the fact that the proclamation of a crucified Messiah continued to be foolishness to enlightened Greeks and a scandal for orthodox Jews (see 1 Cor. 1:23). From the very start the cross of Jesus drew a dividing line between Christian existence and every other type of religion, even though the latter might profess some sort of belief in a dying and rising God.

Curiously enough, however, theological reflection on the cross of Jesus is very infrequent; and when it is carried out, it rarely reaches the level of showing that the cross and the proclamation of a "crucified God"[1] embody the authentic originality of the Christian faith. Such reflection usually remains on the level of pious contemplation. It does not bring out the fact that the cross of Christ implies a new and revolutionary concept of God on both the theoretical and practical level.

In practice such reflection usually focuses on the notion that we have been saved through Jesus' cross. Thoughtless reiteration of that point has led to a more or less magical conception of redemption, one which ends up eliminating the element of scandal in the historical cross of Jesus.

Tradition has also tended to elaborate a mystique of the cross. Indeed it would be more correct to call it a "mystique of sorrow and suffering," as I hope to bring out. Christianity has come to be seen as a religion espoused by grief-stricken people obsessed with suffering (Nietzsche) and totally devoid of *joie de vivre* and a sense of responsibility to bring about a better, more humane world. In recent times theology has tried to counter that accusation, which ultimately derives from a particular conception of the cross. It has sought to elaborate a theology of the resurrection, looking to it as the paradigm of triumphant liberty and the joy of living which was lost in the cross. In short, theology has tended to sidestep the task of reflecting on the cross itself.

In Latin America the cross has traditionally been the main focus of popular festivity. For peasants and oppressed groups in general, their great Christian feast has been Good Friday, not Easter Sunday or Christmas. A profound insight underlies that emphasis, but it has been counterbalanced by the utilization of Good Friday as a substitute for responsible effort in the cause of liberation. Popular intuition has rightly grasped the authentic element of Christian faith in Good Friday, but it has often grasped it in very passive terms. The present-day situation in Latin America has brought out a somewhat different focus, particularly among groups more deeply involved in the effort for social change. This new Christian focus on the cross of Jesus is much more activist in character. While the resurrection remains the paradigm of liberation, the cross is no longer seen simply as a symbol of suffering or as the negative dialectical moment which immediately and directly gives rise to the positive moment of liberation. People now realize that a whole process of analysis is required before the latter positive phase can be viable. From their concrete experience in the effort to achieve liberation, people are now beginning to realize that they cannot prescind from the cross of Jesus if their experience is to be truly Christian.

The present situation rules out any merely romantic conception of Jesus' resurrection. It forces us to reflect theologically on the death of Jesus, and ultimately on the crucified God. Without the cross, the resurrection is idealistic. The utopia of Christian resurrection becomes real only in terms of the cross, and theological reflection on the death of Jesus must probe deeper on at least two levels.

The first level is *theological* in the strict sense. Theology must consider how the cross of Jesus, as a real happening in history, affects God himself. Any consideration of Jesus' death remains partial and incomplete if it fails to reflect on that issue; for it stops at the very point where it could be most revolutionary, where it could become a theology of the crucified God.

The second level of reflection on this issue would consider the suppositions and implications of this particular conception of God *for Christian life*. It should lead us to see the necessity of liberation in history and its Christian import. If reflection on the cross does not reach the theological level of asking questions about God, if it stays simply with the death of Jesus, then it will be ignoring the issue at its deepest level. For both Jesus and the present-day Christian, "God" embodies the ultimate expression of their life and their history. Some conception of God underlies every historical praxis, whether one adverts to it consciously or not. A task of the utmost importance is to spell out that conception and, in our present context, to see whether the notion of a "crucified God" should not have some impact on the way we configure our historical praxis.

I think there are two main obstacles to any attempt to grasp the cross of Jesus in all its profundity. One is the danger of isolating that cross from the concrete history of Jesus; the other is the danger of isolating it from God. To make my treatment more readily understandable, then, I have divided it into three main sections. The very setup of these sections outlines the main problem and the proper way to solve it:

1. After the resurrection of Jesus, there was a tendency to focus on the positive benefits of the cross for humankind. That is to say, stress was placed on the salvific and soteriological aspects of the cross. Unfortunately this approach subtly detached the cross from the person of God, thereby robbing the cross of its power and impact. This we shall consider in the first section of this chapter.

2. One way to begin to recover the pristine value of the cross is to consider it as the historical outcome and consequence of

Jesus' own life, to view the cross in terms of what happened *before*. This approach will be truly theological if we view Jesus' journey to the cross as a process leading toward the truth of God, a process to which Jesus bears witness throughout his journey in life by challenging the truth of other religious and political gods and entering into conflict with them. This we shall consider in the second section of this chapter.

3. The two stages of reflection just described are not radical and thorough enough, however. Our theology of the cross becomes radical only when we consider the presence (or absence) of God on the cross of Jesus. It is at this point that we face the alternatives posed by Moltmann: Either the cross of Jesus is the end of all Christian theo-logy or else it is the beginning of a truly Christian theology, one that is both a critical theory and a liberative praxis. This we shall consider in the third section of this chapter.

In these three sections I will put the more important points and formulations in the form of theses. They will deal with the hard content of a theology of the cross as well as with its presuppositions and consequences. Hopefully this will make my treatment more readily comprehensible to the reader.

THE POST-RESURRECTION VIEW OF JESUS' DEATH

Faith in Christ blossoms fully only after Jesus' resurrection, and only then does it become fully conscious of itself. The fundamental points of this new post-resurrection faith can be summed up in three basic statements, points that cannot be denied because they stand at the very core of the living tradition handed down to us.

First, after the resurrection there is a basic affirmation about God. In the light of God's action in resurrecting Jesus, we get a new historical definition of God which, as historical, is in line with the Old Testament but which also goes beyond it. In the Old Testament God is the one who hears and sees the afflictions of the oppressed (Exod. 3:7; 6:5). In the oldest Hebrew creeds he is the one who liberated Israel from bondage in

Egypt (Deut. 26:5–9; 5:6; Exod. 20:2). In the New Testament we get the definitive historical action of God. He is the one who "raised Jesus our Lord from the dead" (Rom. 4:24), who "restores the dead to life and calls into being those things which had not been" (Rom. 4:17). Historically speaking, then, God is the one who has the power to liberate and revitalize all reality. This new definition of God, however, is also rendered concrete on the basis of Jesus' cross. God appears not only in his historical power but also in his historical love. In history the Father delivers up his Son to death (John 3:16; 1 John 4:9f.; Rom. 8:32; 5:6–11; etc.). In this historical action he reveals his ultimate essence as love: "God is love" (1 John 4:8, 16).

Second, after the resurrection the soteriological import of Jesus' history becomes clear to Christian understanding. Jesus "was handed over to death for our sins and raised up for our justification" (Rom. 4:25). Right from the first of his apparitions as the risen one, Jesus shows himself as a benevolent being intent on reconciliation. The expressions in the Gospels ("Do not be afraid"; "Peace be with you") point up the experience of his disciples. They now realize that God's ultimate word for them is one of love rather than of condemnation. They also realize that what happened to Jesus is the destiny of all human beings. Jesus has been resurrected as "the firstborn of many brothers" (Rom. 8:29; 1 Cor. 15:20; Col. 1:18; Rev. 1:5; Acts 3:15). This triggers a radical hope in a radically new person, a hope that can and should be turned into a reality here below in history through a life of loving self-surrender: "That we have passed from death to life we know because we love the brothers" (John 3:14).

Third, and finally, after the resurrection we get an assertion about Jesus himself: Jesus of Nazareth is really the Son of God. The true and authentic nature of the Son has been revealed in the historical process of one man's life, career, and death on the cross. This faith-inspired intuition is gradually elaborated in various titles that spell out the dignity of Jesus and his character: e.g., Prophet, Lord, High Priest, and Logos. It is also elaborated through the Christian interpretation of certain events in Jesus' life that point up his special relationship of oneness with the Father: e.g., his virginal conception, his birth, his baptism, and his transfiguration.

Now all of these assertions are legitimate and necessary. They ultimately assert that in the historical life of this particular man, Jesus of Nazareth, there has been revealed the ultimate meaning of history, the way to realize that meaning, and the way to approach the Father. But what we want to consider here primarily is something else, something that begins even in the New Testament itself. We want to note how people gradually began to overlook the import of the cross, both as a real fact in itself and as a revelation of God.

Thesis 1: Christian faith has its origin in the resurrection of the crucified one. Even as far back as the New Testament itself, however, it was hard for people to preserve the scandal of the cross, though the cross typifies Christianity. This is evident in the fact that the very death of Jesus as one abandoned by God is mollified. It is also evident in the fact that the title "Servant of Yahweh" is soon dropped as a title embracing the overall figure of Jesus. It is soon replaced with titles that point more directly to Jesus as risen from the dead.

In the various descriptions of Jesus' death in the New Testament we can already detect a trend toward mollifying the death in theological terms. In Mark's version, the most primitive and original one, his death is described in sober terms of tragedy: "Then Jesus, uttering a loud cry, breathed his last" (Mark 15:37). While still alive on the cross, Jesus recites a phrase from Psalm 22:2: "My God, my God, why have you forsaken me?" It may well be that Mark himself put those words on Jesus' lips, but he would not have dared to have put such scandalous words on Jesus' lips without some solid historical basis for doing so. Moreover, this description does correspond with other data in his Gospel, such as the agony in the garden (Mark 14:34–42), as well as with the whole theological context of Jesus' life (as we shall see later on).

What about the other Gospel accounts? Matthew's Gospel follows the same basic scheme in describing Jesus' death, particularly insofar as the feeling of God's abandonment is concerned. But in the Gospels of Luke and John we can detect efforts to soften the edges of this scandalous happening. The theological dimension of Jesus' death is prettified. In Luke's Gospel, the scandalous phrase of Psalm 22 is replaced with the triumphant strains of Psalm 31: "Father, into your hands I commend my spirit." The Gospel of John does not mention Psalm 22 either. There Jesus dies majestically, completely in charge of the situation right up to the very end: "Now it is finished" (John 19:30). Instead of uttering the final cry described in Mark's Gospel, Jesus serenely gives up his spirit.

The point we want to emphasize here is that the event of Jesus' death itself begins to lose its cutting edge in the very first efforts to interpret it. Somehow or other it was difficult right from the start to maintain the scandalous fact of abandonment by God that was embodied on Jesus' cross. Jesus is depicted as a confident martyr (Luke's Gospel) or as the Son of God who consciously realizes that he is fulfilling the will of God (John's Gospel). The divine abandonment on the cross, which is very important for any reflection on the Christian God vis-à-vis all the crosses of history, is stripped of its force. The scandal is maintained by Paul (1 Cor. 1:23) and by the Letter to the Hebrews, the latter explicitly mentioning Jesus' prayers, supplications, loud cries and tears (Heb. 5:7). But on the whole we can detect a tendency to bypass and overlook the element of scandal. For if the Father resurrected Jesus, then it becomes hard to realize that he abandoned Jesus on the cross.

Another indication of this difficulty can be seen in the elaboration of the various honorific titles that the New Testament used to interpret the figure of Jesus. As the various Christologies begin to develop in the New Testament we can notice an ever greater concentration on those titles that express his personal dignity and the nature of his mission in positive terms. Jesus is described as the Messiah, the Lord, the Son of God, and the Logos. As the work of interpreting Jesus proceeds, we find that the titles which primarily describe his work on earth tend to disappear from the vocabulary of theology. Particularly noteworthy is what happens to the title that has to do most directly with his death, the one that associates him with the suffering Servant of Yahweh in the Old Testament.

The suffering Servant is crushed with infirmity (Isa. 53:10), counted with the wicked, and subjected to death of his own free will (Isa. 53:12). We find various references to this figure of Second Isaiah in the Synoptic Gospels. After the resurrection, however, we find very few passages that interpret the figure of Jesus in terms of that Servant of Yahweh. There are three such passages in the Acts of the Apostles (Acts 3:13, 26; 4:27, 30; 8:26f.). In some of these passages we see that the term "servant" is being turned into a technical term to describe Jesus, which suggests that we are dealing with a very old form of Christology. It may well derive from Peter himself, because two of the passages are discourses of Peter and the others are prayers of the community recited in Peter's presence. We also find three references to the text of Isaiah 53 in the First Epistle of Peter (1 Pet. 2:22–24). The importance of the connection between Peter and this Christology of the Servant lies in the fact that it was Peter who was confronted most baldly with the scandal of Jesus as a suffering rather than a victorious Messiah (see Mark 8:32). He managed to preserve the scandalous nature of his own concrete experience by picturing Jesus as the Servant of Yahweh.

The important point here, however, is that the "Servant of Yahweh" title, which is the most direct pointer to Jesus' cross, soon disappeared as the most basic explanation of Jesus' person. It is replaced by other titles that stress his existence as one already exalted in heaven. In the dialectics of cross and resurrection it is the latter that comes to be more and more basic in considering the figure of Jesus. The cross of Christ recedes more and more into the background. It is viewed more and more as a preliminary and provisional stage leading up to the resurrection, and so it becomes less important in trying to grasp Jesus' own understanding of God.

Thesis 2: Another way to emasculate the cross in the New Testament is to reduce it to a noetic mystery, paradoxical as that might seem. For this noetic mystery supposedly can be explained in terms of God's design and its salvific value for human beings. Thus the cross does not produce a crisis for all knowledge of God, a crisis which might then lead us to a knowledge of the Christian God.

In the New Testament the cross is viewed in soteriological terms, in terms of its salvific implications for human beings. It shifts from being something scandalous to being something *positive* for human beings. Now there is no reason to object to what is said positively about it, as when Paul tells us that in Christ on the cross God "was reconciling the world to himself" (2 Cor. 5:19). The problem lies in the fact that one-sided soteriological consideration of the cross draws our attention away from the theological dimension of Jesus' death. In focusing excessively on the cross insofar as it brought benefits to humanity, we tend to forget the relationship of the cross to God himself. What is at stake, in the last analysis, is a conception of God. Does the death of Jesus affect God himself? Did the incarnation of God go so far that God himself had to be affected by the cross and death?

In the New Testament we can detect an effort to evade this basic question, not by getting rid of the question but by turning people's attention to other perspectives that tend to make the cross of Jesus anything but scandalous. The note of scandal begins to disappear ever so subtly as attention is focused on the *why* and *wherefore* of the cross. Contrary to what one might think, the resurrection of Jesus does not eliminate the scandal of the cross; instead it elevates it to the level of a mystery. Precisely because Jesus had risen from the dead, the question as to why Jesus had to die and what God was doing on the cross became all the more pointed. In the New Testament we can detect a tendency to try to clear up this ultimate "mystery"; but since it is the mystery of God, it really cannot be explained or further analyzed.

The first approach in attempting to clear up the mystery was to ask about the *why* of the cross. To answer that question would be to provide some sort of initial explanation, to find some meaningful connection between the cross and the purpose of life. It was obvious that one would have to look to God for this *why*; and so the New Testament tells us that Jesus "was delivered up by the set purpose and plan of God" (Acts 2:23; 4:28; Mark 8:31). Luke's Gospel goes a step further, maintaining that it was *necessary* for the Messiah to die on the cross (Luke 24:26). Moreover, this was predicted in the Scriptures (Luke 24:25; 1 Cor. 15:4). A further step was taken in the process of clarification when the death of Jesus was equated with that of a prophet (Matt. 23:37; Mark 12:2ff.; Rom. 11:3; 1 Thes. 2:14f.). That is certainly true enough, but it does not say enough since it does not bring out what *typifies* and distinguishes the death of Jesus. Jesus dies *as the Son*, as the one who proclaimed the nearness of his heavenly Father and then died completely abandoned by that Father. Thus the unfolding logic of the attempted explanation in the New Testament gradually converts the *real-life* scandal of Jesus' cross into nothing more than a *noetic* scandal. Once we correctly interpret the Scriptures, we presumably will not find anything surprising in the cross of Jesus.

This whole logical schema in which the New Testament frames the question of the cross presupposes a particular knowledge of God at the very start. It is this that will explain and justify the meaning of the cross. Such an approach might well have been possible for the very first Christians, given the fact that they lived in a *socio-cultural* milieu where the notion of "God" as such did not presuppose any problem. But such an approach cannot be taken for granted as self-evident in Paul's *theological* situation nor in ours. The silence of God in connection with Jesus' cross tells us at once that we must break completely with the inertial human way of thinking about God. We must break with every logical schema we had entertained previously insofar as knowing God is concerned. We cannot explain the cross *logically* by appealing to God, who supposedly is known already, because the first thing the cross does here is raise questions about God himself and the authentic reality of the deity. The first thing the cross unmasks is people's selfish interest in seeking to know God.

However, let us get back to our analysis of the New Testament for the moment. Even if we were to explain the why of the cross in terms of some God presumably known at the start, we would still be left with another question: If Jesus really was the Son of God, why was it specifically God's plan that Jesus should die on the cross? If his plan is not purely arbitrary and cruel, we must move on from a logical explanation of the cross to show that there is something eminently positive in the cross of Jesus despite its scandalous appearance. Now in the New Testament this positive element is not viewed in relation to God himself. The cross is not seen as revealing some authentic though unsuspected image of God. Rather, the death of Jesus is seen to be eminently positive insofar as it brings salvation to human beings. Jesus dies on behalf of all humankind.

At the start Christians seemed content with the general idea that Jesus was crucified "to bring repentance to Israel and forgiveness of sins" (Acts 5:31). As time went on, however, various schemes were elaborated to explain how the cross could be salvation, and various models based on the Old Testament were introduced. Jesus dies to *expiate* sin (Mark 10:45). He *sheds his blood* for us (Mark 14:23f.; Luke 22:20). He dies as an *expiatory victim* (Rom. 3:25). These motifs derive basically from a certain conception of cultic worship and they attempt to point up the internal connection between death on the cross, salvation, and the forgiveness of sins.

Other explanatory motifs picture Jesus' death as a new *covenant* (Mark 14:24; Matt. 26:28). The making of such a covenant called for the blood of victims. In Paul's writings we find another model. On the cross Jesus took upon himself the accusing power of the law and thus liberated us from it (Gal. 3:13); he thus eliminated the curse of the law (Col. 2:13f.; Eph. 2:14ff.).

It is important for us to realize what is positive and what is negative about this process of explanation. It is of positive value in that it stresses that Jesus' cross did bring salvation: "God so loved the world that he gave his only Son" (John 3:16). It is also positive in that it seeks to provide models that will help to explain what salvation is and make it more understandable to people. What, then, is negative about it? It is negative insofar as its exclusively soteriological interest in the cross draws our attention away from God himself and his relationship to the cross. It tells us *that* God loved us, but it does not say *how* God himself loved us and liberated us.

That is not a superficial distinction, for what is at stake here is the kind of solidarity that God has with human beings. Does his solidarity with us mean that God himself must go by way of the cross in the midst of countless historical crosses, or in the last analysis does God himself remain untouched by the historical cross because he is essentially untouchable? We shall consider that question in more detailed fashion in the third section of this chapter. The point I want to make here is that the New Testament itself unwittingly draws our attention away from the scandal of the cross insofar as it relates directly to God. Maintaining the element of scandal in the cross is not easy, and even as far as the New Testament era we find people trying to evade the issue. At bottom the cross challenges us to say what sort of God we believe in. Insofar as salvation is concerned, it does not simply ask how people are saved passively; it also asks how God saves people in a world where there is no salvation.

The danger of the explanatory models discussed above is that they tend to interiorize salvation. It is not just that they tend to center salvation around the individual, nor is that the main problem. The real problem is that they tend to treat salvation in terms of inner life, explaining how the cross can bring forgiveness for one's sins, while neglecting to treat of salvation in relationship to the world outside and the problems of externalized injustice and sinfulness. The issue at stake is not just how God can *pardon* an "offense" against him insofar as it is an internal human act; it is how God can *take away* an external sin that leads to the cross of his Son and to all the crosses of history.

Thesis 3: In the history of the church and of theology we find a similar tendency to bypass the scandal of the cross. This is due to two

erroneous presuppositions that were taken for granted: (1) a concep-
tion of God that does not derive from the cross and (2) a conception of
cultic worship as sacrifice that does not derive from Jesus.

It would take a great deal of time and space to trace the
reasons for the abandonment of the crucified God in the history of the church and of theology. Here I should simply like to
make three points to show how the death of Jesus continues to
remain the touchstone of the Christian faith and how attempts
have been made to eviscerate it by the use of theological
schemas that have never been called into question by the cross
itself.

First of all, there is the fact that God's abandonment on the
cross of Jesus was not taken seriously by later tradition, on the
supposition that such abandonment was impossible. Even
back in the early centuries of Christianity, some theologians
maintained that the use of Psalm 22 (verse 2) by Jesus could
only have been metaphorical. Jesus was not speaking for himself; he did not feel abandoned by his Father. He was speaking
in the name of sinful humanity; in his person, therefore, all
sinners are abandoned by God. Such was the view expressed
by people like Origen, Cyril of Alexandria, and Augustine.
Among the Latin Fathers this interpretation might also have
been due to an incorrect translation of Psalm 22:2, whereby the
"words of my cry" was mistakenly interpreted as the "words
of my *sins*." Since Jesus could not have spoken of himself as a
sinner, his talk about God's abandonment must have been
allegorical, referring to real sinners rather than to his own
person. Other Fathers of the Church, including Epiphanius
and Eusebius, interpreted Psalm 22 in its Gospel use as a
dialogue between Jesus' human nature and his divine nature.
In other words, the man Jesus is complaining that the divine
Word is going to abandon his human nature in the tomb. With
the aid of this subtle distinction, then, one could say that the
Father, the God of the New Testament, did not abandon the
Son in any strict sense. Finally, another group of Fathers (e.g.,

Tertullian, Ambrose, and Thomas Aquinas) admitted that Jesus suffered abandonment by God, psychologically speaking; this caused him great anxiety, but not despair.

This brief overview should make it clear how difficult it has been for people to maintain the scandal of the cross. The difficulty lies in accepting the notion of God's absence on the cross, which then prompts people to elaborate theological schemes that will avoid the scandal. There are two aspects to the scandal. One is the fact that Jesus, who was the Son, died in disaster. The other aspect is even harder to take, even if one is willing to accept the first point. It is that the Father was passive on Jesus' cross. Since God is normally conceived in terms of power, even Christian theology finds it almost impossible to ponder his passivity in the face of Jesus' cross.

My second point has to do with the classic medieval interpretation of the salvific meaning of Jesus' death. It is Anselm's theory of vicarious satisfaction. In the background of his view are categories derived from the legal system of the Germanic tribes: e.g., offense, satisfaction, the dignity of the one offended and of the offender, and so forth. Using these concepts, Anselm goes on to say that the offended dignity of the Father could only be placated by the satisfaction of someone who could worthily repair for it. This could only be someone who could heal the infinite distance between God and creature. It could be no one else but the Son of God made man. Due reparation is made to the Father through the cross of his Son, and thus the sins of humankind are forgiven.

The positive feature of this interpretation is that the love of the Son certainly does represent the maximum glorification of the Father. In our present context, however, the important thing to note is that Anselm's explanation is framed in a context that takes the ultimate realities already known and hardly able to be questioned: i.e., Who or what exactly is God? What is sin? What is salvation?

Let us consider what these suppositions are in the concrete. Influenced by the Greek conception of *apatheia* rather than by the biblical notion of God, Anselm's view assumes that God cannot be affected by evil. It also assumes that salvation con-

sists in the pardon of sins, overlooking the much broader
biblical conception of salvation as the reign of God and integral
salvation. It also views the death of Jesus in isolation from the
rest of his life. It suggests that the Father arbitrarily chose the
cross of Jesus for reparation, thereby ignoring the intrinsic
relationship that exists between Jesus' proclamation of liberation, his denunciation of oppression, and his historical death
on the cross. Anselm's theory, like many others, "knows far
too much" to be able to grasp the unique and typical aspect of
Jesus' historical cross. And since it is the explanation that has
been most commonly used in traditional theology and pastoral
preaching, it serves as a fine example of the tendency to bypass
and ignore the deeper reality of the cross.

The ultimate flaw in that theory is that it is ahistorical. The
nexus between Jesus' death and salvation is viewed from the
outside. It is interpreted in terms of God's overall design,
which in turn is viewed speculatively in terms of God's "offended dignity." It never gets inside the historical reality of
Jesus and his cross. It never views the matter in terms of the
power of real sin in history, which brings death to the
Son—not in idealistic terms but in real terms. In Anselm's
theory Jesus' death is obviously framed in the context of a
pre-existing theological schema. There is no thought of asking
whether Jesus' death on the cross should oblige us to break
with all such theological schemas, however traditional they
might be. In trying to explain the cross on the basis of certain
universal schemas, one causes its unique and irrepeatable
distinctiveness to disappear altogether. One seeks to arrive at
knowledge of the cross on the basis of some previously held
conception of God, when in fact one should try to arrive at
God on the basis of Jesus' cross.

My third point dealing with the evisceration of Jesus' cross
relates more to practice than to any theoretical explanation. It
has to do with Jesus' historical cross as the precondition for
any authentic Christian worship. The religions of Antiquity
clearly attest to the fact that people respond to the transcendent power of the deity through some act of self-surrender and
submission. In cultic worship this submission is celebrated

through some symbol that serves as a vicarious representative. As the early church began to integrate itself more and more into the religious schemas of the peoples among whom it lived, it found itself forced more and more to give way to their demands for cultic worship and sacrifice. Christianity certainly transformed the whole idea of cultic worship and desacralized it to some extent. But the unbloody repetition of Jesus' own sacrifice stepped in to fill the vacuum that had been left when the pagan sacrificial cults fell out of favor.

At the very start we find that the Christian liturgy consisted of an agapic meal, a grateful celebration of salvation, and a recollection of Jesus who was now present in the midst of the community through his Spirit. Gradually, however, it was turned into a sacrifical liturgy by the end of the first century. Instead of viewing the cross in all its irrepeatable and scandalous uniqueness, people were now tempted to view it in terms of the already existing notion of a "sacrifice" that could be represented in cultic worship. More and more the cross took on a "religious" character. It became the factor that made possible a Christian cult with sacrifice understood along the lines of other religions. Once the cross was translated into cultic terms of that sort, the danger increased that it would end up as a "de-historicized" cross and that "worship" would end up replacing the real following of Jesus.

From all that has been said above we can arrive at one basic conclusion: The cross of Jesus was a scandal even for the first Christians, and so we see the witting or unwitting elaboration of theological models designed to eviscerate it. As I see it, the basic tack in this assault on the cross was to forget that the person who died on the cross was the Son of God, that the cross therefore affected God himself. If in fact the Father is the ultimate correlate of the Christian's life, then we run into serious difficulties to the extent that we prescind from the Father in reflecting on the death of Jesus. For we then ignore the relationship between Jesus' cross and the ultimate meaning of Christian life, though we may continue to hearken back to it in our speech, our asceticism, or our cultic worship.

Before we go on to consider what an authentic theology of

the cross might be, we should focus on certain presuppositions that have been blocking out the radical meaning of the
cross for Christian existence. They are not explicitly theological; rather, they have to do with general attitudes or people's
overall philosophical outlook. In this connection we must remember that in the first centuries of its existence, and particularly in the second century, Christian theology made explicit its thinking through Greek patterns of thought and
philosophy. Those patterns have continued to exert influence
right up to today, and often they are taken over uncritically.
We simply must get beyond those patterns if we want to
understand the cross of Jesus. More indirectly, we must also
get beyond them if we want to appreciate what a historical
theology of liberation might be.

*Thesis 4: The Greek metaphysical conception of God's being and
perfection renders any theology of the cross impossible. A truly
historical theology of liberation must view suffering as a mode of being
belonging to God.*

The death of Jesus had no positive impact on the formulations about God and Jesus that were elaborated in the first few
centuries of the church's existence. That was no accident. It
was due to the inability of Greek thought to contemplate the
negative pole of reality. Within the Greek horizon of understanding, the task was to clarify the relationship between
disorder and order. The notion of *nothingness*, which is much
more radical than that of disorder, did not appear on that
horizon at all. Hence there was no Greek notion of creation as
the overcoming of nothingness. Christian theology got
beyond that Greek horizon through the biblical view of creation; but it did not know how to incorporate the kind of
nothingness that is death into its conception of God. Here we
can detect the influence of Greek philosophy and its inade-
quacies. Death was not pondered in itself, though it might be
viewed as the transition to another kind of existence (Plato) or
as the end of existence (Epicurus). These two conceptions
ignore the reality of death in itself. For this reason the death of

Jesus, in itself, could not be considered as God's mediation in early Christian theology. We had to wait for Hegel, though his conception of Good Friday is speculative rather than historical.

This point is of the utmost importance for any historical theology of liberation. We live in the presence of so much death. There is the reality of definitive, physical death and of the death that people experience in the toils of oppression, injustice, and sinfulness. Any consideration of God that ignores such a basic datum of life is idealistic, if not downright alienating. In Europe the theological horizon of understanding in recent years has centered around the "death of God." We shall see what that means a bit further on. In Latin America the concrete mediation of the "death of God" has been the "death of the other human being"—that is, the death of the peasant, the native Indian, and so forth (E. Dussel).

When we say that the oppressed human being is the mediation of God, we must get to the heart of that statement and analyze the exact nature of that mediation. It is a complicated task, needless to say, and here I simply want to bring out one point. Why does the "oppressed' person serve as the mediation of God? Is it not because in that person we find expressed what Hegel called "the monstrous power of the negative"? It is quite correct to view God as the *power* over the negative, as its *contradiction*. But such a view remains too abstract if we do not go on to ask how and in what sense God is the power over injustice, oppression, and death. Is it from outside history or from within history?

In this respect liberation theology must get beyond Greek thought. It must ask itself in what sense suffering and death can be a mode of being for God. Bound up with this difficulty in Greek thought is its conception of perfection. That conception, as we have already seen, associates perfection with immutability. Something that is perfect is also eternal and ahistorical. Those traits must therefore be of the very essence of the deity. Suffering implies some form of passivity and mutability, hence it must be alien to God. Greek thought cannot picture suffering as a divine mode of being because that would imply a contradiction.

People in Latin America, however, seem to feel almost automatically what Dietrich Bonhoeffer expressed in intuitive, poetic terms: "Only a God who suffers can save us." Paradoxical as the statement might seem, we should not relegate it to the realm of pious thinking or rhetoric. It must be analyzed carefully because the very essence of the Christian God is at stake. For Aristotle, God is the thinking process which thinks about itself, but which is apathetic with respect to history. For Saint John, God is love. Is that statement real? Is it supposed to be comprehensible in historical terms, not just in essentialist terms? Is it something more than a mere analogy, whereby we take the basic notion of love and then apply it to God in eminent terms? If our answer to those questions is yes, then we must ask ourselves how God can express that love, his ultimate word to human beings, in a world of misery without himself being affected by that misery.

The problem in talking about God as love is that we must not trivialize this ultimate statement of revelation. So we must insist that love has to be *credible* to human beings in an unredeemed world. That forces us to ask ourselves whether God can really describe himself as love if historical suffering does not affect him. It is not at all self-evident to human beings that suffering because of love is an imperfection, since in our world love passes through suffering. If we are going to talk about God in our own language, and that is the only meaningful language for us, then we must say what Moltmann says: "We find suffering that is not wished, suffering that is accepted, and the suffering of love. If God were incapable of suffering in all those ways, and hence in an absolute sense, then God would also be incapable of loving. If love is the acceptance of another without taking thought for one's own well-being, then it contains within itself the capacity for compassion and the freedom to suffer the otherness of the other. An inability to suffer would contradict the basic Christian assertion that God is love."[2]

As I see it, a theology of historical liberation should not restrict its consideration of God to the programmatic moment or aspect of hope and liberation as they appear in God's work of resurrecting Jesus. It must go deeper and explore the credibility of the one who proclaims that liberation. In the eyes of human beings this credibility is bound up with the change that is part of any perceptible love. Hence we must get beyond the older view of God's immutability and apathy and move closer to the concrete reality of history. We must consider the possible revelation of God in the cross of Jesus.

Thesis 5: Greek epistemology, which was based on analogy and wonder, makes it impossible for us to recognize God in the cross of Jesus. Liberation theology must add further principles here. To the principle of analogy it must add the principle of dialectics; to the principle of wonder it must add the notion of suffering as a font of knowledge leading us to the concrete practice of transforming love.

Alongside the metaphysical considerations treated above we find certain epistemological considerations that have made it impossible for us to give Jesus' cross its full revelatory character. Greek thought is analogical. Prescinding from the various shadings of that analogical approach in the different schools of Greek thought, we can say that the basic underlying principle is that like is known by like (Plato), and hence all cognition is at bottom re-cognition. Something new and unknown can be grasped and understood on the basis of what is already known. The basic theological implication of this view is that the reality of God is to be recognized through what is positive in his creatures: their beauty, order, intelligence, power, and so forth.

Now if that is the case, then obviously the cross cannot reveal anything about God. We cannot recognize anything in it that we readily associate with the deity. In it we do not find any beauty, order, intelligence, or power. Hence liberation theology must complement the principle of analogical knowledge with the principle of dialectical knowledge: i.e., knowing something means knowing it through its contrary. If God really is present in the cross of Jesus, then he is there first and foremost as someone contradicting the world and all that we consider to be true and good. God appears on the cross *sub specie contrarii.* It is not at all self-evident that there can be life in death, power in impotence, and presence in abandonment. For the Greek that is nonsense; for the Christian it is a necessity. The very first consequence of Jesus' cross for Christians is a complete break with their customary epistemology. The cross shatters the self-interest that motivates us to gain knowledge of the deity. The cross breaks the inertia of analogical thinking and transforms it into dialectical thinking.

On the other hand it is certainly true that knowledge would also be impossible without some kind of analogy. Greek thought assumes that analogy is possible because some correlation exists between the object to be known and the knowing subject, that correlation is grasped in the sense of *wonder* (Aristotle). There is something in things that triggers the process of cognition, that leads people to search for the correspondence between what is known already and something new. This knowledge produces joy and pleasure. Here, however, we must ask ourselves what joyful "wonder" might mean in the face of Jesus' cross, in a situation where there is little place for joy or wonder. As I see it, the wonder involved in the process of grasping the truth of the cross is a highly qualified sort of wonder. Specifically, it is sorrow. The cognitive attitude that allows for some sort of authentic analogy between the believer and Jesus' cross is that of sorrow in the presence of historical crosses. Here we get a sym-pathy and a con-natural knowledge that enables us to grasp some sort of divine presence on the cross of Jesus and in the overall suffering of the oppressed. "Suffering precedes thought," says Feuerbach; and Moltmann points out that human beings, who can only feel attracted by something that captures their interest, find their interest attracted only when they have the painful experience of reality as something distinct from and alien to themselves. The passion of their thinking is rooted in the feeling of pain and sorrow.[3] Only in the concrete form of sorrow can wonder help us to grasp what happened on the cross; only in that form can it turn our theological discourse on the cross into something real rather than something illusory or demagogic.

Moreover, by its very nature and structure sorrow, as the wellspring of knowledge, has its own distinctive and peculiar dynamism. Sorrow wells up in the presence of the evil embodied in oppression and injustice. When faced with this negative reality, however, sorrow cannot rest content with contemplation; it must issue into some sort of action. Sorrow must be active, and so knowledge tends to be transformed into *agape*. It is transformed into a love that not only re-creates itself with what is like itself (Aristotle) but also re-creates what is unlike itself by transforming it. Who can comprehend the aspect of divine revelation in the cross of Christ? The person who feels sorrow in the face of another's misery and who tries to overcome it by bridging the distance between self and the other's misery. Here we have the only authentic kind of analogy for recognizing God in the cross. Mere cognitive analogy and wonder will not suffice. They are not ample enough to allow us to comprehend the cross of Jesus and to lay hold of the God who may very well be present precisely in Jesus' abandonment.

Let me briefly summarize what we have discussed in this section. After Jesus' resurrection we find Christian faith initiating a theological movement in which it formulated certain basic assertions. Its most basic assertion was that the man Jesus of Nazareth, who died a failure on the cross and abandoned by God, is really and truly the Son of God. Gradually, however, emphasis came to be placed on the latter part of that statement: Jesus is *the Son of God*. Christology was increasingly elaborated in terms of the positive elements to be found in the resurrection of Jesus, so that Jesus was pictured predominantly as the Lord wielding power. In the New Testament we do find some theologians trying to maintain a proper balance by upholding the first part of the basic assertion. Yet the scandal of the cross tended to be forgotten as that datum was integrated into various soteriological schemes. Thus a fundamental Christian statement came to be ignored: i.e., that God himself, the Father, was on the cross of Jesus.

This whole trend was accentuated when Christian theology was framed in the categories of Greek thought. Neither metaphysically nor epistemologically was Greek thought prepared to ponder or believe in a crucified God. So Christian faith was gradually losing its own original character and substance, though its statements about the Trinity and the incarnation of the Logos did really distinguish it from the other religions in its environment. Those statements are certainly true. But in view of Jesus' death on the cross, they do not adequately spell out the radical novelty of the new faith in Jesus and in Jesus' God.

The ultimate outcome, which we shall explore further on, is that a particular understanding of Christian existence derived quite logically from a particular conception of God. Overlooking the death of Jesus as one abandoned by God may or actually did lead people to stop looking for God where he really is. And where is he? In the Christian view his locus is not only the resurrection but also the cross of Jesus. In historical terms God is to be found in the crosses of the oppressed rather than in beauty, power, or wisdom. As Miranda notes, it is not a matter of looking for God or not looking for him, but rather of looking for him where he himself says that he is.

In the next two sections I shall be looking for a theological standpoint that will permit Jesus' death on the cross to recover the importance it should have for both the Christian theory of God and the proper understanding of Christian existence. In this quest we shall try not to forget that the cross can be eviscerated at the very point where Christian faith makes its supreme assertion about Jesus: i.e., that Jesus is the Son of God, most obviously after the resurrection.

JESUS' CROSS AS THE HISTORICAL CONSEQUENCE OF HIS LIFE

Thesis 6: Our theology of the cross must be historical. Rather than viewing the cross as some arbitrary design on God's part, we must see it as the outcome of God's primordial option: the incarna-

tion. The cross is the outcome of an incarnation situated in a world of sin that is revealed to be a power working against the God of Jesus.

One initial way to recover the original meaning of Jesus' cross is to see it as the historical consequence of his life. Jesus was not exactly a prophet, but he was a prophet among other things and was crucified for that reason. If we want to appreciate the import of positioning the cross in history as we are doing here, then we must first consider what we mean when we talk about God's "design" or "plan." It can be understood in completely ahistorical terms, as was the case in Anselm's theory of satisfaction. Such an approach would suggest that God arbitrarily chose one event in Jesus' life to carry out the work of redemption. God's "plan," then, would come down to manipulating history in order to get to the one and only thing that interests him: Jesus' crucifixion as a work of redemption. As I see it, however, God's "plan" can and should be understood in terms of the real, authentic incarnation of God. If God did become incarnate in history and accepted its mechanisms, ambiguities, and contradictions, then the cross reveals God not just in himself but in conjunction with the historical path that leads Jesus to the cross.

At bottom the issue at stake here is our conception of God's revelation. Is God revealed only at key highpoints in Jesus' life such as his baptism, his transfiguration, his crucifixion, and his resurrection? Or does the revelation of God take place all along in the revelation of the Son, in the process whereby Jesus *becomes the Son* through his concrete history?

This latter view presupposes a certain conception of incarnation as well. Following Chalcedon, tradition has maintained that the Logos assumed a human *nature.* Here we do have a fundamental statement: i.e., that Jesus was truly human. At the same time, however, it is much too abstract. To be a human being is to be a historical being and, more concretely, to find oneself immersed in a given situation. Jesus is a human being insofar as he finds himself in a particular situation and responds to it. Hence an analysis of that situation is basic to any understanding of his humanness.

What characterizes and structures Jesus' situation? On the one hand there is the hope that prompts him to proclaim the coming of the kingdom; and there is also the eschatological expectations of his listeners. On the other hand, however, there is the existence of sin. Jesus' situation is dominated by sin, so that his concrete life is meaningful only insofar as he confronts and reacts against that sin. This means that sin is not just something inside a person. It cannot be described adequately if we simply see it as an interior offense against God. Sin has an external embodiment that gives shape and structure to the overall situation. Sin is sin against God insofar as it is sin against the reign or kingdom of God.

The situation presents itself concretely to Jesus as a structure laden with contradiction, and Jesus involves himself in it. Further on we shall consider the concrete contradiction that actually brings Jesus to the cross. Here we simply want to characterize it in theological terms. The contradiction in which Jesus' life is situated and by which it is affected is not merely biographical. It is not just that the person of Jesus made a bad impression on those in power. The contradiction is structured as a theological one. Through his basic outlook, his preaching, and his denunciation, Jesus was raising the question of the authentic reality of God. He did not inject the question on his own from outside, however. It arose from the contradictory character of the situation in which he lived.

Jesus' accusation against those in power is that they are manipulating the true God in the name of a false deity; and that manipulation takes the concrete form of power and its use. Those with religious and political power try to cover the sinfulness of the situation in the name of the deity. Jesus is faced with a contradictory situation, which ultimately comes down to a choice between two deities: either a God wielding oppressive power or a God offering and effecting liberation. Framed in this context of a basic theological conflict, Jesus' trajectory to the cross is no accident. He himself provokes it by presenting the basic option between two deities. His course is also a trial of the deity, with Jesus appearing as a witness on one side and those in power as witnesses on the other side.

Now before going on to a concrete analysis of Jesus' conflict, I want to make two assertions. First, the cross is not simply *the end of any biographical career;* it is the end of the career of Jesus, who seeks to be a faithful witness to God in a world of contradiction. Second, this career is simultaneously *a trial* of God himself. For that reason Jesus' cross cannot be understood on the basis of some notion of God already held. The path to the cross is nothing else but a questioning search for the true God and for the true essence of power. Is power meant to oppress people or to liberate them?

Thesis 7: Jesus is condemned to death for blasphemy. Jesus' journey to the cross is a trial concerned with the true reality of God. Is God the God of religion, in whose name one can subdue human beings? Or is he the God whom Jesus proclaims in the good news about human liberation? The cross leaves open the whole question of the authentic essence of the deity.

Jesus was condemned to death for blasphemy. According to Mark's Gospel, at the end of his interrogation the high priest declares solemnly: "What further need do we have of witnesses? You have heard the blasphemy. What is your verdict?" And "they all concurred in the verdict 'guilty,' with its sentence of death" (Mark 14:63–64). Jesus was judged by the legitimate defenders of his people's religion and condemned to death for blasphemy. This passage is important, not because it enables us to see whether the condemnation was correct in the light of the theology and laws of the day, but because it enables us to see the historical causes that led to Jesus' condemnation.

Jesus was a nonconformist and a liberal insofar as Jewish religious law was concerned. On the one hand he preached a demanding ethical rigorism and called for total detachment from everything commonly regarded as good. His followers were to give up their families, possessions, and many other things. On the other hand Jesus relativized the demands of the Jewish law. The important thing to note here is that it was his particular conception of God that underlay his ongoing conflict with the Jewish religious authorities.

It is in Mark 2:23–28 that we find the classic formulation of Jesus' opposition to mere ritual and to a conception of God that does not liberate. The Pharisees are scandalized that his disciples would pick grain stalks on the Sabbath. Jesus replies: "The Sabbath was made for man, not man for the Sabbath" (v. 27). Even more important than the fact of his conflict with the Pharisees is his frontal assault on the mechanisms they use to manipulate God to their own ends. He criticizes them for injecting human interpretations of the law into the law of God (Mark 7:1–8); under the guise of religion they have found cute alibis for ignoring real religion. Jesus then goes on to criticize their conception of religious ethics: "Hear me, all of you, and try to understand. Nothing that enters a man from outside can make him impure; that which comes out of him, and only that, constitutes impurity" (Mark 7:14–15). Here Jesus breaks with the view that would force people into external ethical schemes based on already established laws. *Everything* outside the person—not just that which is defined by law—becomes an object of morality only insofar as it is interiorized by the person. The implications of Jesus' view are brought out by Käsemann: "In questioning the notion that impurity enters man from the outside, a person is attacking the underlying suppositions of Antiquity's whole cultic practice with its expiatory victims. In other words, one is eliminating the basic difference espoused by Antiquity between *temenos* ('the sacred sphere') and the profane realm."[4]

These arguments about the true essence of religion take on a concrete and graphic tinge in his dealings with the Pharisees as official representatives of Jewish religion. Here Jesus appears in a prophetic role, as someone from the outside who fights them in God's name. The Pharisees are "blind leaders of the blind" (Matt. 15:14). The lawyers are oppressors who "lay impossible burdens on men" (Luke 11:46). The Pharisees use the cloak of religion to justify avoiding duties to which they are bound by justice (Mark 7:11f.). In the parable of the Good Samaritan Jesus levels fierce criticism at the alienation to which the priest and the levite have fallen prey. Faced with the dire need of a beaten and wounded human being, those who were most bound in duty to observe the law of charity "went on" (Luke 10:32).

Jesus did not elaborate a philosophy of religion, nor did he speculate on the potentially alienating role of religion as a structure. He practiced his religion as an orthodox Jew, but he condemned the de facto situation of religion in his words, his actions, and his own attitudes. With his conception of God, then, Jesus was a liberal on religious matters and that led him to the cross. His historical attitude toward religion and its representatives must be understood in the light of his conception of God. At bottom he sought to unmask a way of manipulating the "mystery of God" that served to oppress human beings and to justify such oppression. Some people assumed that ritual and cult were automatically justified because they expressed due reverence to God; Jesus felt that they, too, had certain limits. As Käsemann puts it: "The will of God is not mysterious, at least insofar as it concerns one's fellow man and love. Any Creator who can be set in opposition to his creature is a false God, and false gods can turn even the pious into inhuman people."[5]

Here, I think, we come to the crux of the matter. In the last analysis Jesus is hostile to the religious leaders of his day and is eventually condemned because of his conception of God. More concretely, the issue at stake is the way we find access to the true God. In religion as it actually presented itself to his eyes Jesus saw a scheme whereby people responded to God through the fulfillment of certain obligations. God was pictured as distinct from human beings and greater than them, but he also stood in some sort of continuity with them. In philosophical terms the continuity lay in the fact that God explained the world; in religious terms the continuity lay in the fact that God stood surety for the established order. Insofar as access to God was concerned, there were privileged locales for it: the temple and cultic worship. Jesus noted that human beings were only too happy to accept such a scheme and enter into it. Despite its demands and obligations, it offered some ultimate feeling of security; it could also be manipulated in such a way that one need not heed the pleas of the oppressed. Such a religous scheme offers immunization against the deity since it clearly defines and circumscribes God's demands. It also leaves room for casuistry designed to justify oppressive situations.

By immersing himself in this situation, Jesus *necessarily* introduced conflict into the heart of his life. If incarnation means accepting and then reacting to a given situation, then Jesus' polemics with the religious authorities were not just a didactic exercise; they flowed naturally from the inner dynamism of the incarnation. Jesus presented people with a God who stands in complete contradiction to the existing religous situation. His God is distinct from, and greater than, the God of the Pharisees. On the horizontal level Jesus expands the locale of our access to God enormously, no longer maintaining the temple as the privileged place of such access. In Jesus' eyes the privileged locale of access to God is people themselves. More specifically, it is the person who is poor, who has been forced into impoverishment.

There can be no doubt about that particular point insofar as Jesus' own preaching and action are concerned. Access to God is to be found in making contact with the very people that the religious mentality of the Jews saw as completely estranged from God: the alien, the heretic, the ritually impure person, the sinner, the disinherited, the poor, the orphan, the widow, and the enemy. They are not simply the "passive material" on which one works to attain access to God through virtuous dealings with them. They are the authentic medium through which one draws near to God, as the parables of the Good Samaritan and the Last Judgment make clear (Luke 10:25–37 and Matt. 25:31–46). Jesus unmasks the folly of those whose notion of approaching God flows from some preconceived idea of God as someone already known. It is wrong to assume that we get closer to the numinous mystery of the deity by concentrating on beautiful or solemn realities. The mystery of God is accessible only to those who draw near to the poor.

The greater God proclaimed by Jesus is also described in terms of the vertical dimension. The reign of God draws near as a grace, not as a matter of justice related to people's good works. Here we find something completely new in Jesus' preaching. It has no parallel in the preaching of John the Baptist, in rabbinic tradition, or in the prophetic and apocalyptic tradition outside Jesus. Paradoxically enough, it is this teaching of God's kingdom as grace that proves to be the major obstacle for accepting Jesus. Jesus unmasks the effort of "religious" people to ensure themselves against God. If God's approach is an act of grace, then no human disposition can force his coming. God does not aim primarily to recompense people according to their works but rather to re-create the situation of every human being. It is a wholly gratuitous action, and the "religious" person feels insecure in the face of such a God. It is those who are legally "just" that cannot accept a "greater" God, a God of surprises; it is sinners and non-religious people who are willing to put their hope in such a God.

Jesus' polemical discussions with the Pharisees can be understood only against that backdrop. It is the radical difference in their two viewpoints that explains the tragic end of Jesus. It is not a question of analyzing whether the final verdict of the Sanhedrin was juridically correct or not. Instead we must grasp the deeply contradictory nature of the situation in which Jesus found himself. If Jesus remains faithful to his incarnation, if he does not try to evade the situation in which he finds himself, then his proclamation of God will necessarily give rise to much conflict; and in the end it will lead him to the cross.

To say that Jesus died according to God's design is, in my opinion, to say much too little. We do much better to say that Jesus died because he chose to bear faithful witness to God right to the end in a situation where people really wanted a very different type of God. Their condemnation of Jesus indicates that they clearly saw the option he was posing to them. They would have to choose between the God of their religion and the God of Jesus, between the temple and human beings, between the security provided by their own good works and the insecurity of God's gratuitous coming in grace.

Jesus' cross is no accident. It flows directly from the self-justifying efforts of the "religious" person who tries to manipulate God rather than letting God remain a mystery. As Käsemann puts it, "The cross would be incomprehensible and inexplicable if it were not for the cooperation of the pious Jews."[6]

But if we view the matter in that light, then we are faced with another unanswered question prompted by the cross itself: Who is God exactly? What God really triumphed in Jesus' cross? Either the cross is the end of "religion" or it is the end of the kingdom of God as Jesus understood it. Either it is the end of people's subjugation by other human beings in the name of religion or it is the triumph of Moloch and his demand for human victims. Paradoxical as it may seem, it was "religion" that killed the Son. So we are left with the question as to why the Father allowed his death. Is it possible that he accepted Jesus' death on the cross so that he might overcome the old religious schema once and for all, so that he might show that he is a completely different sort of God who serves as the basis for a completely new kind of human existence?

Thesis 8: Jesus was condemned as a political agitator. Jesus' journey to the cross is a process that raises questions about the kind of power that truly mediates God. Is it the kind of power advocated by the Roman Empire and the Zealots, or is it the kind of power exemplified by Jesus? Jesus' power is that of love immersed in a concrete situation, hence it is a "political" rather than an idealistic love. The whole question of the true nature of power becomes acute when one views it in terms of Jesus' cross.

As we know, Jesus preached the coming of God's reign rather than simply preaching God. In the Old Testament, this reign of God involves two forms of reconciliation: personal reconciliation with God and social reconciliation between human beings. People longed for the day when swords would be turned into plowshares (Isa. 2:4), when wild and tame animals would lie down together (Isa. 11:6), and when tears would disappear from the face of the earth (Isa. 25:8). During his lifetime Jesus performed deeds signifying this new reality of reconciliation. But since his proclamation of the kingdom was not idealistic, it was accompanied by denunciations of the social organization existing in his own day. At the very least he denounced societal life as it was structured in the Palestine of his day.

In Jewish tradition the "reign" of God had to mean one of two things. Either it would be a theocratic political order or, at the very least, it would involve some form of social organization that would necessarily take society and politics into account. One cannot assume a priori that there is no relationship between the kingdom of God and the political realm, for at the very least both have something to do with structuring the way human beings live together. The only real point of conflict, and the one that came to the fore in Jesus' case, was the use of power. What kind of power should be used to organize a society in accordance with God's wishes?

Jesus did look for the imminent arrival of God's kingdom (Mark 9:1; 13,30; Matt. 10:23), but it is worth noting that he was not indifferent to the organization of society in the brief interval remaining. If we try to explain Jesus' view of the kingdom in purely individualistic terms, then we are not doing justice to the overall data of the New Testament. Jesus was not a priest in the strictly juridical sense, yet his activity touched directly on the religious sphere because he had a specific conception of God. The same holds true for the socio-political sphere. Jesus was not a professional politician, but his conception of God's kingdom inevitably involved him in the socio-political realm. Jesus condemned oppression, both the oppression advocated in the name of religion and the oppression advocated in the name of the existing socio-political order; but he did not speculate on the essence or nature of the two.

It is historically certain that Jesus did situate himself in the political situation of his day and react against it in a definitive way. Why? Because he suffered the punishment imposed on political agitators (crucifixion) rather than the punishment dealt out to religious blasphemers (stoning). The inscription on his cross alludes clearly to the reason for his condemnation: "Jesus of Nazareth, king of the Jews."

Bultmann claims that it is very difficult to see his death as a necessary, intrinsic consequence of his activity. His death, says Bultmann, was the result of a misunderstanding; people misconstrued his activity as being political. Jesus' cross was a lamentable error on Pilate's part, and nothing more. We must question Bultmann's view here on both the historical and the theological level. Let us see whether Jesus' death was due to a misunderstanding or not.

There are now many works dealing with the political activity of Jesus in terms of his historical situation. Here I shall simply summarize some of the more solidly based exegetical conclusions. It is historically certain that Jesus lived his life during a highly politicized period of Palestinian history. His own prophetic activity in opposition to all forms of oppression is also quite clear. His anathemas against groups are particularly noteworthy. Jesus does not attack individual egotism as much as he attacks the collective manifestations of egotism that create an atmosphere wholly hostile to the kingdom of God (Luke 6:24f.). He hurls anathemas at the Pharisees for disregarding justice (Matt. 23:23), at the lawyers for imposing intolerable burdens (Matt. 23:4), at the learned for stealing the keys to knowledge (Luke 11:52), and at the rulers of this world for governing despotically (Matt. 20:26).

In the Gospels we do not find Jesus' relationship with the political realm treated explicitly. They deal more explicitly with his relationship to the religious realm and the social realm. One reason might be that when the Gospels were being written, Christians still did not have a clear understanding of the overall nature of Jesus' mission (Acts 5:37; 21:38).

A comparison with the Zealot movement may give us some idea of Jesus' position vis-à-vis the political realm. It is interesting to note that in the Gospels the Zealots are not rebuked as harshly as other social groups such as the Sadducees, the

Scribes, and the Pharisees. The silence of the Gospels in their regard is significant. Jesus shared some of the basic views and outlooks of the Zealots. Both saw their mission as the establishment of the kingdom of God, and they claimed its establishment was imminent. Both demanded unconditional commitment to their cause. Jesus told his followers to take up their cross and follow him, and the Zealots had numerous martyrs also. Both regarded the publicans as sinners for collaborating with the Roman forces of occupation. Some of Jesus' disciples were Zealots: certainly Simon the Zealot (Luke 6:15), probably Judas Iscariot, and perhaps even Peter. Some of Jesus' actions were in the spirit of the Zealots. His expulsion of the merchants from the temple took place after his Galilean crisis according to the Synoptic Gospels, and hence close to his own final end. He entered Jerusalem as a crowd acclaimed him with titles alluding to a political Messiah (Mark 11:1–10). In Luke 13:1 Jesus is warned that Pilate has executed several Galileans, the warning obviously meant to put him on guard for his own safety. Jesus criticizes Herod in the Zealot vein (Luke 13:31f.) and talks ironically about rulers who oppress their subjects (Mark 10:42f.). He bids his followers to trade in their cloaks for swords (Luke 22:36), and that is precisely what they have with them in the garden of Gethsemane (Luke 22:49).

On the other side of the coin we must note that Jesus also admits a publican into the ranks of his disciples (Mark 2:13f.). He eats with publicans (Mark 2:15f.) as an eschatological sign of the arrival of the kingdom. He also condemns the use of the sword (Matt. 26:52). Finally, when faced with the issue of paying taxes to the Romans, Jesus does not come out clearly against tax-paying as the Zealots did (Mark 1:13–17).

This brief historical overview leads us to certain conclusions. We may assume that Jesus did not belong to the Zealot party and that he did not advocate a strictly Zealot line of conduct. On the other hand the Zealot movement is one of the keys for understanding both his life and his death. As Oscar Cullmann puts it: "Jesus' whole ministry was in continuous contact with Zealotism. . . . This formed the background, so to speak, of his activity and . . . he was executed as a Zealot."[7]

Jesus does not disagree basically with the Zealots on the idea that there must be some historical and socio-political mediation of the kingdom of God. That is why he could be, and in fact was, identified as a Zealot. But Jesus was not a Zealot because his conception of God was very different from theirs. What history tells us is not that Jesus was apolitical but that he offered a new alternative to Zealotism. Yet his alternative also had political implications and repercussions. Jesus' crucifixion was not due to a misunderstanding because he was undermining the very foundations of the political view held by the Roman Empire and the rulers in society. Historically speaking, then, we can say that Jesus' death was occasioned by his work on behalf of God's kingdom, which symbolized a particular form of societal life for human beings.

These historical observations must be pushed further with more strictly theological reflections. Jesus did not calculate that the kingdom would come in accordance with some neat scheme or law, as other groups did. The rabbis urged asceticism and fulfillment of the law, advocates of apocalypticism urged close attention to the signs of the times, and the Zealots favored armed insurrection. According to Jesus, however, God's coming was an act of grace. He did not espouse religious nationalism or political theocratism. The basic temptation facing him and others was the temptation to establish God's kingdom through the use of political power. The only true power in Jesus' eyes was the power embodied in truth and love. That is why he broke down the old dichotomy between friend and enemy, calling for pardon and love of enemy rather than vengeance.

His theological critique of the Roman Empire was much more radical. Jesus thoroughly desacralized the concept of power. The power of the Roman Empire and its organized realm, which had turned the Mediterranean into a Roman lake and produced the *pax romana,* was not divine. The emperor, who stood as the visible embodiment of that power, was not God.

It is here that we confront the real issue: What sort of power is it that really and truly renders the deity present? Human beings automatically think of God as someone who possesses and wields power. Jesus forces people to consider whether that deeply rooted conviction is true or not. In historical terms it is readily apparent that power, left to its own inertial tendencies, tends to be oppressive in fact. So it cannot be the ultimate mediation of God, though human beings might tend to think so.

Over against the notion of God as power Jesus sets the notion of God as love. It does not mean that love is apolitical. By the very fact that love is situated in an unredeemed world, it can unfold and develop only by confronting the oppressive weight of power. Jesus' love, then, is not idealistic or Docetist. Jesus' universal love is "political" in that it seeks to be real and effective in a given concrete situation. That is why Jesus' *universal* love takes different concrete forms, depending on the situation. He manifests his love for the oppressed by being *with* them, by offering them something that might restore their dignity and make them truly human. He manifests his love for the oppressors by being *against* them, by trying to strip away all that is making them less than human. In short, Jesus' love is political because it is situated in the concrete. It is proclamation and hope, denunciation and anathema. And that conception of political love led him perforce to the cross.

So now we see that the cross of Jesus cannot be properly understood and appreciated unless we view it in terms of Jesus' whole life. His life is a journey that leads to the cross, a journey that also raises basic questions about the authentic nature of God and of power as the mediation of God. Jesus proclaims that God is love, and that the only authentic use of power is by way of truth and love. The cross is not the result of some divine decision independent of history; it is the outcome of the basic option for incarnation in a given situation. That entails conflict because sin holds power in history and takes the triumphant form of religious and political oppression. Jesus had to choose between evading all that or facing up to it squarely. He chose the latter course, challenging the idolatrous use of power to oppress people and the idolatrous conception of God that justified such use. Power that subjugates human beings has nothing to do with the true God.

Now if we consider Jesus' path to the cross in these terms, we are faced with a pointed question: Doesn't the cross prove that any conception of God as incarnate love is totally illusory? Doesn't the cross represent the triumph of the other kind of power? Is God's love impotent in the face of evil in history? These are important questions that we shall consider in the next section of this chapter. Here I want to draw one more conclusion from what we have already said insofar as Christian spirituality is concerned.

Thesis 9: The cross is the outcome of Jesus' historical path; hence Christian spirituality cannot be reduced to a mystique of the cross. Christian spirituality must consist in following the path of Jesus.

If the cross is the consequence of a fundamental attitude on Jesus' part, then Christian spirituality of the cross cannot simply concentrate on the doleful aspects of human existence. Spirituality based on the cross does not mean merely the acceptance of sadness, pain, and sorrow; it does not mean simply passivity and resignation. Of course the crucified Jesus can also give us inspiration when we face trials in life, but that is not what characterizes Christian spirituality as such. Incarnation situated in a concrete context comes before the cross. Hence Christian spirituality must entail imitating the attitude Jesus had when he incarnated himself in a concrete situation. That means we must take a stand vis-à-vis the sinfulness that gives configuration to a given situation. Christians must take a stand in the face of power and be willing to de-idolize it when it tries to pass itself off as God. It is only in that way that our positive proclamation of the good news and its insistence on the primacy of love can be concrete and effective rather than merely idealistic.

The cross is the most peculiar and distinctive feature of Christian faith, but Christian spirituality is not formally a spirituality of suffering; rather, it is a spirituality focused on the following of Jesus. Not all suffering is specifically Christian; only that which flows from the following of Jesus is. The latter is what Jesus demands of his followers after the Galilean crisis (Mark 8:34). Realizing that his proclamation of the good news and his signs have not sufficed to bring the kingdom in, and that he has only been brought into ever deeper conflict with those in authority, Jesus accepts the full situational implications of his course and does not speak to his followers in idealistic terms. If they are going to be his disciples, they must follow him to the cross. His summons to discipleship is now "situated" in the concrete context, with all the consequences entailed.

The value of political theology can be seen more clearly in terms of what has just been said. Its worth lies in the fact that it seeks to give expression to a truly "situated" spirituality. Its direct intention is to proclaim and live out the good news of love, but it fully realizes that love must be "situated." To say that political theology embodies a spirituality of discipleship is to say that all proclamation of the good news must be fully aware of the sinfulness that is in fact oppressing and suppressing our proclamation and effective realization of the good news. Political theology is also a real *theo-logy* because it is the political realm that serves as the medium for discerning the true nature of the deity. Taken in the broadest sense here, the political realm is the realm where power unfolds its workings. Hence every political conception presupposes some theology, and it would be interesting to study the substitutes for theology that are used in atheistic governments. Insofar as it is *theo-logy*, then, political theology seeks to clarify the essence of power and to unmask all forms of power that seek to pass themselves off as God.

We are not using a mere shibboleth when we say that "political theology is a theology of the cross." The point of that assertion is that the meaning of any authentic *theo*-logy cannot be dissociated from the final end of Jesus' own path. It is in the light of the cross that we learn how to raise questions about God in the right way and what approach we should follow to make sure that our questioning is truly meaningful rather than abstract. The spirituality of the cross is a spirituality of "situating oneself," of following Jesus, and in this sense it is a political spirituality. A spirituality of the cross rules out any identification with the crucified one by way of intention alone, for that would be self-contradictory. Identification with the crucified must take place on the way of the cross. If it strays off that path, then the spirituality of the cross will turn into something else: e.g., stoicism, masochism or, worst of all, an excuse for not taking the way of the cross on the assumption that one is already doing so. As explained here, the cross is the *end* of a process. If we do not go through that process, then the cross to which we offer our acceptance may not be the Christian cross.

THE PRESENCE OF GOD ON JESUS' CROSS

We have now pictured Jesus' death as the historical consequence of the position he took in a concrete situation and lived through to the end. This conception of his death is an important step forward in trying to recover the original, pristine sense of the cross. But we do not get to the deepest core of the cross and its meaning if we do not proceed to theological consideration of it in the strictest sense. We must probe into the reality of God on the basis of Jesus' cross, attempting to get beyond the Greek categories of thought and action mentioned earlier. Present-day theology has been exploring the insight that the future is God's mode of being (Pannenberg). What I propose to ponder here is suffering as a mode of being for God. This will give concrete reality to the most profound intuition of the New Testament concerning God: i.e., that God is love.

Thesis 10: What typifies the death of Jesus, and what differentiates it from the death of other religious and political martyrs, is that Jesus dies in complete rupture with his cause. Jesus feels abandoned by the very God whose approach in grace he had been preaching.

There have been many martyrs for religious and political reasons, both before and after Jesus' time. Their deaths, too, were the result of their stand vis-à-vis society. In many instances those martyrs died in a spirit of enthusiastic heroism, or with the quiet wisdom of Socrates, or with Stoical resignation.

Jesus, too, died as a prophet. But there was nothing beautiful about his death, nor was he just another martyr: "Jesus' death-cry was not an expression of pious surrender; it welled up from his feeling that he had been abandoned by God."[8] His death differed from that of other martyrs and prophets, for they died with the intention that their death should serve as their last act in defense of their cause. Thus their death often stood in *continuity* with their life and their cause. It had real meaning for them, and hence their psychic or physical suffering was secondary. By contrast Jesus dies in total *discontinuity* with his life and his cause. The death he experienced was not only the death of his person but also the death of his cause.

We discover the distinctive nature of Jesus' death by considering three elements: his message concerning the imminent approach of God, his cry on the cross, and his abandonment by the Father. Moltmann sums up the point:

Jesus preached God's approaching nearness in grace as no one ever had before in Israel. He preached it to those without God, to the violators of the law, the alienated, and the rejects of society. Someone who had lived and acted in that way, who was wholly conscious of the nearness of God, could not experience death on the cross as confirmation or as mere misfortune. He could only experience it as hellish abandonment by the very God whose loving nearness he had proclaimed. For the experience of being abandoned by God can only be rooted in the realization that God is not far away but near, that his action is grace rather than judgment.[9]

It is this discontinuity that characterizes the death of Jesus: He has a vivid expectation of God's coming on the one hand but experiences God's seeming absence on the cross. The discontinuity surfaces only when we take note of Jesus' peculiar and distinctive awareness of the one he calls "Father." Hence Jesus did not die like any other prophet might. Nor did he die solely because the religious and political authorities misunderstood him—or better, understood him only too well.

Nor can his death be considered solely as the consequence of the world's sinfulness, which God permitted for some unsuspected reasons.

Jesus died in theological abandonment, and the psychological texture of his death takes second place by comparison. The scandal of this death in theological abandonment is irretrievable even after the resurrection, for resurrection does not eliminate it. Instead the resurrection turns the cross into an ever open question about God. It is only when that question is left open, even after the resurrection, that we grasp the proper tension of the theory and practice of the Christian faith.

Theological consideration of Jesus' death prompts us to begin by reformulating all our conceptions of God. The first effect of the cross is to break down the self-interest that prompts us to ask questions about the deity and indirectly about his reality as a human being. As Moltmann puts it, there must be a revolution in our whole conception of God if we want to comprehend him in the crucified Jesus abandoned by God: "In the presence of Jesus' dying cry to God, theology either becomes impossible altogether or becomes possible only as a specifically Christian theology."[10]

Thesis 11: In Jesus' cross we find fulfilled the prohibition against fashioning human images of God and also the Christian eschatologization of God. God's transcendence is reformulated in the categories of power, suffering, and love.

The first thing to be reformulated on the basis of Jesus' cross is our conception of God's transcendence. In the Old Testament we find two basic ways of expressing that transcendence, both of them operational and practical rather than metaphysical. First, there is the prohibition against fashioning images of God (Deut. 5:8). Second, there is the formulated belief that the authentic reality of God will only show up at the end of history, thanks to some definitive action on God's part (Isa. 65:17). This belief in some total renovation of history implies that present reality is not capable of revealing God fully, that an unredeemed world cannot bear God's holiness.

The prohibition against images of God seeks to safeguard the authentic transcendence of God—not so much his inaccessibility as the fact that he cannot be manipulated. It is not that God is transcendent and unable to be manipulated because he is remote, but rather that his unmanipulability appears in his summons to the human conscience and in his insistence on justice as the ultimate human value (Miranda).

Much the same holds true for the eschatological aspect. To situate the ultimate revelation of God at the end of history is not simply to replace a spatial notion of divine transcendence with a temporal one. Rather, it dissociates Yahweh from every conception of God that grounds and justifies the present order of things (Pannenberg). Yahweh is the God of the future, not the God of beginnings in the distant past. It is the new creation that gives meaning to the old, not vice-versa. *Re*-ligion (looking to the past) becomes *pro*-ligion (looking to the future).

Both of these Old Testament perspectives are retained in the New Testament. Even after Jesus' appearance there is no intuitive image of God: "No one has ever seen God" (John 1:18). Paul realizes that God will be "all in all" only at the end (1 Cor. 15:28). However, the New Testament cross gives concrete shadings to the biblical way of expressing God's transcendence, going far beyond the classic Old Testament perspectives. It radicalizes human intuition of God's transcendence in terms of three categories: power, suffering, and love. On the cross God does not seem to have any visage at all, or at least no visage that human beings might conceptualize. On the cross there is no image of God. The prohibition against fashioning images of God is realized in concrete action rather than in a mere commandment. On the cross there is no evidence of God's perfection, beauty, or power.

The cross also radicalizes the eschatological view of God and his transcendence. As the Old Testament saw it, God draws near in absolute, universal *sovereignty*. On the cross the relationship between God and power appears in very different terms. God is not simply the one who holds and wields power, as he was defined by various religions and philosophies. On the cross God does not show up as one who wields power over the negative from *outside;* rather, on the cross we see God submerged *within* the negative. The possibility of overcoming the negative is realized by submersion within the mechanisms and processes of the negative. The new relationship between God and history, between transcendence and immanence, is formulated in a definitive and totally unsuspected way.

Thesis 12: The cross calls into question all knowledge of God based on natural theology. Knowing God means abiding with God in the passion. The question of knowing God must be posed in terms of theodicy, in terms of our experience of evil in the world.

By "natural theology" I mean here every attempt to gain access to God on the basis of what is *positive* in existence —whether we view it as nature, history, or human subjectivity. As I pointed out earlier, all natural theology operates by way of analogy. On the cross, however, we find nothing similar to what is usually regarded as divine. If there is some knowledge of God to be found on the cross, then some other principle of knowledge must be operative because the deity appears totally unlike anything we know.

Now the dissimilarity evident on the cross does not simply come down to some sort of inadequateness or lack of correspondence between the deity and the knowing subject. There is actually a *contradiction* between the true God and the knowing subject who approaches the cross. The first thing that the cross reveals about God is human *hubris:* People fashion images of God that are in direct contradiction to the real God. As a mechanism for our approach to God, natural theology is nothing else but a way for us to justify ourselves in the face of the true God, to turn aside so that we need not confront the crucified God (Barth).

The cross criticizes every notion of our having some natural access to God. Bonhoeffer expressed the point succinctly in a few poetic lines. The real choice is not between theism and atheism but between two very different and irreconcilable ways of approaching God:

Men go to God when they are sore bestead,
Pray to him for succour, for his peace, for bread,
For mercy for them sick, sinning or dead:
All men do so, Christian and unbelieving.

Men go to God when he is sore bestead,
Find him poor and scorned, without shelter or bread,
Whelmed under weight of the wicked, the weak, the dead:
Christians stand by God in his hour of grieving.

("Christians and Unbelievers,"
Letters and Papers from Prison
[New York: Macmillan 1962], pp. 224–25).

This conception of God presupposes a kind of transcendence never contemplated or imagined by any philosophy. It is a transcendence based on the cross. It is the cross that forces us to reformulate the whole problem of God. God is to be recognized through what seems to be quite the opposite of divine: i.e., suffering. God on the cross explains nothing; he criticizes every proffered explanation.

The cross is not a response; it is a new form of questioning. It invites us to adopt a radically new attitude toward God. On the cross it is not so much people asking questions about God; rather, it is primarily people being called into question concerning themselves and their self-interest in trying to hold and defend a specific form of the deity. To use a classic text here by way of example, we might cite the beautiful words of Augustine. The natural person has a restless heart that will find rest only in God. However, it is not so much that our restless heart pushes us toward an encounter with God. Rather, it is the cross that makes our heart truly upset and restless; and the repose we find there will be very different from that which human beings regard as repose. Hence the cross renders all natural theology impossible, in the sense just described. Natural theology embodies our questioning search for God. The cross, rather than answering any such questions, prompts us to a very different sort of questioning.

The systematic importance of this point for any historical theology of liberation lies in the fact that the privileged mediation of God ever continues to be the real cross of the op-pressed, not nature or history as a totality. It is there that we find something totally other than a "natural" conception of God. Oppressed persons are the mediation of God because, first of all, they break down the normal self-interest with which human beings approach other human beings. Merely by being there, the oppressed call into question those who approach, challenging their "being human"; and this radical questioning of what it means to be a human being serves as the historical mediation of our questioning of what "being God" means. That is why those who do approach the oppressed get the real feeling that it is they who are being evangelized and converted rather than those to whom they seek to render service.

What we are saying here in the language of systematic theology is what comes across in the famous Gospel passage concerning the last judgment: Going to God means going to the poor. The surprise felt by human beings on hearing that the Son of Man was incarnated in the poor is the surprise we must feel to comprehend the divinity of God on the cross. Without such "surprise" there is no knowledge of God, there is only our manipulation of God. It is when that surprise is maintained, when service is rendered to the oppressed, that we "stand by God in his hour of grieving." The resultant knowledge of God is not "natural" but "con-natural"; it is knowledge born of shared communion with the sorrow and suffering of the other person.

Putting it in more traditional language, we would say that it is more a matter of theodicy (justifying God) than of theology (talking about God). All serious thinking about God develops out of a basic quandary. If "God" is the ultimate, and if in this world the "ultimate" synthesis and reconciliation is impossi-ble, then all serious thinking about God unfolds in the pres-ence of an ultimate quandary. Traditionally this quandary has been expressed in many different ways. Platonists tried to reconcile eternal Ideas and sense forms by appealing to the Idea of God, the Good, or the One. Hegel appealed to Abso-lute Spirit to reconcile history and the Absolute.

The cross of Jesus poses this quandary in a different and more radical way, so that human thinking about God may go to its ultimate depths. It is the quandary of theodicy which, in the face of the cross, becomes the problem of love's impotence vis-à-vis sin, of the impotence of good vis-à-vis evil. It is the quandary expressed in Horckheimer's wish that the murderer might not triumph over his victim. The whole question of God finds its ultimate concretion in the problem of suffering. The question rises out of the history of suffering in the world, but it finds its privileged moment on the cross: If the Son is innocent and yet is put to death, then who or what exactly is God?

Though it may not always be made explicitly clear, that is the ultimate context in which liberation theology is elaborated. Liberation theology concretizes theodicy. First, the meaning of history is called into question, not so much by natural catastrophes as by the catastrophes that human freedom unleashes when it organizes society in an oppressive way. Theodicy is thus *historicized*. Second, Latin American theology turns theodicy into anthropocity, into the question of justifying human beings rather than God, much as secularized Europe and North America did in the decade of the sixties. The question is not so much how we can find a benevolent God (Luther) as how we can find a benevolent human being (J. Robinson). Last, and most important, the possibility of justifying God is not to be found in speculating about some possible logical explanation that will reconcile God with suffering history. It is to be found in a new realization of Jesus' cross, so that we may see whether that will really give rise to a new resurrection. And with that consideration we come to the very heart of our reflections here.

Thesis 13: On the cross of Jesus God himself is crucified. The Father suffers the death of the Son and takes upon himself all the pain and suffering of history. In this ultimate solidarity with humanity he reveals himself as the God of love, who opens up a hope and a future through the most negative side of history. Thus Christian existence is nothing else but a process of participating in this same process whereby God loves the world and hence in the very life of God.

Paradoxical as it may seem, there is a real point to the notion of the "crucified God." Even after the resurrection of Jesus, it suggests, God's relationship to unredeemed history is not idealistic and external but truly incarnate; it is through the cross that the definition of God as love receives its ultimate concretion.

If a deity does not respond to the historicized problem of theodicy, then we can assume that it has discredited itself. There is only one possible response on God's part. God himself must be part of the whole process of protest rather than remaining aloof from it. So the question is: Do we find any theological experience where God himself is against God? The answer is yes: the cross. On the cross we find a process within God himself. The Father surrenders the Son, abandoning him to the power of sin. It is not people who first question God in the presence of human misery. It is God himself who questions God, to use language that is anthropomorphic of necessity. As Luther put it: "No one against God except God himself." This questioning of God takes the form of abandoning the Son to the inertia of a world that really ought to be called into question. God "bifurcates" himself on the cross, so that transcendence (the Father) is in conflict with history (the Son).

In God's abandonment of the Son, however, we find not only God's criticism of the world but also his ultimate solidarity with it. On the cross God's love for humanity is expressed in truly historical terms rather than in idealistic ones. Historical love presupposes activity, but it also presupposes passivity because it is love situated in a contradictory structure that makes its force and power felt. The passivity involved here is that of letting oneself be affected by all that is negative, by injustice and death. On the cross of Jesus God was present (2 Cor. 5:19f.) and at the same time absent (Mark 15:34). Absent to the Son, he was present for human beings. And this dialectics of presence and absence is the way to express in human language the fact that God is love. The cross is the contradiction of humanity, but it is grounded on an ultimate solidarity with it. In the Son's passion the Father suffers the pain of abandonment. In the Son's death, death affects God himself—not because God dies but because he suffers the death of the Son. Yet God suffers so that we might live, and that is the most complete expression of love. It is in Jesus' resurrection that God will reveal himself as a promise fulfilled, but it is on the cross that love is made credible. From the standpoint of the cross we can reformulate all the important problems of theology: Who is God? What are we? What is the meaning of history? What is salvation? -

The Christian belief in God as a Trinity takes on a new and dynamic meaning in the light of the cross. God is a trinitarian "process" on the way toward its ultimate fulfillment (1 Cor. 15:28), but it takes all history into itself. In this process God participates in, and lets himself be affected by, history through the Son; and history is taken into God in the Spirit. What is manifest on the cross is the internal structure of God himself. The eternal love between Father and Son is seen to be historically mediated in the presence of evil, and hence it takes the paradoxical form of abandonment; but from this trinitarian love, now historicized, there wells up the force that will ensure that external history can be a history of love rather than a history of domination. In God himself the Spirit is the fruit of the love between Father and Son, as tradition tells us. In history, however, this love takes a historical form: It becomes the Spirit of love designed to effect liberation in history.

The work of the Spirit can be described as the incorporation of the human individual and of all people into the very process of God himself. The Spirit makes us children of God, but it does not do so in any idealistic way. It does so through the structure of the Son. It introduces us into God's own attitude toward the world, which is an attitude of love. But since the world is dominated by sin and hence riddled with conflict, it makes us co-actors with God in history. Alongside the notion of God as a "process," then, we have Christian existence as a "way" based on the following of Jesus. When we view Christian existence as the following of Jesus, we are not simply viewing it in ethical terms that flow from a prior faith. Strictly speaking, we are viewing it as a participation in the very life of God himself. We are not made children of God by some

expression of intent or by some mysterious supra-historical
reality (akin to what has traditionally been called the "supernatural"). We are made children of God by participating in the
very process of God. Following Jesus means taking the love
that God manifested on the cross and making it *real* in history.

In this light we can appreciate the deeper underlying significance of a traditional notion; namely, that we have been saved
by the cross. The usual explanations assume we know who
God is and what salvation is at the start, suggesting that
salvation is something added to a human being who is already
fully constituted as such. In my opinion, however, we are
saying two things when we say that the cross brings salvation:
First, we are saying that in it is revealed God's unconditional
love. Salvation is both gratuitous and possible in historical
existence. If God has loved us first (1 John 4:10; Rom. 5:8), then
there is some ultimate meaning to history. Second, we are
saying that the culmination of our being loved by God is his
work of preparing us to be introduced into his own historical
process, to move from passive love to active love.

The cross, in other words, does not offer us any explanatory
model that would make us *understand* what salvation is and
how it itself might be salvation. Instead it invites us to participate in a process within which we can actually experience
history as salvation. It is the same point that we have already
reiterated several times: Our knowledge of God and of Jesus as
the Son is ultimately a con-natural knowledge, a knowledge
based on sym-pathy within the very process of God himself
rather than outside it. The Son reveals himself to us as the Son
insofar as we follow his path. The Father reveals himself to us
as Father insofar as we experience the following of Jesus as an
open road that moves history forward, opens up a future, and
nurtures a hope in spite of sin and historical injustice. It is
through that experience that we sense that love is the ultimate
meaning of existence and feel an unquenchable hope arise
within us—a hope against hope because it wells up from
suffering.

What we have just formulated in systematic terms is what is
brought out clearly in the theology of the Johannine writings.

First, it historicizes God's love on the basis of the cross: "God so loved the world that he gave his only Son" (John 3:16; 1 John 4:9f.). This love for people must be converted into an active love: "If God has loved us so, we must have the same love for one another" (1 John 4:11). It is this experience that gives meaning to the unshakable hope that "God is love" (1 John 4:8,16). John does not explain the logical steps involved here. He simply states them because the inner logic can only be understood from within the process itself. If the start of it all is the love of God, which is historicized on the cross, then Christian existence is structured as a gratuitous gift. The gratuitousness never becomes reality, however, unless we move from acceptance of the gift to self-giving out of love. I believe that we have frequently made the mistake of seeing the experience of gratuitousness solely in terms of what we have received and our thankfulness for it. In reality the gift is experienced as such only in one's own self-giving. Where that takes place, human life is really a journey with God toward God, even though "no one has ever seen God" (John 1:18).

It is important to realize that these considerations are not purely apologetic in intent. I have spoken here about God as an open-ended process that will reach its culmination at the end of history, and about human life as a journey undertaken with Jesus. I am not simply trying to talk meaningfully about God in a milieu that bears witness to the "death of God" and the "death of the poor." I believe that this is one way to express a fundamental Christian intuition, namely, that knowledge of God cannot be dissociated from the way that leads to God—a way that passes through the cross.

I should like to close this section with a long quote from Moltmann, which lends itself more to meditation than to analysis. I think it tells us what it means to abide with God in his "hour of grief":

The content of the doctrine of the Trinity is the real cross of Christ himself. The form of the crucified Christ is the Trinity. In that case, what is salvation? Only, if all disaster, forsakenness by God, absolute death, the infinite curse of damnation and sinking into nothingness is in God himself, is community with this God eternal salvation, infinite joy, indestructible election and divine life. The "bifurcation" in God must contain the whole uproar of history within itself. Men must be able to recognize rejection, the curse and final nothingness in it. The cross stands between the Father and the Son in all the harshness of its forsakenness. If one describes the life of God within the Trinity as the "history of God" (Hegel), this history of God contains within itself the whole abyss of godforsakenness, absolute death and the non-God. *"Nemo contra Deum nisi Deus ipse."* Because this death took place in the history between Father and Son on the cross on Golgotha, there proceeds from it the spirit of life, love and election to salvation. The concrete "history of God" in the death of Jesus on the cross on Golgotha therefore contains within itself all the depths and abysses of human history and therefore can be understood as the history of history. All human history, however much it may be determined by guilt and death, is taken up into this "history of God," i.e., into the Trinity, and integrated into the future of the "history of God." There is no suffering which in this history of God is not God's suffering; no death which has not been God's death in the history on Golgotha. Therefore there is no life, no fortune and no joy which have not been integrated by his history into eternal life, the eternal joy of God.[11]

Thesis 14: The cross is not the last word on Jesus because God raised him from the dead. But neither is the resurrection the last word on history because God is not yet "all in all." Christian existence in history draws its life from the dialectics of Jesus' cross and resurrection. This translates into a faith against unbelief, a hope against hope, and a love against alienation.

The cross is not the last word of God. God raised the crucified Jesus from the dead. The resurrection proves that the cross is really the first step toward life, that on the cross, God really was taking history unto himself and saving it. In that sense we can agree with Bultmann when he says that the resurrection manifests the meaning of the cross.

But neither is the resurrection of Jesus the last word of God. That will only be spoken at the very end, when God becomes all in all (1 Cor. 15:28). It is the way toward that final consummation that is expressed in the dialectics of cross and resurrection. That is why the dialectics must be maintained in any Christian outlook.

There is a messianic conception of Christianity, but that is not what characterizes it as such. Messianism existed both before and after Jesus' cross. We find some sort of hope in every religion (E. Bloch), so we have not said anything distinctive when we affirm that Christian faith lives for a utopia. It is certainly true enough that Jesus' proclamation of the kingdom of God was utopian. The presentation of Jesus' resurrection as that of the "firstborn" who will be followed by the rest of the universe is surely utopian. So is the concept that God will be all in all. And it is certainly true, as Boff points out, that the utopia has already been realized in Jesus through his resurrection: "Insofar as the Christian is concerned, with the resurrection of Jesus there was no longer any *u-topia* (Greek, 'no place') but only *topia* (a real place). Human hope is realized in the risen Jesus and is in the process of realization in every human being."[12]

Christianity cannot renounce utopia, nor the belief that it has been realized in Jesus. But for us who remain in a sinful world still, the problem remains. Utopia is still *u-topia* ("no place"). For that reason I do not think we can state the matter too simplistically. We cannot simply say that Christianity is a religion of hope or a messianic vision of the universe based on some sort of philosophical anthropology stressing human openness or self-transcendence. All that allows for the potential existence of Christianity, but the latter cannot be reduced to the former. Christianity does affirm such a hope and it locates the *topia* of *utopia*. But it also pinpoints the locale from which we can appraise that utopia, the concrete negation through which the final transformation appears as utopian rather than merely ideological.

That locale is not merely contingency or human limitedness; it is the cross of Jesus and all the crosses of history. The *u* of utopia becomes real through the cross. Paradoxically enough, the more we plunge into the cross, the more we plunge into the resurrection; the more deeply we experience the "against hope" of the cross, the more deeply we live the "hope" of the resurrection. The ultimate reason behind these reflections is not that the cross provides a dialectical complement to the resurrection but rather that it radicalizes every statement about the resurrection. Either all faith, hope, and theology come to an end with the cross, or else the cross makes all of them specifically Christian.

The resurrection of Jesus should be viewed in connection with his cross. God's active presence in the resurrection should be viewed in connection with his absence from the Son on the cross. If that is done, then Christian existence can be described as a journey toward God the Father that takes seriously both aspects of the paschal mystery. This journey has a dialectics all its own. It is not simply the dialectics to be found in every human life, where people must go through the negative to reach the positive. It is a characteristically Christian dialectics since it is motivated by the very nature of the cross rather than by dialectical schemes of a universal cast.

Christian existence has been traditionally described as a life of faith, hope, and love. What the cross does here is force us to give up any ingenuous or merely intentional conception of these three dimensions and see them as concretely Christian. It tells us that in human life they not only fall short of perfect completion and fulfillment but also call for the complete fulfillment of the passion: "In my own flesh I fill up what is lacking in the sufferings of Christ" (Col. 1:24).

Christian existence is determined first and foremost by the dialectics of faith and unbelief. The full and complete revelation of God is not to be found amid the evil that still exists in the world. So long as the world remains unredeemed, faith cannot help but be attacked by unbelief, and the whole problem of theodicy will remain an open question. There is the abandonment by God that Jesus felt on the cross and the abandonment by God that we experience in the history of injustice and oppression. There is the cry of Jesus on the cross and the cry of countless victims in history. They do not allow us to nurture an ingenuous faith in God; it must be a faith that overcomes the world (1 John 5:4). That is why the God of Jesus stands above and beyond the conventional beliefs of theism and atheism. Neither the affirmation nor the denial of God's transcendence explains the evil in the world. The transcendence of Jesus' God must be grasped, not as an explanation, but rather as an appeal to human conscience to overcome the sinfulness and injustice in this world (Miranda).

Christian faith in God is always linked with the mournful plaints of history. In the Exodus God heeded the cries of the Israelites in Egypt (Exod. 3:7; 6:5). On the cross of Jesus he seemed to be deaf to Jesus' cry (Mark 15:34). Even after the resurrection "all creation groans and is in agony even until now" (Rom. 8:22). Christian faith is not independent of those groans and cries. So long as they continue to exist, there can be no naive faith in God. Viewed in the light of Jesus' cross, Christian faith is a process that takes shape through the attacks of unbelief. It is not a merely noetic process but rather the very life of the Christian. It is there that we get beyond theism and atheism; it is there that we elaborate our faith in the God of Jesus.

This characteristically Christian way of life has two basic dimensions: hope and love. Christian hope is no more ingenuous than Christian faith. It takes shape in the dialectical interplay between hope and death. As Paul puts it, it is a "hoping against hope" (Rom. 4:18). Christian hope is not a hopeful optimism which looks *beyond* injustice, oppression, and death; it is a hope *against* injustice, oppression, and death. When the New Testament asks Christians to give an account of their hope (1 Pet. 3:15), it is in the context of persecution. It is in a situation where injustice seems to triumph over goodness: "If it should be God's will that you suffer, it is better to do so for good deeds than for evil ones" (1 Pet. 3:17). This simple verse expresses a profoundly Christian intuition: Hope arises precisely at the moment when it would seem obliged to disappear, at the moment when love and goodness fail to triumph.

The specifically Christian element in this conception of hope lies in the experience of gratuitousness. Hope take its life from a gift that paradoxically derives its nourishment from the cross of Jesus and from service rendered to those who are crucified in our own day. If the cross of Jesus does not put an end to hope, then we experience the realization that it is through his cross that we have been given something that cannot be torn away from us (Rom. 8:31–39). This hoping against hope cannot really be analyzed further. The cross may lead us to scepticism or despair, and the resurrection may lead us to optimism. Hoping against hope is a third approach that arises out of the resurrection of the crucified one.

Neither is Christian love ingenuous. It too draws its life from the dialectical interplay between love and alienation. Christian love has to be real and effective because it lives in the presence of concrete forms of alienation. It must positively fashion a new person and a new society, hence it is not only personal but also structural. That is why Christianity is the font of partial and functional ideologies (Boff), though it itself is not an ideology; it must be concrete and effective.

The cross of Christ reveals that Christian love also has another dimension. Its ultimate depths are lost to view. It draws life from its conviction even before it sees results. It is not idealistic because it stands in need of all the concrete historical embodiments and mediations provided by science, analysis, and organization if it is to be truly effective. But neither is it pragmatic because the cross of Jesus seems to show that death accepted out of love is the ultimate that humanity can say, or better, do. Christianity tells us that many penultimate words are needed in the lives of human beings: organization, ideologies, dogmas, intuitions, and so forth, but it also says that the ultimate word lies hidden beneath all such mediations, that it is love embodied in service.

There were many penultimate words in Jesus' own life (proclamation, action, miracles, and so forth), but the ultimate word was uttered on the cross: "There is no greater love than this—to lay down one's life for one's friends" (John 15:13). The same holds true in the life of the Christian. Concrete alienation will have to be overcome through concrete mediations, but the ultimate value is to be found in loving service. The resurrection offers us the hope of universal reconciliation. The final goal of the Christian is to "be with" human beings both in social mediations now and at the final eschatological end. But the cross tells us that we cannot possibly "be with" human beings unless we choose to "be for" them.

To conclude these reflections, I would simply say that it is the cross that makes Jesus' resurrection *Christian*. It is by maintaining the scandal of the cross that we can conceive of a Christian God, of the Father of Jesus. Today people look at the resurrection of Jesus and then offer a new formulation of God's transcendence. They usually say that God is "ahead of us." Viewing that transcendence from the cross, however, we might well say that it is expressed historically as love. Thus the God "ahead of us" can only become the God "for us." This transcendent God clearly showed us on the cross that he is a God in history who is on the side of history.

The cross suggests that the reality of God may be viewed as a process that is open to the world. Through the Son, God actively incorporates himself into the historical process; through the Spirit, human beings and history are incorporated into God himself. Thus human life can be described as a participation in God's process. That would serve as a modern translation of the classic view about participation in the divine life. The human way of participating in that life was revealed in Jesus; it is the way of the Son.

Christians, like other human beings, have no direct insight into the reality of God. They, too, must maintain the mysteriousness of God and let God be God. But Christians do know how we may respond to this mystery and what way leads to it. We must join with Jesus and do as he did. We must put everything that we have in the service of the kingdom. We must preserve the divine abandonment that Jesus experienced on the cross, for now we ourselves live in a history that remains one of injustice and crucifixion. With Jesus we must follow the road of self-surrender and service through to the end. Because of Jesus, we can die in the hope of resurrection; we can look forward to a new heaven and a new earth.

A symbol serves as food for thought (Ricoeur). The symbol of the cross forces us to change our way of thinking (Moltmann) about the most human realities: liberation, the meaning of history, and God. This particular symbol, however, is also a slice of real history. It is something that happened to a concrete human being who lived the nearness of God and a life of service to human beings as no one ever had before. Hence this particular symbol forces us to change our way of living as well as our way of thinking. Thus understood, there is nothing alienating about the cross. Those who are oppressed will instinctively look to it to find a response to their own lives; so long as oppression continues to exist, there is nothing necessarily alienating about that. But the cross is also more than that. It eternally calls Christian life into question, and it makes it possible for history to keep moving forward toward the kingdom of God in hope and love: "Not every life is an occasion of hope, but that of Jesus certainly is. Out of love he took upon himself the weight of the cross and death."[13]

NOTES

1. This term was popularized recently by Jürgen Moltmann, and many of the thoughts in this book are due to his suggestive formulations. For Moltmann's treatment of the theme, consult the following works: *Der gekreuzigte Gott* (Munich, 1972), see note 10, chap. 1 in this volume; "Dios y la resurrección," in *Esperanza y planificación del futuro*, see note 14, chap. 2 in this volume; his article on "the crucified God" in *Concilium* 76 (New York: Herder & Herder/Seabury, 1972).

2. J. Moltmann, *Der gekreuzigte Gott*, p. 217.

3. J. Moltmann, *Esperanza y planificación del futuro*, p. 69.

4. E. Käsemann, *Exegetische Versuche und Besinnungen*, 3rd ed. (Göttingen, 1969), 1: 207; Eng. trans.: *Essays on New Testament Themes* (Naperville, Illinois: Allenson, 1964); *New Testament Questions of Today* (Philadelphia: Fortress, 1969).

5. Käsemann, *Der Ruf der Freiheit* (Tübingen, 1968), p. 32; see note 4, chap. 3 in this volume.

6. Ibid., p. 36.

7. O. Cullmann, *El Estado en el Nuevo Testamento*, Spanish trans. (Madrid, 1961), p. 64; Eng. trans.: *The State in the New Testament* (New York: Scribner's, 1956).

8. J. Moltmann, *Umkehr zur Zukunft* (Hamburg: Siebenstern, 1970), p. 137.

9. Ibid., p. 137.

10. Moltmann, *Der gekreuzigte Gott*, p. 145f.

11. Ibid., p. 233; Eng. trans., p. 246.

12. L. Boff, *Jesucristo el liberador*, Spanish trans., p. 145; see note 9, chap. 3 in this volume.

13. Moltmann, *Umkehr zur Zukunft*, p. 76.

7.

The Resurrection of Jesus:
Hermeneutic Problem

Whatever investigation we may undertake into the historicity of the traditions concerning Jesus' resurrection, that does not solve the problem as to how we are to *understand* his resurrection.[1] Even if we have established the historicity of an event that took place in the. past, we must still ask what meaning it might have in the present here and now. Today we can no longer identify with the horizon of understanding possessed by the earliest Christians. We are faced with the hermeneutic problem as to what the happenings surrounding Jesus might mean today and what standpoint we must adopt if we want to unlock their meaning for our time and place.

This basic problem, the need for some sort of hermeneutics in general when dealing with Jesus, becomes extremely acute when we confront the resurrection event. The New Testament makes it quite clear that Jesus' resurrection is not the resuscitation of a cadaver. The resurrection does not mean that Jesus is restored to the normal state of life. It is an *eschatological* event in which the final reality of history makes its appearance in the midst of history—whatever that final reality may be understood to be. That is precisely why we pose the question of hermeneutics in the face of this particular concrete event. We wish to know what exactly is the correct horizon for understanding the resurrection of Jesus.

I shall begin by presenting some of the sample solutions offered by various modern exegetes who attempt to say what the proper understanding of the resurrection might be.

Rudolf Bultmann does not deny the resurrection, but he interprets it in such a way that the historical issue is simply ignored. His understanding of the resurrection is wholly independent of the question as to whether it is "historical" or not. As an exegete, Bultmann maintains that the empty tomb is a legend. He also maintains that the traditions that deal with Jesus' bodily apparitions are later inventions of the Christian community. There is no hint of them in Paul, the author whom he regards as most trustworthy insofar as Jesus' resurrection is concerned.

The resurrection of Jesus is a mythical event insofar as it means the return of a dead human being to life. As such it is unacceptable to the people of our day, and its possible meaning can be brought out only through an existential hermeneutics: "The Easter event, insofar as it is Christ's resurrection, is not a *historical event*. The only thing that can be grasped as a historical happening is the paschal faith of the first disciples."[2] The apparitions can be understood as subjective visions that the historian can explain historically.

What is the conclusion to be drawn from such a hermeneutics? If "Christian paschal faith is to be uninterested in the historical question,"[3] then the only access to an understanding of this "event" is *faith*. But here "faith" does not mean simply the acceptance of a truth; it means our understanding of our sinful selves and our corresponding choice between two possible alternatives. Either we choose to close ourselves up in our sinful lives or else we open up to God and allow God to give meaning to our lives. In that sense the resurrection can be interpreted as "the meaning of the cross." To have faith in the resurrection means to believe that the cross is a salvific event.

Thus Bultmann offers an existential interpretation. In the cross our lives are revealed as sinful, but also as accepted by God. Jesus' resurrection is viewed in anthropological rather than strictly christological terms. Bultmann can say that "Christ is resurrected in the kerygma." By this he means that Christ "lives" insofar as he is preached, thereby forcing us to choose between two potential alternatives: a sinful life closed up in itself or a life open to God.

Willi Marxsen maintains that it is the faith of the disciples that is historically verifiable.[4] Jesus' resurrection is an interpretation of that faith, not a reality pertaining to Jesus himself. The interpretation itself was rendered possible by the apocalyptic expectations that the disciples had as Jews. On Hellenic soil the interpretation would have been different. There it might have proclaimed that Jesus had been liberated from the prison of the body. The hermeneutic process for understanding the resurrection, then, is one's own faith; but faith itself is a process of arriving at faith rather than some static or self-evident reality.

Besides this *personal* interpretation of Jesus' resurrection, Marxsen also mentions a *functional* interpretation. Indeed he sees the latter as more original and productive than the resurrection. It has to do with the unleashing of a mission, and Marxsen sees this in 1 Corinthians 15. The resurrection simply says that "Jesus' cause continues to make progress." It is the meaning of the historical Jesus' person, doctrine, and activity. Hence an existentialist interpretation is not enough to capture the meaning of Jesus' resurrection. The proper hermeneutics must include an attitude toward the attendant mission, toward the kind of praxis that will move the cause of Jesus forward (though the exact nature of that praxis may not be spelled out clearly).

Wolfhart Pannenberg starts off from a basic presupposition: Theology cannot affirm anything that is not historically attested.[5] It cannot affirm anything that is based on faith, revelation, or inspiration—not to mention some sort of magisterium. Either the resurrection of Jesus is historical and hence able to be laid hold of by some historical methodology, or else we cannot talk about it at all.

For Pannenberg, a historical event or fact has three characteristics: (1) It is engrafted in a tradition; (2) it can be expressed in some language; and (3) it responds to some metaphysical expectation of human beings. In the case of the resurrection, the horizon of hermeneutic comprehension is a radical hope reaching beyond death (characteristic 3).[6] It finds verbal formulation in "the resurrection of the dead" (characteristic 2). And it can be understood because it is framed in an apocalyptic tradition (characteristic 1).

Pannenberg maintains that the phrase "resurrection of the dead" expresses the *final* end and culmination of history, from which vantage point we can comprehend history as a whole. This comprehension of history as a whole enables history to serve as the mediation of God and enables Jesus' resurrection, as the anticipatory appearance of history's final end, to be the definitive revelation of God.

Implied in this view is a hermeneutics that considers the meaning of an event from the standpoint of history as a whole; a historical methodology that rejects anthropological prejudices and the supremacy of analogy, maintaining that the apparitions of the risen Jesus are explicable only insofar as they can be deduced from the reality of Jesus' resurrection itself; and a universal hope that makes it possible for someone to view the resurrection as the finale of history.[7] Thus Pannenberg rejects both the existential hermeneutics of Bultmann and the practical hermeneutics of Marxsen. One need only verify the facts historically to see that Jesus did rise from the dead, and one must have a radical hope to realize that his resurrection reveals both the final end of history and hence God.

Leonardo Boff views Jesus' resurrection in terms of the proclamation of God's kingdom as liberation and in terms of the cross as an alternative to that kingdom. "Is death to be more powerful than that great love? Is death, not life, to be God's final word on the destiny of Jesus of Nazareth and all human beings?"[8] Boff then proceeds to spell out the necessary presuppositions for understanding the resurrection. I shall quote him here, underlining some of the key words and expressions in his presentation:

We are essentially beings on the way toward selfhood. We try to fulfill ourselves *on every level:* biological, spiritual, cultural. In this effort we are *continually blocked* by frustration, suffering, lack of love, and lack of union with self and others. The *hope-principle* in us compels us to keep elaborating *utopias:* e.g., Plato's Republic, Campanella's City of the

Sun, Kant's City of Eternal Peace, Marx's Proletarian Paradise, Hegel's Absolute State, and Teilhard de Chardin's Omega Point. The same tendency is evident in the utopian myths of native Indians in South America. *We all* join in the groaning of St. Paul: "Who can free me from this body under the power of death?" (Rom. 7:24). With the author of the book of Revelation *we all* yearn for a world where "there shall be no more death or mourning, crying out or pain, for the former world has passed away" (Rev. 21:4). The resurrection of Jesus purports to be that utopia realized here inside our present world. . . . In it are annihilated all the alienating elements that lacerate our life: death, suffering, pain, hatred, and sinfulness. . . .[9]

Here the hermeneutic principle for understanding Jesus' resurrection is the realization of a hope that is utopian, that covers all levels of personal and historical life, and that is not naive because it takes on flesh and blood amid the groaning and suffering of human beings.

Now I should like to propose another focus for understanding the resurrection of Jesus. [10] Let us assume that the resurrection of Jesus is not simply the resuscitation of a cadaver or some great "miracle" performed by God. Let us assume that it is *the event that reveals God.* In that case our talk about the resurrection and our hermeneutics of the resurrection bring us to the same set of problems we face with regard to knowledge of God in general. In other words, we cannot assume at the start that we already know who God is and move from there to an understanding of the resurrection. As was the case with the cross of Jesus, we can only learn who God is from the cross and resurrection of Jesus.

This basic focus leads us to another option of the utmost importance. If the problem of the resurrection is the problem of God, then our hermeneutics of the resurrection will have to be one that takes in all aspects of reality. It will have to be the most comprehensive and all-embracing hermeneutics possible. Granting at the start that this is only one possible option, we may try to work out such a hermeneutics by asking three basic questions: What may I hope for? What can I know? What should I do?

WHAT MAY I HOPE FOR?

The Horizon of Hope in the New Testament

All Jesus' activity was performed in an atmosphere of apocalyptic expectation. The end of history would soon appear, re-creating all of reality.

In the Old Testament this expectation was expressed in the notion of the "resurrection of the dead," a metaphor taken from everyday life. Rising again meant passing from the state of sleep to a state of alert wakefulness. It implied a *change* that is *radical,* producing *a new situation superior to the old.*

We do not find this idea of resurrection, of a radically new kind of existence, in the early stages of the Old Testament. Belief in some survival after death was influenced by Greek philosophy (Wisd. 3:1–5,16; 2 Macc. 7:9; Job 19:25). The typically Israelite conception appears in the writings of the prophets (Ezek. 37:1–14; Isa. 26:19), in apocalyptic writings in particular (Dan. 12:1–4), and in such non-canonical books as Enoch and Baruch. Some currents of thought held that the resurrection was simply a prerequisite for the final, universal judgment; others maintained that the resurrection itself was the final saving event, so that only the just would be raised from the dead.

When Jesus' disciples experienced apparitions of him, they did not simply say that Jesus was "alive" or "with God." They said that Jesus "had been resurrected by God." Thus the New Testament uses the technical formulation of apocalyptic literature. For the disciples this apocalyptic expectation served as the horizon for understanding what had happened to Jesus, the event they had experienced in his apparitions.

The case of Paul is important here because we can glimpse what this horizon of understanding was *prior* to his experience on the road to Damascus. For him resurrection meant a radical change (1 Cor. 15:35–56; see Isa 25:8; Dan. 12:3), which simultaneously safegarded the continuity of the bodies involved. It was also a salvific event in itself, and hence Paul seems to lean toward the view that only the just will be resurrected (1 Cor. 15:22f.; see Isa. 26:7–10; on the opposite side see Dan. 12:1–3).

Thus the New Testament tells us that Paul (and the rest of the disciples) were able to formulate some idea of what had happened to Jesus *because* they possessed a prior horizon of understanding, which was nothing else but *hope*. Without it they would not have been able to describe the Jesus-event as "resurrection."

Here we must consider the whole matter of apocalyptic thought and its relationship to any understanding of Jesus' resurrection. Several points must be brought out.

First, in the apocalyptic strain of thought we do not find the expectation that only "one" human being would be resurrected. For this reason the first generation of Christians believed that Jesus' resurrection marked the start of a universal resurrection (1 Thess. 4:15,17; 1 Cor. 15:51). It was the second generation of Christians who became aware of the temporal tension existing between the resurrection of Jesus and the final parousia. That is why Jesus is seen as one who was resurrected as "the first-born of many brothers" (Rom. 8:29; 1 Cor. 15:20; Col. 1:18; Rev. 1:5; Acts 3:15).

It was possible to grasp the resurrection of Jesus only by cherishing a hope for all, for the world. Even after Jesus' resurrection people had to focus on the future of their own history, for whose fulfillment they were hopefully waiting (1 Cor. 15:13; Rom. 8:11; 1 Pet. 1:3). Of its very essence Christian faith in the resurrection cannot be separated from a hope in the future of history.

Second, the discontinuity noted above between apocalyptic thought and Christian hope is not a radical one, however. Even in apocalypticism we find legends about the disappearance or hiding of "one" individual (Elijah and Enoch, for example), though that in itself is an unimportant detail. The real break between apocalypticism and Christian hope lies in the fact that the basic situation of the witnesses to Jesus' appearances was defined by three specific factors: (1) the preaching of Jesus and his summons to discipleship; (2) the cross of Jesus and its destruction of their faith in him; and (3) the general apocalyptic expectation of contemporary Judaism. This means that the horizon of expectation shared by the witnesses to Jesus' resurrection was not simply apocalyptic hope but a well defined type of hope.

The real continuity between apocalypticism and Christian hope is not to be sought in the notion of *anticipation;* it is not that both look forward to some final end of history that will renew everything. The real continuity lies in the deeper underlying *intention* of apocalypticism. Its formulated notion of the "resurrection of the dead" does not simply express an anthropology of hope; it looks forward to the vindication of God's justice. To put it another way, apocalypticism is not just concerned with the end of history; it is concerned with the issue of theodicy.

That issue cannot be resolved simply by affirming that "someone" has been raised from the dead. We must ask "who" that someone is. There is a continuity between apocalypticism and Christian hope in that both are concerned with the justice of God. The discontinuity does not lie in the fact that someone or other was resurrected ahead of everyone else; it lies in the scandalous fact that the one who was raised from the dead was Jesus, who had been condemned, executed, and abandoned.

Thus we can say that apocalypticism is the horizon for understanding the resurrection insofar as it expresses a hope. Several observations are in order, however. First of all, apocalypticism was a syncretist movement, but its core did not lie in some anthropology of hope or in a conception of universal history based on some final end or culmination (e.g., the resurrection of the dead). Second, Jesus' own preaching was *formally* apocalyptic, but he superseded its *material* side insofar as he proclaimed God's coming in grace. Formally speaking, Jesus' activity is anticipatory; it points toward the end of time; materially speaking, however, it is a test and trial of the truth of the power of God's love in a world of injustice. Third, the postpaschal kerygma formally comprehends the resurrection as an anticipation of the end of history and in that sense it is indeed eschatological; materially speaking, however, emphasis is placed on the fact that this anticipation of the end is embodied in the crucified Jesus, not in just anyone at all. The resultant faith cannot be adequately translated into anthropological hopes or some universal tendencies of history; it must be translated into a hope for some new justice in an unredeemed world. Fourth, the hermeneutic locale for understanding the resurrection of Jesus is not to be found simply in hope. It is to be found in the questioning search for justice in the history of suffering. We cannot bypass that issue, or give it a satisfactory answer, by simply stating that someone has been raised from the dead. Fifth, basic discussion about Jesus' resurrection does not have to do with the possibility of envisioning it in physical, biological, or historical terms. It has to do with the triumph of justice. Who will be victorious, the oppressor or the oppressed?

Systematic Consequences

We can see clearly what the hermeneutic principle for understanding the resurrection was in the New Testament. It was the apocalyptic horizon that looked forward to God's revelation at the finale of history. This suggests that we need the same horizon today. We must be oriented toward the future because the truth is not adequately embodied in any past origins. In anthropological terms it means that without a radical hope, against which *nothing* serves as a real barrier, we cannot understand Jesus' resurrection. That disqualifies any merely existential interpretation that ignores the *temporal* horizon of hope.

Even as far back as the New Testament, however, the horizon for understanding the resurrection of Jesus is not just hope but a *qualified* hope (as was noted in the previous section). The more general conception of hope as openness to the future is *merely* a necessary precondition for understanding the resurrection of Jesus.

The nature of the hope in question must be defined in terms of the concrete situation of the disciples after the cross. For us it means that the Christian hope required to understand the resurrection can arise *only* in conjunction with our questioning search for justice in an unredeemed world (the *intention* of apocalypticism). *Anthropological* hope is not enough. It must be concretized in *theological* terms. We must ask about the power of God over injustice, and that finds its ultimate concretion in *Christology*. In other words, the resurrection is grasped as hope insofar as it gives rise to a hope, precisely because the one who rose from the dead is none other than the one who was crucified.

The *first and primary* hermeneutic consideration for comprehending Jesus' resurrection is the fact that there does exist a hope which, even after his resurrection, is a hoping *against hope*. That leads us on to another question that we shall consider further on. Where do we find the locale where this hoping against hope arises in authentic Christian terms?

Apocalyptic expectation finds its counterpart in the Greek conception of the immortality of the soul and in the more modern conception of radical openness to the future. This apocalyptic expectancy must also be possible today, but it has to be concretized in Christian terms. As Moltmann points out:

> The specifically Christian element becomes visible only when we move from the formal categories of anticipation to the material content embodied in Jesus' preaching and the Christian kerygma concerning the resurrection of the crucified. In my opinion, it is only in the questioning search for justice amid the suffering caused by the evil and misery of the human world that we come to grips with the perduring question of apocalypticism, which cannot be ignored, and with the answer of Jesus and his history which cannot be dismissed.[11]

Expressing it in christological terms, then, we must say that Jesus' resurrection cannot be grasped *solely* from the standpoint of apocalypticism. The horizon of Jesus' cross must also be kept in mind. There can be no comprehension of Jesus' resurrection without apocalyptic expectation and utopian thinking. But the locale of that u-topia ("no place") is none other than the cross, which seems to close off the road altogether. It is not to be found in any simple anthropology stressing an unfinished or open human nature. To put it in classic theological language, the resurrection is the *terminus ad quem* of utopia, but the cross is the *terminus a quo* of utopia. In that sense utopian hope is the condition which makes it possible for us to know the resurrection of Jesus.

WHAT CAN I KNOW?

Here we want to consider the role and function of "historical" knowledge in trying to comprehend Jesus' resurrection.

A Hermeneutics for Grasping the Historical as Such

In the previous section we were dealing with the problems connected with the *historicity of the traditions* concerning the resurrection of Jesus (the apparitions and the empty tomb).[12] Now we must consider another side of the story. First of all, there is no historical tradition in the New Testament that deals with the resurrection *event itself*. Second, if we attempt to deduce the historicity of the resurrection itself from the historicity of Jesus' appearances, then we are making an inference that presupposes a certain understanding of what history and historical method is. Third, there is another difficulty here aside from that of verifying something as historical on the basis of an inference. The difficulty has to do with the content of the event in question here. While it is narrated as a historical event, the resurrection is an eschatological event.

In that context we must ask ourselves what it means to *know* that the resurrection is a historical event. What presuppositions underlie our effort to raise the question of historical knowing here?

Here, if anywhere, we have a theological problem surrounded by prejudices and presuppositions that should be clarified at the very start. We can present the prejudices in the form of contradictory alternatives regarding people's understanding of history and the relationship between historicity and faith.

There are two stances with regard to the first issue. One

alternative maintains that Jesus' resurrection is ahistorical. The reality of the resurrection is viewed in such a way that it can be an object of faith (see Bultmann, for example). The other view maintains that the modern sense of history deriving from historicism is ahistorical, curiously enough. It proposes a new conception of historical methodology that would enable us to say that the resurrection is historical (see Pannenberg, for example).

This whole problem arose with the appearance of a new science of history in the eighteenth and nineteenth centuries. If that science is correct, then the resurrection is not historical. If the resurrection is historical, then the newer concept of historical science cannot be true.

There are also two basic stances with regard to the second question i.e., the relationship between historicity and faith. One position maintains that the resurrection must be established historically, otherwise faith in it is impossible (Pannenberg). The other position maintains that it *should not* be established historically, otherwise faith in it would be impossible (Bultmann).

To some extent this problem flows from the previous one. If one accepts the challenge of the Enlightenment, as does Pannenberg, then the only way to salvage "faith" in the resurrection is to ground it on historical knowledge. If one feels that this is impossible, as does Bultmann, then the only way to safeguard "faith" in the resurrection is to lay down the principle that faith should not look to history for its support.

Before we try to resolve the dilemmas just proposed, I should like to consider what the New Testament meant by "historical" when it talked about the resurrection. First of all, it is important for us to note the problematic situation in which the disciples found themselves after the crucifixion of Jesus and their own experience of his appearances. This is important if we are to form a judgment about their statements that Jesus had been resurrected.

Second, if we are going to affirm that the resurrection was historical, we must spell out the content of that event in precise terms. The disciples did not simply say that "Jesus was raised

from the dead." They did not restrict themselves to the christological dimension of the resurrection. Instead they specified
three points: (1) God raised the crucified Jesus from the dead;
(2) on him is grounded the whole future of justice for sinners
and those subjected to injustice, oppression, and death;
(3) the disciples are not merely spectators to this event. They
are *witnesses*, which implies they are summoned to a faith and
a love that is meant to overcome the world.

In the New Testament, then, the historical problem does not
come down simply to affirming whether or not the tomb was
vacant, or whether or not Jesus was "alive." The truth of the
resurrection must be affirmed in the three dimensions just
indicated. It is the resurrection understood in that sense that
we are asking about here. What do we mean when we say that
it is historical, and how are we to understand its historicity?
Before we tackle that question, let us consider some of the
difficulties posed by various conceptions of history.

Prejudices Surrounding Historicity and the Concept of History

Critique of historical positivism. As the natural sciences arose
and developed in the last few centuries, there also appeared a
new historical science that sought to be *objective.* It advocated a
fetishism of historical facts.

This understanding of history looked to the Enlightenment
for one of its presuppositions. The philosophy of history was a
philosophy of crisis: It sought to liberate humanity from the
past by reducing the past to *nothing more than* the past. Historical methodology would enable us to dominate the events of
the past so that they could no longer summon people today:
"The continuing relevance of a past ever alive and evolving,
ever perduring in human memory, gave way to a past that was
nothing more than an object to be precisely defined, dated,
and localized."[13]

The criteria of the new historical method derive from this
positivistic conception of history. Historical statements are
correct and accurate, unlike artistic statements. Those state-

ments can be checked and verified, and hence one can understand new situations on the basis of something already known.

The ultimate suppositions of this theory can be reduced to two. First, on the epistemological level our knowledge of history is analogical. This means that we come to understand the new on the basis of the old. Second, on the theological level it is human beings, not God, who are the carriers of history.

According to this conception of history, it is impossible to designate the resurrection as a *historical* event. The *anthropological* supposition that human beings are the ultimate subject of history makes it impossible for us to comprehend Jesus' resurrection as an action of *God*. The *analogical* supposition makes it impossible for us to grasp the eschatological character of the resurrection: i.e., its *radically new* character. And the *rational* supposition makes it impossible for us to verify the practical character of the resurrection, the fact that it is an event to which people must bear witness; for in this case those who perceive it are not merely observers but witnesses.

We would offer the following criticism of that method. It does not do justice to the historians themselves because they are inside history, not above and beyond it. This means that the ideal of historical objectivity that flourished in the nineteenth century is highly questionable. The analogical supposition that the new is to be known on the basis of the old is wholly gratuitous, if not false. At the very least it is inadequate insofar as it seems highly likely that human beings can be defined as open to novelty and the future. The assumption that humanity is the authentic carrier is one option, but it is not the only possible one. The Bible's anthropology and philosophy of history show us another option, and it was on that basis that the resurrection of Jesus was formulated.

Critique of the existentialist conception of history. The existential outlook does get beyond historical positivism. Bultmann does not define the essence of a historical event in terms of what it is "in itself" or of its accidental context. He sees it in relation to the future, and he sees the present as somehow responsible for the future. However, Bultmann does not grasp the future in temporal terms; instead he sees the end of history already operative in the present. Historical reality is viewed in positive terms insofar as it is a summons to a decision: "Don't look around you in universal history. Instead you must focus your attention on your own history. The meaning of history always lies embedded in the present. You cannot look upon it as a spectator; you can only grasp it in your own responsible decision-making."[14]

This view is simply an attempt to avoid the reefs of historical positivism, and in fact it is merely the other side of the coin. In a crisis-ridden era people drew a sharp distinction between objective history on the one hand and its wholly subjective meaning on the other. The view of Bultmann makes it impossible for us to recognize Jesus' resurrection as an action by God and a happening that points toward a *temporal* future. Its history would come down to the third point noted earlier: i.e., the resurrection is historical because it is something to which witness must be borne in preaching so that it can set in motion the historicity of the listeners. The listeners must make a decision for or against the new vision of existence with which they are presented when they hear the kerygma about the resurrection.

My criticism of this position is the general one levelled against the partial or one-sided nature of existentialism. Since it eliminates the temporal dimension of history, we can find salvation even now in the unredeemed world. That is a very questionable view, however, because temporality entails at least the intention of making salvation *real* in the objective structures of the real world, not just in the inner structures of the subject.

Critique of a one-sided conception of universal history. Pannenberg's conception is positive in that it assumes that a historical event can be understood only in a context that ultimately takes in history as a whole. In other words, an event is recognized as historical insofar as it is seen in terms of universal history. Since history has not yet come to an end, the meaning of an event can be understood only in terms of the end of history. Since that end has been anticipated in the event of the resurrection, however, we can have an understanding of universal history. Thus Pannenberg maintains two things: The whole of history can be conceived from the standpoint of the resurrection on the one hand, and the resurrection-event as historical can be understood from the standpoint of history as a whole.

Our most serious criticism of this view is that Pannenberg does not seem to realize that the *negative* side of history cannot be comprehended readily in the horizon of a universal history because it is in fact the negative aspect which seems to rule out any possibility of giving some total meaning to history. The negative side cannot be inserted without further ado into a dialectical schema. It is only through the concrete overcoming of some concrete negative aspect that history is opened up further, though we cannot decide in advance what the full result of such opening up might be. History cannot be comprehended as a whole so long as suffering, misery, and injustice exist. Even after Jesus' resurrection it can only be grasped by way of hope.

History in Terms of Promise and Mission

Here I propose to elaborate a concept of history that would satisfactorily allow us to understand the resurrection as an historical event.

If reality is to be history rather than some eternal present understood in cosmological or existential terms, then the future must be viewed as something more than a possible "plus" added to an incomplete present. It must be viewed as a *promise,* and here I shall quote Moltmann to specify what that means:

A promise is an offer that proclaims a reality that does not yet exist. . . .

The promise links us with the future and furnishes us with the meaning that will enable us to grasp history. . . .

History defined and inaugurated by the promise is not the eternal return of the same thing. It possesses a definite thrust toward the promised fulfillment yet to come. . . .

When the word is a word of promise, it means that it has not yet found its guarantee in reality. On the contrary, it stands in contradiction to the reality that can be experienced now or that could be experienced in the past. . . .

The word of promise always creates an intermediate space charged with tension, a space lying midway between the giving of the promise and its fulfillment. It thus provides us with a distinctive area of freedom to choose between obedience and disobedience, hope and resignation. . . .

If the promise is considered to be God's promise, then it cannot be verified by human criteria. The fulfillment of it can contain something new even within the boundaries of what is hoped for, and it can supersede in reality what had been imagined in human categories. . . .

The "not yet" of expectation exceeds any fulfillment that has intervened so far. Hence every real fulfillment so far becomes the confirmation, interpretation, and liberation of a greater hope. . . . The constant element of surplus and excess in the promise, its perduring overflowing of history, is rooted in the inexhaustible character of the God of the promise.[15]

The point is that grasping reality as history is ultimately not a matter of grasping temporality and the unfinished nature of history; it is a matter of grasping the future as a promise. Comprehending the resurrection as historical, then, means understanding it to be the definitive promise of God.

The resurrection is a still unfinished reality. It is still in the process of fulfillment insofar as its saving efficacy is concerned. In its historical structure, then, the revelation of God effected in Christ's resurrection is a promise. His resurrection cannot be comprehended by broadening the meaning of some conception of history because it is not a possibility *in* the world and *in* history but a possibility *for* the world and *for* history.

Hence the only things that can be verified historically are the person of the crucified one, the time and place where the disciples claim to have experienced apparitions, and the credibility of the disciples. The hard reality of the resurrection itself escapes all historical verification, remaining as yet unknown and hidden in obscurity. It is beyond the bounds of historical judgment to lay hold of the resurrection as such. The *historical* aspect of Jesus' resurrection is to be grasped insofar as we see it in terms of a promise that opens up a future. Relating it to Jesus' disciples, Moltmann has this to say: "The paschal happening is not an event that has been definitively consummated and that already belongs to the past. It is not something that anyone can verify so long as they take the trouble to investigate it methodically. It is primarily a happening belonging to the future. In all its historical ambivalence it already provides the foundation for a universal hope that is capable of renewing the world and that is therefore necessarily bound up with the risk of faith."[16]

Laying hold of history as a *promise* ultimately comes down to taking cognizance of a mission. Historical consciousness is consciousness of a mission. Grasping a historical fact or event means realizing the mission that it sets in motion. As Moltmann puts it, we should not say that the resurrection is "historical" because it happened *in* history. It is "historical" because "it *founds* history that can and ought to be lived out, by pointing out the channel leading toward the future as a happening. The resurrection of Christ is historical because it opens up an eschatological future."[17]

That thought leads us to our third question: What should I do? If we do not found a new history, then we cannot comprehend the fact that Jesus' resurrection does found history. And we must view that history in realistic rather than idealistic terms. We must see it as history in an unredeemed world. In investigating the resurrection of Jesus *historically,* the work of the theologian is not to secure the faith against the conflicts of history (see Pannenberg). Rather, it is to place faith in the midst of the historical conflict triggered by Jesus' resurrection.

WHAT SHOULD I DO?

Here I want to consider praxis as a hermeneutic principle for understanding the resurrection.

In the New Testament the notion of praxis as a hermeneutic principle for understanding the resurrection is presented in a highly stylized way, but it is there. All the accounts of Jesus' appearances stress a mission. Jesus does not appear simply to show himself to people. His appearances are always bound up with a vocation to a mission.

In the New Testament this mission moves in two directions. First, it is a work of service designed to proclaim Jesus as the risen Christ. Second, it is a work of service to the concrete content to be found in Jesus' resurrection: i.e., to the new creation. This means that the resurrection itself cannot be understood apart from service to the mission given. It is no accident that the resurrection was proclaimed in a missionary way. As Moltmann points out, that evidently is "part of the reality of the resurrection itself."[18]

This mission should not be restricted to proclaiming what happened to Jesus, however. It also has to do with the transformation of the world. In mission terms it is not a matter of comprehending humanity in a different way but of seeking to bring something new to the world. The resurrection texts are not primarily narratives of the past but a form of creative witness. This desire and intention to bring something new to the world is the common horizon which is shared by both text and interpreter and which makes it possible for us to comprehend the resurrection. Only in that case will the interpreter be following in the footsteps of the texts.

To put it in modern terms, it means that for us today the resurrection of Jesus is an event that establishes a new history. If we are to grasp it as such, we must have the attitude that we are going to establish a new history. The mediating link between past history and future history is forged through a historical mission that propels history forward.

In general terms then, the hermeneutics of the resurrection is the apostolate itself. It is in the determined effort to carry on the hope that appeared in Jesus' resurrection that the very same hope becomes comprehensible to us.

Preaching the resurrection-event itself is not the only action or work of service set in motion by Jesus' resurrection. We must also serve the reality for which we are allowed to hope by virtue of his resurrection. We cannot preach the resurrection of

Jesus if we do not have the active *intention* to flesh out in reality the hope that finds expression there. The service of preaching seeks "to point out to human beings their work in the world and their hope in the future of Christ."[19]

In the last analysis the resurrection sets in motion a life of service designed to implement in reality the eschatological ideals of justice, peace, and human solidarity. It is the earnest attempt to make those ideals *real* that enables us to comprehend what happened in Jesus' resurrection.

In general we can say that the resurrection is laid hold of not only in hopeful expectation for the end of history but in here-and-now love. Love anticipates what is promised in the resurrection amid the concrete conditions of present history. We can specify this a bit more concretely from three complementary standpoints:

First of all, the hermeneutics designed to comprehend the resurrection must be political. This means that it is possible to verify the truth of what happened in the resurrection only through a transforming praxis based on the ideals of the resurrection. The elements of misery and protest in the biblical texts can be *understood* only in an active process of change which transforms the present, in a concrete effort to implement the promises of history here and now. We see this point spelled out programatically in Paul's work. His preaching destroys all the structures that oblige people to live as oppressed beings. His gospel of justification is a protest against the oppression exerted by religion and the existing deities. This political hermeneutics does not look for some merely noetic correspondence between text and interpreter. Given the fact of a world that is presently unredeemed, the resurrection can be understood only through a praxis that seeks to transform the world. This means that our *approach to the resurrection is continually in process of formation*.

Second, political hermeneutics must take into account the theology of the cross, for the work of transforming reality goes on in the presence of the power wielded by evil and injustice. Christian transforming praxis is characterized by the acceptance of suffering in the face of contradiction. Christian praxis must go by way of the cross; it must be a hoping against hope. It is both utopian and paradoxical for that reason, but it is also the correct hermeneutic principle for understanding Jesus' resurrection.

Third, we can summarize everything we said above in Moltmann's phrase: "Not every life is an occasion of hope, but that of Jesus certainly is. Out of love he took upon himself the weight of the cross and death."[20] The mission inaugurated by the resurrection can be viewed as an apostolate or a transforming praxis. But in sum it is the following of Jesus.

We can now describe the nature of this following or discipleship. First, it is a praxis, a line of action similar to that of Jesus himself. The following of Jesus is a summons to collaborate with the kingdom of God. Second, this action is structually akin to that of Jesus, and here we have an unvarying constant in Christian praxis. It is directed toward the public sector, toward the concrete manifestations of politics, bodily life, and the cosmos. Third, its applications will vary with time and place. New forms of sin, misery, and alienation will keep cropping up in history, and they will call for new ways of overcoming them in practice. Fourth, the following of Jesus is a praxis in which one experiences the same sort of structural conflicts that Jesus did. One encounters the power of evil over truth and love on the political and religious level, and even on the level of God himself. One confronts God's silence and relative historical impotence in the face of evil. It is this that gives rise to a hope against hope. Fifth, the one outstanding difference between the follower and Jesus is that Jesus suffered and died in solitude whereas his followers suffer and die in communion with him.

CONCLUSION

In this chapter I have tried to show how it is possible to understand the resurrection of Jesus. Three basic requisites were set forth: a radical hope in the future, a historical consciousness that grasps the meaning of history as a promise, and a specific praxis which is nothing else but the following of

Jesus. In my opinion, the last requisite is the most important one for several reasons. First of all, it is praxis based on love that concretizes hope and makes it specifically Christian hope. Second, love is the only thing that keeps opening up the horizon of history.

Like knowing God, knowing the resurrection of Jesus is not something that is given once and for all. We must keep creating our horizon of understanding, and we must keep alive our hope and praxis of love at every moment.

NOTES

1. Here we shall not deal with the strictly exegetical question concerning the historicity of the New Testament literary traditions dealing with Jesus' resurrection. There is an abundance of literature on the issue. See, for example, E. Ruckstuhl and J. Pfammatter, *Die Auferstehung Jesu Christi* (Luzern: Rex, 1968); Spanish translation published by Ediciones Fax in Madrid (in the series entitled *Actualidad Bíblica*). For a very brief summary of conclusions with regard to the exegetical problem, see chap. 11 in this volume, theses 8.1 to 8.6.

2. R. Bultmann, *Kerygma und Mythos* (Hamburg, 1948), p. 46f.; Eng. trans., *Kerygma and Myth: A Theological Debate*, edited by Bartsch, revised edition (New York: Harper & Row, 1961).

3. Ibid., p. 47.

4. Willi Marxsen, *Die Auferstehung Jesu als historisches und als theologisches Problem* (Gütersloh: Mohn, 1963); *Die Auferstehung Jesu von Nazareth* (Gütersloh: Mohn, 1968); Eng. trans.: *The Resurrection of Jesus of Nazareth* (Philadelphia: Fortress, 1970).

5. Pannenberg, *Fundamentos de cristologia*, pp. 82–142, see note 6, of chap. 2 in this volume; "Dogmatische Erwagungen zur Auferstehung Jesu," in *Kerygma und Dogma*, 14 (1968), pp. 105–18.

6. Today there is general acceptance of hope as the hermeneutic horizon for understanding the resurrection. See, for example, K. Rahner, W. Thüsing, *Christologie—systematisch und exegetisch* (Freiburg, 1972), p. 38f. This shift is noteworthy and important because Rahner focused on the resurrection from the standpoint of the incarnation in his earliest works on Christology. Thus in his earlier works the meaning of existence went back to some event in the past. The new emphasis on the resurrection as the key moment in Jesus' existence shifts the hermeneutic stress from the past to the future.

7. Pannenberg, *Grundfragen systematischer Theologie*, pp. 91–158; see note 12, chap. 2 in this volume.

8. L. Boff, *Jesucristo el liberador*, p. 113; see note 9, chap. 3 in this volume.

9. Ibid., p. 114f.

10. My objective position and proposed solution of the hermeneutic problem derives basically from the theology of Moltmann, particularly as it is

258   *The Resurrection of Jesus*

presented in two works of his: *Teología de la esperanza*, pp. 123–392, see note 31, chap. 2 in this volume; and *Der gekreuzigte Gott*, pp. 147–83, see note 10, chap. 1 in this volume.

11. *Der gekreuzigte Gott*, p. 164.

12. See note 1 of this chapter.

13. J. Moltmann, *Esperanza y planificación del futuro*, p. 193; see note 34, chap. 2 in this volume.

14. R. Bultmann, *Geschichte und Eschatologie*, p. 184; see note 23, chap. 3 in this volume.

15. Moltmann, *Teología de la esperanza*, pp. 133–36.

16. Moltmann, *Esperanza y planificación del futuro*, p. 80.

17. Moltmann, *Teología de la esperanza*, p. 237.

18. Ibid., p. 246f.

19. Ibid., p. 264.

20. J. Moltmann, *Umkehr zur Zukunft* (Hamburg: Siebenstern, 1970), p. 76; see *El lenguaje de la liberación*, Spanish trans. (Salamanca: Sígueme, 1974), pp. 91–98; Eng. trans.: *Gospel of Liberation* (Waco: Word, 1973), pp. 71–77; German original: *Die Sprache der Befreiung* (Munich: Kaiser, 1972).

8.

The Resurrection of Jesus:
Theological Problem

If the starting point of Christology is the historical Jesus, its culmination is reached in the resurrected Jesus according to the New Testament. In the previous chapter we considered *how* to grasp his resurrection. Here we shall consider *what* really took place in that event.

The kernel of the New Testament kerygma about the resurrection involves three dimensions. *Theologically* it affirms that *God* raised Jesus from the dead (see 1 Cor. 15:3a,4b; Acts 2:24, 3:15, 4:10, 5:30, 10:40, 13:30). *Christologically* it affirms that the ambiguity of Jesus' life is overcome in the resurrection, that its authentic reality is made clear by that event: "Let the whole house of Israel know beyond any doubt that God has made both Lord and Messiah this Jesus whom you crucified (Acts 2:36). *Anthropologically* it makes clear the meaning of life with respect to human beings, society, and the cosmos. Put negatively, the point is that "if Christ has not been raised, our preaching is void of content and your faith is empty too" (1 Cor. 15:14). Put positively, the point is that Jesus was "raised up for our justification" (Rom. 4:25).

Here we want to consider all three dimensions. But we particularly want to explore the christological dimension, which we shall treat last.[1]

THE THEOLOGICAL MEANING
OF JESUS' RESURRECTION

Even back in the Old Testament we find that the essence of God is not manifested by way of epiphany but in connection with some action in history. The credos of the Old Testament are historical credos. Some such summary credo always introduces the decalog: "I, the Lord, am your God, who brought you out of the land of Egypt, that place of slavery" (Deut. 5:6; see Exod. 20:2; for the most ancient historical credo see Deut. 26:5–9).

In the course of Old Testament history we find that the historical action of Yahweh that will reveal his essence is gradually moved to the future (see 1 Kings 20:13, 20:28; Ezek. 25:6, 8). This trend reaches its high point in Second Isaiah: "Lo, I am about to create new heavens and a new earth; the things of the past shall not be remembered or come to mind" (Isa. 65:17).

Prescinding from the question as to whether the resurrection-action is to be viewed as an event or a promise, we can say that the New Testament sees that action as the most fundamental one of Yahweh. The new historical credo now says: "Our faith will be credited to us also if we believe in him who raised Jesus our Lord from the dead" (Rom. 4:24). God is the one "who restores the dead to life and calls into being those things which had not been" (Rom. 4:17).

Several things should be noted about this new definition of God. First of all, it follows the historical focus of the Old Testament. Thus it contrasts sharply with later theology, which was influenced by Hellenic essentialism and which sought to define God in terms of *properties* rather than actions.

Second, both in the New and Old Testaments we find a tension existing between God's action in the present, which is incorporated into the historical credo, and some expectation of a definitive divine action in the future. It is worth noting that even *after* the resurrection of Jesus Christians still hopefully await some definitive action on God's part: "When, finally, all has been subjected to the Son, he will then subject himself to the One who made all things subject to him, so that God may be all in all" (1 Cor. 15:28). In christological terms this means we must ask ourselves whether Jesus' resurrection is the definitive *action* or the definitive *promise* of God.

Third, the new definition of God in terms of his power over death is also in danger of picturing the essence of the deity simply as power. That is what religions typically have done. The danger can be overcome only if we consider God's *passivity* on the cross in conjunction with his *activity* in the resurrection: "In the self-surrender of Jesus there takes place the self-surrender of God himself. In the suffering of Jesus, God himself suffers. In the death of Jesus, God himself tastes condemnation and death."[2] The sovereign omnipotence of God can be comprehended only through the cross. He is not just the one who gives life to things that have not yet existed; he is also the one who died under the power of sin and injustice.

God's omnipotence in the resurrection cannot be known solely through analogy with his omnipotence at the creation. In the latter instance he demonstrates his power over *nothingness*. In the case of the resurrection, however, he must overcome not only nothingness but also the death that is caused by *injustice* and *evil*. He does not exercise power over those two realities from somewhere outside; instead he immerses himself in them on the cross.

Fourth, God is revealed not just by the *abandonment* of Jesus on the cross or by his *active work* in the resurrection, but also by his *fidelity* to Jesus in those two events. What reveals God is the resurrection of the crucified, or, the cross of the resurrected one. It is the two-sided nature of all this that enables us to know God as an open *process* that will eventually find its synthesis in the *eschaton*.

Fifth, it is this same duality that allows the New Testament to give God a new and definitive name without giving way to banality. It tells us that "God is love" (1 John 4:8,16), but we must appreciate what that means. Without the resurrection love would not be authentic power; without the cross this power would not be love. And we should note that the definition of God as *love* continues to be a historical one: "God so loved the world that he gave his only Son" (John 3:16; see 1 John 4:9f.).

THE SOTERIOLOGICAL MEANING OF JESUS' RESURRECTION[3]

We have already noted how the cross was interpreted in soteriological terms on the basis of different explanatory models. Yet the resurrection, too, manifests salvation, and Bultmann is right when he says that "the resurrection is the meaning of the cross." What Paul states in more general terms (see Rom. 4:25) shows up quite clearly in the very structure of the post-resurrection apparitions. The risen one approaches those who had fled from his passion, those who had betrayed and denied him. His very approach is a sign of God's benevolence, of his pardoning and reconciling love. This benevolence comes across in the very words of the resurrected Jesus, even though these may have been made up by the later Christian community. For when he approaches them, he tells them not to be afraid and to be at peace.

The New Testament makes it clear that reconciliation with God must be understood in an entirely new way on the basis of the cross. Otherwise it might be turned into what Bonhoeffer calls "cheap grace." The reconciliation has cost "blood beyond price" (1 Pet. 1:19). Jesus' resurrection does not allow for any merely nominal reconciliation because one's experience of being reconciled to God must go hand in hand with a realization of its cost. Here we have no magical conception of reconciliation, but a down-to-earth one. There is reconciliation because there was love; and there was love because there was suffering and death.

Here we might do well to turn aside briefly and consider the matter of *grace*. The basic nature of grace is described in very simple terms in the New Testament. Grace is a way of life. At bottom it is a way of life prompted by love. The New Testament assumes that such a life of love is possible because love existed even before us: "If God has loved us so, we must have the same love for one another" (1 John 4:11). Our new life based on love is made possible by God's love.

The relationship between being loved and loving others actively is not a strictly logical one, but it is the only real one. Human transformation was made possible by love, and so that love is creative. Human love, in turn, consists in transforming others.

This simple description of grace was grasped intuitively by Ignatius Loyola when he wrote the following passage in his *Spiritual Exercises:* "Imagine Christ our Lord present before you upon the cross, and begin to speak with him, asking how it is that though he is the Creator, he has stooped to become man, and to pass from eternal life to death here in time, that there he might die for our sins. I shall also reflect upon myself and ask: 'What have I done for Christ? What am I doing for Christ? What ought I to do for Christ?' " (n. 53; see Appendix in this volume). Christ's love transforms us leading us to active work of transformation in turn.*

Bonhoeffer, too, vividly described the meaning of grace by contrasting "cheap grace" with "costly grace." The former is something of which one can be objectively sure because of Jesus' resurrection; the latter takes Jesus' cross seriously:

Cheap grace means grace as a doctrine, a principle, a system. It means forgiveness of sins proclaimed as a general truth, the love of God taught as the Christian "conception" of God. . . . Cheap grace means the justification of sin without the justification of the sinner. Grace alone does everything, they say, and so everything can remain as it was before. . . . Costly grace is the gospel which must be *sought* again and again. . . . Such grace is *costly* because it calls us to follow, and it is *grace* because it calls us to follow *Jesus Christ*. It is costly because it costs a man his life, and it is grace because it gives a man the only true life. It is costly because it condemns sin, and grace because it justifies the sinner. Above all, it is *costly* because it cost God the life of his Son. . . . Above all, it is *grace* because God did not reckon his Son too dear a price to pay for our life, but delivered him up for us.[4]

Jesus' resurrection inaugurates a liberative future. It was understood to be the anticipation of a universal resurrection. Christ is to be the firstborn of many brothers.

This means that we cannot turn the resurrection into nothing more than a past event. The risen one cannot be turned into "an origin myth that grounds the present."[5] Even after Christ's resurrection, humanity, by its very nature, is oriented toward the future of its own history and expectantly awaits its fulfillment (1 Cor. 15:13; Rom. 8:11; 1 Pet. 1:3). This hope must also leave its mark on the present (Rom. 6:4). The essence of the Christian faith cannot be reduced to affirming the truth of past events. It must affirm what already is insofar as it has not yet been fulfilled for all. Jesus' resurrection makes human beings truly ec-centric and their lives truly an ex-odus.

THE CHRISTOLOGICAL MEANING OF JESUS' RESURRECTION[6]

After Jesus' resurrection we see the start of a process of faith and theological reflection on Jesus. It leads to the definitive formulation that "Jesus is the Son of God." The process of reflection developed over a period of time, and it had different theological strains among different communities and different theologians of the New Testament.

What about faith in Christ during his own lifetime? There is much debate as to whether Jesus evoked faith in himself in his lifetime, in the sense that even then his disciples came to see a very special relationship between Jesus and God. In any such discussion the following points should be taken into consideration.

It is possible that in the first stage of Jesus' public life his disciples somehow thought that Jesus was a messianic figure or the Son of Man. But when the Galilean crisis occurred (see Mark 8:27–33), it was obvious that the content of their faith in Jesus had not grasped the typifying features of his person. Whatever their faith in Jesus might have been, the cross posed a fundamental crisis and they abandoned him there. It is important for us to realize that the crisis of faith was not merely anthropological but also theological. It was not just that the disciples were disillusioned and frightened into disloyalty.

They simply could not see how they could relate Jesus to God when God left him to die on the cross.

In the life of Jesus we find a structural feature of anticipation.[7] It seems to suggest that faith in Jesus would be possible only if God himself verified that faith. At the start of his public ministry Jesus preached about the kingdom of God, a reality which was already familiar to his listeners; his truthfulness, then, would depend on the arrival of the kingdom. We also find this element of anticipation in Luke 12 (vv. 8f.), where people's present relationship to Jesus will determine their *future* salvation or condemnation. There is also the fact that Jesus refused to work certain signs. This might suggest that he himself could not work the definitive sign in the present, that it would be worked by God in the future (see Mark 8:11f.; Matt. 12:38–42; 16:1–4; Luke 11:16,29,32; 12:54ff.).

This leads us to conclude that both in fact and in principle there was no elaboration of Christology before the resurrection and could not be. In fact the disciples did not reach any full or clear understanding of Jesus, and in principle his life was pointed toward the future.

The chronological development of the basic statements about Jesus might have gone something like this.[8] If Jesus had arisen from the dead, then God had confirmed his concrete preaching and life, including his death on the cross. (At first there may not have been too much reflection on the cross and its relationship to Christology.) By his resurrection from the dead Jesus came to closely resemble the expected Son of Man. This suggested the idea that the Son of Man was none other than Jesus himself, who would come again. And so we get two basic ideas in the earliest Christology: (1) There is in fact a distinctive relationship between Jesus and God, and it is expressed in the term "Son of Man"; (2) the parousia is imminent and people must wait expectantly for it.

The next step was a fundamental one. If the risen Jesus was exalted in glory by God, then God has manifested himself definitively in Jesus. Jesus' relationship with God is no longer bound up with the "Son of Man" model. This opened up the possibility of exploring the relationship more deeply, and in fact Christians did just that. They ended up professing that Jesus was the Son of God.

Alongside this process of universalizing the significance of Jesus there arose the possibility that Jesus ought to be preached to all human beings. Thus we get the movement toward the Gentiles.

Reflection on the person of Jesus took two basic forms. On the one hand it examined and elaborated honorific titles, applying them to Jesus; on the other hand it sought to theologize the events of Jesus' life. This was the main issue of the earliest Christology and its reflection on Jesus.[9]

It was perhaps due to the apocalyptic milieu in which the disciples lived that their first attempt to bring out the distinctive character of Jesus involved associating him with the figure of the Son of Man who was to come at the parousia. The *functional* oneness of Jesus and the Son of Man before Easter was now turned into a *personal* oneness. New Testament Christology would begin with the meaning and relevance of Jesus' future, and we see a clear reflection of it in Acts 3:20ff: "Thus may a season of refreshment be granted you by the Lord when he sends you Jesus, already designated as your Messiah. Jesus must remain in heaven until the time of universal restoration which God spoke of long ago through his holy prophets" (Acts 3:20–21). The same sense of future expectation can be found in the cry "Maranatha," which is regarded as quite early in time. It sums up the original understanding of the Eucharist as an anticipation of the *eschaton* in communion with Jesus. In that cry, "O Lord, come!" the emphasis is not on the title "Lord" but on the expectation of his coming. One confirmation of this view may well be those passages in the Synoptic Gospels where Jesus speaks of his person in terms of the coming parousia (see Matt. 25:31–46; Mark 14:61f.; Luke 12:8f.).

In all likelihood this focus on the future gradually led the early Christians to explore the relationship and reality of Jesus' person in terms of the present. Jesus is seen as the exalted one

(Acts 2:33,36; 5:31; 13:33; Rom. 1:4). He now sits at the right hand of God. The future lordship of Jesus was gradually shifted toward the present under the influence of Psalm 110: "The Lord said to my Lord, Sit at my right hand until I make your enemies your footstool" (Acts 2:34–35).

Quite aside from the exegetical question as to whether the most primitive Christology concentrated on the future parousia or Jesus' exaltation here and now, there is a serious systematic question. Is the figure of Jesus to be viewed in terms of the future or is it to be viewed solely in terms of the eternal present of Jesus as exalted Lord? The important point is that we must not break the tension evident in the two early forms of Christology. Unfortunately that is precisely what has happened. Preference has been given to the Christology that focuses on the exaltation of Jesus here and now, and hence to a liturgy that sees cultic worship as the proper way to approach that Christ. This has led people to de-emphasize the importance of the other aspect, to slight the note of expectant waiting for a Christ who is yet to come (see the previous chapter).

Jesus' relationship to God is brought out in two titles attributed to him, and they are given special stress in Pauline theology.

First of all, Jesus is the *Lord*. His lordship extends to everyone and everything (Rom. 14:9), but especially to the community that celebrates it in cultic worship (Phil. 2:11). Paul also appeals to the Lord's words (see 1 Cor. 7:10f., 25; 9:14) to give a basis for certain Christian obligations. Paul thus uses the title "Lord" to bring Jesus into the closest possible relationship with God. Both have parallel functions. Jesus holds lordship, and that is really typical of God himself.

Second, another important title points up Jesus' relationship of oneness with God. He is the "Son of God." Paul is inclined to see Jesus' work as that of an envoy. The Son is sent by the Father on a mission (Rom. 8:3; Gal. 4:4–6). That is how Paul explains the work of salvation: God "did not spare his own Son" (Rom. 8:32).It is as God's beloved Son that Jesus brings about our reconciliation with God (Gal. 2:20; Rom. 5:8,

10). When Paul uses the title "Son of God," it means that Jesus has a very special relationship with God. It practically means that Jesus himself is divine.

Jesus' union with God is also spelled out through the theological interpretation of the events in his life. One current of interpretation is *adoptionist* in tone and seems to be more primitive. It suggests that Jesus became the Son of God at some point in his life through some special adoption by God (Rom. 1:3f.). The event in question might be the resurrection, or it might even go back as far as his baptism (Mark 1:11). A second current of theological interpretation sees Jesus' union with God as something that has always existed. We find this in the notion of Jesus' pre-existence as espoused by Paul and John, for example. Its basic model is the theological view of pre-existent wisdom (Wisd. 9:9–12) and the various gnostic notions of a pre-existing savior.

This model led to the classical formulation of the doctrine of the *Incarnation*. It is a useful model, but certain things about the Incarnation must be kept clearly in mind. First, the Incarnation cannot serve as the *starting point* for theological reflection on Jesus; both logically and chronologically it is the *culmination* of such reflection. Second, the Incarnation cannot be viewed in natural categories, as if the Son took on some human *nature* once and for all. It must be viewed in historical categories. Jesus becomes fully human in an ongoing process, and it is that process that serves to mediate his divine sonship. We should view his sonship in terms of Jesus' concrete self-surrender to the Father through the vicissitudes of his historical career rather than in terms of some initial descent alone.

The whole matter of his virginal conception and birth falls midway between other currents of theological interpretation. On the one hand it seeks to move his union with God back before his resurrection or baptism. On the other hand it is not so radical as the tradition that stresses his divine pre-existence. It goes beyond adoptionism and points up Jesus' union with God from the very start of his life, but it does not imply any notion of God being incarnated.

Here I should like to offer some systematic observations on

the development of faith in Christ. They presuppose a study of the real-life development of that faith.[10] Thanks to the resurrection, the disciples experienced the fact that God had not abandoned Jesus on the cross after all, that God had confirmed Jesus' life and the cross in particular. Jesus' relationship with God came to be examined closely, and that process of examination may have gone something like this. First of all, after the resurrection it was no longer possible to think about Yahweh without thinking of Jesus also. Then it seemed that one could not contemplate the action of Yahweh without taking into account Jesus' activities. This realization was ultimately expressed in ontological categories which asserted that God does not exist as such without Jesus.

It is in some such process rather than in any explicitly trinitarian formulas that we find the first reflection on the triune reality of God.[11] The historical reality of Jesus is part of God, and so is the possibility of following Jesus. The basic experience of the first Christians is that God, the Father, continues to be the transcendent, nameless God of the absolute future. The Son is the historical appearance of the Father. More precisely he makes clear in history how one responds to the Father. The Spirit is God interiorized in the believer, more precisely in the community of believers.

The nature and content of Jesus' divinity can be understood only in terms of his concrete relationship to the Father. Rather than starting off from some a priori conception of divinity, we must consider Jesus' active and passive relationship to the Father. It is passive insofar as he is resurrected by the Father; it is active insofar as the historical Jesus embodies total trust in, and self-surrender to, the Father.

The various honorific titles give positive expression to the intuition which we have just formulated in negative terms. They are explanatory models based on the theology of the Old Testament and Hellenism. Some titles stress Jesus' relationship to the kingdom of God: e.g., Son of Man, Messiah, and prophet. Others put more stress on his relationship with the person of God: e.g., Son of God and Logos. Some titles concentrate on Jesus' earthly life (Prophet, High Priest, Servant of

Yahweh) while others stress his divine reality (Lord, Logos, Son of God). It was the one-sided emphasis on the divine title and the gradual de-emphasis of the earthly ones that paved the way for Docetism.

Of particular importance in this respect was the failure to elaborate the title "Servant of Yahweh." In my opinion it is not just another title. When we set it over against the title "Lord," we have the dialectics needed to understand the authentic sovereignty of Christ and to concretize the abstract notion of divinity as "power" in truly Christian terms. Equally important is the fact that such expressions as "Christ crucified" (1 Cor. 1:23) and the "slain lamb" (Rev. 5:6) are not normally regarded as titles of Christ. The obvious reason for this lies in the fact that such terms were not used in the theology of the Old Testament and Hellenism to point up a human being's peculiar or distinctive relationship with the deity. But they should serve as sources for christological reflection precisely because of their distinctiveness.

The use of titles in the New Testament moved in two different directions, as did that of the soteriological models mentioned earlier. In one case honorific titles were applied to Jesus in order to explain his importance. This was a movement from the universal to the particular, from Christ to Jesus; and the underlying assumption is that we can get to know Jesus on the basis of realities and concepts already known. In the other case the titles were explained and interpreted on the basis of Jesus. Moving from the particular to the universal, from Jesus to Christ, people would seek to discover and explain the uniqueness of Jesus. For example, Paul stresses that the risen and exalted one is none other than the Jesus who had been crucified. The Epistle to the Hebrews affirms, not that Jesus is a priest, but that being a priest means being like Jesus. The Joannine writings affirm, not that Jesus is God, but rather that the Son of God is none other than the Jesus whom witnesses have seen and heard and touched (1 John 1:1).[12]

After the resurrection Jesus becomes the one who is proclaimed rather than the one who does the proclaiming. Rather than being the one who talks about God, he now becomes the one whom others talk about as they would of God. There is a discontinuity here which could prove fatal for Christianity. It would be very serious if Jesus ceased to be the way to God, as he was in his earthly life, and simply became the goal. The fact is that even after the resurrection Jesus is seen in relationship to the Father, not in terms of himself alone (1 Cor. 15:24–28; Rom. 6:10; 1 Cor. 3:23; 11:3; Rom. 15:7, etc.).[13]

Finally, the resurrection does not cause the disappearance of the eschatological outlook. It is not as if the grand finale had taken place in the resurrection. Jesus preached the coming of God and Paul preached justification. There is continuity between the two because both are eschatological and hence call for the very same sort of life. The following of Jesus cannot be set up in opposition to justification by grace. What Paul sees in fact is that grace has come about through Jesus and that eschatological life is modelled after him.[14]

NOTES

1. In the brief compass of this chapter I can only offer a brief summary of the more important theological motifs involved in the "resurrection of Jesus." To them one could add the trinitarian and cosmic implications as well as the implications for salvation history insofar as they are based on the statements of the New Testament. What I want to stress here is the mistake in proposing to reduce or restrict the resurrection to its christological aspect. That would amount to abandoning the focus that has guided our reflections so far, i.e., the *relational* aspect of Jesus and his life. That aspect must be maintained even with respect to the resurrection. If the resurrection is the great eschatological event, then its importance must extend beyond the figure of Jesus himself. "The various aspects of the resurrection event should not be isolated or absolutized; nor should they be understood to define Jesus' resurrection in such a way that they can provide an exhaustive inventory of that happening" (B. Klappert, *Diskussion um Kreuz und Auferstehung* [Wuppertal: Aussaat, 1967] p. 40).

2. J. Moltmann, *Esperanza y planificación del futuro*, p. 85f; see note 34 of chap. 2 in this volume.

3. See L. Boff, *Jesucristo el liberador*, pp. 144–48; see note 9 of chap. 3 in this volume.

4. D. Bonhoeffer, "Costly Grace," in *The Cost of Discipleship*, Eng. trans. (New York: Macmillan Paperbacks, 1963), pp. 45–48.

5. The point here is that myth is essentially a conception of existence and history based on origins. "Myth" signifies some event that took place in primeval time, and that therefore is fundamental for the whole order and regulation of life. See W. Pannenberg, *Christentum und Mythos* (Gütersloh:

Mohn, 1972); also my article, "Mito, antropología e historia en el pensamiento bíblico," in *Estudios Centroamericanos,* San Salvador, 305-6 (1974), pp. 170–79.

The resurrection of Jesus should not be conceived as a way of fixing Christ in the past in such a way that the present is already explained and justified in relation to that past. Instead the resurrection, by its very nature, points toward the future of humanity.

6. See L. Boff, *Jesucristo el liberador,* pp. 160–65.

7. See W. Pannenberg, *Fundamentos de cristología,* pp. 67–82; see note 6, chap. 1 in this volume.

8. Ibid., pp. 82–92.

9. That reflection was based on the experienced happening of Jesus' resurrection, but it then moved on to reflect on the reality of Jesus himself in relation to God. It could have moved in two directioñs in trying to relate him to God. One would entail reflection of the figure of the future Son of Man. The other would entail reflection on the already exalted Son of God (see R. Schnackenburg, "Cristología del Nuevo Testamento," in *Mysterium Salutis,* III/1 [Madrid, 1969], pp. 268–76). The point is that we must put stress on the *process* of reflection itself. That process of reflection on the truth of Jesus' person is where we now recover, in theologized form, the figure of the historical Jesus.

10. See Schnackenburg, ibid.; O. Cullmann, *Die Christologie des Neuen Testaments,* see note 29, chap. 3; F. Hahn, *Christologische Hoheitstitel,* see note 29, chap. 3.

11. F.J. Schierse stresses the point that our understanding of the Trinity cannot come from interpreting New Testament passages on the basis of dogma, or even from starting with the trinitarian formulas we find already elaborated in the theologies of Paul and John. Instead we must go back to the way revelation took place in the life of Jesus himself ("La revelación de la trinidad en el Nuevo Testamento," in *Mysterium Salutis,* II/1 [Madrid, 1969], pp. 117–65).

12. Thus the creation of new titles is justified and even required. In accordance with what was said earlier in this section, they would spell out the significance of Jesus today. Thus Karl Rahner calls him "the absolute bearer of salvation," and Teilhard de Chardin calls him "the omega point of evolution." In doing so, they are simply continuing the logic of the New Testament. For the very same reason there is a need for new titles to be applied to Jesus in Latin America. L. Boff, for example, calls him "the Liberator."

In creating new titles, however, we must remember that it is from the figure of Jesus himself that we know what it means to be "the absolute bearer of salvation," "the omega point of evolution," "the liberator," and so forth. Obviously we are dealing with a hermeneutic circle here, but what is at stake is the christological concentration of theology.

13. See W. Thüsing, "La imagen de Dios en el Nuevo Testamento," in *Dios como problema,* edited by J. Ratzinger, Spanish trans. (Madrid, 1973), pp. 80–120.

14. See J. Moltmann, *Der gekreuzigte Gott,* pp. 107–19; see note 10, chap. 1 in this volume.

9.

The Historical Jesus and the Christ of Faith:
The Tension Between Faith and Religion

It is common knowledge that the whole problem of the historical Jesus arose when modern exegesis discovered that any talk about a biography of Jesus of Nazareth was naive. Such a biography could not come from the Gospels because they were written after Jesus' resurrection and based on the faith of the first Christians. Kahler concluded that the authentic Christ is not Jesus of Nazareth but "the Christ who is preached."[1] Bultmann pushed that insight further and popularized it.[2] He asserted that the reality of Christ is identical with the reality of preaching about Christ. When the message of Christ's death and resurrection is proclaimed, we are confronted with the obligation of acknowledging ourselves to be sinners. We are forced to realize that we are closed up in ourselves, trying to give meaning to our lives on the basis of ourselves alone. We must either stay with that option and be sinners, or else become believers and allow God to provide us with the meaning of our lives. The Christ of Bultmann is the Christ of faith.

In recent decades the view has changed in Europe. Exegetes such as Jeremias[3] and Käsemann[4] became much less skeptical about the possibility of ascertaining the fundamental facts and features of the historical Jesus, though they had no illusions about reconstructing his complete biography. A strictly theological interest went hand in hand with this exegetical interest, stressing the importance of the historical Jesus for

Christian faith as well as for historical science. Bonhoeffer made an important contribution here with his notion of Christ as "the man for others."[5] Bonhoeffer himself did not have time to elaborate the notion, but he did point up the need to explore it further. If Jesus was a man "for" others, then obviously we could not simply rest content with the Christ of faith. We would have to go back to the concrete figure of Jesus and see how he expressed his commitment in real-life history. Only on that basis could we comprehend and appreciate his saving life as the risen one.

Today studies on the historical Jesus abound in Europe. Surprisingly enough, some of them are being written by Marxists. Desiring to be truly "radical," to go back to the roots, they hope to find in Jesus of Nazareth one of the roots that must be incorporated into present-day Marxism if it is to gain further self-understanding and to be more relevant here and now.[6]

In Latin America liberation theology has turned almost spontaneously toward the figure of the historical Jesus.[7] Latin American bishops have not hesitated to invoke that figure at the Synod of Bishops in Rome. This interest is not merely exegetical or historical. Latin Americans are not interested solely in ascertaining the historical facts. They regard the historical Jesus as the most satisfactory theological focus for all the different themes in liberation theology. The following quote from J.P. Miranda nicely sums up the importance of the historical Jesus for liberation theology: "No authority can decree that everything is permitted: for justice and exploitation are not so indistinguishable. And Christ died so that we might know that not everything is permitted. But not any Christ. The Christ who cannot be co-opted by accomodationists and opportunists is the historical Jesus."[8]

When the problem of the historical Jesus is posed in those terms, we move beyond any merely noetic interest in Christ. We no longer simply want information about his historical life and his present-day existence as the risen Lord. Without forgetting all that, we now focus our interest on a somewhat different question: What exactly is the correct way to gain access to Christ? Simplifying the matter somewhat, we can say that this question leads us to some conclusion such as the following. We can gain access to the Christ of faith, the resurrected Lord, through some sort of direct intentional act: e.g., a profession of faith, a doxology, a prayer, or cultic worship. However, we cannot gain access to the historical Jesus that way, as the Gospels make clear. We gain access to him only through a specific kind of praxis, which the Gospels describe as the "following of Jesus" or "discipleship."

Thus there is a tension existing between the historical Jesus and the Christ of faith, between cultic worship and discipleship. It does not mean that we are faced with an either-or situation, that the two dimensions are mutually exclusive and we must choose between them. My point here is to point up where the logical priority lies, and it lies with what is prior chronologically. It lies, in short, with the historical Jesus. This means that access to the Christ of faith can only come through access to the historical Jesus, through discipleship. And the ultimate reason for this is that the Christ of faith is not just some vague, exalted Lord but the very man who lived a certain kind of life and died a certain way because of that.

In this chapter we shall take for granted the main features of the historical Jesus that were spelled out in previous chapters. Instead of reiterating them here, I want to show what has happened in the history of the church when the historical Jesus has been overlooked or forgotten. I propose the following thesis: *Whenever Christian faith focuses one-sidedly on the Christ of faith and wittingly or unwittingly forgets the historical Jesus, and to the extent it does that, it loses its specific structure as Christian faith and tends to turn into religion.*[9]

To appreciate the point of this thesis, we must briefly consider the distinction between faith and religion. By "religion" here I mean a conception of the world and humanity, a conception of reality, in which the meaning of the whole is already given at the start because the reality of God is satisfactorily shaped and defined from the very beginning. The reality of God is characterized by omnipotence, omniscience, and retributive justice. Normally associated with that conception of God is an anthropology focusing on origins in the distant past rather than on the future. The truth about humanity, its meaning, and history has already been spoken; it is already constituted in principle. We can only hope to construe it literally, so logically history becomes quite superfluous.

Religion also assumes that there is some privileged locale for direct and immediate access to the deity. In the classic religious version that locale is cultic worship; in the philosophical version of people like Aristotle, it is reason. Though the deity is unknown and awesome, he can in principle be manipulated. He is particularly open to such manipulation through legalistic and moralistic requirements. Though God can be totally demanding, there is a code of obligations articulated by religion which, if carried out, does summon the deity to give a certain recompense. In short, there is a mechanism that allows people to secure themselves against God. The fulfillment of certain dictates, demanding though they may be, allows people to retain the security that they prize so highly.

The structure of Christian faith is essentially different. First of all, the essence of the deity does not appear in genesis myths but at the end of history. It will appear with the establishment of the kingdom of God and "a new heaven and earth." Thus the meaning of the whole is not given from the very start. Second, God does not appear in history to explain the world or to justify a specific regimen of life. He appears in a very specific context, namely, when he "hears the cries of the oppressed." This means that we cannot talk about the meaning of the world or history so long as injustice and the cries of the oppressed continue. The Christian God does not guarantee our security through any legalistic mechanism. He guarantees it in a most paradoxical way, demanding that we give up all our security and abandon ourselves to God. We see this in the Bible when Abraham is asked to leave his father's house and live solely by hope. The classical concepts of divinity, omnipotence, and justice are fleshed out concretely in a surprising way when Jesus appears. In him they are presented as grace and love. God does not display his omnipotence by conquering the negative reality of the world from outside. Instead he does so by immersing himself wholly within it and thereby displaying the power of love.

Christian faith also rejects the idea that there is any direct access to God in cultic worship. It can come only indirectly through service to human beings, specifically to those who can represent and embody the total otherness of God in historical terms, namely, the poor and oppressed. Finally, the ethical side of Christian faith is not like that of religion. It does not come down to fulfilling certain prescriptions in order to secure oneself against God and win a reward in some other life. The fulfillment of Christian obligations embodies the only way to gain access to God. It verifies the fact that we are participating in God's life and hence makes the reality of God "truly real." Rather than securing ourselves against God, we turn the history of the world into God's own history.

On the basis of that description we can say that Christian faith does not have a religious structure. It has its own distinctive structure, which we learn from the way God reveals himself in the Old Testament and especially in Christ. A religious conception of Christianity would therefore go against the very nature of Christianity. When and if the Christian faith takes on a religious structure, it ceases to be Christian and becomes something else. It becomes a religion, a worldview, a philosophy, or one of the many other substitutes that we latch on to when we face the question of life and its meaning. [10]

Now I am not going to analyze the terms "historical Jesus" and "Christ of faith" to prove the truth of my thesis. I am not going to consider whether they essentially relate to a religious structure as opposed to a real structure of faith, or vice versa. My aim here is one that might seem more modest. I simply want to undertake a brief historical investigation to show how forgetfulness of the historical Jesus and one-sided concentration on the risen Christ has in fact led Christian faith to take on a religious structure in the pejorative sense. Such an investigation could and should be expanded to take in the history of the church right up to our own day. But here I will concentrate on the early history of the church. It should not be difficult for the reader to see that the tendencies noted here have cropped up throughout the history of the church.

I shall begin with a seemingly paradoxical statement. The resurrection of Christ is the major event that serves as the ultimate ground for faith in Jesus of Nazareth. It cannot be ignored by any faith or theology that purports to be Christian. At the same time, however, it is also what makes it possible for Christians to forget Jesus of Nazareth. Hence it is what makes it possible for Christian faith to stop being Christian and turn into a version of religion. I want to show historically that the most radical temptation facing Christianity is the temptation to focus one-sidedly on the risen Christ, and that the way to overcome the temptation is to go back once again to the historical Jesus.

I shall do this in terms of four points I regard as basic. In the first section I shall consider the tension existing between Jesus of Nazareth and the Spirit of the risen one; in present-day terms it is the problem of "pentecostalism." In the second section I shall consider the tension existing between faith and metaphysical theology of an explicative sort; it is the problem of orthodoxy. In the third section I shall consider the tension existing between two different types of political theology, one espousing the acquisition and use of power and the other espousing prophetic witness and denunciation; it is the problem of power as the mediation of God. Finally, in the fourth section I shall consider the tension existing between cultic worship and discipleship; it is the question as to whether and where there is some privileged locale of access to God.

THE TENSION BETWEEN JESUS OF NAZARETH
AND THE SPIRIT OF THE RISEN LORD

A generation after the resurrection, Christians found themselves in a new historical and theological situation. Historically speaking, they no longer lived with Jesus himself; most of them had not even known him personally. Theologically speaking, Jesus was no longer the one doing the preaching but the one whom they preached about. Jesus was no longer preaching about the kingdom of God, and people might be tempted to believe that the definitive kingdom had already arrived.

The consequences of this new situation can be seen clearly in the Christian communities of the Hellenistic world. Unlike the Christologies which arose in the Palestinian communities, the christological hymns of the Hellenist communities (see Phil. 2:6–11; 1 Tim. 3:16) stress the enthronement of Jesus as Lord wielding power and dominion. They no longer talk about the historical Jesus in all his concreteness. The Christian community seems to be living in heaven already, and salvation is viewed as total liberty in the present: "By virtue of the resurrection . . . Christ was for them the new God in the pantheon of mystery religions; and they shared his lordship through baptism."[11]

This situation is reflected clearly in Paul's two epistles to the Corinthians. The Christian communities in Corinth lived in an atmosphere of religious enthusiasm over their newfound total freedom in Christ, and it found spontaneous expression in their liturgical gatherings. So strong was their sense of freedom in the present that they did not invest their hope in expectant longing for the final resurrection. Thus their church "saw itself as another kind of mystery religion—the authentic one of course—and turned Jesus into their cultic God—an incomparable God of course."[12]

The important thing to note is that this liberty and enthusiasm of the mystery-religion type derived from a false theology of the resurrection. It was based on a one-sided understanding of the Christ of faith. The risen and exalted Christ became so exclusively important that all interest in the historical Jesus disappeared. Emphasis was now placed on the Spirit of the risen Christ and his presence in the community. The critical nature of the situation is brought out clearly by the fact that Paul had to rebuke them sharply: "Nobody who speaks in the Spirit of God ever says, 'Cursed be Jesus' " (1 Cor. 12:3).

Christology was thus being turned into an enthusiastic but abstract orthodoxy that was more inclined to reflect the desires and aspirations of the surrounding milieu than anything associated with Jesus. Union with Christ was no longer effected through concrete discipleship but rather through participation in the sacraments. Through the sacraments, baptism and the eucharist in particular, Christians were already living in heaven with Christ. Forgetfulness of the earth went along with forgetfulness of Jesus. Societal relations were idealized in the name of the freedom stemming from the risen Lord. The lordship of the risen Christ was interpreted in such a way that Christians could concentrate solely on what he was already giving his disciples and could overlook the demands he laid upon them. The basic problem of the Christian community, then, lay in a false theology of the resurrection and hence a false conception of Christian liberty and praxis.

Paul's reaction. Faced with this situation, Paul had to speak out against a false and alienating theology of the resurrection. His basic tack is to recover and rehabilitate the historical Jesus, though of course Paul himself does not use the term in our modern sense. From the very start of his first epistle Paul stresses the historical Jesus, concentrating on his most concrete and scandalous aspect: i.e., the cross (1 Cor. 1:23). It is the crucified Jesus that Paul now preaches in the present.

His intention is clear enough when we realize that Hellenistic religion was also familiar with dying and rising gods, and even with a descent into hell. As Käsemann puts it: "If the cross is simply the shadowy entrance way into heaven, the final supreme obstacle before eventual triumph, then the Christian message does not differ basically from what other rival religions might say."[13] In Paul's eyes the cross is not simply a passing episode leading to the resurrection; it is the other side of the resurrection. The cross cannot be understood without the resurrection, but neither can the resurrection be understood without the cross.

The christological aspect of Christ's present lordship and dominion is also reworked thoroughly by Paul, Christ's lordship should not be interpreted in enthusiastic or emotional terms because it has not yet destroyed "every sovereignty, authority, and power" (1 Cor. 15:24), nor the last enemy, death (verse 26). Only at the end of time will all things be subjected to Christ (verse 28). For Paul, then, the cross is not simply a passing stage prior to the resurrection, an event that loses all meaningfulness once the resurrection has taken place. For Paul, "the exalted Lord continues to bear the marks of the nails he received on earth; otherwise he would not be identical with Jesus."[14]

Operating on those basic premises, Paul attempts to correct an erroneous understanding of the sacraments based on excessive enthusiasm (1 Cor. 10:1–22). He stresses the ambiguity of the ecstatic gifts that the Corinthians attribute to the Spirit. Spiritual gifts are worthless in themselves unless they help to build up the community (1 Cor. 12:5) and are inspired by authentic love (1 Cor. 13). These two criteria go back to the historical Jesus who lived "for" others and fulfilled the commandment of love. Authentic Christian life must be based on the example of Jesus and his cross, as Paul points out with respect to his own life (2 Cor. 6:4f.; 11:23f.; Gal. 6:17). Jesus' authentic power is revealed in his frailty and impotence (2 Cor. 13:3f.).

As Paul sees it, what is at stake in the Corinthian community is not just a proper conception of liturgy and service within the Christian community but the very essence and existence of Christian faith itself. He insists that Christian faith is not basically the cultic proclamation of the risen Lord and the enthusiastic liberty that flows from him. Christian faith basically comes down to following Jesus and configuring our lives to his (Rom. 6:5f.). If it is not that, then Christianity runs the risk of turning into a religion like that of the other Hellenistic mystery religions. It will try to satisfy people's needs and yearnings, to give meaning to their lives, by transporting them from their cross-laden lives in this world to some realm of enthusiastic belief, ecstasy, and freedom. Such a transposition cannot be justified in the name of Jesus, according to Paul.

Paul thus sets his own theology over against the theology of the risen Christ held by the Corinthians. The liberty flowing from the resurrection finds its concrete content in the liberty of the crucified Jesus. It is a freedom to serve and to suffer in the service of human beings even as Jesus did. In affirming the identity of the risen Christ with the crucified Jesus, Paul is saying that the historical way of living as resurrected beings here and now—which is what the Corinthians want to do—is to live a life of service under the aegis of the cross. Christians must follow Jesus in discipleship.

The basic mistake of the Corinthians lay in the fact that they held a dualistic view. They did not think that the resurrection could be lived amid the negative circumstances of human life here in history. They felt that they would have to live as if they were no longer part of this world if they wanted to live as resurrected beings, and they seemed to experience such a transposition in the spiritual gifts and charisms they received. Paul corrects them sharply. Living as resurrected beings here in history means living a life of service and self-surrender that leads to the cross. Christians must immerse themselves in this world, serving other human beings in order to overcome evil. We can subsequently celebrate our life of service and discipleship in liturgical acts of thanksgiving, but discipleship itself cannot be replaced by cultic worship or ecstatic union with the Lord.

I think Paul is telling the Corinthians the same thing that I expressed above in systematic language. He is talking about the danger of the Christian faith being turned into a religion. When the figure of Christ is separated from his concrete life and death, all we have left is a "divine" residue that can easily be assimilated to the general notion of divinity in vogue. Christianity would then become a new religion based on some "deity," but not on Jesus of Nazareth. Placed at a distance by history and divinized by a theological process, Jesus would become nothing more than a symbol signifying idolatrous overcoming of the law, victory over death, and triumph over the demons. Such a Jesus could be celebrated in cultic worship, but no one would know for sure how or in what way he differed from other Hellenistic deities such as Attis and Hermes. We would be back with the old scheme of religion, and only the name of the diety would have changed. Our ties with the concrete history of Jesus would be lost in a new deity who embodied all that is eternal and ahistorical. Jesus would be turned into an abstract principle. As time went on all could find what was of interest to them in the figure of Jesus, and Jesus could pave the way for a new religion. No longer would the figure of Jesus call into question the whole scheme of religion, as Jesus of Nazareth did in his own time. Instead religious people could appeal to Jesus and fashion him after their own needs and desires.

Thus the example of the Corinthian community shows us how the risen Christ could be used by Christians to do away with Jesus himself.

The general reaction of the New Testament. Needless to say, we would have to scour the whole New Testament if we wanted to treat this topic exhaustively. In particular we would have to consider the treatment of Docetism in the Johannine writings and the Christology of the Letter to the Hebrews. I shall refer to the latter a bit later on, but here I simply want to offer two general observations. They will help the reader to see how the New Testament focuses on the problem of the historical Jesus and his relationship to the Christ of faith. I used the example of the Corinthian community earlier because it is a classic case.

My first observation is a historical one, but it also has theological value. It has to do with the very existence of Gospels. We now realize that those writings do not purport to be biography when they describe the life of Jesus. We also know that they were written after the resurrection and in the light of that event; hence they are basically professions of faith in Christ. To confine our attention to the earliest Gospel, that of Mark, we find that even in it Jesus is already depicted as the Son of God, God's epiphany on earth, and one who has power over evil spirits. Yet that is not the most noteworthy characteristic of Mark's Gospel. As E. Schweizer has pointed out, the most remarkable thing is that Mark's Gospel *was written at all.* [15] What is of great interest to us here is the logic underlying the effort to write Gospels in the first place.

We should remember that when Mark was writing his Gospel other sources and writings were already in existence, e.g., various professions of faith in Jesus, the fairly well developed theology of Paul, collections of Jesus' sayings, some miracle accounts, a summary narrative of the passion, and a compilation of polemic sermons and segments of Jesus' apocalyptic discourse. We must also realize that in contemporary Hellenistic culture we find compilations of the opinions of various philosophers and biographical data concerning them.

The significance of Mark's Gospel in that overall context is that it is not primarily interested in anthologizing Jesus' sayings. Instead it purports to narrate the deeds of Jesus that gave historical embodiment to his sayings. It is also surprising to note how much space Mark gives to Jesus' passion in view of the fact that Christians now professed faith in him as the risen Christ. Mark is the evangelist who has Jesus die totally abandoned by God, and we cannot help but wonder what is the logic underlying this interest in the concrete details of Jesus' passion and death. The answer is not hard to find. Mark clearly is anxious to make sure that the concrete figure of Jesus of Nazareth is not dissolved into some abstract symbol. He is out to combat the threat of Docetism and Gnosticism. However much the Gospels may be imbued with theology, they are descriptions of the historical Jesus. The early Christian communities were not content with the existing versions of theology and Christology. At the very least this suggests that they sensed the danger of ending up with an abstract deity and sought to combat it by turning once again to the historical Jesus. And in doing this they placed great stress on the most concrete and scandalous fact of his life, namely, his passion and death on the cross.

My second observation is theological. In the writings of Paul two words are joined that have very different connotations and functions in themselves. The two words are "Christ" and "Jesus." Accustomed as we are to using these words together, we tend to overlook the theological meaning of the name "Jesus Christ." "Jesus" is a proper name belonging to a concrete individual who lived a concrete life and died a concrete death. "Christ" is not a proper name at all. It is a descriptive term that basically means "the anointed one." Various traditions of the Old Testament specified this meaning somewhat, so that it referred to someone who had a specific mission from God and a unique relationship to the kingdom of God. The theological importance of the name "Jesus Christ," then, is that the two words are brought together. The abstract term cannot be separated from the concrete name. Isolated from the proper name, the term "Christ" is an abstract honorific into which people can project all sorts of ideas and yearnings. It could become the basis for some new religion, in the pejorative sense of the term. But the term loses its abstract air if it is linked with the proper name "Jesus."

We can detect an important two-way movement in the effort to bring together the name "Jesus" and the title "Christ." On the one hand the early Christian communities attempted to specify the concrete meaning of Jesus by investing him with honorific titles whose import was already familiar to them from the Old Testament and Hellenistic religion. Using such titles, they sought to make clear that Jesus was not just another human being, that they professed faith in him for certain reasons. Even more important for our purposes here is the other movement, however. For the early Christians also sought to comprehend the meaning of the honorific titles on the basis of Jesus and his concrete life. Thus the New Testament does not say that Jesus is the Christ, implying that the a priori meaning of the term "Christ" makes it clear who Jesus was. Instead it says that it is in fact Jesus who is the Christ, implying that the meaning of the term "Christ" can be understood only through the concrete figure of Jesus.

If we were to follow the first approach and try to figure out who Jesus was on the basis of the general meaning of the term "Christ," then we would fall victim to the typical religious scheme of things. We would be using some abstract universal term, whose meaning was supposedly known already, to figure out who Jesus was. Jesus would simply be a concrete application of the abstract universal. When Paul uses the name "Jesus Christ," he is trying to preclude that danger. The real meaning of the term "Christ" is to be found in the concrete figure of Jesus. This prevents us from giving way to the inertial tendencies of religious thought, because the concrete name of

Jesus cannot be easily manipulated and turned to improper uses.

The same basic point holds true for all the other honorific titles that the New Testament uses to point up the significance of Jesus. The meaning of such epithets as "Lord" and such concepts as "omnipotence" cannot be deduced from the meaning they had in Judaic or Hellenistic thought. The meaning of "lordship" can be discerned only through Jesus' concrete exercise of lordship. The same holds true for the loftiest epithet that John applies to Jesus: Logos. John tells us that Jesus is the Logos, the Son of God, indeed God himself. However, he is not making Jesus "one" particular instance of the deity, implying that the nature and character of God is already known from Judaic and Hellenistic thought. Instead he is saying that the nature of the "deity" can be known only through Jesus. The most evident proof of the New Testament way of approaching the whole matter can be found in its trinitarian conception of God. In principle it breaks with the old scheme of the existing religions.[16]

So far I have been talking here about Christology, noting the temptation to transform Christian faith into religion in this area. But the same point applies to other features of New Testament thought. It is not surprising that Christianity should be tempted to transform itself into just another religion, since it has lived in the midst of other religions and cultures. The point is that it can give way to that temptation only by separating itself from the historical Jesus and focusing exclusively on the Christ of faith. When the Christ of faith is viewed in abstract, universal terms, then he can serve as a bridge between Christianity and the more classic forms of religion.

THE TENSION BETWEEN FAITH AND AN EXPLICATIVE, METAPHYSICAL THEOLOGY

Though it was not a straight-line development, we find a shift in the conception of faith that is quite well developed by the time of the second-century apologists. Originally faith was viewed as the following of Jesus and worshipful acclamation of the risen Lord. Gradually that conception changed, and faith came to be regarded as an overall explanation of reality. Here I can only point up some of the things that paved the way for such a development.

The christological supposition underlying such a development was the conception of the risen Christ as the Logos—i.e., as the authentic and definitive word of the Father. The wisdom of the cross and the figure of the historical Jesus came to be forgotten when Christians began to interpret the term "Logos" in a one-sided way, and this tendency was heightened when the early Christian apologists entered into debate with Hellenistic philosophers and sought to elaborate the cognitive status of Christianity.

The first structural step in this direction is to be found within the New Testament itself, where we note a gradual shift of interest from Christology to ecclesiology. To be sure, Christ does not disappear from the picture altogether; but more and more the church takes center stage. Its organizational aspect is treated in the pastoral epistles, among others, and there are attempts to define its essential nature in such epistles as that to the Ephesians. The underlying problem was that Christians wanted to integrate the figure of Christ into a doctrine of the church. The danger was that the church would overshadow Christ. As Käsemann puts it: "The church took center stage to such an extent that the figure of Jesus paled into insignificance. He became a shadowy figure, an ecclesial icon. He became the church's founder and cultic hero."[17]

Christian reflection began to shift from consideration of the ultimate truth of the crucified and risen Jesus to consideration of the church as "the pillar of truth" (1 Tim. 3:15). Feeling that it possessed the truth about Jesus, the church began to nurture conceptions of the faith that were more and more removed from the following of Jesus and more and more like those held by surrounding religions. The faith became "sound doctrine" (2 Tim. 4:3), and people began to talk about the many concrete items that went into its content. This conception was not clearly formulated in the beginning (Acts 6:7; Rom. 10:8), but

later preaching came to be regarded as the transmission of
doctrine (Acts 11:26) and faith was seen to involve a variety of
propositions (Heb. 11). Timothy is told: "If you put these
instructions before the brotherhood you will be a good servant
of Christ Jesus, reared in the words of faith and the sound
doctrine you have faithfully followed" (1 Tim. 4:6).

The lifestyle of the ecclesial community began to be described with a technical term. It was the "way" (Greek *hodos*;
Acts 9:2; 18:25; 19:9,23; 22:4; 24:14,22). This new "way"
marked Christians off from the followers of Judaism first of all.
But the fact is that in using such a term to differentiate Christians from Jews, Christians were actually suggesting that their
lifestyle was analogous to other religious ways. The Christian
way was allegedly "the" way, but it was now being pictured in
terms like those of other religions. Commenting on the term
"way," Bultmann notes that it could refer to the Christian
community as such or to Christian doctrine. In either case it
shows clearly that the Christian community sees itself "as a
new religion alongside Judaism and paganism."[18]

We see the same development at the start of the second
century when Ignatius of Antioch coined the term *chris-
tianismos* ("Christianity"). The term was used to differentiate
the Christian way from that of the Jews, but in fact Christianity
came to be regarded as a new religion in the polemical debate
against Judaism. Faith is no longer viewed as that which satisfactorily and adequately describes the Christian life: "Faith
now comes to be regarded as the first step, to be followed by
a way of life in accordance with Christianity. . . . The neol-
ogism of Ignatius clearly articulates a new self-understanding in which Christianity views itself in terms of
the surrounding religions."[19]

The adoption of religious nomenclature also helped to foster
the view that Christianity was indeed a religion. It is already
evident in Paul's speech in the Areopagus (Acts 17:22f.),
which may not in fact have been spoken as such by Paul
himself. There we find a missionary preaching style very much
like that of late Old Testament Judaism (Wisd. 13). Pagan
religious terms and notions are introduced to make the

speaker's message comprehensible. The reader should note the way faith is presented in this speech of Paul's. Here it seems to correspond with what is commonly regarded as religion, whereas in his letter to the Romans (1:18–23) faith is the very antithesis of religion.

The adaptation of existing religious terminology by the Christian faith can be seen in the use of the term *eusebeia*. Its original Greek meaning was "attention," "religious fear and awe," "scrupulous concern." It is used in Acts to describe the religious piety and reverence of such people as the pagan Roman centurion, Cornelius (10:2), his escort (10:7), and the Jew, Ananias (22:12). Later, however, it is also applied to the perfect Christian (2 Pet. 2:9); and it is in general use in the pastoral epistles (Tit. 2:12; 2 Tim. 3:12). This usage paved the way for an outlook that would judge the faith in terms of general religious piety and practice. By the time that the first letter of Clement was being written, faith (*pistis*) and piety (*eusebeia*) "were mutually complementary if not actually interchangeable terms."[20] Faith was no longer being seen as suffering-laden service to the crucified Jesus. It was being turned into the more general notion of piety as one of the virtues that people are obliged to practice toward the deity.

The process of intellectualizing the faith in an extensive way reached its culmination with the apologists of the second century. They sought to defend the Christian faith in a world where the very notion of faith was suspect, if not completely despised. The difficult task facing the apologists was to uphold the position that faith is real knowledge and wisdom so that it would be acceptable to the Hellenistic world. They carried out that task, but at a price: Once more faith was brought closer to what was commonly understood to be religion.

Paul's concept of revelation was a very different one. He said that the good news of God had been revealed to Christian believers whereas God's wrath would be revealed to the pagans (Rom. 1:17–3:21). The apologists replaced this notion of revelation with the Hellenistic one. They borrowed the Stoic concept of revelation to explain God's revelation in Jesus Christ, thus ensuring the univeralism of the faith while disregarding the most characteristic features of Jesus. The apologist Justin, for example, maintained that even in the Sybilline oracles it was clear that Christianity was the true religion. Universal revelation in the cosmos, the Old Testament, and pagan religions manifested the truth of God's revelation in Jesus.

It should be noted that there was criticism of religion to be found even within paganism. It was particularly evident in Epicureanism, and we do well to note the two-edged strategy that the apologists adopted with respect to it. On the one hand they joined it in combatting polytheism and myth; on the other hand they allied themselves with the established religions to attack Epicureanism. We can readily understand why the apologists would look for points of contact between Christian faith and the established religions. The faith was under attack, and all sorts of accusations were being levelled against it. But in their effort to prove that Christianity was the true religion, they overstepped the historical boundaries set by Jesus. To achieve universality and hence its own justification, Christianity had to be inserted into the mold of an explicative Logos that spelled out the meaning of the universe. Only in that way could it be viewed favorably by its opponents and prove its right to exist. While it continued to criticize myth-based cultic worship, it had to take on the form of a world-explaining religion.

The apologetic need to justify the Christian faith in the face of the Greek *logos* meant that the Christian faith would be intellectualized, not only in the heretical gnostic movement but also among loyal Christians. Even though it sought to combat gnosticism, Christianity was influenced by the formulations and attitudes of that movement. As Clement of Alexandria put it: "The truth sought by philosophers is identical with the divine revelation brought by Christ."[21] Faith, the ideal of human existence, is really faith enlightened by knowledge. It is the faith of an explicative Logos, and that is why it was called "philosophy" by the apologists. Faith, then, was turned into a theory of Christianity, a theory that sought to explain the whole of reality. It brought together a whole series of specific truths and doctrines, elaborating them in such a way that they might serve as an overall explanation.

So we can detect the gradual disappearance of the notion of faith espoused by people like Mark and Paul. The new line of development was not wrong because it attempted to ponder the faith, to seek out its objective nature and its congruence with philosophy and human knowledge. Its error lay in its underlying christological conception. After his resurrection Christ could rightfully be called the Logos, the Word of God. But if one overlooks the historical Jesus, then one also overlooks the fact that on the cross we find God's silence rather than God's spoken word. Faith is then turned into a theory that utilizes the same techniques and mechanisms used by natural humanity. When we forget that the wisdom of God appears on the cross (1 Cor. 1:24), we tend to turn the Logos into nothing more than an explicative Logos.

We must remind ourselves that the wisdom of the cross is not just a paradoxical or pietistic discourse. It tells us what a truly Christian theory should be. It tells us that such a theory must be critical, not simply explicative, because the cross is a criticism of all the cognitive presuppositions and the self-centered interests that prompt human beings to fashion theories. If the Logos is the Logos of someone who was crucified as well as resurrected from the dead, then we are confronted with a revolutionary concept of God. God is not someone who simply explains the origin and course of history. God is someone who does all that by criticizing history and immersing himself in it so that it might progress further. The cross rules out any merely explicative theory of the faith. It calls for a critical and practical theory, and such a theory is possible only if the reality of Christ is not reduced to that of a risen, divine Logos capable of explaining everything. The historical, crucified Jesus must be part of the picture if we want to get beyond intellectualist gnosticism.

The norm of truth is the historical Jesus. We must apply some sort of hermeneutics to that figure if his truth is to be relevant and operative today. We cannot evade the hermeneutic issue by appealing directly to some eternal Logos that is universal by very definition and hence capable of explaining all of reality *sub specie aeternitatis*. Faith must be a critical, praxis-oriented theory based on some hermeneutics and embodied in discipleship. It is through such a concrete theory that we can gradually fashion reality and come to understand it in the process.

THE TENSION BETWEEN PROPHETIC POLITICAL THEOLOGY AND POWER-CENTERED POLITICAL THEOLOGY

As Logos, the risen Christ made it possible for Christians to view faith as an explicative philosophy like that to be found in the religious framework of gnosticism. As Lord, the risen Christ made it possible for Christians to picture faith as somehow connected with political power. The influence of Greek thought prompted Christians to associate faith with philosophy. The influence of Roman culture prompted Christians to associate faith with the political state. In both instances they were led to imitate the traditional tendencies of religious thought, to turn faith into a new form of religion.

The mutual interrelationship between religion and the political state is quite apparent in earlier religions. The relationship between the two institutions is twofold. To begin with, power itself has a certain allure. Embodied in the political state, it takes on a certain numinous and sacral quality. One of the classic ways of trying to comprehend power, which of its very nature is associated with the deity, is to consider its manifestations in the realm of political power. By the same token the state itself needs some sort of ideological support to hold society together. Religion has often provided that support, and it certainly did in Antiquity, for example, in the political theology elaborated by the Roman Stoics, who profoundly influenced the first generation of Christians.

In Antiquity there could be no state without a deity, and no deity without a state. The two went together in ancient political theory and practice, and so the words associated with societal organization and virtue had clear-cut religious overtones. As Moltmann puts it: "The first and foremost obligation of the state was to acknowledge and venerate the gods of the homeland. That was the way to ensure peace and well-being to one's country, and the citizens of a country were joined together by a common religion."[22] When Christians began to spread out through the Roman Empire, they were confronted with political religions that helped to give solidity and cohesiveness to the political state. Those religions provided a mythical account of national origins and glorified the history of their peoples.

We have already considered Jesus' stance vis-à-vis political power and authority. Basically he desacralized political power, finding nothing numinous or divine about it. It certainly was not a religious manifiestation of God's power in Jesus' eyes. The power of God was reflected in those who seemed weak and powerless (Matt. 6:28; Luke 12:27f.), and Jesus' followers were not to act as leaders of nations and people with power did (Mark. 10:42).

In the first few decades after the resurrection there seems to be some ambiguity in the relationship between Christian faith in Jesus and the political state. The representatives of Roman rule are treated with some degree of respect in the gospel accounts of the passion and in the Acts of the Apostles. Christians are also told to be submissive to legal authority (Rom. 13:1), to pay government levies (Rom. 13:6; 1 Pet. 2:13), and to pray "especially for kings and those in authority" (1 Tim. 2:1–2). At this point no serious problem has arisen between the Christian faith and the political state; their relationship is one of relatively peaceful coexistence. Nor does the political state seem to represent any great temptation for the faith.

Toward the end of the first century A.D., the situation of peaceful coexistence changes radically. The state is now subjected to harsh criticism, not because of any theoretical reasoning but because of the persecution unleashed against Christians by Domitian. The Roman state is depicted as a "beast" (Rev. 13) and personified in one man (Rev. 13:18). Far from being the medium of God's power in action, the exercise of political power is now viewed as something quite the opposite. Faith in Jesus is wholly in opposition to such political power (Rev. 14:12). In the eyes of a church undergoing martyrdom, "the state was *predominantly* an embodiment of 'this world' in the pejorative sense."[23] The temptation posed by power was overcome by virtue of the very situation in which the Christian church found itself. Christians had expected that their faith would penetrate the whole world. The situation in which they now found themselves was very different, and "just the opposite had happened."[24] Persecution helped to bring out the true dimensions of Jesus' lordship. Jesus is "the lamb that had been slain" (Rev. 5:6). It is because he is that lamb that he is worthy to receive "power and riches, wisdom and strength, honor and glory and praise" (Rev. 5:12). In the book of Revelation, therefore, we find that the real situation has nullified any temptation to join Christian faith with the state as a political religion. In line with the thought of Paul, Jesus' lordship as the risen one is viewed in terms of his concrete, historical cross.

Succeeding generations began to give way to the temptation of viewing Christianity as a political religion that was useful to the Roman Empire. We can understand why they might succumb to such a temptation. Persecution lasted for a long time, though it was somewhat intermittent, and Christians could not help but be interested in coming to peaceful terms with the imperial government. No such settlement was possible, however, so long as Christianity purported to be faith in Jesus. As a faith, its status was inferior to that of all the officially recognized religions. This fact "undoubtedly reinforced the tendency to propagate Christianity as a religion and to point up its positive contribution to the state as other cults might."[25] Understandable as the motivation might be, it is surprising to see how quickly Christians fell into the whole schema of religion in trying to point up the positive relationship between Christianity and the state. While the voices of church leaders do express certain reservations, they basically picture the relationship between Christianity and the state in terms of the classic model of the relationship between religion and the state.[26] The basic argument is that Christianity is the best religion for the empire and its welfare.

Though this process reached its culmination with Constantine, it had begun much earlier. In the later half of the second century Melito of Sardis pictures the relationship between church and state in very enthusiastic terms. He reminds the emperor, Marcus Aurelius, that Christian philosophy has brought blessings and good fortune to the empire; and he promises the same for future generations of emperors if they protect the Christian religion. In the middle of the third century Origen goes so far as to promise military victories for the Roman Empire if its soldiers become Christians. He asserts that the prayer of Christians is even more powerful than that of Moses in winning victory over one's enemies. Thus Christianity is the most efficacious religion in the realm of politics. Eusebius of Caesarea (c. 263–340) views Constantine's edict as the fulfillment of the Old Testament promises. The church has now integrated into itself all the religious aspirations of humanity. Around the same time Lactantius, a convert, saw the Christian religion as the leaven that would help to bring about an ordered and convivial form of societal life. In short, Christians now maintained that Christianity would perform a useful moral function in society, helping to provide stability amid the vicissitudes of history.

To be sure, there were other voices expressing different views. Yet the opinions noted above do indicate the growing trend within Christianity. When Constantine finally adopted Christianity as the state religion, he was fulfilling a desire that had been voiced by many in earlier generations. The various edicts of the fourth century confirmed the growing tendency of Christians to view their faith as a politically useful religion. In 311 the emperor Galerius adopted an edict of toleration that assumed that Christianity was a religion. His edict made Christianity a licit religion, as the term was understood by the political state. Constantine's conversion was not a conversion to the Christian faith but rather a change of religion. He was interested in the deity, and he was probably a monotheist. The gnostic influences of his day may have had a profound impact on him. Constantine felt that religion could and should help him to consolidate his empire. The Christian church would be expected to perform functions like those performed by the various pagan cults. The validity of other cults is made clear in the Edict of Milan (313), but it is also obvious that he expects the Christian cult to guarantee the safety and security of his empire. Constantine envisioned his own reign as a religious mission. He sought to be the overseer or bishop of all, and he felt he had the right to the last say with regard to any conciliar decisions: "The emperor was viewed as 'God's lieutenant.' "[27] And once the emperor became a Christian, other Christians were ready to accord him the sacral character they had denied to earlier emperors even in the face of persecution. An air of divinity now surrounded the emperor and everything in his vicinity. His palace was a sacred precinct, and refusal to venerate him was akin to sacrilege. According to Athanasius, one who refused him such veneration could justifiably be punished with death.

With the edict of Theodosius in 380, Christianity went from being a licit religion to being the official state religion. The edict does talk about the Christian religion as one based on the Father, the Son, and the Holy Spirit; but it is clear that the functions envisioned for it are those of any other state religion. Acceptance of it now becomes obligatory, and those who do not practice it are to be punished not only by God but also by the emperor.[28] Thus Christianity was turned into a religion structurally, completing the process that had been going on for some time. The norm of truth in Christianity is no longer faith in the scandalous reality of the crucified Jesus but its usefulness to the state.

I am not suggesting here that this was the only development in Christian faith during the first four centuries of its existence. The point here is that this development certainly did take place, and right down to our own day we can see how political power has been a temptation for the Christian faith. The church has sustained and sometimes wielded political power.

It has served to unify a given society or nation, just as the old pagan religions did.

Undoubtedly there are many reasons behind this development. The thing that interests us here is the underlying theological cause of it. What has made it possible for the faith to take on the forms of religion more and more over the course of time? As I see it, the theological roots of this development are to be found in a specific conception of Christian universalism, one based on a particular understanding of the risen Christ. The notion of a universal mission was keenly felt by the early Christians, and it derived logically enough from their belief in Christ as the savior of all human beings. But that in itself does not explain why Christian universalism should be linked with political power and view its mission in terms of power.

It is a fundamental dictum of Christian faith that the risen Jesus is the Lord and hence wields power. But how are we to picture this power and its exercise? One conception would follow Paul and the book of Revelation. If the risen Lord is viewed as the crucified Jesus or the slain lamb, then power is manifested through the miraculous praxis of discipleship. In their words and activities Christians will necessarily practice a political theology, but its lineaments must be clear. On the negative side it will entail prophetic denunciation and maintenance of a certain eschatological reserve. On the positive side it will entail efforts to organize society along the lines demanded by justice and preached by the historical Jesus. Thus we will get a prophetic and active political theology. It will not be a total all-embracing ideology based on power. Instead it will serve as the font of different functional ideologies of a more incomplete nature that will help us to organize society according to the values of justice and community. Each concrete situation will require a hermeneutics of its own if we are to flesh out our ideals and draw closer to the kingdom of God. But we must never forget what sort of power really mediates God and helps to construct a better society. It is love embodied in self-surrender and service, as we see in the case of Jesus.

The risen Jesus and his lordship may be pictured in different terms, however. Suppose he is pictured as Lord but somehow in isolation from the historical reality of his life on earth. In that case we may picture his power in the vague, general terms usually ascribed to the deity. Christianity would have a natural affinity with every religion that tends to support the exercise of power or to wield power in its own right. Rather than a political theology centered around prophetic praxis, it would espouse a political theology centered around submissiveness, an absolutist view of society, and the exercise of totalitarian power. And all that would be guaranteed by the absolute truth and power of the risen Lord.

Ultimately, our Christian analysis of any given socio-political order (the Roman Empire, medieval Christendom, etc.) will depend on our christological conception of Christ's resurrection. If we picture it solely in terms of power, sovereignty, and omnipotence, then our view of the Roman Empire, for example, will be a favorable one. Despite the persecutions to which Christians were subjected, it will be viewed as the means used by divine providence to ensure the expansion of Christianity and its ultimate integration into the political state. It is a fact that Christian poets and thinkers have praised the Roman Empire for paving the way for the later politico-religious state known as Christendom.

Power is an inevitable and necessary reality, but it is also ambiguous. The resurrection of Jesus allows for its use in theological terms, but it does not eliminate the ambiguity. The ambivalence of power disappears only when we view it in terms of the historical Jesus; it is he who embodies its meaning in terms of truth and love. Power is truth when one engages in prophetic denunciation. Power is love when one serves the needs of society and one's fellow human beings. In both cases it must be situated in the context of a concrete historical situation; it cannot be defined in abstract terms.

Focusing one-sidedly on the Christ of faith, Christians have forged a Christian religion, a political religion like those of Antiquity. In the name of the historical Jesus we can and should live a life where faith is politically relevant, but where it is prophetic and praxis-oriented rather than merely a matter of words.

THE TENSION BETWEEN CULTIC WORSHIP AND CONCRETE DISCIPLESHIP

By virtue of their faith in Christ's resurrection, Christians necessarily had a relationship with him in the present. It was only natural that they should sense his presence here and now and acclaim him as Lord. Faith, love, and thanksgiving must be given expression and so Christian liturgy is legitimate and even necessary in principle.

The problem begins when we ask ourselves what sort of model underlies the Christian liturgy. Has it maintained its original Christian cast as a thanksgiving celebration in which people hear the word of God, acknowledge that salvation comes through Jesus Christ, and choose to follow him by promoting the same ideals in the vicissitudes of history? Or has it perhaps taken on the same cast as the cultic worship of world religions? Does it suggest that cultic worship provided a privileged locale for approaching God or the risen Christ, quite apart from the concrete demands of discipleship?

In other words, my concern here is to see whether the Christian liturgy has maintained its original nature. Is it possible that over the course of time it has come to be viewed in the same way that cultic worship is viewed by most religions? Obviously the question did not confront the first Christians in the systematic way posed here. Many different elements went into their liturgy and existed side by side. The point there is to see which elements gained dominance and in what direction the Christian liturgy tended to move as time went on.

In Jesus' day Judaism was formally a religion based on observance rather than on cultic worship. The synagogue was the place where interpretation of the law had a profound impact on one's daily life, and so it had come to diminish the importance of the temple. There was cultic worship, to be sure, and the Jews engaged in it. But the formal value of cultic worship lay in concrete observance of prescribed law rather than in cultic worship itself. Jesus did not attack cultic worship itself, and he participated in the liturgical celebrations of his people. He had harsh things to say about legalistic ritualism (Mark 7:6f.; Matt. 23:25–28) and hypocrisy (Mark 7:9–13), and he made it clear that cultic worship was no privileged locale for access to God. Love, embodied concretely in love for the oppressed and downtrodden (Matt. 25:31–46), was the true locale for access to God.

After Jesus' resurrection, the earliest Christian communities in Palestine tended to view their day-to-day life in terms of Judaism. They "went to the temple area together every day" (Acts 2:46). They brought their gifts to the altar (Matt. 5:23f.) and paid the temple tax (Matt. 17:24–27). Thus they shared the cultic worship of the Jews readily, while still injecting some of their newfound Christian beliefs into it: "They devoted themselves to the apostles' instruction and the communal life, to the breaking of bread and the prayers" (Acts 2:42).

A fundamental change in the conception of cultic worship gradually came about in the Christian communities of the Hellenistic world. From the very beginning they did have liturgical reunions. Whether or not they were cultic gatherings depends on how you define the word "cultic." In the beginning we certainly do not find some of the characteristic features of cultic worship: e.g., sacrifice, priests, sacred places, and set times of worship. These Christian gatherings were dominated by the spoken word and its interpretation. Sermons were delivered, and people tried to read and interpret the Old Testament (1 Tim. 4:13), the writings of the apostles, and the gospel accounts (1 Thess. 5:27; Col. 4:16; Rev. 1:3). To this were added hymns, prayers, and chants of various sorts. So while some of the typically cultic elements do not appear, it would seem that these gatherings simply cut down some of the features of cultic worship rather than eliminating it entirely. Bultmann sees the import of cultic liturgy in the fact that the attending community implores and prays for *the presence of the deity* in its midst. In that sense the liturgy of the Christian

community would have to be described as cultic, too.[29] The
deity made his presence felt through the Spirit. What distinguishes the worship of the Christian communities in the Hellenistic world is the fact that Christ was included in their
doxologies (Rev. 5:13; 7:10).[30] It is here that we can detect a
difference between the Christian communities in Palestine
and those in the Hellenistic world. In the former communities
Christ is now regarded as the Son of Man or Messiah who will
come at the end of time; in the latter the risen Christ is now
viewed as the exalted Lord who is rendered present in cultic
worship.

As Bultmann sees it, the decisive shift toward a religio-cultic
conception of the Christian liturgy took place toward the close
of the first century. It was then that the Eucharist came to be
viewed as a sacrifice and that the word began to lose its
importance in liturgical reunions. No longer did the liturgy
express the eschatological consciousness of the community as
an assembly in which the Spirit was present to guarantee
salvation. Instead the celebration of the Lord's supper was
viewed as a medicinal remedy guaranteeing immortality. As
Bultmann puts it, "Eschatological awareness was over-
shadowed by a new emphasis on sacramentalism."[31] As this
new understanding of the liturgy took shape, the officials of
the Christian community took on a more cultic character. The
episkopos ("overseer"), whose function was not cultic at first,
now became a priest. He now took on a character that separated him from the rest of the community, and we see the
gradual rise of a distinction between the priest and the lay
person. Such a distinction was not present in the early days of
the church. Now the leader of the liturgical worship is viewed
in the same terms prescribed by most religions. The same
happens with respect to other concepts such as *ekklesia*
("church"), *presbyteros* ("elder"), and *apostolos* ("one sent
out"). Originally those terms were taken from the terminology
of civil society and did not have any sacral connotation. Indeed
it is worth noting that the authentically sacral notion of priest
(hiereus) is scarcely used in the New Testament.

Hére, then, we find the decisive transition that led to the

transformation of Christian faith into cultic worship. Sacred times and places are established, a distinction is made between priests and lay people, and later a distincton is made between bishops and plain priests. Eventually this gives rise to a church law of allegedly divine origin. Here we cannot follow all the details of the process. The point is that the Christian liturgical community gradually came to see itself in the same terms that most religions saw cultic worship. Cultic worship became a privileged locale for access to God and the risen Christ, and the church began to see itself as the mediator of salvation by the very fact that it possessed certain institutions and living patterns· like those of religions in general. This whole line of development was further enhanced when the church became an integral part of the political state.

Here again the gradual cultualization of Christian faith was due to a specific conception of the risen Christ. Since he was the Lord, it was possible to establish a relationship with him in the present; more and more cultic worship came to be regarded as the locale where that relationship was established. Once that happened, cultic worship could take predominance in Christianity over every other aspect of Christian living—specifically, over the concrete obligation of discipleship.

The New Testament work that is most critical of any one-sidedly cultic elaboration of Christianity is the Epistle to the Hebrews. Interesting enough, it also elaborates a Christology that is solidly based on the historical Jesus. The author of that epistle denounces any attempt to turn Christianity into a cultic religion similar to that of the Old Testament. His fundamental thesis is that God's grace can no longer be obtained through any sacrifices offered by human beings, and that priests in the Old Testament sense are no longer needed to serve as mediators between God and human beings.

The author of Hebrews bases his thesis on Christology: Christ is the one and only authentic priest. It is interesting to note, however, how the author of Hebrews views Christ's priesthood. In general the New Testament does not refer to

Jesus as a priest, though certain passages seem to allude to his salvific work in quasi-cultic terms. In 1 Cor. 5:7 Jesus is called the paschal lamb, and in several places Jesus is presented as one who shed his blood for humankind (Mark 14:24; Rom. 3:25; 5:9). It is curious to note that, apart from these few references, the early Christians went along for years without appealing to cultic terms to explain or understand the work of Jesus. Yet such terms are ordinarily an integral part of any religion. Only in the Epistle to the Hebrews is the concept of cultic worship used to explain the work of Jesus. And there, surprisingly enough, the author uses sacral, cultic terminology to affirm that Jesus has put an end to cultic realities.

Hebrews tells us that Christ was called to be a priest by God. However, this "priest" does not perform cultic worship in the temple. He offers up his own life, not incense or sacrificial animals. Christ is a "priest" by virtue of his historical life and death. His new kind of priesthood fulfills the aim of the Old Testament priesthood, but it is so different from it that it actually brings that priesthood to an end. Cultic worship based on some vaunted separation between the realm of the sacred and real-life history in the world is not the locale for access to God. It is Jesus' new way of being a priest that establishes the new and definitive covenant. Now that Jesus has lived his life, we must look to him to discover the real meaning of cultic worship and access to God through such worship. Jesus was the mediator between God and humanity through his concrete way of living in history, and he continues to be that here and now.

Thus the Epistle to the Hebrews shatters the age-old religious view of cultic worship and its allied institutions. We cannot understand the mediation of Jesus and later Christian liturgy by regarding them as some particular applications of a more universal religious notion of cultic worship. It is Jesus who teaches us what being a priest means and what access to God through cultic worship means. Jesus' work of mediation takes place in the profane realm of real history, thereby terminating the validity of the Old Testament priesthood and its cultic worship. Jesus was a layman. He belonged to the tribe of Judah, not to the priestly tribe of Levi. His work was carried out among the people, not in the precincts of the temple. Instead of offering libations and holocausts, he approached the oppressed and offered them hope while condemning their oppressors. His work of mediation was to advocate justice and love between human beings, to put his whole life and energy into the service of God's kingdom. The major sacral concept of "victim" is completely desacralized by Jesus. He makes no vicarious offering. The cross is not an altar, and there is no sacrificial lamb on it. Instead we find there the body and the life of a human being. It is in this way that Jesus, a layman living in the profane world, effectively and concretely manages to do what priests had been vainly trying to do in symbolic, sacral terms, namely, to render present here among human beings God's love and the desire for human solidarity.

The Epistle to the Hebrews poses the whole issue of what Christian cultic worship might really mean. On the one hand it is true that Jesus is the risen, exalted Lord here and now. He lives now in the present, and so he can and should be acclaimed. It is that fact that allows for the existence of a Christian liturgy. At the same time, however, it should not turn into just another religious liturgy. What is the essence of Christian cultic worship? How does it provide access to God? What is the nature of priestly mediation in the Christian sense? The Epistle to the Hebrews stresses the fact that we must look to the historical Jesus to find answers to these questions. Mere cultic representation of the risen Lord's death is not enough to guarantee God's presence among people in any infallible way. The Christian way to obtain union with God is to follow in the footsteps of the historical Jesus. It is he who shows us how we are to lead a Christian life and thereby gain access to God. We can celebrate his life and journey with doxologies, but it is even more important to follow in his footsteps: "Let us keep our eyes fixed on Jesus, who inspires and perfects our faith. . . . Remember how he endured the opposition of sinners; hence do not grow despondent or abandon the struggle" (Heb. 12:2–3).

CONCLUSION

Having come to the end of this chapter, I should like to sum up some of the conclusions to which we have been led and to point up the reservations that rightfully apply to our study.

It is obvious that a far more complete and well documented study would have been in order if we wanted to prove conclusively that a particular understanding of Christ can exert a profound influence on the way Christian life is understood and lived. Yet even granting that, I think we have seen enough to realize that a one-sided Christology can have a deleterious impact on the Christian way of life. I would formulate my thesis in these modest terms: *to the extent that Christians tend to overlook or forget the historical Jesus, they tend to structure Christian life more and more as a religion in the pejorative sense.* This holds true even though they may still profess faith in Jesus, thus distinguishing their belief from that of other religions insofar as words and concepts are concerned.

Strictly speaking, I have not spelled out *the relationship existing between the historical Jesus and the Christ of faith.* Nor have I considered how access to Christ as a historical figure is related to access to Christ as the risen Lord. I would describe the basic relationship in some such terms as the following. The historical Jesus raises the whole question of history's meaning by proclaiming the coming of God's kingdom. Structurally speaking, the definitive answer to that question comes with the resurrection. If we are to grasp the resurrection as the answer to that question, however, we stand in need of some specific hermeneutics. That hermeneutics is nothing else but the following of Jesus. The resurrection can be comprehended only in terms of hope, but not a neutral, anthropological hope. It must be the "hoping against hope" of which Paul speaks, and that can emerge only in a concrete praxis designed to effect liberation. It is only from within such a praxis that human beings can come to comprehend the resurrection as a response to the whole question of history's meaningfulness. Thus *access to the Christ of faith comes through our following of the historical Jesus.*

There are other issues that I have not dealt with explicitly here. I have not considered the possible value of an explicative theory, a Christian theology, from the standpoint of the historical Jesus. I have not considered the whole problem of power and its use in trying to organize a society oriented toward the kingdom of God. I have not dealt with the explicit meaning of a Christian liturgy. All these topics need to be explored further and worked out fully.

I have also disregarded a structural difficulty that confronts any Christology centered around the historical Jesus. The fact is that the following of Jesus (discipleship) does not clear up all the difficulties involved in trying to explain Christian existence, nor does it spell out all the obligations of such an existence. There is a very simple reason for this, which goes back to the historical Jesus himself. Jesus expected the imminent end of history, the imminent arrival of God's kingdom. The long delay in the arrival of the parousia puts the Christian in a situation that is fundamentally different from that of Jesus himself. The difference is not fundamentally theological, because God ever lies in the future both for Jesus and the Christian. The difference lies in the fact that Christians must look for a hermeneutics that will take due account of the way in which their situation differs from that of Jesus. It must explain the following of Jesus in the context of a history that does not seem to be near its end as yet, and that therefore will require all sorts of analyses if we are to organize history on our way toward the kingdom of God. We must now engage in religious, social, economic, and political analyses. Thus the following of Jesus must take due account of Jesus' own basic attitudes and motives, but it cannot come down to any mere "imitation" of Jesus.

Despite all the reservations and qualifications noted above, I think we can draw the following important conclusion: *The very reality that serves as the foundation for faith in Jesus is also that which allows for the disappearance of that faith.* On the one hand proclaiming the resurrection of Jesus means affirming that the historical Jesus is the Son of God, that the truth was embodied in that figure, and that liberation is to be found in following him. On the other hand the resurrection is also that which makes it possible for people to overlook or forget the concrete reality of the historical Jesus. The process of universalizing faith in Jesus begins with the resurrection, but that very process can end up as a process of abstraction. The risen Christ may be viewed and interpreted in the framework of such abstract concepts as deity, omnipotence, explicative Logos, and so forth.

Christianity may turn into religion insofar as the process of universalizing its faith is based on abstraction rather than on the concrete history of Jesus. The risen Christ, viewed as an abstract deity, can serve as an excuse for theology's failure to come to grips with the perduring value of Jesus' concrete history. As Paul points out, we are faced with the task of knowing the God who reveals himself in Jesus Christ specifically. Jesus revolutionizes the existing structure of religion, the way in which people view God's revelation in the world, and our notion of the proper access to God. God appears in the concrete context of history when heeding the cries of the oppressed. History is not fashioned and completed once and for all at the very start. It is an ongoing quest for liberation. In Jesus we see what that liberation entails. Its ultimate paradigm is to be found in his own resurrection. In Jesus' approach we also discover how to carry out that task. There is no privileged cultic or philosophical access to God. We gain access to God by trying to fashion history, and we experience that process as both a grace and a concrete line of praxis.

Whereas religion claims that we can make contact with the deity through some direct act of intention, faith maintains that we make contact with God by journeying toward him and trying to fashion his kingdom. In Christ's resurrection we find the definitive promise of the goal toward which we are striving; but it is in the figure of the historical Jesus that we discover how to journey toward that goal. Going to God means making God real in history; it means building up God's kingdom here and now. No abstract concept of the diety can teach us that fact, however; we must learn it from the concrete figure of the historical Jesus.

NOTES

1. *Der sogennante historische Jesus und der geschichtliche, biblische Christus,* 1892, p. 22; see note 11, chap. 1 in this volume.

2. *Glauben und Verstehen,* 1:274; see note 15, chap. 3 in this volume.

3. Consider his intense interest to get back to the *ipsissima vox* of Jesus, to the core of his preaching and activity: "Die zentrale Bedeutung des historischen Jesus," in *Theologie der Gegenwart,* 4 (1961), pp. 66–72; summarized in *Selecciones de Teología,* 33 (1970), pp. 13–16.

4. "Das Problem des historischen Jesus," *Zeitschrift für Theologie und Kirche,* 51 (1954), pp. 125–53; in Eng. see *The Problem of the Historical Jesus* (Philadelphia: Fortress, 1964); summarized in *Selecciones de Teología,* 42 (1972), pp. 87–103.

5. See D. Bonhoeffer, *Letters and Papers from Prison,* Eng. trans. (New York: Macmillan Paperbacks, 1962).

6. There has been renewed interest in the historical figure of Jesus ever since K. Kautsky wrote his book on the origin and foundations of Christianity in 1908 (reissued in English as *Foundations of Christianity* [New York: Monthly Review, 1972]). Kautsky sought to explain the rise of Christianity in terms of social and production relationships. Interest in the historical Christ is strongly evident now among Marxists and atheists. See Ernst Bloch, *Atheismus im Christentum* (Hamburg: Rowolt, 1970); Eng. trans.: *Atheism in Christianity* (New York: Herder, 1972). The theme has been developed more explicitly by V. Gardavsky, *Dios no ha muerto del todo,* Span. edition (Salamanca, 1972); Eng. edition: *God Is Not Yet Dead* (Baltimore: Penguin Books, 1973); M. Machovec, *Jesús para ateos,* Spanish edition (Salamanca, 1974); Eng. edition: *A Marxist Looks at Jesus* (Philadelphia: Fortress Books, 1976); and R. Garaudy, *La alternativa,* Spanish edition (Caracas, 1972); Eng. edition: *The Alternative Future* (New York: Simon & Schuster, 1974).

7. See the works of Gutiérrez and others cited in note 25, chap. 1 in this volume.

8. J.P. Miranda, *El ser y el Mesías* (Salamanca, 1973), p. 9; Eng. trans.: *Being and the Messiah* (Maryknoll, New York: Orbis, 1977).

9. The notion of a contrast between religion and Christian faith has a long history. In this century it was brought up again by Karl Barth, who opposed knowledge of God through revelation to all so-called natural knowledge of God. But the problem takes on a different cast when access to God is posed in terms of a direct, intentional act on the one hand and the concrete following of the historical Jesus on the other—the latter leading to subsequent knowledge of God and access to him in the liturgy. The latter perspective was elaborated by Bonhoeffer, and more recently by Moltmann. See, in particular, the following works of Moltmann: "Critica teológica de la religión política," in *Ilustración y teoría teológica* (Salamanca, 1973), pp. 11–45; *Hope and Planning,* Eng. trans. (New York: Harper & Row, 1971); and *The Crucified God,* Eng. trans. (New York: Harper & Row, 1974).

10. There is no reason why the contrast between religion and faith should be equated with the contrast between popular religiosity and "enlightened" religion. In both latter spheres one can find elements of both faith and religion.

In this book I have not tackled the pastoral problem of trying to detect those elements. My concern here is to point out what sort of structure and values should give orientation to Christian existence. Obviously the concrete form they take will depend on the sociological milieu in which they originate and are practiced.

11. E. Käsemann, *La llamada de la libertad*, p. 54; see note 4, chap. 3 in this volume.

12. Ibid., p. 79.

13. Ibid., p. 89.

14. Ibid., p. 91.

15. E. Schweizer, "Die theologische Leistung des Markus," in *Evangelische Theologie*, 24 (1964), pp. 337–55; summarized in *Selecciones de Teología*, 33 (1970), pp. 50–61.

16. The cross of Christ is the culminating point where the Gospels break with any notion or schema of some knowledge about an abstract divinity. Jesus is put to death because he committed himself to the cause of God's kingdom, to the liberation of the oppressed. His basic weapons had been those of truth, love, and service. On the surface at least, the cross seems to suggest that truth proved to be sterile and love to be impotent. This situation, grounded in the most historical reality of Jesus himself, is what destroys any self-interest that people might seek to use as a way of coming to know God (see J. Moltmann, *Umkehr zur Zukunft* [Hamburg: Siebenstern, 1970], p. 135f.). It forces us to ask: "Who exactly is God in the light of the cross of Christ, who there was abandoned by God? . . . Who is man really in the light and presence of the Son of Man, who was first rejected and then resurrected in the freedom of God? . . . Either Jesus abandoned by God is the end of all theology, or else he is the start of a specifically Christian theology and existence that are both critical and liberative" (J. Moltmann, *Der gekreuzigte Gott*, see note 10, chap. 1 in this volume). As Käsemann puts it: "Only the God of the cross is our God. Our God is never the one that the world accepts without undergoing conversion. Those who minimize or reduce the significance of the cross for Christianity and the world are obscuring the truth of God and the scandal introduced by grace. Even if they affirm some theology of the resurrection, they will still be falling into the realm of superstition" (*La llamada de libertad*, p. 98f.).

17. E. Käsemann, *La llamada de libertad*, p. 120f.

18. R. Bultmann, *Theologie des Neuen Testaments*, 6th ed. (Tübingen: Mohr, 1968), p. 468; Eng. trans.: *Theology of the New Testament* (New York: Scribner's, 1970).

19. P. Stockmeier, *Glaube und Religion in der frühen Kirche* (Freiburg: Herder, 1973), p. 34.

20. Ibid., p. 56.

21. Clement of Alexandria, *Strom*. 1, 32, 4.

22. J. Moltmann, "Crítica teológica de la religión política," p. 20.

23. H. Mühlen, *Entsakralisierung* (Paderborn, 1970), p. 200.

24. E. Käsemann, *La llamada de la libertad*, p. 175.

25. P. Stockmeier, *Glaube und Religion in der frühen Kirche*, p. 81.

26. Ibid.

27. H. Mühlen, *Entskralisierung*, p. 207. "Constantine completed the task of recognizing Christianity officially and integrating it into the religious and spiritual scheme of the Roman Empire. Clearly he did this largely in terms of his own conceptions. Whatever his personal experience had been, his conceptions were largely in line with Roman tradition. He accorded Christianity equal rights as a religion specifically; and though it was a religion of a somewhat special character, it was gradually brought under submission to the state" (P. Stockmeier, *Glaube und Religion in der frühen Kirche*, p. 92f.).

28. P. Stockmeier, p. 101.

29. Bultmann, *Theologie des Neuen Testaments*, p. 125.

30. Ibid., p. 126.

31. Ibid., p. 462.

10.

The Christological Dogmas

The topic of christological dogmas is exceedingly complicated on both the historical and the systematic level. Here I can only offer a few basic ideas about the subject.

Liberation theology has not concerned itself greatly with the task of dealing with theological themes from a strictly dogmatic standpoint, though that does not mean that it has not dealt with the basic contents that are enshrined in dogmatic formulas. Nor is this present book of mine on Christology structured around dogma. Still, that does not absolve me from the responsibility of considering the whole problematic issue of Christology from the standpoint of dogma. There are several reasons why the task cannot be evaded.

First of all, it cannot be evaded because my Christology purports to have an ecclesial significance, as I defined that notion in the Preface to the English edition. The first and most basic feature of such a Christology is that it reflects on Christ from within the context of the life of ecclesial communities. But there is a second side to an ecclesial Christology. It must also consider the authoritative declarations of the magisterium, which are solemnized embodiments of the christological reflection based on the aforementioned ecclesial life.

Second, the task cannot be avoided because of the pastoral use to which dogma is put. On the one hand dogma may be used to give legitimate unity to the expression of the Christian faith that is required of us. On the other hand dogma may be pastorally abused or misused to impose uniformity on professions of faith that derive from different ages and places and which, for that very reason, should be varied and different. Nor can we overlook the fact that dogma is systematically ignored, if not rejected outright, by some groups of Christians because they do not find it to be an adequate vehicle for the expression of their faith. It is my belief that in so doing they are losing an important historical perspective as well as some of the precious content of dogma at its core level.

Third, we must consider Christology from the standpoint of dogma because dogmatic formulations are, in my opinion, a historical necessity for a church composed of human beings. We need words and an authoritative word if we are to give expression to our faith and share it through reciprocal communication. I also feel that dogma, correctly understood, is highly valuable within the church.

For all these reasons I think it is wise and necessary to offer some preliminary remarks on the nature of dogma, and then to proceed to a consideration of the various christological dogmas. In my preliminary remarks I shall first consider the notion of "dogma" in terms of its historical development, then consider the whole problem of the "interpretation" of dogma, and finally try to say something about the positive value of dogma. That should help us to see how dogma might be put to correct pastoral use and how it is now misused.[1]

PRELIMINARY REMARKS
ON THE NOTION OF "DOGMA"

Historical Development of the Notion of "Dogma"

The notion of "dogma" is one of the most fundamental notions in theology. At least indirectly it is also one of the most basic notions in the pastoral life of the church, particularly since Vatican I. For the past century theology has been basically a "dogmatic" theology. It is most important, then, that we realize that this particular conception of theology is a *historical* one. By that I mean that theology has not always been conceived in those terms. So we must have some idea how the whole notion of "dogma" developed in the church and what it has meant at various times.

The Greek word *dogma* basically means something that someone thinks is true (an "opinion"); it can also mean a "resolution" or a "decree." It is not used in the New Testament in the same sense that it is used by the church today. There it may refer to an imperial decree (Luke 21:1; Acts 17:7; Heb. 11:23) or to the precepts of the Jewish law (Eph. 2:15; Col. 2:14).

However, we do find an ecclesial reference in several passages of the Acts of the Apostles (16:4; 15:22,28). "As they made their way from town to town, they transmitted to the people for observance the decisions *(dogmata)* which the apostles and presbyters had made in Jerusalem" (Acts 16:4). In this passage dogma does not refer to some dogmatic formulation about the Creed; instead it refers to an authoritative indication as to the proper *modus vivendi* between Jewish and pagan Christians (see Acts 15:22,28f.). The importance of the term here lies in the fact that the church shows an awareness of having *the power and the duty to make decisions* on important matters in the name of the Holy Spirit (Acts 15:28); but we do not find the *doctrinal* connotation which the word dogma now has.

In the writings of the early fathers of the church, *dogma* may mean the mandates and moral recommendations of Christ (the Didache, 1 Clement, Ignatius of Antioch). The early apologists, however, gave it a more intellectual connotation, though still not the one we envision today. For them dogmas are the fundamental doctrines in the faith of Christ's disciples. As yet dogma is not distinct from ecclesial faith; rather, it is the normal expression of that faith. "Liturgy is dogma at prayer and, by the same token, theology is doxology."[2]

For a long time the term "dogma" was not used in western theology. One exception is a piece written by Vincent of Lerins (died c. A.D. 440), which was attributed to Augustine and read as such by medieval theologians. Noteworthy is the fact that the term "dogma" was hardly used at all in the Middle Ages, and that it certainly did not have any theological importance.

Thomas Aquinas uses it rarely, and Bonaventure never does. Instead of talking about dogmas, the medieval theologians talk about the articles of faith, which are simply the articles of the Creed. All that exists for them are the dogmas of the primitive church, which have become part of the Creed.

It was during and after the Council of Trent that the adjective *dogmaticus* began to gain currency in both Catholic and Protestant circles. Both now began to talk about *fides dogmatica* and *theologia dogmatica.* The growing use of the noun "dogma" in the period of the Counter Reformation was influenced by the *Commonitorium* of Vincent of Lerins, which was much translated in the sixteenth century. Caught up in fruitless polemics against the Protestants, Catholics found in Vincent's work a criterion for settling questions. The "universal and ancient faith" is what "has always and everywhere been believed by all." Now it is called "divine, celestial, ecclesiastical dogma," and set in contrast to the "new dogma." Thus the use of the term "dogma" and its sudden rise to prominence was occasioned by a polemical atmosphere, and it was designed to resolve doctrinal questions. We must realize this if we want to appreciate the way in which dogma has been understood and used in the last two centuries, right up to the recent present.

The modern conception of dogma appears for the first time in the work of Philip Neri. Disillusioned with the prevailing theology of controversy, he appealed to firm and solid judgments for the profession of truth: "The dogma of faith is nothing else but the doctrine and the truth revealed by God, which is put forward to be believed with divine faith by the public judgment of the church, the contrary doctrine being condemned by the church as heretical" (*Regula fidei,* 1792). At the time this opinion was branded as too "minimalist," and it was even put on the *Index.* Nevertheless it gained widespread recognition during the nineteenth century. This concept of dogma was used by Vatican I, by Pius IX in his *Syllabus* (1864), by Pius X in his *Syllabus* (1907), and by Pius XII (1950).

It is worth noting that the concept of dogma, understood in this sense, played no role in the Councils of the church before Vatican I. The first Council of Nicea used "dogmas" only in the sense of disciplinary decisions (D 127). For its Creed it uses such terms as *ekbesis* and *pistis*. At the Roman Synod in the Lateran (649), there was reference only to *haereseos dogmata* (D 520). It is only in the eighth century that the concept of dogma appears in provincial synods in connection with the doctrine of faith, but there it does not have a specifically technical sense. Even Trent touches upon it only lightly (D 1505; 1825). Summing up the matter, Kasper writes:

We are faced with the surpising fact that a concept so central to the Catholic church's way of thinking today as is the concept of dogma was first used in Catholic theology only around the start of the eighteenth century, and in the official language of the church only in the nineteenth century. We also must note that this term appears in a problematic context which is quite clearly defined. First it was defined by the attempt to delimit Catholicism over against Protestantism. Then, in Vatican I, the context was an attempt to defend the church against certain rationalist currents within it. This was followed by efforts to combat certain modernist errors. The concept of dogma, as currently understood, does not include all the elements that are associated with it in ecclesiastical tradition—not at all.[3]

In considering briefly the development of the *notion* of dogma here, we are not simply interested in an analysis of the term itself. What really interests us is the reality behind the term. But our analysis is important insofar as it sheds light on the concrete truth of the technical term "dogma" which is in use today. In our day, as opposed to what was the case in earlier ages, pronouncing the word "dogma" seems to imply that we are uttering the deepest and most profound statement about the Christian faith. That was not the implication in earlier ages, as I have just tried to show. Our brief analysis makes it clear that the present-day conception of dogma represents an impoverishment vis-à-vis that held by earlier tradition. Our analysis, then, will help us to restore full ecclesial value to the reality hidden behind the dogma. Its full ecclesial value is hidden by the term "dogma" as currently used.

I said that an impoverishment of the Christian faith occurred when people came to suppose that its profoundest realities were concentrated in "dogma." We can observe this impoverishment taking place in three changes that have occurred in the history of the church and of theology. First, there has been a shift from a more general concept of dogma to a technical concept of dogma with a very strict sense. Right up to the time of Trent, the concepts of "faith" and "heresy" were used to describe the life of faith *as a whole*—both in its objective aspect (what is believed) and in its subjective aspect (the act of believing and living accordingly). Then there was a shift to a concept of dogma in the stricter sense. People wanted to objectify the content of faith in concrete formulas.

Second, there was a shift in the grounding and justification offered for the faith-content which found expression in dogma. In an earlier day dogma was grounded and justified in terms of its relationship to the content of faith. Now it is grounded and justified on the basis of its *formal, juridical nature.* Interest shifted from a real, comprehensive profession of faith to acceptance of dogmatic formulations. This was the shift to what we today might call a Christianity based on mere orthodoxy.

Thirdly and finally, there was a shift in attitude toward the proper hierarchization of the realities of faith as expressed in human formulations. Whereas earlier the church did tend to distinguish between more and less important truths, and to maintain a hierarchy of faith-realities, a levelling now set in. Any truth of faith was important insofar as it had been declared a dogma, and all such truths took on uniform importance.

With this brief historical analysis I am not trying to deflate the importance of dogma—not even its doctrinal importance. My purpose is to warn the reader against an overly simplistic notion of what dogma is. This will pave the way for a correct understanding of dogma, of its function within the life of the church, and of its correct pastoral use.

The Problem of the "Interpretation" of Dogma[4]

We have gone into a brief historical analysis of the notion of dogma in order to gain a better understanding of what the contents of dogmas mean today and how we must interpret them if we want to use them properly. This in turn will help us to acquire a positive understanding of dogma, as we shall see in the next section.

When we combine historical and systematic reflection on the content of dogma, we come up with some basic conclusions. They might be spelled out as follows:

a. A dogma is an affirmation of faith formulated as doctrine and authoritatively put forward by the church's magisterium in order to defend the faith against some heresy. The first thing worth noting is that the intention behind dogma, or behind the conciliar and papal statements that are now regarded as dogmas, has almost always been polemical. That is the case historically, it would seem, except possibly for the dogmas about Mary. All the other important dogmas arose out of polemical encounters with heresy. This historical fact has great systematic importance. It means that the intention behind dogma is not to exhaust the content of faith but to defend some aspect of it, some aspect regarded as basic, against some error that threatens it. To put it another way: Dogma is not the source of what is positive in the faith; generally speaking, we can say it is a formulation designed to defend the faith against error. Hence the very formulation of many dogmas, and of conciliar canons in particular, is in negative terms.

That brings us back to an even more fundamental issue: the way in which the faith was originally formulated and the ways in which the church may propose it to us. Here I suggest three possible ways in what I regard as the proper order of importance. First of all, the faith can be expressed as gospel and kerygma, calling for an individual and communitarian response that embraces the whole reality of the listener. Second, faith can be expressed as a teaching or catechesis, calling for reflection and acceptance on the part of the listener. Third, in polemical situations faith can be expressed in dogmas that likewise call for acceptance on the part of the listener.

This hierarchical arrangement of the ways in which the faith can be presented to people is of great importance in the real life of the church. Dogma is the most forceful expression of the faith on the *juridical level;* but it is *not* the most forceful expression of the faith on the level of real life because its contents are dependent on what has already been preached as gospel message or on what has already been taught as catechesis.

b. The faith spelled out in Scripture has given rise to traditions. Some of the latter, in turn, have been converted into dogmas. This means that in principle a dogma can neither ignore nor go beyond what has already been said in Scripture. Dogma is an explanation of Scripture, not vice-versa, though pre-Vatican II theology seemed to assume the contrary.

Strictly speaking, the dogmatic explanation does not add anything to what was already known from Scripture. It is a *logical* explanation which explains and makes explicit what is really in Scripture for a new historical situation and culture; and it does this by using the concepts familiar to those in the new situation and culture. Take the formula of Chalcedon, for example. From it we do not learn *more* about Jesus than we gain from studying his life, activity, and teaching in the New Testament. The function of dogma is not to provide us with *additional* knowledge. What it should do for us is provide us with *better* understanding and knowledge insofar as the data of Scripture is spelled out in a conceptual framework more suited to a given age.

It is precisely here that we see the limitations of dogma insofar as it is meant to serve the faith of Christians. For even when a dogma says something very fundamental, it always says *less* than Scripture does. Let us consider the Council of Chalcedon once again. Even though it is of major importance and validity, everyone would have to admit that we learn less about Jesus from a reading of the Council than we do from a reading of the Gospels. But there is a further point here. At a given point in time a dogmatic formulation may offer a *better* expression of some fundamental point of faith; but if that formulation is maintained unchanged over a long period of time, then it may end up being a *worse* historical expression of that same point. It is not that what is expressed in the dogmatic formula is not true. It is that the historical and cultural situation has changed so much that the conceptual formulation of the dogma, which was associated with one epoch, has become inappropriate for another epoch.

c. The above remarks should make it clear that we have a compelling obligation to "interpret" a dogma. Today that is admitted by all theologians. Such interpretation is not a move backward into the past, a regressive step. It is not a matter of educating today's Catholics so that the formulas of a past age are comprehensible to them. That is obviously the work which belongs properly to specialists. Interpretation is really a move forward, a progressive step. Here and now today we must find a different way to affirm what was said in the past in different terms. And we must do this precisely out of fidelity to the message of the past.

I would propose two criteria for helping us to interpret a dogma correctly. In my judgment they are of great theoretical and pastoral importance. One has to do with the proper hierarchization of dogmas; the other has to do with the historical analysis of a dogma.

d. The typifying feature of dogma, as it is conceived today, is that it has been declared as such; but it is its content that remains basic. That is why there is great theoretical and pastoral danger in talking unthinkingly about dogmas in the plural. Such talk implies that there is a multiplicity of truths but it gives no hint that there is some sort of hierarchy among them. Awareness of the differences between the various contents of the faith has always existed in the church. In dealing with the problem of ecumenism, Vatican II recognizes a hierarchy of truths even though it is not dealing with dogmas specifically. It proposes the following criterion: "There exists an order or 'hierarchy' of truths, since they vary in their relationship to the foundation of the Christian faith" (*Unitatis redintegratio*, no. 11).[5]

Here I will propose one possible model for the proper heirarchizing of the truths of faith. At the very least it will prevent us from reducing all dogmas to the same level and enable us properly to interpret one in relation to the other.

First of all, we have *central* dogmas. They express what is fundamental in the Christian faith. These are the dogmas that have something to say about the reality of God, Christ, and the Spirit. They also include those dogmas that say something about the relationships between God and human beings: e.g., the dogmas concerned with creation, redemption, and grace. Equally central, though with a different shading, would be the dogmas that express the negative but all-embracing aspect of human existence: e.g., the dogma of original sin.

Second, we have *peripheral* dogmas. Their truth and meaningfulness is bound up with their relationship to the central dogmas. They can be divided into three groups: mariological dogmas (except the dogma of her divine motherhood, which is related to the reality of Christ himself); ecclesiological dogmas; and dogmatic statements about problematic moral areas.

This hierarchization provides us with a criterion for interpreting a given dogma, which ceases to be isolated with an autonomy of its own; it is brought into relationship with what is most fundamental in Christian reality. The importance of such hierarchization can be seen even in the case of the central dogmas, for it establishes a necessary, reciprocal relationship between the reality of human beings and the reality of God. On the one hand it relates the reality of human beings expressed in such central dogmas as creation, redemption, and grace, to the reality of God and human beings. Or, to put it in more relevant terms for today, it introduces dogma into the hermeneutic circle of salvation history on the one hand and salvation in history on the other.

e. Historical analysis of a dogma means that we apply to dogmatic formulations the analytic techniques that are now recognized and used in the interpretation of historical texts. Such analysis would include such things as literary criticism and the determination of the surrounding historical, social, economic, and political context. Such analysis attempts to make a clear distinction between what is being said and the way in which it is being said. It seeks to discover the deepest underlying intention behind a dogma, the truth which was enforced as a definitive one at some point in time and which cannot be ignored by later generations.

Thus the interpretation of dogma does not aim simply for a literal, or even a conceptual, translation of a given dogmatic formulation. What it seeks to translate is the original intention behind a given dogma. In this effort, then, we must take due account not only of the truth that is affirmed in a dogma, but also of the *meaning* of that truth. Interpreting a dogma does not simply mean laying hold of its historical truth. It also means offering a suitable hermeneutic approach so that the truth can be understood and rendered truly operative. Formally speaking, then, the problem of the interpretation of dogma is the same problem involved in the interpretation of scriptural texts. I have already touched upon the latter theme in discussing the resurrection of Christ, so I will not repeat the hermeneutic steps required to make a dogmatic text comprehensible.

The Positive and Necessary Significance of Dogma

Here I offer my systematic understanding of the positive and necessary value of a dogma, presupposing that the aforementioned work of interpretation has been done. Hence I am not presenting what dogma signifies in other theologies, nor am I saying that this notion of dogma is assumed in the present-day language of the magisterium. I am simply trying to consider why what we now call dogma arose in the history of the church, though it may have gone by a different name in other ages; and I am also trying to evaluate that fact at its true worth.

Focusing on the central dogmas, which would include the christological dogmas of course, we first notice that they affirm limit-realities. In other words, they deal with realities such as God, creation, and grace, which are not comprehensible in themselves and which cannot be adequately grasped by human understanding, even if the human being in question is a believer. In these central dogmas, then, human beings and the church are fashioning ultimate formulations about reality, history, and their meaningfulness; they can be expressed, but they cannot be analyzed further.

To say that these realities are limit-realities is not to say that there is no rationality in the formulations dealing with them. It simply means that they cannot be grasped directly in themselves. They can be grasped only on the basis of other realities, a knowledge of which makes the limit-formulations reasonable. Strictly speaking, this is not a peculiarity of theological discourse. We find it in other realms of human reflection as well. For example, human beings talk about such things as "liberty," "love," and "utopia." None of the latter realities can be intuited in itself, even though we may offer nominal definitions of them. But it is reasonable and meaningful to talk about them insofar as certain real-life experiences lead people to formulate the ultimate meaningfulness of life and history in those terms.

The first application of this point to the positive understanding of dogma is that the content of dogma ever remains incomprehensible, which is to say that it can never be adequately grasped. The formulation of a central dogma is possible only if the believer's process of coming to know its content—the process which leads to the dogmatic formulation—is integrated into the content of the dogma. In other words, the content of the dogma cannot be laid hold of directly; it can be obtained only on the basis of some other reality, a knowledge of which enables us to formulate a dogma that is meaningful.

The point which I have just made in formal, abstract terms can be illustrated in more concrete terms. Consider how language about God is used in Scripture. In Scripture we find two kinds of statements about God. Following the conventional terminology of Pannenberg and Schlink,[6] I shall call them historical statements and doxological statements. The liberation of the Hebrews from Egypt can be taken as a historical statement about God. In such a statement we find, first of all, a historical event that is verifiable in principle. The Hebrews, who had lived as slaves in Egypt, went out of that land and settled down in Palestine. Historically speaking, we can say that they were liberated. This merely historical statement becomes a historical statement about God when the whole historical process of liberation is attributed to God's intervention.

In this kind of historical statement about God, we do not talk specifically about God in himself but about God in relation to some historical event. This is the structure of the historical creeds of the Old Testament. It is a structure that does not relate God with some abstract adjective describing his essence but rather with some action. Such statements say: God is the one who led us out of Egypt, who brought us to the promised land, etc.

Besides these historical statements we find others that claim to say something about God in himself. Their structure is quite different. In them God is described by some adjective. The Canticle of Moses and many of the Psalms might serve as our example here. After the Exodus Moses says: "God is my savior; God is glorious in his wondrous deeds." The Psalms repeatedly tell us that Yahweh is just, merciful, and so forth. We apply the term "doxological statements" to such affirmations, which seek to describe the intrinsic reality of God. In historical statements we talk about God in relationship to some historical event; in doxological affirmations we claim to be talking about the very essence of God.

We can say much the same thing about the language of Christology. In it we find creeds that are structured as historical statements, and we also find creeds that are structured as doxological statements. The latter would include hymns, some aspects of the liturgy, and dogmas. Dogma is a doxological statement in which we seek to formulate the mysterious reality of God himself.

The value of this definition, of course, does not lie in any attempt to solve the problem of dogma in some nominalist fashion. Its value lies in the fact that it points us toward the concrete meaningfulness and the concrete possibilities of dogma. In line with the example of the Old Testament, doxological statements cannot be intuited in themselves; they are possible only on the basis of historical statements. This enables us to draw two conclusions that are of basic importance for the understanding of a dogma.

First of all a dogmatic formulation embodies the end result of an epistemological or cognitive process. Just as Moses was able to formulate the reality of God as Savior after he had gone through the personal experience of saving events, so the reality of God in himself can be formulated on the basis of concrete historical experiences of God. What is more, the content of a doxological affirmation derives from the content of a historical affirmation. Our first conclusion, then, is that a dogma is a doxological formulation that marks the culmination of a whole process of Christian living and Christian reflective thinking.

Second, even though the historical statement may make the doxological statement reasonable, it does not strip the latter of its character as a mystery. This means that the doxological statement is not a straight-line continuation of a historical statement. To reach the point of making a doxological statement, the one making it must experience a rupture, must take a leap; and this leap from a historical statement to doxological statement about God must take the form of an act of self-surrender. In every doxological statement we find the surrender of the finite "I" of the human person. We can no longer verify or maintain control over the content of our affirmation about God; we sacrifice our ego and allow ourselves to be controlled by the mystery of God. Thus a dogma, insofar as it is a doxological statement about God in himself, presupposes the surrender of the thinking "I" to the mystery of God. This surrender of the ego on the rational level parallels the surrender of the ego in chanting liturgical hymns on the one hand and in the leading of life of true discipleship on the other.

In my opinion, then, the positive feature of dogma lies in the fact that it is a doxological affirmation about God in himself, the content of which expresses the deeper, underlying meaning of reality: i.e., that God "is" the Father, the Savior, and so forth. As a doxological statement, it is made possible by historical statements about God. I would also add that the dogma will have a true and profound Christian sense if the surrender of the ego on the rational level goes hand in hand with the authentic surrender of the ego in real life. Without the latter, the former has no real meaningfulness. It would simply come down to the humdrum repetition of seemingly orthodox formulas; it would not be a real doxological statement.

Having said this, I think we have at least enunciated the fundamental hermeneutics of dogma: Without some real-life surrender to some concrete content there can be no surrender of the thinking ego to some content about God. In its very essence, then, the ultimate truth of dogma cannot be separated from the liturgy and the following of Jesus. We are not simply spouting a fashionable modern slogan when we say that ortho*doxy* is *doxo*logy and praxis. Dogmas cannot be understood outside the context of doxology and praxis. In that sense we can say that the positive function of dogma is to express in theological language the same thing that is expressed in the liturgy in hymns of praise and joyful thanksgiving and that is expressed in real life in the language of concrete praxis.

Finally, I should like to say something about the Christian necessity of dogma. First of all, we can consider the matter on the basic human level. Even on the level of ideology human beings are always obliged to take their fundamental statements about their life and existence and to concentrate them in certain basic points. As an organization of human beings, the church has this same need and obligation. Moreover, as we intimated above, the church is faced with the historical necessity of making pronouncements about basic points at moments of crisis and controversy.

Here, however, I am talking about the *Christian* necessity of dogma insofar as dogma is a doxological affirmation, and that may not be so evident at first glance. The problem does not have to do with the cognitive impossibility of understanding God; it has to do with the basically impoverished and wretched situation of reality. Christian faith encounters its greatest difficulty in composing a doxological formulation insofar as it confronts the wretchedness and misery of reality: "How could we sing a song of the Lord in a foreign land?" (Ps. 137:4).

It is in the presence of this difficulty that the Christian need for dogma as a doxological statement appears dialectically. It is a need that wells up from the concrete experience of gratuitousness. The historical and noetic process that leads to the formulation of a dogma is not one that is necessary in any automatic or mechanical way. It is possible only if the Christian and the church can utter a doxological word about God through that process and despite it. Dogma becomes necessary only if the Christian and the church, living in the process of history, maintain a hope against hope, a hope that does not die.

It is in that sense that we can apply Moltmann's comment about theology to the understanding of dogma as well. He says:

Theology is at once necessary and unnecessary. It becomes relevant for us in the realm of misery and dire necessity, even though it wells up from our wonder at the history of Christ and our joy over God's unmerited grace that speaks to us out of that history. . . . Under the first aspect Christian theology is therefore the *theory of a praxis* that transforms misery. . . . Under the second aspect, by contrast, Christian theology is at the same time overflowing joy in God. . . . Under the first aspect it is *the theory of a praxis.* Under the second aspect it is *pure theory:* i.e., contemplation that transforms the one contemplating into what is being contemplated—hence *doxology.* [7]

Here, then, we understand Christian dogma to be a doxological statement. In terms of the object, its possibility resides in the historical actions that can be traced back to God. In terms of the subject, its possibility resides in the surrender of the thinking ego to the mystery of God. Its meaningfulness lies in the fact that it uses limit-formulations to assert the meaningfulness of existence and history on the basis of the mystery of God. And the need for it arises when people maintain hope in that meaningfulness even when history calls it into question. It is our way of expressing, on the noetic level, the gratuitousness of the experience of God that has been granted to us.

THE CHRISTOLOGICAL DOGMAS

I think the above clarifications are necessary if we wish to understand the significance of the dogmas concerning Christ. What I propose to do now is twofold. I want to verify the truth of the christological formulas on the basis of the things said about the person of the historical Jesus and his destiny; to do that is to carry out our *theological* responsibility. And I also want to verify the truth of the things said about Christ on the basis of the christological formulas, that being our *ecclesial* responsibility.

Here I do not propose to offer a direct historico-dogmatic analysis of the genesis of christological dogmas in the early centuries[8]; nor do I propose to offer an interpretation of the dogmatic formula in terms of itself,[9] for that is precisely what I maintain to be impossible. I simply want to show that the Christology presented so far in this book is in accord with the dogmatic formulas. Thus reflection on Christ can continue to move forward by bringing together the truth that is contained in both and confronting one with the other.

The Basic Christological Dogmas

The basic dogmas of Christology were formulated in the fourth and fifth centuries. In the fourth century Arius denied the divinity of Christ, using the following line of reasoning. Christ is a composite of the Logos and the *flesh* of Jesus, not a composite of the Logos and the *man*, Jesus. The spiritual principle of Jesus is not the *soul* but the eternal Logos itself. This means that the one who suffered and died on the cross was the Logos. The Logos cannot be divine, for that would imply the mutability of God. Against this view the Council of Nicea formulated the first dogmatic definition about Christ:

We believe . . . in one Lord Jesus Christ, the Son of God, the Only-begotten, Begotten of the Father, of the Father's substance, God of God, Light of Light, true God of true God, begotten not made, of one and the same substance as the Father . . . " [DS 125].

What is affirmed directly in this formula is the divinity of the Logos. The most important consequence or conclusion is that God is not just the Father alone, that the Logos is also part of God, though in this formula it is not yet clear what is the exact relationship between the Logos and Jesus.

Reflection on the relationship between the divine Logos and the humanity of Jesus led to the crisis of the fifth century. The two opposing positions were those of Cyril of Alexandria and Nestorius of Constantinople. *Cyril* stressed the unity of Christ's divinity and humanity. But his famous formula, "one single nature of the Word incarnate," seemed to suggest something in the line of deprecating Christ's humanity. *Nestorius* defended the authentic humanity of Christ, but his view made it difficult for people to comprehend the unity of the person of the Logos. The Council of Chalcedon put an end to this debate:

Following the holy Fathers, we are unanimous in teaching that the Son, our Lord Jesus Christ, is one and uniquely perfect with regard to divinity, perfect with regard to his humanity, true God and true man, composed of a rational soul and body. He is essentially equal to the Father in divinity, and essentially equal to us in humanity, . . . "yet never sinned" (Heb. 4:15) . . . [DS 301].

We profess a Christ, one and unique, the Son, the Lord, the Only begotten, who consists of two natures without confusion, without change, without division, and without separation of the two natures. The distinction of natures never eliminates their union; rather, it preserves the peculiar distinctiveness of each one of them, bringing them together harmoniously in one person and hypostasis. We do not profess a separate Son divided into two persons, but one, unique, only begotten Son, the divine Word, the Lord Jesus Christ . . . [DS 302].

These formulations basically assert that Christ, the Son of God, is true God; and stress is placed on the fact that he is true man. The second segment attempts to explain *how* the two dimensions—natures—coexist in the one single divine person of Christ. The union is a personal one. In other words, there exists in Christ only one person, one ultimate principle of subsistence; but on the other hand the two natures are not separated nor intermingled.

Criticism of the "Formulation" of These Dogmas[10]

Before I consider what is positive and eternally valid in these formulas, I want to offer a criticism of them. I do this precisely because I want to better serve the basic intention that underlies them. What perdures in these formulas for the history of the church is a generic truth. It continues to remain a truth, but only on the condition that it can be mediated historically in and through every kind of cultural, sociological, philosophical, and theological analysis. If the eternal truth of these formulations is to succeed in becoming concrete truth, then it must pass through all those mediations.

The necessity of such mediating factors becomes more obvious when a new cultural and social situation arises in the church, with all its consequent repercussions on philosophical and theological reflection. The rise of a novel situation is always accompanied by a crisis of meaning that directs our attention to the overall conception of existence and history. In the new situation we come to see the need to restore meaning to the age-old formulations, 'but we also glimpse something that now lacks meaningfulness. That is why I choose to begin by criticizing the dogmatic "formulations" about Christ. It is quite apparent that our present situation is markedly different from that of the Greco-Roman world of the fourth and fifth centuries in which the christological dogmas were formulated.

Viewed from the standpoint of our own situation now, those formulations suffer from a lack of concreteness, historicity, and relationality. The first and most basic difficulty for people today is not the difficulty of understanding certain terms such as nature, person, and hypostatic union as they were used by the council fathers and understood against the backdrop of the Greek mentality. That certainly is a practical difficulty, and hence of pastoral importance. But the most basic difficulty is that the formulas give the impression that one knows at the very outset who God is and what it means to be a human being. Thus the only remaining problem lies in the assertion that these two dimensions, already known from the very start, are united in the person of Christ. But the problem that Christology poses to us is quite the opposite. For it tells us that it is on the basis of Christ that we know who God is and what it means to be a human being.

God is not just any deity: God is first and foremost the Father of Jesus. To be a human being is not simply to possess the essence of a rational animal; it is to be like Jesus. That does not rule out the trinitarian problem that we shall broach further on, but it does put us on the scent of the formula's limitation that we wish to bring out.

The crucial point about Christology is that it calls into question the very thing that the natural human being takes completely for granted. Natural human beings assume that they know what human nature is and what divine nature is. This assumption, which today is clearly felt to be a weakness, is the danger I see in the Chalcedonian formula if it is taken in too abstract a manner.

It cannot be denied that there is a danger. In earlier systematic theology we can note a strong tendency toward abstract formalization. Insofar as theology tends increasingly to stress the abstract side of its terminolgy, it also tends to dilute the concrete content of the human subject, Jesus of Nazareth, the theological features of "the God and Father of Jesus Christ," and the dramatic nature of their oneness. In large measure the synthesis of systematic theology ended up being little more than an elaboration of one single type of Christology. It elaborated the ancient christological dogma along lines that were markedly ontological.[11]

The formulations also suffer from lack of historicity, another feature that is characteristic of the Greek mentality. The concepts of nature and person are used to explain the mystery of the Incarnation, but the concept of history is missing entirely. They state that Christ really is true God and true man, but the humanity of Christ is subsumed under the conceptual category of nature. In particular, the formula does not do justice to the humanity of Christ. Reading it from our vantage point today, we must agree with the criticisms that Paul van Buren makes with just a touch of irony. He points out that the way in which Jesus Christ's humanity was defined by earlier theology seemed to threaten the place of Jesus of Nazareth in the world of real human beings. The problem can be seen as far back as the writings of Justin Martyr. Justin stresses that Jesus was a human being with body, soul, and spirit; but he seems to suggest that Jesus did not have any real historical relationship with the rest of humankind. He was *like* us, but not really *one of us*.[12]

In the Chalcedonian formula we do not find the historical categories that are typically highlighted in the New Testament: the conflict-ridden reality of Jesus, his temptations, his ignorance, and the internal and external process of development that he experienced. It does say that he was like us in everything except sin, but once again the resemblance is established on the formal, abstract level of nature. But the Logos assumes a truly human history, through which the man Jesus becomes a real human being; and the revelation of the Son takes place gradually through the revelation of Jesus' human history.

Finally, the formula suffers from a lack of relationality. It does talk about Christ as the Son, and that implies a relationship with the Father. But its analysis of the reality of Christ stresses the relationship between humanity and divinity in Christ himself. The formal relationship with the Father is preserved in its reference to "God of God" and "Light of Light" and "true God of true God"; but that seems to be only a pale reflection of what is implied in Jesus' essential relationship to the Father. The problem may have been that the category of "relationship" seemed to be a weak conceptual vehicle for affirming the divinity of Jesus, so the categories of "nature" and "person" were chosen instead. But in that choice theology lost sight of a fundamental datum in the Synoptic Gospels: i.e., that the truth about Jesus is not to be found primarily by relating him to the eternal Logos, but rather by relating him to the Father. This difficulty is heightened insofar as the formula does not mention the "kingdom of God" as Jesus' ultimate pole of relationship.

Posed on this level, the whole issue may seem to be overly abstract and speculative; but its consequences can be readily noted in the structuring of traditional Christologies. "Preoccupied with Christ's dignity, dogma and theology have talked about his divinity in such a way that it could not help but seem more and more closed in upon itself."[13] It is the logical presupposition that lies behind the growing distance between ordinary dogmatic Christology on the one hand and the Christology of the New Testament on the other. "It is precisely in his incomparable relationship with God, in his knowledge that his power comes from God and a life lived wholly in and for the Father, that the New Testament reveals the dignity of Christ and his oneness with God."[14] Insofar as the dogmatic formula centers on the relationship between divinity and humanity in Christ himself, it prompts us to overlook or forget the more basic relationship in Jesus' life: i.e., his unconditional trust in the Father and his complete obedience to the Father in his mission of proclaiming and realizing the kingdom of God.

The kind of shortcomings we notice in the various dogmatic formulations are not just of one sort. It is not just that it is difficult for people of different ages and cultures to understand them. The central problem is that these formulations do not bring out fundamental data about Jesus that appear clearly in his own history. The old dogmatic formula may express a basic point of the New Testament *better* for those of Greek mentality by explaining the distinctive reality of Jesus of Nazareth in terms of his being God and man and the eternal Son of the Father. But it pays a price for this insofar as it says *less* than the New Testament does. For the latter tells us that the humanity of the eternal Son has a concrete, well defined history; and that the reference-pole of that history is the Father and the kingdom of God.

The Dogma of Chalcedon as a Doxological Statement About Christ

I do not think we can overcome the difficulties described above by trying to work solely and completely from within the dogmatic formulas themselves. In my opinion, the only way to overcome the difficulties is to regard the dogmatic formulas as doxological statements in the sense that I have explained earlier.

In the dogma we make a statement about Christ in himself. The basic content of that statement is that Christ, the one whom his contemporaries wondered about and wanted to identify, is a distinctive and unique person because he is simultaneously God and man, without confusion or distinction. Thus this christological statement is, first and foremost, a pre-eminently positive statement about Christ. This is the basic value of the dogma, both for what it positively asserts and for the boundaries it sets. Those boundaries must be respected by every ecclesial Christology.

But since it is a doxological statement, the truth that is affirmed in it cannot be intuited in itself. Its reasonableness cannot be grasped simply by considering the formula in itself. Tradition has repeatedly stressed this by pointing out that the hypostatic union is a mystery in the strict sense. More recently Karl Rahner has made the same point in trying to ensure that we do not trivialize the doxological statement about Christ:

When the orthodox Christology of descent says, "This Jesus *is* God," that continues to remain true *if* the phrase is understood correctly. Put in this way, however, it could be understood in monophysite terms. Such phrases are formulated and are to be understood according to the norms governing the *communicatio idiomatum* ("communication of attributes"). Nothing in them makes it explicitly clear that here the copula "is" must be understood in a sense that is completely different from the sense it usually has for us in phrases that seem to contain the exact same copula. When we say, "Peter is a man," the phrase affirms a real and true identification of the content of the subject and the predicate. When the copula "is" is used in phrases based on the *communicatio idiomatum* in Christology, however, its meaning and validity is *not* based on any such real identification. Instead it is based on a unique, irrepeatable unity that does not occur in any other form and that ever remains profoundly mysterious. . . . Between it and the other realities so linked there ever remains an infinite abyss. Jesus in and according to his humanity, which we see when we say "Jesus," *is not* God; and God in and according to his divinity *is not* man, in the sense that there is a real identification. [15]

This passage points up what I earlier referred to as the subjective precondition for making a doxological affirmation—in this case, for affirming that Christ "is" God and man. Rahner is telling us that we can make this statement meaningfully only if we are willing to submit to noetic self-surrender.

For here the human mind is being asked to give up nothing less that its usual understanding of the copula "is"—apart from any sort of analogical interpretation. We can profess this christological dogma only insofar as we are willing to give up the idea that we can confer ultimate meaning on that which is really ultimate: i.e., "being."

But if the christological dogma is a doxological formulation, then we must also analyze its objective presupposition. In an earlier section of this chapter I pointed out that doxological statements can be formulated meaningfully only on the basis of historical statements. This means that we must first analyze the history of Jesus, his work on behalf of the kingdom, his unconditional trust in the Father, and his loyalty to the destiny that leads him to the cross and the resurrection. It is only if those historical realities are referred back to God that one can make the doxological statement: "Jesus is the eternal Son of the Father." At that point human thinking no longer has control over what it says. Yet people can make this statement meaningfully *if* they have reflected on the history and destiny of Jesus within the framework of the hermeneutics described earlier.

The point is that dogmatic statements about Christ can only be obtained *indirectly* through the history of Jesus. Jesus' divinity is not self-evident, and the dogmatic formula does not make it so. We can profess that Jesus is the eternal Son of the Father, but only indirectly on the basis of historical happenings that can be laid hold of in themselves (e.g., his preaching, his activity, and his death) and on the basis of the eschatological happening of his resurrection. Once again this shows that the proper logical order of Christology is the chronological order. We are justified in starting our Christology with the historical Jesus because that is the only way in which our dogmatic formulas can have any real meaningfulness. It is literally impossible to begin with the Council of Chalcedon because the meaningfulness of its statements is made possible only insofar as it takes in the whole process of cognition and praxis that led to Chalcedon.

Finally, the fact that the dogmatic formula is a doxological statement means that it is an ultimate statement; hence it cannot be used as the premise of a syllogism in order to prove something. In concrete terms this means that what is asserted in DS 302 about the relationship between the two natures in Christ is not, strictly speaking, an explanation of what is said in DS 301 about Christ's divinity and humanity. It is an explicative model of a doxological sort, which means that it does not tell us anything more than what was already said in the preceding paragraph (DS 301).

Of even more basic importance is the methodological implications of the fact that the dogmatic formula is a doxological statement. It means that the formula cannot serve as either the starting point or the end point of Christology. We have already seen that it cannot be the starting point. Neither can it be the end point, however, for it is a doxology of the fifth century. Its methodological importance lies in the fact that the Christologies which must be elaborated later must incorporate its essential core, however they might be formulated. They, too, must affirm that Christ is unique and irrepeatable as the mediation between God and humanity.

Jesus' Personal Oneness with God

If doxological statements cannot be intuited in themselves, then it is worth our while to work out theoretical models that will help us to understand them. What we elaborate or describe in such models will help to spell out the ultimate meaning of the doxological statement. With reference to the divinity of Jesus, then, I propose his personal union with God as an explicative model. [16]

In the New Testament the clearest and most obvious category for expressing Jesus' oneness with God is the category of relationship. Jesus' distinctiveness and uniqueness shows up first and foremost in his distinct and unique relationship with the one he calls his Father. To the latter he shows complete confidence. To him he offers perfect obedience in carrying out his mission to proclaim and realize the kingdom of God. This relationship can be described as one of filiation or sonship. Here we have our first systematic category, a category verified in Jesus' own history, that may help us to explore more deeply his unique mysteriousness. In and through Jesus' radical surrender to the Father, which was confirmed by his resurrection, a special relationship between Jesus and the Father is established. That is the historical background that moves us toward doxologically affirming the divinity of Jesus in relationship to the Father.

This relationship is a personal one. Here again I must offer some theoretical clarification as to what I mean by "person." In the history of philosophy and theology we find two basic ways of understanding what it means to be a person. One way conceives person in terms of the individual's possession of self. The other way stresses the relational character of the person as this has been brought out within Christian theology. We note that Augustine defined the persons within the Trinity in terms of relations, and that Richard of Saint Victor defined the person as an ex-sistence. This line of thought was explored more deeply by Duns Scotus and systematized by Hegel into the following basic idea: abstract personhood is acquired concretely in self-surrender to another.[17]

What, then, are we talking about when we talk about the personal unity of humanity and divinity in Jesus? First of all we are saying something that is verifiable. We are saying that Jesus is a person who becomes the person he is precisely through his surrender to the Other who is the Father. The divinity in Jesus is the modality of this personal relationship with the Father, which takes place in history and amid the conflict-ridden reality of history. In loyal self-surrender to the Father right to the very end, Jesus gradually took on his concrete personhood. Jesus' peculiar relationship with the Father shows up and develops insofar as it is maintained to the very end. As Pannenberg puts it: "The surrender of Jesus to the Father was in the nature of a self-abandonment. It was not surrender to a mission lived out in full clarity and accepted wholeheartedly. Rather, it was surrender to the will of God amid all the obscurity surrounding his path to the cross, and the cross represents the complete failure of Jesus' mission."[18]

In this theoretical model for understanding the divinity of Jesus, then, we make two kinds of statements. Some statements are historical: e.g., about Jesus' trust in, and obedience to, the Father. Other statements are doxological: e.g., when we say that this relationship is "uniquely distinctive and unrepeatable." That is a doxological statement couched in non-dogmatic language. What dogma does specifically is state in trinitarian terms what we have so far described simply as Jesus' distinctive and unique relationship with the Father. The dogmas formulate this distinctiveness and uniqueness by saying that Christ *is* the eternal Son of the Father. At bottom the mechanism of shifting from historical statements to doxological ones is the same, but the formulation is different.

Thus the identifying of Jesus with the eternal Son is done indirectly, on the basis of the man Jesus' tangible, historical filiation with the Father.[19] The identification is not an affirmation that can be intuited in itself. The relationship between the two stems from what can be observed historically with respect to Jesus' sonship. The doxological aspect, which cannot be verified by human thought, enters the picture when we identify Jesus' historical filiation with the eternal filiation of the Son.

Thus the Christology elaborated here maintains the dogmatic statements, but it offers a different approach to understanding them. Instead of beginning with the doxological affirmation of the incarnation of the eternal Son in Jesus of Nazareth (the theology of *descent*), it ends up with the doxological statement that this Jesus of Nazareth is the eternal Son. Both approaches involve a shift from the historical to the doxological. The advantage of my approach here over that of the traditional Christology of descent is that it regards the history of Jesus as basic and essential to the dogmatic assertion that Christ is the eternal Son.

Jesus as the Way to the Father

Classical and dogmatic Christology begin with the doxological statement that the eternal Son of God became man. They begin with the Incarnation, and so they are called Christologies of descent. In them we have at least an implicit category of evolution or development, but it is an evolution from above to below. Part of the mystery of the doxological statement consists in the assertion that the Son became man. In the Christology presented here, the movement would seem to go in the opposite direction, from below to above. Jesus gradually fashioned himself into the Son of God, became the Son of God.

This may strike some readers as shocking. It may sound like some sort of adoptionism that was condemned back in the early centuries of the church. But we must be clear about what is being said here. Both in the classical theology of descent and this Christology of ascent there is an element of mystery that cannot be satisfactorily explained. Both must include some kind of becoming in order to make explicit the mystery of Christ. In the last analysis both types of explanation share the limitations of the human mind in trying to understand what "becoming" might mean in God.

The difference between the two explanatory models might be put in these terms. In the first model (the classic model), the eternal Son becomes a human nature. Thus there is a historical movement in time in which the Son becomes man. But once that basic historical movement is granted, we cannot see clearly what exactly is historical in the nature assumed by the eternal Son. In the second model (the model proposed here), we assert that the human being, Jesus of Nazareth, becomes the Son of God in and through his concrete history. The advantage of this model is that it does justice to the history of Jesus as it is presented in the New Testament. Jesus is someone who learns obedience and arrives at perfection (see Heb. 5:8f.).

Both statements are doxological: i.e., the statement that the eternal Son becomes man, and the statement that Jesus of

Nazareth becomes the Son of God. The question is whether the first doxological statement is possible without the second, at least in the light of the New Testament. When we look at the attempts to reflect theologically on the unique oneness of Jesus with the Father in the New Testament, we notice an advance in them. At first Jesus' oneness with God is situated in the parousia, or else in the resurrection. Then this moment of oneness is moved back to Jesus' transfiguration or his baptism. Then it is moved back to his conception in Mary's womb. Finally, a doxological statement asserts that Jesus was united with the Father from all eternity.[20] That is what is implied in the New Testament references to his pre-existence, and to the fact that the eternal Son became man. Such a doxological statement would not have been possible, however, if the New Testament theologians had not pondered the concrete life of Jesus and come to realize that its growth in filiation went hand in hand with his developing historical self-surrender to the Father.

The believer who has gone through the whole process of reflection as just described can and should end up with the doxological statement that the Son became man. But one must have first observed how Jesus went through the process of becoming the Son for the process of reflection to be possible at all. An authentically orthodox Christology must end up with the ontological affirmation of the Incarnation. Epistemologically, however, it must work in the opposite direction. It must examine the divinization of Jesus.

This seemingly abstract discussion has important consequences for systematic theology. Let me suggest what I see them to be. I pointed out above that we cannot understand the divinity of Jesus without mentioning his relationship to the Father and the kingdom. Now I would say that we cannot understand that relationship without analyzing its historical development, as we did in earlier chapters. The relationship of Jesus of Nazareth to the Father has a history, and hence I would maintain that Jesus is not only the Son of the Father but also the Way to the Father. This means that he is not directly or simply the sacrament or the epiphanic manifestation of the

Father. Instead he is the revelation of the Son, of the correct way to approach and correspond to the Father. The statement that Jesus is the eternal Son incarnate is a doxological statement, the perceivable meaning of which lies in the fact that the concrete history of Jesus is the historical version of the Son's eternal filiation. The latter cannot be intuited in itself, but it does have meaningfulness if it is formulated on the basis of the history of Jesus' filiation.

The most concrete and practical systematic consequence should be added here. The Son does not simply reveal the potential filiation of all human beings with God. He also reveals the very process of filiation, the concrete way in which human beings can and do become children of God. If Jesus is the Son, then human beings can be children of God. But Jesus went on to reveal a very concrete sort of filiation, with a concrete path all its own; hence human beings have been shown the path to filiation. Human beings cannot simply stop with the doxological statement that they are children of God, or that they can become such. They must go on to follow the concrete path to filiation. Herein lies the ultimate importance of analyzing the figure of Jesus in historical categories, in terms of concrete becoming. Otherwise our abstract statements about filiation may remain abstract and wholly inoperative.

The Verification of the Truth of Chalcedon's Dogmatic Formula

From everything that has been said so far, it should be clear that in a strict sense we cannot verify the dogmatic christological formula because it is a doxological statement. However, that does not mean that it does not need any verification at all. If that were true, then it would be a purely arbitrary formula. The verification should take place on several different levels that I shall now enumerate.

First and most obvious is the fact that the doxological formula must be verified through the historical statements that make it possible. Here that means specifically that it must be verified through the history of Jesus narrated in the Gospels.

Basically we have done that already by linking what is fundamental in the dogmatic formula with what is fundamental in the New Testament—even with the limitations and reservations described above.

Second, the doxological formula must be verified on the basis of the history of the ideas to which it gives rise. If the christological formula makes a statement that is universally valid at its core, then this means that it must be subsequently interpreted in different historical situations and cultures. Let me put this as pointedly and as graphically as I can: If the christological dogma of the fifth century were an ultimate and definitive *formulation* from every point of view, that would constitute the formal negation of its truth; for that would mean that its supposed universality were reduced or restricted to a given age and place. If Christ really is the eternal Son of God, as dogma says he is, then there must be a history of Christology.[21]

However, the criteria of verification that follow below seem even more important to me than the ones above. Third, then, the formula finds verification in the fact that throughout history people do actually continue to make doxological statements about Christ that reflect the fundamental nucleus of the earlier dogmatic formulas. The Chalcedonian formula would cease to be true if it turned out that people merely repeated it, if we did not find the surrender of the finite ego which prompted people to utter some type of doxological confession in the presence of Jesus and his history. The later doxological formulations might well appear to be quite different from those of Chalcedon, but they can and should retain the core points of the latter. For example, Teilhard de Chardin talked about Christ as the "Omega Point"; Karl Rahner has called him the "absolute bearer of salvation"; and Latin Americans have begun to talk about him as "the Liberator." If people come to uttering such formulas, and if in them they wish to point up his ultimate role as mediator between the divine and the human, transcendence and history, then the formula of Chalcedon continues to remain true. For even though the formulations are different, it means that we still find Christian human beings who are compelled to express the ultimate truth about Christ in doxological terms.

That brings us to the final and most important criterion of verification. The Chalcedonian formula continues to be true insofar as there really continue to be followers of Jesus, people whose concrete discipleship professes Jesus as the Christ. Let me put the point negatively, first of all. It would be absurd to profess that Christ is the eternal Son of God if his reality were not capable of unleashing a history of sonship. The dogma of Chalcedon could hardly be eternally valid if, historically speaking, the Christ of Chalcedon did not generate Christians. To put it positively, the ultimate verification of the truth of Chalcedon's christological dogma lies in the course of later history. It is true if we continue to find Christians in later history and in very different cultures and societies, if we continue to find people whose life finds its meaning in pursuing and continuing the life of Jesus and thereby becoming children of God.

Thus, in viewing christological dogma as an ultimate affirmation about Christ, we come back again to our starting point: i.e., the relevance of the historical Jesus in opening up concrete paths for other human beings to gain access to the Father. Precisely because dogma asserts that Christ is the Son, the most urgent task of Christology is not to re-interpret christological dogma directly. That ever remains an important task, to be sure. But the most urgent task of Christology is to reposition the path and course of believers so that their lives can be a continuing, advancing discipleship, a following of Jesus, and hence a process of concrete filiation as his life was.

NOTES

1. See W. Kasper, *Dogma y palabra de Dios*, Spanish trans. (Bilbao, 1968); German original: *Dogma unter dem Wort Gottes* (Mainz: Matthias-Grünewald, 1965); J. Finkenzeller, *¿Fe sin dogma? Dogma, desarrollo de los dogmas y magisterio eclesiástico*, Spanish trans. (Estella, 1973); German original: *Glaube ohne Dogma?* (Düsseldorf: Patmos, 1972).

2. G. Gloege, *Religion für Geschichte und Gegenwart*, 2:222, cited by Kasper, *Dogma y palabra de Dios*, op. cit., p. 36.

3. Kasper, ibid., p. 41.

4. In an earlier work on the dogma of the real presence and transubstantiation, I tried to spell out how a dogma might be interpreted analytically. On more recent discussion of the real presence and transubstantiation see *Ecclesiastica Xaveriana*, n. 2 (1970), 20:3–87. On the problem of the interpretation of dogma in progressive, postconciliar theology see K. Rahner, "Considerations on the Development of Dogma," in *Theological Investigations* (Baltimore: Helicon, 1966), 4:3–35; idem, "What is a Dogmatic Statement?" in *Theological Investigations*, 5:42–66. On the problem of the development of dogma and the historicity of theology, see his articles in Volumes 1 and 8 of *Theological Investigations*. Also see E. Schillebeeckx, *Revelación y teología*, Spanish trans. (Salamanca, 1968), especially pp. 163–210; Eng. trans.: *Revelation and Theology* (New York: Sheed and Ward, 1967); *Glaubensinterpretation: Beiträge zu einer hermeneutischen und kritischen Theologie* (Mainz, 1971), especially pp. 48–82; in English see *The Understanding of Faith* (New York: Seabury, 1974); *La presencia de Cristo en la eucaristía*, Spanish trans. (Madrid, 1968), especially pp. 25–125; in English see *The Eucharist* (New York: Sheed and Ward, 1968); P. Schoonenberg, *Die Interpretation des Dogmas* (Düsseldorf: Patmos, 1969); B. Welte, "Ein Vorschlag zur Methode der Theologie heute," in *Gott im Welt* (Freiburg: Herder, 1961), 1:271–86; F. Schupp, *Auf dem Weg zu einer kritischen Theologie* (Freiburg, 1974), especially pp. 70–87; Z. Alszeghy and M. Flick, *El desarrollo del dogma católico*, Spanish edition (Salamanca, 1969); W. Pannenberg, *Grundfragen systematischer Theologie*, especially pp. 159–251, see note 12, chap. 2 in this volume.

In Latin America the topic has been examined critically rather than treated in any novel way. For example, one might read the critical observations of H. Assmann in *Theology for a Nomad Church*, English trans. (Maryknoll, New York: Orbis Books, 1976).

5. In practice, the hierarchization of dogma is being based, not on the dogmas themselves, but on one's theological position. But it is important to notice the trend toward a proper hierarchization. As in many other areas, Rahner paved the way with his statement that theology says only one thing: i.e., that the mystery eternally remains a mystery (see *Theological Investigations*, 5). He thus reduced all theology to the mystery of God and the mystery of God's communication in history, the latter with its two highpoints in Christ and humanity. Rahner's importance does not lie in the way he determines or defines the fundamental "dogma" or "mystery." It lies in his stress on the fact that the "plurality" of mysteries is quite secondary, that it takes on meaning only in the framework of some hierarchizing principles.

After that a movement arose in Europe to find brief formulas of the Christian faith. See Rahner's article on the need for such a brief formula in *Concilium* 23, 1967 (English edition, New York, Paulist Press). Latin American theology has not been preoccupied with elaborating such brief formulas, but it draws its life from the same basic intuition. In fact it has sought to hierarchize theology around the mystery of "God the Liberator."

6. W. Pannenberg, *Fundamentos de Cristología*, pp. 227–32, see note 6, chap. 1 in this volume; idem, *Grundfragen systematischer Theologie*, pp. 181–200, see note 12, chap. 2 in this volume; E. Schlink, "Die Struktur der dogmatischen Aussage als ökumenisches Problem," *Kerygma und Dogma*, 3 (1957), pp. 251–306. These two authors distinguish between doxological statements and kerygmatic statements. I call the latter "historical" statements for the sake of a more readily understandable nomenclature. E. Schillebeeckx also alludes to the ultimately doxological character of theological statements; see *Glaubensinterpretation*, pp. 10f., 96–109.

7. J. Moltmann, *Sobre la libertad, la alegría y el juego*, Spanish trans. (Salamanca, 1972), p. 44f.; in English see *Theology of Play* (New York: Harper & Row, 1972), and *Theology and Joy* (London: SCM, 1974).

8. For a study of the history of Christology up to the formulation of Chalcedon, see A. Grillmeier, *Christ in Christian Tradition* (New York: Seabury, 1976); P. Smulders, "Desarrollo de la cristología en la historia de los dogmas y en el magisterio eclesiástico," in *Mysterium Salutis*, III/1 (Madrid, 1971), pp. 417–503; J.I. González Fauss, *La humanidad nueva, Ensayo de cristología* (Madrid, 1974), 2:375–517. For more summary treatments see C. Duquoc, *Cristología*, pp. 250–72, see note 23, chap. 4 in this volume; and L. Boff, *Jesucristo el liberador*, pp. 191–201, see note 9, chap. 3 in this volume.

9. There are many different works that have attempted to reinterpret the christological dogmas and work out a Christology accordingly. Here I mention only a few sample ones: K. Rahner, *Christologie—systematisch und exegetisch* (Freiburg: Herder, 1972), pp. 51–69, where he sums up and presents the basic intuitions that underlie his articles on Christology in Volumes 1 and 2 of *Theological Investigations*; P. Schoonenberg, *Un Dios de los hombres*, Spanish trans. (Barcelona, 1972), pp. 59–119; Eng. trans.: *The Christ: A Study of the God-Man Relationship in the Whole of Creation and in Jesus Christ* (New York: Herder & Herder, 1971); O. G. de Cardedal, *Jesús de Nazaret: Aproximación a la cristología* (Madrid, 1975), pp. 349–603; J.I. González Fauss, *La humanidad nueva*, pp. 625–59; P. Faynel, *Jesucristo es el Señor* (Salamanca, 1968), pp. 189–247; French original: *Jésus Christ-Seigneur* (Paris: Ligel, 1965); D. Wiederkehr, "Esbozo de cristología sistemática," *Mysterium Salutis*, III/1 (Madrid, 1971), pp. 505–667.

Among Protestant studies see: P. Van Buren, *The Secular Meaning of the Gospel* (New York: Macmillan, 1963), pp. 1–79, 157–71; J. Moltmann, *Der gekreuzigte Gott*, pp. 214–36, see note 10, chap. 1 in this volume; and above all, Pannenberg, *Fundamentos de Cristología*, pp. 351–492.

10. Various criticisms of the dogmatic formulations and the systematic theology based on them can be found in the works cited above. For example: Wiederkehr, "Esbozo," pp. 517–26; Schoonenberg, *Un Dios de los hombres*, pp. 59–75; K. Rahner, *Christologie*, pp. 55–58; Pannenberg, *Fundamentos de Cristología*, pp. 356–63; and González Fauss, *La humanidad nueva*, pp. 509–12.

11. Wiederkehr, "Esbozo," p. 517.

12. Van Buren, *Secular Meaning of the Gospel,* p. 38.

13. Wiederkehr, "Esbozo," p. 518.

14. Ibid., p. 519.

15. Rahner, *Christologie,* p. 55f.

16. See Pannenberg, *Fundamentos de Cristología,* pp. 403–15.

17. See W. Pannenberg, "Person," in *Religion für Geschichte und Gegenwart,* V, col. 230–35.

18. Pannenberg, *Fundamentos de Cristología,* p. 416.

19. Ibid., pp. 414–33.

20. Ibid., p. 165f.

21. Referring to the task of reflecting seriously on the historical rise of different Christologies, Pannenberg has this to say: "The realization of this task on a grand scale will take on the character of a theory of christological tradition. That theory will be simultaneously historical and systematic since the succeeding course of interpretations is part of the historical essence of the subject matter that calls for interpretation. For the subject matter, by virtue of its intent to have universal significance, constantly fosters the inclusion of new viewpoints and thus constantly gives rise to new interpretations" (ibid., p. 22).

11.

Theses for a Historical Christology

1. PRESUPPOSITIONS FOR CHRISTOLOGY

1.1. Theology in general and Christology in particular deal with themes that sum up the full, all-embracing meaning of existence and history. This comprehensive meaning derives from the very realities under study: God, Christ, liberation, and the sinfulness of the world. It is the option of faith that these themes are viewed as recapitulating and expressing the total meaning of life and history. If they were viewed as incomplete and partial, then our christological study would not be Christian. It would be motivated by some other set of reasons: e.g., apologetic intent, intellectual curiosity, political concerns, or mere sympathy for the figure of Jesus.

1.2. From such a standpoint, then, the theme "Christ" is a limit-theme, a reality around which all human limit-realities revolve: transcendence, liberation, love, truth, justice, the sinfulness of the world, and the meaning of history. If they are limit-realities, however, then Christology cannot intuit them in themselves; and the same applies to the figure of Jesus himself, who christianizes them. Our affirmations about them cannot be isolated from the path and process that leads us toward knowledge of them. Our statements about such realities draw life and breath from historical experience itself, and only to that extent do they have a meaningfulness that can be formulated. This leads us to conclude that the real approach of theology is none other than the path of faith itself. No Christology can or does explain the reality of Christ from outside. Theology in general and Christology in particular have a maieutic task to perform. They must help us to draw out those viewpoints that enable us to do a better job of explaining how the faith is to be lived in real life. They must also help us to frame those questions, at least on the theoretical level, that will enable us better to comprehend Christ as the limit-reality that provides the total meaning of life and history and that will also help us to interpret our historical experience as a Christian experience. This will involve both criticizing historical experience on the one hand and marking out its Christian channels on the other.

1.3. We are looking for those viewpoints that will enable us to study Christology as something that offers the total meaning of life and history. I would propose the following points to help us in that search:

a. Wittingly or unwittingly every Christology is elaborated within the context of a specific situation. The need for a "new" Christology is felt in a "new" situation, where people clearly feel the meaninglessness of the existing situation and glimpse the direction in which a new meaningfulness might be found. The interaction between Christology and a new concrete situation can take place on various interrelated levels: on the intratheological level, as a reaction to the unsatisfactory nature of some particular Christology (scholastic Christology, for example); on the philosophical level, as a critical or positive reaction to new philosophical currents (such as existentialism, evolutionism, personalism, and Marxism); on the cultural level, as a critical or positive reaction to the cultural milieu (which may be sacral or secularized); and on the level of concrete reality itself, where one may face such structured situations as that of the Third World, the consumer society, or the socialist state.

Christology must take cognizance of what sort of situation it finds itself in and on what level it is situated. In passing we might note here one fact that can be verified historically. When the level of discussion has merely been theological, philosophical, or cultural, Christology has preferred to focus on the resurrected Christ as the symbolic expression of an explanatory and comprehensive vision of reality; but when the level of discussion has been that of concrete reality itself, Christology has naturally tended to focus on the figure of the historical Jesus.

The fact that Christology must be innovative in a new situation does not derive solely from the feelings of dissatisfaction to which an outmoded Christology gives rise. It derives from the very object of christological study: Christ. If Christ could fail to be of novel interest in a novel situation, if he could not be experienced and lived in new and different ways, then he would not be Christ. Thus the reformulation of Christology in a new situation is nothing else but an expression of faith in the universal significance of Christ.

b. Broad segments of humanity today live with a deep yearning for liberation. This movement for liberation found expression as far back as the Enlightenment, which specifically saw it as human liberation vis-à-vis theology. The movement has had two structurally distinct phases. One phase concentrated on the liberation of reason from dogmatic faith (Kant). The other phase championed the liberation of the whole person from a religious outlook that supported or at least permitted social, economic and political alienation (Marx). We might sum up the two phases as a general yearning for reasonableness and for transforming praxis.

Today no Christology can sidestep the challenge posed by the Enlightenment. If it does not respond to that challenge, no Christology is credible or relevant. But every Christology must take cognizance of the underlying interest that motivates it. Is it trying to show that the truth of Christ can be justified before the bar of reason or is it trying to show that it can be justified before the demands and yearnings for a transforming praxis? The two standpoints are not mutually exclusive, of course, but the emphasis given to one or the other will shift the thrust and direction of a given Christology. History indicates that European Christology has been more interested in demonstrating the truth of Christ before the bar of reason, though more recent political Christologies do move in a somewhat different direction. By contrast christological reflection in Latin America seeks to respond to the second phase of the Enlightenment noted above. It seeks to show how the truth of Christ is capable of transforming a sinful world into the kingdom of God.

c. From all that has been said so far, one can readily see the importance of a given hermeneutics for Christology. Specifically one can see its importance for the biblical texts in which the figure of Jesus is presented. Hermeneutics does not simply presume to settle the question as to the truth of statements about Christ. It also entails the task of figuring out a way to make them comprehensible and operational, to turn the tradition about Christ into something that continues to be alive and relevant here and now. The kind of hermeneutics used in Christology must do justice to two realities. First, it must do justice to the real situation today so that Christ will really be *comprehensible.* Second, it must do justice to the history of Jesus himself so that the now comprehensible Christ is not simply a wraith conjured up by present-day Christians. To put it another way, we must try to see what viewpoint is demanded by the gospel texts themselves if the figure of Christ is to be comprehended as such rather than as just another figure in past history. We must investigate to find out whether the gospel texts present themselves as merely to be comprehended by the mind or as words to be realized in practice as well.

d. If the very nature of Christology is to offer some complete all-embracing meaning of total reality, it cannot ignore the element of discontinuity and rupture to be found in that totality. Total meaningfulness and fulfillment does not exist in history, nor is it possible in the strict sense. Hence all serious thinking and all Christology arises in the presence of some ultimate quandary. The problem is to pinpoint the specific quandary that will make christological thinking truly fruitful.

On the theological level we find two basic approaches used to specify and resolve the quandary in christological terms. One approach sees Jesus as the solution to the problem of reconciling God with all that is positive in reality (e.g., nature, history, and human subjectivity); this is the approach of natural theology. The other approach sees Jesus as the embodiment of, and the unexpected solution to, the problem of reconciling God with what is negative in life and reality (e.g., sin, injustice, oppression, and death); this is the approach of theodicy. Every Christology operates on one of these two implicit presuppositions. It either assumes that Christ will prove to be the positive affirmation of humanity insofar as he fulfills all our natural potential; or else it assumes that Christ will affirm humanity by criticizing the natural person and thus helping to generate the new person. Either supposition will have an impact on the resultant conception of Christ and the emphasis given. While one brand of Christology will focus on the risen Christ as the paradigm of human fulfillment, the other will focus on the crucified Jesus as the incarnate criticism of the natural person. In short, the dominant underlying presupposition will profoundly affect the way a given Christology views the relationship between Jesus' cross and resurrection, two basic data about Jesus that no Christology can ignore.

e. Finally, every given Christology must focus consciously on its own role within theology as a whole. Does it see Christology as the Christian concentration of all theology or merely as just another chapter in theology—though admittedly an important chapter? To put it concretely, it must ask itself whether or not its conception of God, sin, liberation, and transcendence are derived from Jesus and hence christological, or whether they are viewed as realities already known logically from some other source quite independent of Jesus' appearance in history. How radically rooted in Christ are all the realities considered by theology? Is Jesus merely a privileged example and embodiment of things that can be learned quite independently of him?

The notion of christological concentration has another aspect that should be clarified right at the start. Even if we acknowledge the radicality of the revelation of Christ, we must go on to ask what this revelation is assumed to be. Do we picture it as a revelation of the ultimate essence of the Father or as a revelation of the Son? In other words, is Christ the sacrament of the Father or the way to the Father? Depending on which alternative we choose, we will get a different christological hermeneutics and a different overall view of revelation. One view will tend to be more epiphanic, stressing that "God" revealed himself in Christ. The other view will be more operational, stressing that Jesus reveals not so much the mystery of God himself as something to be *known cognitively* but rather the way to God that now can and should be travelled by humanity. So we will get two different Christologies. One will logically tend to be more praxis-oriented while the other will tend to be more contemplative, though of course there is no complete disjunction between them.

2. THE STARTING POINT OF CHRISTOLOGY

2.1. Granting that Christology has the task of spelling out the all-embracing meaningfulness of the Christ-reality, we must acknowledge that it is not easy to find some a priori starting point that will shed light on all the features of that reality. However, we certainly must be fully aware of the starting point that we do choose for it represents a hermeneutic principle that will illuminate and also condition all our reflection on Christ. The value of spelling out our starting point is that it puts us on guard against the possible limitations it imposes on us. If we do not spell it out, we may think that we are getting at the full and total reality of Christ when in fact we may be disregarding basic features of it (see 2.4).

2.2. When we talk about our starting point, we must keep in mind both the subjective and the objective aspect. The subjective starting point of Christology is faith as a lived experience, as I noted above. The next problem—which we shall consider further on—is how we are to live the faith so that the figure of Jesus as the Christ may be unveiled to us through that experience.

2.3. Looking for an objective starting point means looking for that aspect of the total and totalizing reality of Christ that will better enable us to find access to the total Christ. Here I propose the historical Jesus as our starting point. By that I mean the person, proclamation, activity, attitudes, and death by crucifixion of Jesus of Nazareth insofar as all of this can be gathered from the New Testament texts—with due respect for all the precautions imposed by critical exegesis. This particular starting point contrasts sharply with any christological approach that *begins* its reflection with the already glorified Christ. Put in positive terms, our approach here asserts that both for reflection and life it is the historical Jesus who is the key providing access to the total Christ.

There are several reasons for adopting this particular point of departure. First, as we noted at the start, the total Christ is a limit-reality in this world and can be comprehended only in connection with Jesus' actual course toward fulfillment as the Christ. Second, Jesus himself demands this, insisting that the fundamental contact with him comes through following his historical life: i.e., through real praxis of faith motivated by hope and love. This same demand holds primacy for any understanding of the total Christ. It takes priority over any "intentional" sort of contact with Christ: e.g., prayer, worship, and orthodoxy. Christian discipleship, however, can be understood only on the basis of the historical Jesus and his life. Third, a look at history makes it clear that things go wrong when faith focuses one-sidedly on the risen, fulfilled Christ and forgets the historical Jesus. It then tends to be turned into a "religion" in the pejorative sense of the term, working against the life of faith and downgrading all that is really and typically Christian (see thesis 9).

2.4. Besides the positive reasons adduced above, the deficiencies evident in other starting points justify using the historical Jesus as the proper point of departure. The dogmatic formula of Chalcedon disregards the concrete features of Jesus and his God. When a biblical Christology is based solely on the titles applied to Christ, it tends to view Jesus in terms of concepts already known: e.g., Messiah, Son of Man, Lord, Logos, and so forth. Instead it really should point out that the proper meaning of those terms can be gleaned only through the figure of Jesus himself. The resurrection of Jesus certainly is the culmination of Christology, but it calls for a hermeneutics if it is to be understood (see thesis 8). Such a hermeneutics is feasible only through a consideration of the history of Jesus. The kerygma about Christ, the proclamation of his cross and resurrection, does place humanity in a crisis. But emphasis on the kerygma has tended to individualize its thrust rather than "personalize" it as it claims to do, thereby ignoring the public aspects of its activity in history. Finally, an approach motivated by soteriological interests tends to disfigure Jesus also insofar as it manipulates him and reduces him to an example of what is of deep interest to humanity in any historical situation.

2.5. There is an important epistemological implication in the fact that we make the historical Jesus the starting point of Christology. It is Jesus himself, in his own historical life, who raises the whole question of his own person. We are forced into a very different position. Instead of asking questions, we ourselves are now called into question by Jesus. Thus it is the historical Jesus who brings Christology into crisis, effecting the epistemological break that is necessary if Christology is not to be simply the outcome of the natural person's inertial wishes and projections.

2.6. It can be historically verified that the various interpretations of liberation theology in Latin America seem to agree on one point: If a Christology disregards the historical Jesus, it turns into an abstract Christology that is historically alienating and open to manipulation. What typifies Jesus as a historical reality is the fact that he is situated and personally involved in a situation that displays structural similarities to that of present-day Latin America. At least we can detect a similar yearning for liberation and a similar situation of deep-rooted sinfulness. It is the historical Jesus who brings out clearly and unmistakably the need for achieving liberation, the meaning of liberation, and the way to attain it.

3. JESUS AND THE KINGDOM OF GOD

3.1. History means activity, change, evolution. A Christology centered around the historical Jesus must follow the characteristic features and events of Jesus' life in chronological order if it is to evaluate them properly as historical realities. The most certain historical datum is that Jesus began his activity by proclaiming the coming of God's kingdom: "After John's arrest, Jesus appeared in Galilee proclaiming the good news of God: 'This is the time of fulfillment. The reign of God is at hand! Reform your lives and believe in the gospel!' " (Mark 1:14).

3.2. To understand the figure of the historical Jesus and his relationship with the kingdom of God, we must differentiate two structurally distinct stages in his life: the period before the Galilean crisis and the period after it (see thesis 5). Here we find a rupture that will affect not only his outer attitude but also the very depths of his person and his conception of God and the kingdom. In this section we shall focus on the characteristics of the first stage, never forgetting that a profound change in Jesus would take place later on.

3.3. We can sum up the characteristic features of Jesus' early proclamation of the kingdom by saying that it was eschatological in character and that it was embodied both in words and in deeds.

3.4. *The eschatological character of the kingdom.* Toward the end of the last century exegetes discovered that Jesus' preaching was eschatological, and also that Jesus preached about the kingdom of God rather than the church.

a. The importance of this discovery lay in the fact that it seriously questioned the figure of Jesus presented by liberal theology or pietistic thought. That figure seemed to embody the ideal of bourgeois society and its value-system. Harnack's book, *The Essence of Christianity*, may be taken as representative of the liberal view. As one writer puts it, it was "the fullest and loftiest embodiment of bourgeois idealism and its age. Inspired by an optimistic faith in the human spirit and the progress of history, it believed it could almost automatically establish unity and harmony between God and the world, religion and culture, divine justice and the human order, and throne and altar. Thus it could look toward the future with confidence" (see note 12, chap. 1 in this volume). Jesus was the one who embodied and fulfilled the yearnings of bourgeois man, but he did not criticize them or call them into question.

The discovery of Jesus' eschatological character was made in the same German-speaking bourgeois milieu. A. Schweitzer and J. Weiss played an important role in this process. In preaching the coming of God's kingdom Jesus brings people into serious crisis. Things cannot go on as before because the end is now at hand. A basic and important step forward was thereby taken by Christology, for it became evident that the authentic historical figure of Jesus had to be looked at in true perspective.

b. The eschatological crisis brought on by Jesus has been viewed in two ways by theology. One views it in temporal terms: The chronological end of history is now imminent. The other view interprets it in anthropological terms: The ultimate reality of humanity and history is now at hand. The common feature in both interpretations is the fact that Jesus offers us the possibility of attaining our true identity by facing up to a crisis and undergoing a conversion. Only in that way can the kingdom come about. The whole process may be viewed in different terms. Bultmann interprets it in existential terms. Pannenberg interprets it in terms of faith and trust. Moltmann interprets it in terms of praxis, insofar as Jesus offers us the possibility of some ultimate and definitive way of behaving. Boff interprets it in terms of liberation, insofar as the proclamation of the kingdom triggers partial but functional ideologies of liberation.

c. A whole series of important systematic conclusions flows from the basic fact that Jesus' preaching of the kingdom was eschatological in character. First, eschatology means crisis. The approaching kingdom is a judgment even though it is approaching as a grace. Second, eschatology has a temporal aspect. The present situation is not the ultimate possibility for us. The future is not simply an extrapolation based on the present; it is an as yet unrealized utopia. Third, eschatology poses the problem of God all over again, but from a different slant. God is now to be viewed in terms of the future rather than in terms of past origins and primeval genesis. The way to approach God is no longer described as some sort of contemplative possession of him; it is through hope, and we must now see whether that hope should be merely passive or active as well. Fourth, eschatology presents the old tensions basic to classical theology in a new light. Where classical theology had talked about God versus creature, nature versus grace, and faith versus works, we must now talk about the church versus the kingdom of God, injustice versus liberation, the old person versus the new person, and the gratuitous entry of the kingdom versus active effort on its behalf.

3.5. *The "words" of Jesus.* To begin with, Jesus expresses his teaching in the terminology of earlier Jewish tradition. Strictly speaking, he did not *say* anything that was totally new. He did not claim to be an innovator insofar as religious ideas were concerned. Instead he was a reformer who radicalized the best traditions of his people. And like any really good reformer, he created something new in the process of seeking out the essence of the old.

We find various Old Testament traditions at work in Jesus' preaching about God and two stand out in particular. One is the sapiential tradition, which stresses God's goodness, providence, and patience on the one hand and people's corresponding response of trust and patience on the other. The other is the prophetic-apocalyptic tradition, which stresses God's renewing love, judgment, and the renovation of reality on the one hand and the corresponding inner crisis produced in people as the means of their own renewal.

Formally speaking, we can say that the latter line of tradition is the more important in the preaching of Jesus. It is the one that molds his preaching into its typical and distinctive shape. Jesus' preaching about God is always framed in the context of his proclamation about the "kingdom of God." Implied in that expression is a transformation of all reality—personal, social, even cosmic—through which the reality of God will be revealed in a definitive way. The essential reality of God is inseparably bound up with the operative reality of the reign of God.

3.6. From his preaching about God we can deduce certain important things about the figure of Jesus. First, Jesus did not preach about himself. His whole preaching is relational in character. The center of Jesus' person is not in himself but in something distinct from himself. Second, Jesus did not simply preach about "God" either. He preached about the "kingdom of God." The correlate of Jesus' person is not God but the "reign of God."

Jesus' view of God, then, is taken from the Old Testament. God does not simply "exist." God exists insofar as he "acts," insofar as he "reigns" in the world. God's revelation is not simply epiphanic, designed to disclose his essence; it is historical, designed to create a wholly new situation. To put it succinctly we can say that in Jesus' view God "is" or "exists" insofar as he creates community and human solidarity. In principle, then, access to God necessarily calls for some sort of historical mediation. There is no access to God except insofar as there is access to the kingdom. To put it another way, our filiation vis-à-vis God is necessarily mediated through brotherhood between human beings. Without the brotherhood, the filiation is wholly and purely idealistic. Brotherhood is not just an ethical consequence deriving from a God already constituted and known; it is the very way in which God really is the Father, and in that sense, God. In Jesus' eyes, a God who does not create brotherhood simply is not God at all.

A third important conclusion about Jesus can be derived from his preaching about God. Jesus preached the good news that God was drawing near in grace and liberative love. Precisely because that was the content of his preaching, Jesus' proclamation could not stop with mere words. A word of love simply must be incarnated in a historical gesture or act. Jesus did not seek to propound a doctrine about the abstract truth of God. He sought to call attention to a reality, namely, God's liberative love for human beings. Hence Jesus' message had to be historicized in acts of love and liberation signifying the gradual fulfillment of the kingdom.

3.7. *The "actions" of Jesus.* The first thing to be stressed here is that Jesus' actions are concrete. They are signs of a reality greater than concrete history, but signs displayed within history. They are actions within a situation characterized by two features: an expectant longing for liberation on the one hand and an objectively sinful situation on the other. It is this situation that rules out any merely idealistic expression of love on Jesus' part, that demands that his love be expressed in concrete acts that take the situation itself into account. Jesus does not perform abstract gestures of reconciliation; he performs concrete acts of reconciliation in a situation characterized by oppression. His basic positive gesture is to draw near to people and situations where there is no reconciliation, to break down the hard and fast barriers that society, religion, and politics had erected, and thus to show in a concrete historical way that God does indeed draw nigh to those whom nobody else will approach. This is the typological import of Jesus' approach to sinners, publicans, prostitutes, lepers, cultically impure people, Samaritans, and so forth. His word of hope has to be fleshed out historically in an act of hope.

Among the actions that Jesus performed in the first phase of his public life, his miracles merit special consideration. The marvelous and unwonted nature of these prodigies is not their typifying feature insofar as the New Testament is concerned. That is why it does not use the Greek word *teras* to describe them. Instead it uses such words as *ergon* ("work"), *semeion* ("sign"), and *dynamis* ("power"). This gives us a clue to the authentic christological import of Jesus' miracles. The important point is that they are signs of God's presence, which is concretely experienced as liberation from some type of oppression. They are active deeds of power performed by Jesus, symbolizing his mastery over the negative power operative in the world—personified in the devil.

This leads us to consider the relationship between Jesus and power. In the first stage of his public life it is concretely embodied in his use of miracles. Jesus utilizes power, placing all that is his in the service of the kingdom: his idea of God and the kingdom, his time and energy, the power of his preaching and of his miracles. At this point, then, Jesus does not ignore power nor underestimate the value of power; rather he simply places it in the service of the kingdom when he uses it.

The second phase of his public life will raise serious questions about such use of power. Is that enough to usher people into the kingdom of God? Is an all-conquering power enough to get across the message that God is love in a concrete situation where sin and injustice triumph over love and justice? Is it possible that the power of love must somehow be broken by evil so that evil can be conquered from within? Jesus' attitude toward power and its use does not change in the sense that he gives up the power with which he was invested as a human being. What happens instead is that the sin-ridden concrete situation strips Jesus of his power, and so Jesus learns something new about the use of power. He knows that the power he exercised in the first phase of his public ministry is very real and ought to be used. But it must become secondary to another sort of power in the second phase of his public life: i.e., the power of truth and of the sacrifice of one's life for others out of love.

3.8. To sum up the first phase of Jesus' public ministry, we may say that the figure of Jesus must be seen against the backdrop of God's kingdom. Jesus begins his ministry with an orthodox view of God and his kingdom that is prior to his own person. Following the logic of the kingdom, he puts all his energy and activity in its service. This basic relationship of Jesus to the kingdom will encounter a serious crisis in the second phase of his ministry, and there will be a real switch in the process of understanding both. Instead of moving from an understanding of the kingdom to an understanding of the figure of Jesus, concrete understanding and realization of the kingdom will have to be based on the concrete journey of Jesus himself (see thesis 5).

4. FAITH AND DISCIPLESHIP
BASED ON THE HISTORICAL JESUS

4.1. One of the demands posed by the historical Jesus is conversion, which finds expression amid a tension that cannot be resolved intellectually. On the one hand Jesus proclaims that the kingdom is drawing nigh as a grace, that it is the work of God; on the other hand Jesus demands radical conversion. Confronted with Jesus' eschatological proclamation, we cannot continue to live on the inertial routine of our past life.

4.2. To appreciate the nature of Jesus' demand, we must consider his conception of God and of God's kingdom. We must also realize that it is a "situated" demand, which is to say that it will be expressed in different ways according to the particular situation in which Jesus proclaims his message. Here the main dividing line which characterizes Jesus' concrete situation is that between oppressors and oppressed. The demand for conversion will have different concrete mediations, depending on different concrete contexts and circumstances. Putting the basic demand in schematic terms, we can say that Jesus calls for radical trust in God and discipleship in the service of the kingdom.

4.3. In the first phase of Jesus' ministry, both faith and discipleship derive their motivation from the notion of God and his kingdom, not directly from the concrete person of Jesus himself.

a. Jesus proclaims a God who is approaching in grace and he calls for complete and total trust in that God. This proclamation is personified in the Gospels by those people who have lost all hope and all possibilities of a future because of social, religious, political, and economic ostracism. Jesus demands that those people believe in a God who is greater than the one presented by the orthodox belief of the standing order. He asks them not to consider their personal situation of ostracism and alienation as the ultimate possibility of their life because in fact it is not the ultimate possibility of God. Even sin against the law does not constitute a barrier for the God who is approaching in grace; hence it should not bar them from hope.

b. In systematic terms this means that we are to accept this greater God, this God who cannot be captured in images, this coming God who opens up a future for us. In concrete terms it is a God of love, who draws near to proffer grace and re-create the poor person rather than to reward people according to their works. Faith in this God, then, must be translated into radical trust in him. This demand of Jesus applies to every human being, though in his own history it seems to be directed mainly to those who have least cause for hopefulness.

c. Since Jesus proclaims the kingdom of God rather than simply God, he also proposes another kind of demand. He asks for active service on behalf of the kingdom, dedicated effort like that which he himself is expending. He selects and sends out disciples to exercise power over unclean spirits, to heal the sick, and to preach the good news. This demand may be considered the summons to discipleship as opposed to the other demand for hope in the coming God. As yet, however, it is not a demand to follow Jesus himself in the strict sense; it is rather a demand to proclaim the good news of the kingdom of God, and it was not a wholly new idea to Jesus' listeners and followers.

4.4. In the second phase of Jesus' ministry we see a change in his demands for faith and discipleship even as his own view of himself and his mission changed. Whereas the demands he made in the first phase of his public life could be deduced more or less logically from the notion of God's kingdom, the demands made in the second phase of his public life must be viewed more strictly in the light of Jesus' own concrete person and destiny.

a. The faith required now is no longer simply confidence in God; it involves one's acceptance of Jesus with all his scandalousness. Jesus seems to be a failure and there is no sight of God's kingdom. The hope and confidence he proclaimed earlier must now become a hoping against hope. Trust in God is now put to the test because Jesus, the one who triggered that trust in the first place, proves to be a failure. Radical hope in God must now encompass not only one's own desperate personal situation but also the scandal of Jesus' failure.

b. The same shift can be seen in the notion of discipleship. It is no longer service to the kingdom that flows from a logic prior to Jesus. Discipleship now means following the concrete person of Jesus in a situation where it is not at all obvious that Jesus himself has very much to do with the coming of the kingdom as people had envisioned it before. Discipleship is no longer the following of some Messiah viewed in older orthodox terms. Now it is the following of Jesus on his journey to the cross, with all the demands that made the journey both possible and inevitable (see thesis 6).

4.5. If we wish to view Christian living as an obligation imposed by the historical Jesus, we must take account of both factors mentioned earlier. While the Gospels seem to make a typological distinction between two kinds of people, both the obligation of faith in God and of discipleship must be brought together in the life of the Christian individual. Both factors, faith and practice, are indispensable and interrelated. They come together through a hermeneutic process that will be spelled out a bit further on (see thesis 11).

It is also important that we take note of the change in Jesus' demands when he moved from the first phase of his public life to the second. If Christian living is viewed as a journey toward God, then the first phase seems to presume that God is somehow already known at the start while the second phase centers wholly on Jesus himself. In the first phase Jesus might be one more possible road to a God already known. In the second phase Jesus is the one and only way to a God not yet really known.

5. THE CONSCIOUSNESS OF JESUS

5.1. One way of coming to know the reality of Jesus is to become familiar with his consciousness. Traditional theology began from the dogmatic supposition that Jesus had to be explicitly aware of his divine sonship. It alluded to certain passages in the New Testament to back up this supposition, focusing particularly on Johannine theology. Since Jesus explicitly said certain things about himself, he must have known exactly who he was from the start; all we have to do, then, is to read what he said about himself. When modern exegesis ruled out that approach, attempts were made to discern the explicit consciousness of Jesus on the basis of the christological titles that he himself used or permitted others to apply to him. Modern exegesis has posed serious obstacles to that approach also. In my opinion the way to solve this whole problem is not to consider the *absolute* consciousness of Jesus (what Jesus explicitly thought about himself) but to focus on his *relational* consciousness. In other words, we should try to deduce what Jesus thought from his attitude toward the Father and the kingdom of God.

5.2. *Jesus' consciousness vis-à-vis the kingdom.* It seems quite apparent that Jesus had a distinctive personal consciousness vis-à-vis the kingdom of God, though it might not be able to be described precisely as a messianic consciousness. Various facts support this contention. Jesus performs certain signs indicating the imminent approach of the kingdom: exorcisms, the forgiving of sins, meals with publicans, and so forth. He comes forward with an interpretation of the law that is even more original than that of Moses. Unlike the earlier prophets, he does not justify his actions by saying that he is acting in the name of Yahweh; instead he speaks and acts on his own authority. He seems to claim that his own person is functionally decisive insofar as salvation is concerned, and he poses a strict and unheard-of demand that people must follow him personally.

All these facts point indirectly to Jesus' distinctive consciousness vis-à-vis the kingdom. He realizes that the arrival of the kingom has its privileged moments and its own proper timeliness (Greek *kairos*), and he is convinced that he himself has a decisive role to play insofar as the "right moment" is concerned.

5.3. *Jesus' consciousness vis-à-vis the Father.* In the Gospels we find that Jesus has an explicit awareness of the Father and his own relationship to him. This awareness differentiates Jesus from all other human beings, though one cannot deduce from it that Jesus knew himself to be the "eternal Son" of the Father. This consciousness of sonship is expressed in relational rather than absolute terms. His felt relationship to the Father finds expression in two characteristic traits: confident trust in the Father and obedience to his mission. Trust in the Father comes out in Jesus' prayer, which expresses both his theological poverty and his theological richness as well as his awareness of sonship. It also finds expression in his fidelity to his mission right to the cross. So we might make this general statement about the psychology of Jesus: Jesus becomes conscious of his distinctive relationship to God through the concrete mediation of his life and the external difficulties he must face.

5.4. This relational view of Jesus' consciousness can cause surprise and give rise to misunderstandings because we have been used to using a concept of person and of perfection that goes back to Greek philosophy. In that view perfection is basically knowledge, so personal perfection and fulfillment means full possession of self through knowledge. If Jesus was perfect, then he had to know that he really was the "eternal Son" of God.

Such a view, however, is grounded on a wholly gratuitous supposition. It does not really correspond with the biblical conception of person or with many current conceptions, though that in itself would not be decisive. The biblical conception of person is quite different. It was further elaborated in discussions about the Trinity and Hegel formulated it in more modern terms. Basically it says that the essence of being a "person" is surrendering oneself to another and finding fulfillment precisely in that other. To know who Jesus really was, then, we do not have to know exactly what Jesus thought about himself. Instead we should find out how and to whom he dedicated himself as a person.

5.5. *Crisis and growth in Jesus' consciousness.* Consciousness is a subordinate feature of the human person. Its development does not take place in some idealistic realm. It takes place in and through some concrete situation outside consciousness itself that is fraught with conflict. The repercussions of such conflicts are abundantly evident in the life of Jesus, and from them we can gather the real growth and development of his awareness. Jesus "had to become like his brothers in every way" (Heb. 2:17) except in knowing sin (2 Cor. 5:21). He "learned obedience" (Heb. 5:8), and it is through the learning process that he became a human being and God's Son. Basically it involved his overcoming of negative influences, and it can be described in terms of the shift that took place between the first and second phase of his public life.

a. The Galilean crisis, which is noted by all the evangelists, marked a sharp break in Jesus' consciousness, specifically with reference to his conception of the kingdom of God. His preaching mission, as he had conceived it, was a failure by any external measure. Now it is no longer simply a matter of dedicating all his energy and activity to the kingdom. Now he must actually surrender all the ideas he had held about God as well as his own person. After the Galilean crisis Jesus moves toward an unknown future over which he has no control. That crisis is what makes it possible for Jesus to radicalize and concretize his relationship to the Father in trust and obedience.

b. The same thing is spelled out programmatically in Jesus' temptations, though the gospel accounts situate them at the start of his public life for theological reasons. The temptations have to do with Jesus himself, with what is most basic to his person and his mission. That is why they are placed alongside the account of Jesus' baptism, for Christian theological reflection saw his baptism as Jesus' decision to accept his mission from God. Temptation is the general atmosphere in which Jesus grows and develops, as is the case with every human being. It is not a matter of choosing between good and evil but of choosing between two very different ways of conceiving and carrying out his mission, of using power, of picturing God, and of rendering the kingdom present to people.

On the historical level Jesus' basic temptation is depicted in his agony in the garden of Gethsemane. Jesus overcomes that temptation by bowing to the Father's will and surrendering wholly to it. It is in that way that Jesus' person, and more indirectly his consciousness, is fashioned and developed.

c. It is, then, through crisis and temptation that Jesus' person is fashioned concretely. Accepting that view, we can see the positive role of Jesus' *ignorance* and *mistakes,* both of which are mentioned in the gospel accounts. It is important to note that Jesus' ignorance is not just in matters of detail; it has to do with something fundamental for him. Jesus does not know when the day of Yahweh will come nor does he know what the future course of his mission will be. He did not envision a "church," though a church could arise as a possible continuation of Jesus' work.

Greek philosophy would regard Jesus' ignorance as an imperfection. In reality it is supremely positive. It makes it possible for Jesus' dedication to the Father to be concrete and real rather than merely idealistic and abstract. Paradoxical as it may seem, it helps to perfect Jesus' dedication and surrender to the Father because it allows God to remain God. Jesus comes to know God precisely in not knowing the day of Yahweh, for he thereby allows God to be the ineffable mystery and the absolute future.

5.6. Jesus' consciousness was fully human, so we are perfectly justified in talking about the faith *of* Jesus. Here we must understand faith in the biblical sense of the term. Instead of picturing it as basically a cognitive act, we must see it as loyal surrender of self to God. Thus Jesus was the first to live faith in all its fullness and originality, as the Epistle to the Hebrews makes clear.

But Jesus' faith was a historical one. It underwent growth and development because it was immersed in history. After the Galilean crisis Jesus did not think about God and his kingdom in exactly the same way, nor did he act in the same way. His view of trust in God and obedience to him was also greatly altered. This movement in Jesus' consciousness, in his faith in God, was viewed as heretical by orthodox Jewish belief. In reality, however, it was the movement that faith must undergo if it is to be concrete, historical, and real. In that sense we can say that Jesus underwent a "conversion." It is not that he had to get beyond some personal sin. It is that he had to get beyond the inertia of a particular way of thinking and acting that was good in itself but was too bound up with his own notion of God and the kingdom. By undergoing a "conversion" in his way of thinking and acting, his sonship would attain fulfillment and perfection.

6. THE EXTERNAL CONFLICTS OF JESUS

6.1. The crisis in Jesus' consciousness was mediated through his external conflicts. It was embodied in his opposition to those who wielded religious, economic, and political power. The import of this feature of opposition and conflict cannot be brought out fully if we simply look at isolated incidents in Jesus' biography. We must consider the following points: (a) Jesus took on a nature that was not only human but also historical. It was "situated" in a concrete context. He became human through finding himself in a given situation and reacting to it. (b) A structurally important feature of that situation was the real sinfulness existing in it. It did not simply exist alongside Jesus' work but reacted sharply against that work. (c) The conflict surrounding Jesus paved a course leading to the cross, to the death of the Son. From the final episode we can see how deep-rooted the conflict was. (d) This course taken by Jesus is simultaneously a test of God's authentic divinity. Two questions stand out: Does the true essence of God find expression in the de facto situation of religion? Is the power of God truly mediated through the de facto situation and use of political power?

6.2. Jesus was condemned for *blasphemy*, not for heresy. Thus his conception of God was not only different from, but radically opposed to, that held by the established religion of the standing order.

a. Jesus unmasked people's domination of others in the name of religion, people's manipulation of the mystery of God through merely human traditions, and the religious hypocrisy that used the mystery of God to avoid the obligations of justice. In that sense the religious leaders were correct in realizing that Jesus was preaching a God opposed to their own.

b. Jesus' religious revolution had to do both with his conception of God and with his conception of the place and means that provided access to God. First of all he preached a God who was drawing nigh in grace, thereby breaking all connections with the works stipulated by the law. Religious people could not feel secure against God simply because they performed certain works. Rather than offering "things" to God, they must offer up their own persons and security as well. Second, Jesus also desacralized the locale that provided access to God. The privileged locus of access to God was not cultic worship, scholarly knowledge, or even prayer. It was service to the lowly and oppressed. Insofar as the oppressed are totally "other" to those who approach them, they serve to mediate the total otherness of God and show how we can gain access to God, namely, through a liberative praxis.

c. Thus Jesus' conflict with the representatives of religion is a deeply rooted one, and he is condemned to death as a result of it. A direct consequence of Jesus' conception of God, the cross poses the whole problem of the true essence of the deity and leaves open the question of who God is and what the meaning of history is. Faced with the cross, we must ask who God is exactly. Is he the God of Jesus or the God of religion? Is Jesus' God an illusion, or is he the real God even though the established religion killed the Son?

6.3. Jesus was actually executed as a *political rebel,* not as a blasphemer. His conception of God necessarily entailed his proclamation of God's coming kingdom, and this could not help but bring him into conflict with those in political power. If the kingdom of God entails human reconciliation, then Jesus could not help but unmask a situation that did not correspond with that vision.

a. Jesus calls attention to the coexistence of oppressors and oppressed, insisting that such a situation is the result of human free will rather than something willed or even permitted by God. Denouncing the situation in the prophetic manner, Jesus says there is poverty because the rich will not share their wealth, ignorance because the learned have stolen away the keys to knowledge, and oppression because the Pharisees have imposed intolerable burdens on people and rulers are acting despotically.

The strongest anathemas voiced by Jesus are collective, aimed against groups. They point up an unjust situation that is the collective fruit of egotism on the part of many individuals. They also point up hypocrisy, suggesting that this oppressive use of power is justified by appealing to God and claiming that it is a legitimate mediation of God and his power.

b. The political death of Jesus makes sense in that Jesus had a different conception of God as power. He shared the conviction of the Zealots that God's kingdom had to be established and hence he bore certain similarities to them, but his conception of God was very different from theirs. God is not simply power, as most people were inclined to think. God is love, and he manifests himself in the dialectics of an impotent love. Moreover, God's approach is an act of grace rather than a result of some law as the Zealots maintained. Even harsher is Jesus' implicit attack on the Roman Empire. The emperor is not God. Jesus desacralizes that kind of power and its claim to be the absolute mediation of God. The *pax romana* is not the kingdom of God. The political organization of Rome might dazzle the world with its power, but it was oppressive; hence there was nothing sacred or divine about it.

c. The issue at stake here was the essential nature of power insofar as it mediates God. That was the deepest underlying question in Jesus' own eyes. He certainly used all the power he had, displaying it in his persuasiveness, his lucid ideas, and his miracles. But gradually he came to realize that the revelation of God as love can only come about when power is subordinated to the law of service in a sinful world. Thus power is transformed into a love willing to accept suffering and defeat at the hands of the world's sinfulness.

d. In Jesus' eyes God's ultimate historical word is love, whereas the ultimate historical word of power in the human world is oppression. Jesus' journey to the cross is a trial dealing with the authentic nature of power. In the penultimate stages love must be fleshed out in schemas and structures that effectively render service to human beings, and so it has need of real power. But the ultimate stage and the last word is simply love. Jesus makes it clear that without love power in history turns into oppression.

e. Jesus does not advocate a love that is depoliticized, dehistoricized, and destructuralized. He advocates a political love, a love that is situated in history and that has visible repercussions for human beings. Rather than simply advocating the complete abolition of the Zealot spirit, he proposes an alternative to Zealotism. Historically speaking, Jesus acted out of love and was for all human beings. But he was for them in different ways. Out of love for the poor, he took his stand *with* them; out of love for the rich, he took his stand *against* them. In both cases, however, he was interested in something more than retributive justice. He wanted renewal and re-creation.

7. THE DEATH OF JESUS

7.1. One thing differentiates Jesus' death from that of other religious and political martyrs: Jesus died in complete rupture with his own cause. At his death he felt completely abandoned by the God whose nearness he had felt and proclaimed. The typifying features of his death can be glimpsed when one considers his message about the approaching kingdom, his cry on the cross, and his abandonment by the Father.

7.2. The distinctive character of Jesus' death does not lie in his biographical finale but in the new questions about God and the new revelation about God that arise from it.

a. The cross radicalizes the transcendence of God, which was already recognized by the Old Testament. It does this in two ways especially. First, the Old Testament prohibition about making images of God is radicalized. There is no image of God on the cross. Second, the cross radicalizes the Old Testament view of God coming in power at the end of history to re-create everything. On the cross there is no hint of divine power as natural humanity might understand it.

b. The cross rules out any access to God by way of natural theology. Natural theology assumes that we can gain direct access to God on the basis of the positive elements in creation: e.g., nature, history, and human subjectivity. The cross challenges such an assumption. Not only does it show up the inadequacy of all human knowledge about God insofar as the actual reality of God is concerned; it also points up the contradiction faced by all human knowledge about God when people actually attempt to think about God. Natural humanity did not and could not have imagined that suffering rather than power might be a mode of being for God. To know God from the standpoint of the cross is to abide with God in his passion.

c. The cross poses the problem of God, not in terms of theology (discourse about God), but in terms of theodicy (the justification of God). On the cross theodicy is historicized. The Son is not crucified by some natural evil that embodies the creaturely limitations of nature or humanity. He is crucified by a historicized evil, i.e., the free will of human beings. What justification is there for a God who allows the sinfulness of the world to kill his Son (and hence other human beings as well)?

7.3. On the positive side the cross presents a basic affirmation about God. It says that on the cross God himself is crucified. The Father suffers the death of his Son and takes upon himself all the sorrow and pain of history. This ultimate solidarity with humanity reveals God as a God of love in a real and credible way rather than in an idealistic way. From the ultimate depths of history's negative side, this God of love thereby opens up the possibility of hope and a future.

7.4. The crucified God, the powerless God on the cross of Jesus, draws the dividing line between Christian faith and every other type of religion. Christian faith lies beyond conventional theism and conventional atheism. But it is quite obvious that it has not been easy for Christians to maintain the scandal of the cross. From the time of God's revelation in Jesus' resurrection there has been a tendency to view the cross as a passing transitional stage leading to the definitive reality in which God is seen as sheer power and Jesus is viewed solely as the exalted one.

a. In the New Testament itself Jesus' death is toned down and stripped of its scandalous aspect: i.e., his abandonment by God. Mark's account, the most original one, is modified by Luke and John. Luke depicts Jesus dying as a confident martyr and John depicts him dying in majestic control of the situation.

b. The title "Servant of Yahweh" fades from the scene relatively quickly. That particular Christology is probably due to Peter himself, who personally had to suffer the scandal of a suffering Messiah. It soon takes a second place to other titles that have more to do with Jesus' glorification than with the cross.

c. Gradually the scandal of the cross was reduced to little more than a cognitive mystery. Jesus died in accordance with some mysterious divine plan that can be discovered in the Scriptures: When we interpret the Scriptures correctly, we will find no reason to be scandalized by the cross.

d. Another way to eliminate the scandal of the cross is to focus solely and exclusively on the cross's salvific value. By focusing all consideration on this positive redemptive value of the cross, people could forget the scandalous fact that the cross affected God himself. The model explanations used to bring out the salvific value of the cross also tended to assume an a priori knowledge of what salvation is (the forgiveness of sin) and who God is.

7.5. It has been equally difficult to maintain the scandal of the cross in the history of the church and its theology. By way of example, we may cite the following instances:

a. Even many of the early fathers of the church took no serious note of Jesus' abandonment by God on the cross. Some fathers explained it allegorically, saying that it was really sinners who were abandoned by God on the cross. Others claimed that Jesus was complaining that the Logos was going to abandon his body in the tomb in the short interval between his death and resurrection.

b. The classic and extremely influential theory of vicarious satisfaction presupposes knowledge of who God is, what sin is, and what salvation is. The cross of Jesus does not call those a priori concepts into question at all, and hence it is completely emasculated. It is fitted into a neat theological scheme when in fact it shatters every such scheme.

c. The repeatable nature of the Mass as a sacrifice has posed a great danger to the cross. There has been a real danger that the Mass might reduce the real, historical cross of Jesus to nothing more than a cultic, ritualized cross. In that case the cross would simply make it possible for Christian faith to become just another religion with a sacrificial worship of its own.

d. There has been a tendency to isolate the cross from the historical course that led Jesus to it by virtue of his conflicts with those who held political religious power. In this way the cross has been turned into nothing more than a paradigm of the suffering to which all human beings are subject insofar as they are limited beings. This has given rise to a mystique of suffering rather than to a mystique of following Jesus, whose historical career led to the historical cross.

7.6. In the last analysis the metaphysical and epistemological roots of this emasculation are to be found in the conceptual armory of Greek thought in which the mystery of God and Jesus was formulated right from the beginning.

a. The cross implies suffering, and hence change. A Hellenized theology could not conceive of suffering as a divine mode of being for that very reason. It saw God as apathetic toward history, and so his love could not be formulated in historical terms that would be credible to suffering human beings who carry on the passion in history.

b. Greek philosophy never pondered death in itself. Death was either the end of life or the transition to another higher state of existence. In no way could death as such serve as the mediation of God.

c. Greek epistemology was based on the principle of analogy: We come to know something through its resemblance to something already known. If the deity is pictured in terms of power or intelligence or wisdom, then one can hardly recognize God on the cross of Jesus because it displays no trace of power or wisdom. The principle of dialectical knowledge, of coming to know things through their seeming contrary, was not developed by Greek philosophy. That is in marked contrast to the gospel scene of the last judgment, where it turns out that the Son of Man was concealed in the oppressed and needy and persecuted. Greek epistemology could not take account of the surprise needed to recognize God on the cross.

d. Greek epistemology saw admiring wonder as the motive force behind human knowledge. It did not envision suffering as a source of knowledge, and hence it did not see that suffering embodied the required solidarity and the authentic kind of analogy for encountering God on the cross. Moreover, admiring wonder can stop at contemplation while suffering cannot. The former approach to knowledge lacks the feature of praxis, which is required if one is to comprehend the cross.

8. THE RESURRECTION OF JESUS

8.1. With the resurrection we come to the culminating point of any historical Christology, even though the resurrection of its very nature points toward some final, ultimate, and hence transcendent fulfillment of history. Three aspects of the resurrection must be considered. They are intimately connected with each other, but their interrelationship presents peculiar problems because the resurrection is an eschatological happening and hence has a distinctive relationship of its own with what is historical. The three aspects to be considered are the historical aspect (what really happened), the theological aspect (what exactly is the significance of the resurrection-event), and the hermeneutic aspect (how is it possible to comprehend the event and its meaning).

8.2. *The historical aspect of the resurrection.* In the New Testament we do not find any canonical tradition that narrates the event of Jesus' resurrection itself. The gospel narrative recounts two types of traditions that deal with it, one dealing with the apparitions of the risen Jesus and the other with the empty tomb. In asking about the historicity of Jesus' resurrection, we are asking first and foremost about the historicity of those two kinds of tradition.

8.3. The historicity of the "empty tomb" tradition is a moot question. It does not appear in the oldest narratives about the resurrection, and this suggests that it might have arisen in the interests of apologetics. It is equally improbable, however, that people would have proclaimed the resurrection of Jesus in Jerusalem if his corpse could have been easily located. This has led some to suggest that Jesus may have been buried in a common grave so that his corpse could not be easily identified in any case. Critically studied, however, the New Testament data does not provide any real foundation for this hypothesis—though it does not rule it out either. Two points are important and noteworthy:

a. In the New Testament itself faith in the risen Jesus does not depend on the existence (or non-existence) of the empty tomb, but on the concrete experience of Jesus' apparitions.

b. Centering the whole discussion around the empty tomb may prejudice one's conception of Jesus' resurrection, leading one incorrectly to envision it as the revivification of a corpse. This view is certainly not shared by the New Testament.

8.4. The traditions dealing with apparitions of the risen Jesus are far more important and decisive. The oldest of these traditions, perhaps going back to 35 or 40 A.D., is the one found in 1 Cor. 15:3–5, 7. Those which talk about Jesus' appearances to the women and the disciples offer more difficulties, contradicting each other on various points such as place of appearance, chronology of events, and the nature of Jesus' new corporeal state. Did Jesus appear in Jerusalem or Galilee? Did the ascension take place on the day of his resurrection or forty days later? Was his resurrected body a solid corporeal mass or a spiritual entity?

Many of these discrepancies can be explained in terms of the theological, apologetic, or kerygmatic motives of the final redactors and the situation in their respective communities. Yet we also do find certain literary schemes shared by both traditions dealing with Jesus' apparitions (to the women and to his disciples). This might indicate the existence of very old traditions that were literally historical but that were then filled out with divergent details.

8.5. All we can deduce so far, then, is the existence of certain *traditions* that are very ancient, at least insofar as their nucleus is concerned. This would point toward their historicity. The next question is whether the *events* narrated in these traditions are historical.

Concretely the problem comes down to the historicity of people's experience of Jesus' appearance. There can be no historical doubt that the disciples had some sort of privileged experience. It is evident not just because they say so but because we can verify the impact it had on their lives and their behavior. The cross was the end of their faith in Jesus, yet shortly afterwards they are preaching about Jesus and are willing to give up their lives for this faith. What took place between those two very different historical situations? The disciples themselves said that they had seen the crucified one "alive." Can that assertion be verified as historical in principle or not? That is a question we shall consider when we get to the hermeneutic aspect below. Here we want to consider the origin of the disciples' new-found faith.

We can pose this issue in terms of an alternative: Either their novel experience can be explained by some natural mechanism or else it was caused by the "presence of the risen one" that made itself known. In the last analysis choosing between these two possibilities is not a matter of historical science at all, because prejudices of all sorts are at work here even more so than they are on many questions. If people do not accept the possibility of resurrection, then they will attempt to prove that the apparitions were hallucinations. If people do allow for that possibility and accept the credibility of the narratives, then they will point out that the atmosphere was scarcely conducive to hallucinations. The disciples could hardly have been disposed in that direction after what had happened on the cross, and Jesus' appearance at different times and places hardly fits the general pattern of collective hallucinations.

8.6. Though it is an extremely difficult task, historical exegesis can show that certain things are historical: i.e., that the disciples did in fact have faith in Jesus after Easter even though the cross had shattered their earlier faith in him; that they tied their new faith to appearances of the risen Jesus (not to the empty tomb); and that the nucleus of those traditions gives indications of being authentic. Thus countless presuppositions underlie any effort to find out in what sense Jesus' resurrection is historical and how it can be understood as such. Those presuppositions must be considered under the hermeneutic aspect of the resurrection.

8.7. *The theological aspect of the resurrection.* The first thing that the resurrection affirms is something very similar to the Old Testament's efforts to define God in historical terms rather than in terms of abstract characteristics. It is a new historical credo that asserts that the new name of God is the one who has raised Jesus from the dead and who brings into being things that have not yet existed. God is defined as a liberative power that has also become a historicized love after the cross of Jesus. God not only raised Jesus from the dead but also handed him over out of love for human beings.

8.8. The resurrection of Jesus also says something about humanity and history. God's action in Jesus has been a salvific action of pardon and revitalization rather than of retribution. Humanity has been offered a new kind of life based on hope and love. Because Jesus rose from the dead as the "firstborn of many brothers," we are now pointed toward our own fulfillment and the revitalization of history. Because the resurrection also confirms the life of Jesus himself, we are now offered the possibility of living a particular way of life in the footsteps of Jesus. We can and should live as new, risen human beings here and now in history.

8.9. Finally, the resurrection says something about Jesus himself. If God did resurrect Jesus, then Jesus stands in a distinctive relationship to God. The various Christologies of the New Testament attempt to determine the nature of that relationship, and we can now try to give a brief overview of the basic stages through which that reflection went.

a. If God did raise Jesus from the dead, then he also gave confirmation to Jesus' concrete way of living, to his preaching, his deeds, and his death on the cross. In the early stages, however, there was not too much reflection on Jesus' cross for its own sake.

b. With his resurrection from the dead Jesus came so close to the awaited Son of Man, the figure who was to come, that people more and more come to the notion that the Son of Man was none other than Jesus himself. Thus Jesus' distinctive relationship to God came to be expressed in terms of people's expectation of the parousia.

c. If Jesus was raised from the dead and then exalted by God, then obviously God has manifested himself in a definitive way in Jesus. Here we have the fundamental step forward.

Rather than adhering to the model of the Son of Man in trying to understand Jesus' relationship to God, Christians now glimpsed the possibility of exploring that relationship further. This they did, and they ended up professing that Jesus was the eternal Son of the Father.

d. Alongside this process of universalizing the significance of Jesus there arose the possibility that Jesus could and should be preached to every human being. We now get a movement toward the gentiles and toward a view of the new community (the "church") as something new and different rather than as the mere continuation or extension of the people of Israel.

8.10. Christian reflection on Jesus' oneness with God took place basically on two levels. On one level it explored the various honorific titles of Jesus. On the other level it sought to develop a theological interpretation of the major events in his life. The earliest reflection began exploring Jesus' special relationship of oneness with God in terms of the parousia yet to come or Jesus' exaltation in the present. It then went on to consider his oneness with God on the basis of Jesus' earthly life, gradually pushing that oneness further and further back toward the very beginning: transfiguration, baptism, virginal conception, pre-existence with God.

The various honorific titles express Jesus' oneness with God in terms of theological models already known. As we have said some focus more on his earthly work ("Prophet," "Servant of Yahweh," "High Priest") while others stress his transcendent character ("Logos," "Lord," "Son of God," "God"). The first set of titles faded out rather quickly, and preference was given to those titles that were grounded on a priori theological models and that related Jesus more directly to God ("Lord," "Messiah," "Son").

It is important to note the twofold movement involved in the New Testament's attempt to attribute titles to Jesus. On the one hand it attempts to spell out the special importance of Jesus' person by giving him titles whose meaning was already familiar to biblical or Hellenic theology. On the other hand the novelty of Jesus is brought out by stressing that the meaning of those titles can be known only through Jesus himself.

The utilization of those titles was simply a way to help people understand the import and relevance of Jesus' person within the context of a specific culture and theology. There is no reason why such titles need be the exclusive prerogative of one particular culture, even that of the New Testament writers. Thus today Jesus could quite rightly be called "the liberator," so long as we remember that it is through Jesus that we learn what liberation really is and how it is to be achieved.

8.11. The New Testament normally does not talk about the absolute divinity of Jesus. It discusses it in terms of Jesus' relation to the Father. Jesus' divinity is relational, and this point is expressed in various terms. In personal terms Jesus is the Son. In functional terms Jesus is the one who holds lordship. In temporal terms Jesus will hand the kingdom over to the Father at the end of time. Thus the divinity of Jesus is depicted in relational terms rather than in terms of his own absolute nature.

8.12. *The hermeneutic problem.* Because Jesus' resurrection is an eschatological happening, it is not readily and immediately comprehensible as such. We must look for some standpoint or hermeneutics that will do justice to all the pertinent aspects. First of all, we must do justice to the fact of the resurrection itself as it is understood by the New Testament; otherwise we will simply be talking about some symbol of utopia rather than about the resurrection of *Jesus* specifically. Second, we must be able to make the resurrection comprehensible today; otherwise it will not be an eschatological event of universal significance.

It is not easy to find such a hermeneutical standpoint, and in the end it will depend on a person's most basic personal options. Here I want to propose one possible hermeneutics that has three characteristics and which, in my opinion, does do justice to both the New Testament texts and the present-day situation.

8.13. First, the expression "resurrection of the dead" is a utopian formulation that derives from the Old Testament and later Judaism rather than from the Hellenic world. The Greek formulation focused on the "immortality of the soul." The biblical formulation suggests the total transformation of the person and history. Thus the first hermeneutic condition for understanding the resurrection of Jesus is a hope in such a transformation, a hope that overcomes all the negative elements of the world. It is a hope *against* death and injustice (the biblical model) rather than simply a hope *above and beyond* death and injustice (the Greek model).

8.14. Second, grasping the meaning of the resurrection presupposes that we grasp history as a promise and are conscious of a mission to be performed. The disciples were aware that they were not simply spectators of an event, that they were witnesses, who necessarily had to give testimony on behalf of what had happened. Thus the resurrection is comprehensible only insofar as one is conscious of building up history and trusts in the promise.

8.15. Third and finally, in the New Testament the appearances of the risen Jesus go hand in hand with a vocation, with a summons to a mission. The disciples realize that something new has entered the world with Jesus' resurrection. Hence his resurrection initiates a praxis that can be described as service to both the work of proclaiming the risen Jesus and to the content of the promise that his resurrection embodies for the world. Like Jesus, they must serve the cause of establishing a new creation. This means that the meaning of Jesus' resurrection cannot be grasped unless one engages in active service for the transformation of an unredeemed world.

8.16. Understanding the resurrection of Jesus today, then, presupposes several things. One must have a radical hope in the future. One must possess a historical consciousness that sees history both as promise and as mission. And one must engage in a specific praxis that is nothing else but discipleship—the following of Jesus (see thesis 11). The last condition seems to be the most necessary because it is praxis inspired by love that concretizes Christian hope as a hoping against hope, and because love is the only thing that opens history up. Like knowing God, knowing the resurrection of Jesus is not a one-time event, something given once and for all. Our horizon of understanding must be constantly fashioned anew. Our hope and praxis of love must be kept alive and operational at every moment. Only in that way can Jesus' resurrection be grasped not only as something that happened to him alone but as the resurrection of the "firstborn" and a promise that history will find fulfillment.

9. THE TENSION BETWEEN THE HISTORICAL JESUS AND THE CHRIST OF FAITH IN CHRISTIAN LIVING

9.1. Jesus' resurrection made faith in Jesus possible. By the same token however, a one-sided understanding of the resurrection made it possible for Christians to give in to the worst temptation facing Christian faith, i.e., the temptation to forget that the Christ of faith is none other than Jesus of Nazareth.

This danger made its appearance very soon after the resurrection, and it had grave implications for the Christian faith. To the extent that the historical Jesus was forgotten, Christian existence lost its identity as "faith" and began to turn into "religion," in the sense criticized by Jesus himself.

9.2. The basic tension can be found in the very notion of Christology itself. It is well exemplified in Paul's arguments with the community in Corinth. Some Christians in Corinth claimed that they could experience access to the risen Jesus directly in their own lives through the enthusiastic celebration of the liturgy and the gifts of the Spirit. They believed that this brought them possession of the Spirit of the risen one, and so they ignored or even disdained the historical Jesus. Some even went so far as to anathematize Jesus.

Paradoxical as it might seem, Paul does not support their theology of the resurrection. He recalls the historical Jesus and reminds them of his cross, the point where his historicity is most concentrated and clear. He criticizes their conception of spiritual gifts, using the basic criteria of the historical Jesus. The one and only authentic gift is that of service to the community performed out of love. The way to verify one's faith and one's possession of the Spirit is to live as Jesus did and follow his journey to the cross. That is the duty incumbent on both the individual and the community as a whole. There is no verification to be found in seemingly supernatural or suprahistorical gifts.

The New Testament as a whole is quite conscious of the danger of breaking with Jesus in the name of the risen Christ. That is why the Gospels were written. Though they are not biographies of Jesus, they do refer the reader to his historical figure rather than to some figure that is or can be easily idealized and hence manipulated. The Gospels are conscious of the danger of ending up with a cultic deity, of maintaining the religious structure common to other religions existing at the time and simply changing the name of the worshipped deity to Jesus.

There is clear evidence of the New Testament reaction to this danger in the name that has perdured as the typical designation of Jesus, i.e., Jesus Christ. The word "Christ" is really an honorific title; but it is also abstract, and in principle it was familiar to people quite apart from Jesus. "Jesus," however, is a concrete name. By bringing the concrete name of Jesus together with the title "Christ," the Gospels are saying that the risen one (the Lord, etc.) is none other than Jesus in all his concrete history, including the scandalous history of his cross.

This also means that in principle there is a criterion that can verify whether the Spirit invoked by Christians is really the spirit of Christ or not. The spirit of Christ is really present where there is love, service, and hope. The liberty that comes from his Spirit is a liberty embodied in service to the crucified one. The joy of the Spirit does not transport Christians to some imagined heaven; it brings them down to earth, where the passion still goes on.

9.3. The tension between Jesus on the one hand and the Christ of faith on the other can also be seen in the Christian conception of faith and theology. The risen one is the Logos, the wisdom of God. But even in the New Testament we can detect a tendency that grew stronger and more evident among the apologists of the second century. More and more divine wisdom is viewed as a general explanation for the cosmos rather than as something that seems foolish and scandalous to most people. Faith is gradually turned into doctrine. Reflection on Christian life becomes an explicative theology rather than reflection focused on a transforming praxis. The Logos is viewed more as a Logos who brings fulfillment to everything rather than as a Logos who brings redemption by criticizing reality instead of explaining it.

9.4. The same tension can be seen in the relationship between Christian life and politics. The older religions were political in two senses. First of all, the state needed some religion to serve as the foundation and guarantee of the social order. Second, political power itself was viewed as a mediation of the divine. In professing faith in Jesus as the Lord, Christians were asserting that he possessed power; but that power could be interpreted in very different ways. The more Christians focused one-sidedly on Christ the risen Lord and his power, the more their faith took on the features of a political religion that supported and even illegally wielded power; throughout history such power had proven to be oppressive. This process came to a head with Constantine, but earlier Christian theologians had paved the way by calling the attention of emperors to Christianity, not as faith in Jesus, but as the best religion for ensuring the stability and success of the state.

So long as the memory of Jesus was kept vividly alive, the relationship of Christianity to the state was respectful for the most part, turning critical only when Christianity was oppressed and persecuted by the state. We see persecution exemplified in the book of Revelation, where Christianity was faced with the reign of Domitian. The "Lord" of that book is the "slain lamb," who possesses the power of the historical Jesus. Rather than being an arbitrary power that dominates rather than liberates people, it is a power embodied in truth and love, in proclamation and denunciation.

9.5. Finally, the same tension can be seen in people's understanding of the liturgy. The earliest Christian liturgies maintained their identity by recalling Jesus. Then they gradually began to take on the cultic features to be found in Jewish and Hellenic religion, and Jesus was turned into a cultic deity.

In the New Testament, the Epistle to the Hebrews reacts

sharply against the tendency to turn the Christian liturgy into a religious cult. It desacralizes and hence christianizes all the key concepts of cultic worship on the basis of the historical Jesus. Jesus was a layman. His work was performed out in the city rather than in the temple. The cross was not an altar, and there was no lamb on it; on it we find the life and body of a human being. The epistle brings out clearly that any sort of cultic worship and priesthood, as those things are understood by "religion," has been abolished. The new, authentic, and definitive cult has made its appearance in Jesus. In the profane realm Jesus succeeded in doing what all the priests of all religions had not succeeded in doing in the sacral realm: i.e., manifesting God's love for human beings and effectively realizing brotherhood among them.

9.6. These brief considerations, prompted by the history of the church in the early centuries, are applicable even up to our own day. Christianity has frequently taken the form of "religion" rather than of "faith" insofar as many of its aspects are concerned: e.g., the liturgy, the notion of faith and theology, and its relationship to the political realm. On the theological level this has been due in the last analysis to a Christology that has preferred to focus on the risen Christ as an abstract symbol of faith rather than on the historical Jesus as the proper key to an understanding of the total Christ. The total Christ is certainly present by virtue of his Spirit. The real question is whether this Spirit is the Spirit of Jesus or some vague, abstract Spirit that is nothing more than the sublimated embodiment of the natural, "religious" person's desires and yearnings. If it is the latter, then it is not only different from, but actually contrary to, the Spirit of Jesus.

10. THE DOGMATIC FORMULATIONS OF CHRISTOLOGY

10.1. When we use the word "dogmas," we must realize that the official conception that prevails today derives from Vatican I. For many centuries, therefore, the church lived its life without that conception, though it has always had formulations in which the Christian faith was made explicit.

To understand a dogma correctly, we must first be aware of its danger. A dogma can be dangerous insofar as Christians are tempted to reduce the expression of their faith, which takes in all of humanity and all praxis, to doctrinal formulations. They are tempted to prefer the juridical cast of a dogma to its concrete content. They tend to forget that the faith, even on the level of formulation, has already been transmitted in the writings of the New Testament, in the first creeds, and in the earliest catechesis—where it appears in a more pristine and basic form than it does in dogmas.

10.2. It seems to me that the positive nature of dogmas is to be found on two levels. First of all, they set certain limits that are sometimes very important and should be respected by all versions of Christian faith. That is why dogmas have arisen in polemical situations for the most part. Second, they are valuable insofar as they are doxological statements quite akin to those of the liturgy, however sophisticated their language might seem to be at times. A dogma expresses in words what the Christian lives out in real life: the surrender and submission of one's own ego to the mystery of God.

10.3. *The christological dogmas in general.* First of all, unlike other dogmas of a secondary or peripheral nature, the christological dogmas undoubtedly have to do with the essence of the Christian faith (see Vatican II on the proper hierarchy of truths).

Second, these dogmas formulate *direct* statements about Christ (e.g., Jesus is God) which in fact can only be understood *indirectly*. Stating that Christ is God does not mean that we can directly intuit the truth of this statement. It is a limit-statement that is rendered possible by the activity and destiny of Jesus that can be observed historically.

Third, the christological dogmas do not say more than can be gleaned from the life of Jesus as it is presented in the New Testament; nor do they necessarily say it better. Hence those christological dogmas are both chronologically and logically posterior to what is narrated about Jesus in the New Testament.

Fourth, the christological dogmas present certain difficulties insofar as they are formulations based on the Hellenic outlook. Let me summarize them here:

   a. They talk about divinity and humanity in abstract terms. They do not indicate that the divinity in question is Yahweh, the Father of Jesus, and that the humanity in question is the concrete person of Jesus.

   b. Their interpretation is ahistorical. They say that Christ is man rather than that he became man in living and reacting against a specific situation, and that he became the Son in and through the process of becoming a man.

   c. They presuppose knowledge of who God is and what humanity is at the start, when they should start at the other end. God is the Father of this particular Son, and so we know who God is insofar as we know how Jesus relates to his Father. We know what it means to be a human being insofar as we know how the eternal Son of the Father fleshed out his life in history.

   d. The divinity of Jesus is formulated in ontic rather than relational categories. In the New Testament, by contrast, the divinity of Jesus is generally deduced from his relationship to the Father.

   e. Finally, the christological dogmas explain Jesus' relational nature in terms of his relationship to the eternal Logos rather than in terms of his relationship to the Father (as the New Testament does).

   10.4. *A positive interpretation of the dogma of Chalcedon.* First, despite the conceptual limitations indicated above, the Chalcedonian formula does affirm the basic truth of Christian faith: i.e., that the ultimate meaning of human existence was revealed in Christ. It is in and through Jesus that we learn what God is, what man is, and where salvation lies.

   Second, the Chalcedonian formula offers a model explanation of the person of Christ, saying that in him God and humanity are united without division or confusion. By affirming this union it is affirming categorically that God is in history and that there is no access to him except in and through history—specifically, in and through human beings. It is also saying that God is not history, thereby affirming the "more" that is an essential part of history and that allows for hope precisely within history.

Third, the Chalcedonian formula states positively that Jesus is the eternal Son of God. The model I propose here to enable us to understand that filiation is the model of Jesus' personal oneness with the Father. This means that we must have some understanding of the notion of person, and in this case a specific notion of person, though neither need be highly technical. Here I do not view the notion of person as meaning the self-assertion and self-affirmation of a spiritual subject. Here "person" represents the end of a long process of self-reconciliation in which the subject surrenders his self to another. Historically speaking, Jesus' surrender to the Father takes place through his complete incarnation in a particular situation. Through this concrete, historical surrender to the Father, Jesus becomes the Son in a real rather than an idealistic way. He does so by facing the conflicts occasioned by a sinful situation that goes directly counter to the reality of the Father. To put it in more concrete terms, Jesus lives "for" the Father by living "for" human beings. These two kinds of living "for" others coincide completely in Jesus. That is why and how he becomes the Son. That is why and how he attains fulfillment both in his relationship to God and in his reality as a human being.

Fourth, we must consider a question that seems highly theoretical but has important practical repercussions. We must take seriously the fact that Jesus is the Son, not the Father. Hence it is not exactly correct to say that Jesus is the manifestation of the Father, the "sacrament" of the Father. The Father is and remains the ultimate mystery of existence and history. The Father is not known in himself; he is known only through the Son.

This consideration should prompt us to reformulate Christology in more operational terms. The Son does not reveal the mystery of the Father in such a way that it can be intuited directly. Instead the Son reveals to us how one may respond to this Father, how one may respond to God. In short, the Son reveals the way to the Father, not the Father himself. He thus radicalizes a basic insight of both the Old and New Testaments: Knowing God means going toward God, and accepting the mystery of God means being on a continual search for him. Paradoxical as it may seem, it is only when we adopt that attitude that we can come to know the innermost reality of God.

10.5. Christian faith accepts the notion that the formula of Chalcedon has a universal significance. But the important feature of that universality is that it derives from the content of the formula, not from its character as a juridical act of the church. This means that the formula must necessarily be translated in different concrete situations. Christian faith affirms both the possibility and the necessity of such translating. Without that process of translation Christ would be universal only for one culture or one specific situation—a contradiction in terms. The formula of Chalcedon is universal insofar as it is rendered universal in different circumstances. Absolute fidelity to the formula itself would be the worst sort of infidelity.

What does this mean in more functional language? It means that every human being in every historical situation is offered the possibility of being a son of God if he or she follows the way of Jesus. Faith considers it impossible that the figure of Jesus could ever fail to be of interest to people or to serve as the path to salvation. But if that should happen at any point, then at that point the formula would cease to be true. At that point Jesus would cease to be the revelation of what human beings are, and hence the revelation of who God is.

11. GENERAL FEATURES OF THE CHRISTIAN LIFE FROM THE STANDPOINT OF CHRISTOLOGY

11.1. The summary reflections presented here are not meant to take the place of a detailed study of Christian ethics which would serve as the concrete mediation of the demands imposed by Christian faith. Such concrete mediation must be carried out in every domain—personal, social, economic, and political. What I propose to do here is to present certain traits that seem to be typical of Jesus himself or to be advocated by him and that also seem to be normative for any kind of life that calls itself "Christian."

11.2. There is obviously one limitation bound up with such a focus, and it is usually pointed up in the distinction between "imitating" Jesus and "following" Jesus. Here I propose the following of Jesus (discipleship) as the general paradigm of Christian existence. As opposed to the imitation of Jesus, the following of Jesus presumably takes more account of the differences between Jesus' own situation and that of present-day Christians. Today's Christians, for example, may live in the Third World. There they find themselves in a basic state of structured dependence, but also in a situation that offers more technological possibilities for liberation than were available in Jesus' day.

The biggest difference between the situation of present-day Christians and that of Jesus is the fact that Jesus himself expected the imminent arrival of the kingdom. The difference here is not theological in the strict sense because for both Jesus and present-day Christians God ever remains a future yet to come and a mystery greater than humanity. The difference here lies in the fact that Jesus' expectation of the kingdom's imminent arrival could have a real impact and influence on the way Jesus might envision the reorganization of society in terms of justice and love, and that his view might differ radically from that of people who see a long history ahead of them which is to be fashioned and organized.

11.3. In this context it is worth noting the limited role that the following of Jesus has played in Christian ethics itself, which has been far more influenced by Aristotelian virtues up to recent times. Even more restricted has been the role of discipleship in Christology itself. The positive assertion I wish to make here is that the following of Jesus is both the concrete embodiment of Christian life as well as that which makes it possible for Christians to know Jesus precisely as the Son.

11.4. Looking at the concrete lifestyle of Jesus, we must first consider the special relationship between orthodoxy and orthopraxis. To begin with, we must consider Jesus as an orthodox Jew who shared the Jewish view that Yahweh was the true God. Jesus did not disdain that orthodoxy. The problem he faced in life was not that of choosing between orthodoxy and heresy but that of choosing between an abstract orthodoxy and a concrete orthodoxy. For Jesus it was impossible to concretize his orthodoxy simply by pondering orthodoxy intellectually. It could only be concretized through a concrete praxis. Throughout his life Jesus would be involved in concretizing the meaning of such realities as "God," "hope," and "love."

Jesus demanded much the same of his followers. Discipleship meant following in his footsteps and proclaiming the kingdom; it was a concrete praxis. Over against this Jesus set any sort of abstract orthodoxy that came down to the mere repetition of verbal formulas; he had nothing but anathemas for that. But he did not oppose praxis to concrete orthodoxy because the latter is merely the expression of the former.

It might seem that a different view of orthopraxis and orthodoxy could have developed after Jesus' resurrection. First of all, Jesus himself now became an object of orthodoxy along with God. Second, with Jesus now present as the risen one, one might be inclined to think that the liturgy could provide infallible access to Christ wholly apart from praxis. However, the New Testament reacts strongly against any such distorted view. Even after the resurrection, Christian life is the following of the crucified Christ (Paul), or a life of service motivated by love (John).

Quite apart from these historical reasons militating against a distorted view of orthodoxy, there is a systematic reason as well. The contents of orthodoxy are limit-realities such as God, Christ, salvation, and sin. They cannot be pondered or intuited in themselves. What we know or learn about them cannot be separated from the historical experiences that allow us to make general formulations that are reasonable. The assertion that Christ is the way to the Father can have meaning only for someone who follows the same road. The notion that God is the absolute future can be grasped only in the midst of a historical experience that makes it clear that following the way of Christ does open up vast new possibilities.

Even from the standpoint of orthodoxy itself, therefore, it is obvious that orthodoxy is impossible without some praxis. Orthodoxy can be rendered concrete and Christian only through a specific praxis. Without this our statements about God, Christ, and salvation will remain abstract. They may express "religious" yearning, but they will not express the Christian faith. Hence they will be not only irrelevant but contrary to the experience of faith.

Viewed from the standpoint of praxis, the ultimate supremacy of praxis over orthodoxy is evident. It is evident in the case of the historical Jesus, who stresses the importance of doing the Father's will over crying "Lord! Lord!" Even after the resurrection, praxis continues to be the supreme norm for Christian living in the eyes of Paul and John.

This assertion is not based just on the natural view that action holds supremacy over knowledge. It is based on the very essence of Christian revelation. What happens in divine revelation? We do not get some abstract knowledge about God or some doctrine; we get a manifestation of God in action. What we get in revelation is the historical and historicized love of God. Viewed theologically, the life of the Christian does not consist in knowing about that love but in receiving it and sharing it. Knowledge of it is subordinate to that process, though it is not to be disdained. To put it another way, it would be a complete contradiction to proclaim God's message solely so that it might be pondered and talked about; for that which is communicated is to be received as a liberating love.

Thus the New Testament proposes (1) the supremacy of praxis over mere thinking and (2) the need for praxis if orthodoxy is to become concretely Christian rather than remain abstract.

11.5. Christian life as a whole can be described as the following of Jesus. That is the most original and all-embracing reality, far more so than cultic worship and orthodoxy. Rather than being opposed to these latter, however, the following of

Jesus integrates and crystallizes them. It can be analyzed in terms of three basic dimensions, which have been traditionally described as faith, hope, and charity ever since the New Testament era.

The three basic dimensions have been called theological. That is correct so long as we historicize them even as the reality of God himself was historicized. God is a trinitarian process that entered into history in the incarnation, immersed itself in the depths of history on the cross, marked out the direction of history in the resurrection, and will attain its ultimate synthesis only when God becomes all in all.

Through the Son, God immersed himself in history, plunging into its depths with all that was negative there. Through the Spirit, God has integrated history into himself in such a way that there no longer are two histories. If we view Christian existence as a participation in God's historical process, then we can say that it comes down to participating in the very life of God himself. It is not some mysterious reality of a supernatural or suprahistorical cast that makes us like God. We become like God insofar as we immerse ourselves in the historical process as Jesus did; for that is the option God chose. It is immersion in that process that constitutes the gratuitous gift of faith, whether one does or does not realize consciously that it is the process of God himself. If someone really believes in the possibilities of history despite all the misery around, if one firmly holds on to hope in spite of so much injustice and death, if one practices love in spite of its seeming ineffectiveness, then one experiences this gratuitousness and realizes that love is the ultimate word of meaningfulness. In Christian terms it means that love stands at the very beginning and the very end of the whole process.

The gratuitous dimension of Christian life is not to be determined by differentiating what is natural and historical from something else. It takes on reality insofar as one lives the reality of nature and history in a different way: in the manner of the Son. What Christ has given us is the possibility of experiencing this gratuitousness and fleshing it out in reality to the fullest.

11.6. Suppose we assume that the life of Christian faith is theologically the life of a person who does not yet possess God definitively, who is ever on the way to God and will find consummation in the process of God himself. In that case Christian life is marked by the dialectical interplay of Jesus' cross and resurrection. This is not some particular instance of some universal dialectical schema; it is the direct consequence of the innermost nature of divine revelation. It is this dialectic that prevents faith, hope, and charity from remaining ingenuous and purely idealistic, that makes them real and Christian.

11.7. Christian *faith* is the acceptance of a God who really is greater, whose approach is a saving grace and a promise that was manifested in the resurrection. However, this faith must also maintain the scandal of God's silence on the cross. It is a faith that is constantly being fashioned amid the temptation to unbelief, a faith that constantly overcomes the world and is never given once and for all.

In the concrete, then, this faith is jeopardized by all the crosses of history that seem to manifest the silence of God. It is constantly confronted with the groanings of history: of the Israelites enslaved in Egypt, of Jesus dying on the cross, of all creation trying to come to birth and awaiting its liberation. Faith in God goes far beyond conventional theism and atheism. It takes its stand where things are happening, where the groaning of history can be heard and touched.

11.8. Christian *hope* is hope in the fulfillment of the universe, but it is not naive either. Rather than directing its gaze above and beyond injustice and death, Christian hope takes a stand against injustice and death; it is a hoping against hope. That this hope does not waver or grow weary is again part of the experience of gratuitousness. Without Jesus' resurrection Christian hope could be skepticism or desperation; without his cross it could be mere optimism. Christian hope is a third possibility arising from the resurrection of the crucified one. It enables people to lay hold of history from the standpoint of a future with promise rather than from a present filled with misery. Christian hope believes in a utopia (a "no place") whose "place" is the resurrection and whose "no place" is the cross.

11.9. Christian *love* is also historical, and it is not ingenuous. It is a love historicized in the very midst of the succeeding train of alienations through which humanity passes. It seeks effectiveness, and hence it is political. Its bottomless depths are lost to view because it believes in itself even when it cannot see any results. It has a relationship with power, though the relationship is fraught with tension. It will use power at every level—organizational, ideological, institutional, etc.; but it is constantly aware of the fact that power and its use tends by its own inertia toward oppression rather than liberation. In that sense Christian life can be said to have the task of denouncing oppressive power and transforming all power into service. And it must be ever conscious of the fact that the ultimate work of love is "giving," even if that means giving up one's life.

11.10. Christian life is to be concretized from the standpoint of the cross, but this does not mean that it is to be a mystique of suffering. The cross was the historical consequence of Jesus' praxis. Hence Christian life is formally the following of Jesus, not some intentional union with the sufferings of the cross.

11.11. All that has been said above makes it clear that Christians, like all other human beings, have no direct intuition or insight into God. Christians, too, must maintain the mystery of God, must let God be God. But Christians do know how to respond to that mystery, how we can go toward God. We must follow the example of Jesus and join him in his journey. We must put all that we have in the service of the kingdom. We must maintain Jesus' experience of God's abandonment on the cross through our own experience of a history that continues to be one of injustice. Like Jesus, we must travel the road of service and self-surrender to the end. And because of Jesus, we can die with hopes of resurrection, with hopes of a new heaven and a new earth.

11.12. The same holds true when we consider the privileged locale that mediates God in the concrete. The gospel account of the last judgment tells us what that locale is to be if Christian life is to be based on the concrete figure of Jesus. Authentic orthodoxy means not knowing God directly, means letting God be God. The locale for access to God is the place where we find everything that seems to be the contrary of the divine. The privileged locale is the oppressed person. The access-route to God is the concrete praxis of love. And the proper way to approach the oppressed is the way of the historical Jesus himself. It is the person who lives thus that truly "knows" God, even without realizing it; for his life is a journey toward God.

The gospel scene of the last judgment is equally important for Christian reflection. It shows us where we can find the proper categories for pondering such things as the Christian God, salvation, and so forth. God's existence as an "other" is not mediated through such realities as beauty and power; it is mediated through the "otherness" of the oppressed in relation to the one who approaches them.

The first consequence of this contact is to raise serious questions about what it means to be a human being. This serves as the historical mediation for later questions about the natural person's ideas concerning God's way of being. Approach to the other person is obviously not a matter of contemplation; it is a matter of liberative action in the presence of evil. It is this access to the other, with all its structured nature, that shows us how to gain access to God. The latter is basically not a matter of orthodoxy or of cultic worship; it has to do with the liberation of the "other" human being. Without an approach to human beings designed to effect their liberation, there can be no approach to the God who is totally other.

11.13. Structurally speaking, then, Christian existence is the following of Jesus in a concrete situation. It is living the law of service "for" God and "for" human beings. But even here and now in history we find a paradigm of the sought-for fulfillment in being "with" God and "with" human beings. This is the dimension of festive celebration, of liturgy, in Christian existence. Liturgy is not opposed to discipleship, but it is the latter that makes the former truly Christian. Jesus was thoroughly "with" human beings because he was thoroughly "for" human beings. If we do live out our hope and love in the following of Jesus, then we can and should celebrate our hope and love in the liturgy as well.

Appendix

The Christ of the Ignatian Exercises

In this Appendix I want to offer a few brief reflections on the figure of Christ in the *Spiritual Exercises* of Ignatius Loyola.[1] I wish to examine the impact of this concrete figure on the overall organization of the Exercises and on Ignatius's conception of Christian existence.

Let me point out right at the start that my remarks are not meant to be a scientific and rigorous exegesis of Ignatius's text. I am not trying to spell out what exactly was Loyola's experience of Christ in all its complexity, nor am I interested in dealing with the whole concrete process that led Ignatius to set down his own experience in a structured form. It might well be that Ignatius had a mystical temperament or certain privileged psychological experiences that are not normally to be attributed to people today who read or go through his Exercises. Our aim here is to ponder the text as it has come down to us, and to consider the repercussions it might have for us today.

It is a basic hermeneutic principle that a text always says more than what seems to be in it on the surface. This "more" unfolds in the very process of interpreting the text. The possibility of a new interpretation depends on the gradual development of a new horizon as history moves on. Insofar as we are concerned, then, the text of Ignatius is of interest to us insofar as we live in the horizon of Latin America today and that horizon may prompt and even demand a new Christian understanding of it. This does not mean that we should engage in an allegorical reading of his text, gleaning from it the a priori conclusions we had hoped for. That has been done often enough. It simply means that any reading of the Exercises is, and must be, a rereading based on a given concrete situation.

Here we are not interested in considering the psychological mechanisms that gave the Exercises their traditional power. Nor are we going to be concerned with ascetical or mystical stimuli designed to bring about a change in one's life. We are interested in the bedrock theological principles that are operative, however unconsciously and even inconsistently, in the broad outlines of the Exercises and its main thoughts.

In other words, I am interested in seeking out the theology of the *Spiritual Exercises*. That theology is all the more valuable in that it is implicit for the most part and therefore not ideologized. Clearly the theology of the Exercises is not some superstructure tacked on to Ignatius's own concrete way of living the faith; it is part and parcel of his own developing experience of the faith. That is a great advantage, I think. Indeed it may serve as a paradigm of what a theology ought to be, for theology should always go hand in hand with the concrete process and experience of faith.

THE EXPLICIT AND IMPLICIT THEOLOGY OF THE EXERCISES

Ignatius was not a theologian. In writing the Exercises he did not feel he was doing theology in the conventional sense. For that reason it is important that we distinguish between certain explicit theological statements, which are more the product of the theological and ecclesial milieu of his time, and the more implicit theological conception that seems to underlie the Exercises. In my opinion the authentic theology of Ignatius is centered around a Christology of the historical Jesus and the following of that Jesus. Imbedded in that theology, then, is a certain understanding of God and of sin.

Before I develop that theme, however, we would do well to consider theological and cultural factors that conditioned his work and might seem to discredit my own thesis. First of all, it is obvious that Ignatius read the Scriptures without the aid of any critical exegesis. In that respect he remained a medieval person, suspicious of the new advances in scholarship that were already embodied by Erasmus. He thought that the Gospels really and truly narrated the life of Jesus. In his meditations, then, he dwelt upon a whole series of details and incidents that we today would not consider historical at all.

Second, Ignatius shared the "monarchical" view that prevailed in his own culture and time. This is reflected in some of the expressions he uses (Jesus as the "eternal king"), and in his conception of the hierarchical church (n. 353) when he tries to lay down rules for thinking in line with the mind of the church (nn. 353–70). In his eyes the church was the kingdom of God. Hence working for the kingdom was equivalent to working for the church. We must remember that the same outlook can be found in Bellarmine, who was younger than Ignatius by a few years. Bellarmine insisted that ecclesiology should defend the monarchical structure of the church, and specifically the papacy. So in Ignatius we do not find our modern distinction between the church as the wayfaring people of God and the eschatological kingdom of God.

Third, Ignatius shared certain conceptions of moral theology that are highly questionable today, and this is important insofar as the following of Jesus is concerned. For example, he made a distinction between "all persons who have judgment and reason" (n. 96) and "those who wish to give greater proof of their love, and to distinguish themselves in whatever concerns the service of the Divine King" (n. 97). He also seems to suggest that the following of Jesus depends on God's free volition (nn. 15, 98, 157, 168), and that there is some distinction between a morality based on commandments that is addressed to all and a morality of discipleship addressed only to a chosen few.

Finally, he shared a view of humanity that was tinged with dualism. He noted the division between body and soul, saying that the former was the prison of the latter (n. 47). Thus salvation applied to the soul, and the Exercises were addressed to individuals. It was individuals who had to save their souls (n. 23), to ponder and break with their past sins.

All these things were certainly part of the intellectual and emotional baggage of Ignatius. The question here is whether they were the most characteristic and fundamental part of his own spiritual experience. My opinion is that alongside those explicit affirmations and others like them we can detect a main guiding thread, which is sometimes explicitly stated and sometimes implied, and which constitutes the core of his own spirituality.

I have already defined it as a spirituality grounded on the historical Jesus, but once again certain preliminary observations are in order. First of all, he did not face the problem we ourselves face in this area. On the more superficial level, the exegesis of his day told him that the preaching of Jesus was historical, just as his descent into hell was. On a deeper and more important level, it was obvious to Ignatius that Christianity had to be a praxis. He never thought there was any real alternative approach to Christ to be found in cultic worship, orthodoxy, or mysticism. Thus Ignatius does not explicate the problem of the historical Jesus because the historical Jesus seemed crystal-clear and self-evident to him.

Given the praxis-oriented nature of the Exercises, we can readily see that Loyola's conception of the whole Christ will appear more clearly in the kind of praxis he demands than in any explicit statements about Jesus. We might be able to understand this fact better if we consider another theological example of primary importance. Some are wont to affirm that Paul was interested in the risen Christ, not in the fleshly Jesus. To support that view, they cite a famous passage in his epistles where Paul says that he no longer knows Christ "according to the flesh" (2 Cor. 5:16–17). Quite apart from the fact that the meaning of that text is somewhat uncertain, and that Paul appeals to the crucified Jesus to combat a one-sided theology based on the risen Christ (see 1 Cor. 7:23), Paul's real understanding of Christ can be gathered from those passages where he seeks to prove the Christian nature of his life and apostolate. His basic proof is none other than the fact that he has lived and suffered as the historical Jesus did (see 2 Cor. 6:4f.; 11:23f.;

Gal. 6:17). He also reminds the Thessalonians that their community is truly ecclesial precisely because it has endured persecution (see 1 Thess. 1:3f.).

The point here is that the Christology of Ignatius Loyola is not to be gleaned from his explicit statements about Christ so much as it is to be deduced from the general orientation of his Exercises and the kind of praxis he equates with truly Christian action. Ignatius would not have understood one word in the modern debate over the historical Jesus and the Christ of faith. He would have acknowledged and accepted the total Christ, just as today's Christian should. But in his Exercises he offers us a quintessential way of understanding and approaching that total Christ through the following of the historical Jesus.

A CHRISTOLOGY OF THE HISTORICAL JESUS

We have already seen the typical features of the historical Jesus, and they are summed up in the previous chapter (theses 3–8). What we want to know here is which of those basic features, if any, had an influence on Ignatius Loyola and his Exercises.

The Life of Jesus

On the formal level the first thing that strikes our attention is that Ignatius does not begin with the conciliar dogmas about Christ when he tries to bring the figure of Christ to life in his Exercises. He certainly could have done that, but he did not. He doesn't begin with the Christologies of Paul or John, which are structured lines of theological reflection that come after the real-life happenings of Jesus himself. Nor does Ignatius stop to dwell on the honorific titles of Jesus, though he does refer to him as "Christ, our Lord."

All this is clearly indicative. Though Ignatius Loyola certainly did believe in the total Christ, the Christ of faith, his attention and insight were focused on the actual life of Jesus when he sought to effect a change in people's lives. In the Exercises he focuses on a stage prior to later theological reflection, assuming that the concrete historical happenings of that life were what could and should effect a change in those taking his Exercises. His fundamental intuition is that of Moltmann: "Not every life is an occasion of hope, but that of Jesus certainly is. Out of love he took upon himself the weight of the cross and death."

Most of Loyola's meditations focus on the real life of Jesus. He does not choose to meditate on such things as the christological hymns of the New Testament (e.g., Phil. 2:6–11). It is not that Loyola did not believe or accept them. It is that these embodied a later stage of theological reflection, that they·did not represent the most primitive and original elements in the life of Jesus.

It is also worth noting that liturgy does not play an important role in Loyola's Exercises. There is no concentration on the Eucharist or the sacraments in general. Once again this certainly does not suggest that Loyola valued them any less. It simply underlines his clear and compelling conviction that it was the actual life of Jesus that could and would change a person's life. Contact with Christ was not to come primarily through cultic worship but through following the real life of Jesus.

The Exercises themselves, of course, are not the concrete following of Jesus. They are simply spiritual exercises, which is to say "every method of examination of conscience, of meditation, of contemplation, of vocal and mental prayer, and of other spiritual activities" (n. 1). But they are oriented toward discipleship, as Ignatius brings out in all the basic meditations and from the very start. They are ways "of seeking and finding the will of God" (n. 1).

The key meditations of the Second Week are designed to help the participants (1) to follow Jesus and (2) to make sure that they are doing that as Jesus would want. It is interesting to note that Loyola's line of argument here differs greatly from that which he uses at the beginning of the First Week. When he is talking about the "First Principle and Foundation" in the First Week, he uses arguments that are accessible to human reason, in theory at least. When he comes to the critical Second

Week, his contrast between the temporal king and the eternal king makes it clear that Christian life is the following of Jesus. His comments on the "two standards" spell out what discipleship means. And his reflections on humility and humiliation underline the fact that it is the person of Jesus, not the salvation of one's own soul, that is the ultimate reason behind the Christian life. Personal salvation comes in as a corollary.

To sum up, then, we can say Ignatius viewed the concrete life of Jesus as the factor that could and should revitalize the life of the Christian. His Exercises were designed to help people absorb nourishment from Jesus' life. Ignatius presents scenes from Jesus' life in many of his meditations. He repeatedly tries to bring out the meaning of the events in Jesus' life, so that the participant in the Exercises will identify ever more closely with Jesus in his prayer and be saturated with his psychology. The aim of these meditations, however, is not mere contemplation or contact with Jesus through meditation. They are designed to arouse in the participant a strong disposition toward following Jesus. Without such discipleship Christian life, even the life of prayer, would be meaningless in the eyes of Ignatius. In the Third Week he tries to arouse "sorrow, compassion, and shame" (n. 193) in the participant. In the Fourth Week he urges the participant "to be glad and rejoice" (n. 221). Such sentiments, however, are not an end in themselves. They are meant to help the participant "not to be deaf to his call" (n. 91).

Concrete Features of the Historical Jesus in the Spiritual Exercises

Jesus is not just the Creator-Logos who unfurls our full human potential. He is also the Redeemer-Logos who takes seriously the negative dimension of human existence: i.e., evil, injustice, sin, and death. In the dialectical interplay between pardoning sin and eradicating it, Jesus clearly stresses the second aspect.

The view of sin in Loyola's *Spiritual Exercises* is clearly marked by features stemming from the theology and ecclesiology of.his own day. Ignatius does view sin primarily in terms of the individual person; he does not spell out its structural, social, or collective dimensions. He also sees the damnation of the individual soul as the basic and ultimate consequence of sin. At the same time, however, there are various elements in the Exercises that indicate that the figure of the historical Jesus is exerting some influence on Loyola's conception of sin. Let us consider them first, before we move on to consider the summons to service and the element of conflict entailed in discipleship.

Eradicating concrete sin. First of all, we do not discover what sin really is on the basis of natural reason or of Pauline theology. We find it out by considering what happened to Jesus. Sin, according to Loyola, is what killed Jesus, the Son. Loyola does not go on to a further consideration that we must add today: i.e., that sin kills not only the Son but also the rest of God's children. But his conception of sin is based on a consideration of its consequences rather than on some abstract view of sin in itself.

To that extent, then, Ignatius does historicize his conception of sin even as he historicizes his conception of Jesus. This holds true, even though his way of doing it reveals his ties with his own age. For example, he considers the consequences of the sin of the angels, the sin of Adam and Eve, the mortal sin of someone who dies unrepentant, and so forth (n. 50f., 56).

Loyola wants sin to be pardoned (n. 44), but that is not his main interest in it. Strictly speaking, he wants sin to be eradicated. He wants the soul to "rid itself of all inordinate attachments" (n. 1). This presumes that sin not only affects the innermost being of a person but also has an external embodiment that must be wiped away, though Ignatius certainly concentrates on the personal, individual embodiment of sin. This point is central for Ignatius Loyola, and it is the key to his spirituality. Spirituality does not come down to "good intentions" or the "purity" of one's intentions. Ignatian spirituality comes down to fleshing out one's inner intentions in history even as Jesus of Nazareth did. Expressed in negative terms, it comes down to eradicating sin.

Finally, Ignatius's consideration of one's own sinfulness and pardon does not lead simply to gratitude (n. 61). It leads one toward a practical attitude that will be fleshed out concretely afterwards. For Loyola there is both a rational and a christological attitude toward sin. The rational view considers sin in all its gravity and malice as an offense against the infinite goodness of God that merits eternal condemnation (n. 52). The christological view is the more important one, however. It sees sin as something that kills the Son. It is this concrete historical incarnation of sin that reveals its true nature and triggers the authentic Christian attitude toward sin. We move from a speculative consideration of sin to a practical view: "What have I done for Christ? What am I doing for Christ? What ought I do for Christ?" (n. 53).

Underlying this is a conception of conversion akin to that of the historical Jesus. Put in New Testament terms, it is the transition from faith to discipleship. Put in present-day terms, it is the transition from feeling liberated to liberating others. In Loyola's terms it is the transition from realizing that sin killed Christ to asking what one can do for Christ. The problem of sin does not end with sacramental confession, personal conversion, and gratitude for being pardoned. All that must lead to a decision to act accordingly, and there is obviously a particular figure of Jesus at work here. The famous Ignatian colloquy between Christ and the retreatant is important mainly because of its actual content. It is not just that one can and should make contact with the risen Christ through prayer. In the colloquy the sinner tells Christ what he is going to do, how he is going to historicize his life. If one neglects this thrust towards historicization, which turns out to be the following of Jesus in the Second Week, then one has overlooked what is most basic in Loyola's conception of sin.

The call to service. It is quite apparent that the most original and typical features of Ignatius' thinking and his *Spiritual Exercises* are to be found in the Second Week. It is dedicated wholly to a consideration of the historical Jesus, but under a very specific aspect. It is concerned with a personal election or decision to render service to the kingdom.

Here again we find certain elements that could be viewed in purely rational terms and quite independently of Jesus himself. The retreatant is reminded that he was created "for the praise of God our Lord and for the salvation of my soul" (n. 169). But the viewpoint that will dominate the Second Week is made clear in the first meditation of that week: "The call of our earthly King . . . will help us to contemplate the life of the eternal king" (n. 91). Here we find two fundamental ideas.

The figure of Jesus envisioned here is that of the historical Jesus as he is depicted by the Gospels—which is to say, a Jesus living in an intimate relationship with the kingdom of God. Jesus is presented as the "eternal king" from the standpoint of his activity (n. 91) and his consciousness of a mission (n. 95). This formulation obviously reveals Loyola's ties to the monarchical conception of his own day, but its actual content has much more to do with the biblical image of the Servant of Yahweh (n. 98). Ignatius offers an image of Jesus whose features are those of the historical Jesus after the Galilean crisis. It is a Jesus who now realizes that the kingdom will not be ushered in by his proclamation and his miracles, that he must sacrifice himself to death on the cross.

It is worth noting why the mission of Jesus is offered for the consideration of the retreatant in the Ignatian Exercises. It is not primarily so that the retreatant might simply contemplate Jesus or understand him better. It is because Jesus issues a "summons" to which the proper response is "discipleship." Here we find the same intuition that modern theology has worked out in terms of a hermeneutics of praxis. It is the realization that there can be no real understanding unless there is a concomitant willingness to engage in concrete action. In the logic of Ignatius, which is implicit rather than explicit, all consideration of Jesus becomes relevant for Christian living only insofar as it is done from the privileged standpoint of discipleship.

Insofar as Loyola's view of discipleship is concerned, we can say that his line of argument is personal rather than rational. The following of Jesus does not flow directly from the basic principles that were elaborated in the First Week. Instead it follows from the concrete, historical appearance of Jesus himself. As Loyola sees it, Christian life means adherence to the person of Jesus. It is not concretized primarily in some sort of emotional, cultic, or mystical union with Jesus. It is concretized in discipleship, in concrete personal adherence to Jesus' historical mission. This leads the retreatant to petition God that he may not "be deaf to His call, but prompt and diligent to accomplish His holy will" (n. 91). Throughout the course of the Exercises Loyola tries to bring out what that will might be for a given individual. But the basic lineaments of discipleship are spelled out at the start: "Whoever wishes to join with me in this enterprise must be content with the same food, drink, clothing, etc., as mine. So, too, he must work with me by day and watch with me by night . . . that by following me in suffering, he may follow me in glory" (nn. 93, 95). Loyola's vivid language might seem to suggest mere imitation of Jesus, but he is really spelling out the basic structural norm of discipleship: i.e., living as Jesus did. While God's will for different individuals may be different, nothing can be God's will if it does not correspond with acting as Jesus did.

In this very first meditation of the Second Week, then, we can detect some important features of Loyola's Christology. There can be no Christian living without the historical Jesus, though Christian life may also find expression in prayer and liturgical worship. Without the historical Jesus there can be no access to the total Christ, the Christ of faith. Without the former, the latter remains abstract and open to manipulation. The typical element in the historical Jesus is his mission, which he suffered through to the end in a spirit of loving service. If we want to grasp this Christology aright, then we should view Jesus as one "who sends out a call" and human beings as people who "are open to discipleship."

It is from that standpoint that the figure of Jesus holds interest for Ignatius Loyola, and it has one basic consequence for his whole spirituality. He readily accepted what had traditionally been regarded as the transcendent dimension of faith, the supernatural, and so forth. But he clearly felt that it could not be isolated or separated from the process of verification once it was introduced into the inner life of the person. Christian faith is verifiable. The inner renewal of the individual can be verified in its external historicization, in the concrete work of discipleship. This is brought out quite clearly in the Exercises—for example, when Ignatius talks about the three classes of people. But the main point here is that this is a theological theme, not just a psychological observation. In the eyes of Loyola, access to the transcendent God is a visible, tangible, historical reality embodied in the following of Jesus. Though he does not formulate it in precisely these terms, Ignatius is very adverse to the idea of concentrating on the interior, transcendent dimension of faith to the point where its external embodiment and historicization is overlooked and left unverified. There is no justification for failing to follow the path of concrete discipleship, and we are only deceiving ourselves if we think there is.

The element of conflict in discipleship. Precisely because it is historical, the following of Jesus has one structural feature of the utmost importance. The historical Jesus acted in an unredeemed world, a world fraught with sinfulness. It therefore could not help but be riddled with conflict. Jesus did not proclaim the kingdom of God as something that fit in well with the inertial possibilities of the world. The kingdom of God would be a new creation and hence it would be in utter contradiction to the existing sinful world. In the time of the historical Jesus himself the contradiction was embodied in the conflict between the power of love on the one hand and the oppressive power of religious and political structures on the other.

Loyola does not analyze the element of conflict in discipleship from the standpoint of present-day political theology or liberation theology. Nor does he analyze it from the standpoint of modern biblical theology as I have done in this book. At the same time, however, Ignatius is well aware of the structural element of opposition and contradiction to be found in discipleship. He brings it out somewhat even in his meditation on the call to the retreatant, though there he deals with it more in psychological terms. He makes it very clear that the person who would respond to God's call must "act against" (n. 97).

The conflictual nature of discipleship is brought out most explicitly in his famous meditation on the "two standards." He uses that sort of language to bring out his point, and his vivid contrasts are worth noting: Christ versus Lucifer; Jerusalem versus Babylon; concrete knowledge of life versus deception and deceit; apostles versus demons; and the desire to help people versus the laying of traps and snares (nn. 136–47).

Underlying all these details is nothing else but the necessarily conflict-ridden pattern that emerges in the process of discipleship. Without such conflict discipleship is merely idealistic and ideological. The relationship between the two standards is not a complementary one; one cannot pick and choose between elements of both. Nor is it a dialectical relationship of thesis and antithesis leading to some sort of sublimated synthesis. The relationship between the two standards is one of total contradiction, as was evident in the life of Jesus himself. Jesus told us that no one could serve two masters.

Loyola describes the content of this conflict in terms of two contradictory views of human life. One view envisions life in terms of haughty pride, wealth, and honor, which bring in their train a whole host of vices. The other sees life in terms of poverty, opprobrium, and humility, which nurtures all the virtues (nn. 142, 146).

There is a certain element of ambiguity in Loyola's view of the worldly way of life. Haughtiness and vice are clearly opposed to Christ and are evil. In Loyola's time, however, there was no structural analysis of the alienation caused by the improper distribution of wealth, and so in theory wealth and honor did not seem to be evil in themselves. I think we will get down to the heart of Loyola's insight if we explore this problem a bit more deeply.

First of all, it seems quite evident that Loyola's reflection is not guided solely or primarily by a merely rational consideration of the essence of wealth. His reflection is historical, and it has two main facets. On the one hand he notes that wealth, whatever it may be in itself, has served as a source of dehumanization in history. It has created antagonism between human beings, though Loyola describes it explicitly as an obstacle to doing God's will (n. 154) and a temptation of the devil (n. 142). What is important is the historical observation he makes: Living in accordance with the world's way and contrary to discipleship is, "as Satan is accustomed to do in most cases," giving in to the desire to covet riches (n. 142). On the other hand it is clear that Ignatius does not offer some rational justification for rejecting riches. The positive motivation for such rejection is to be found in the figure of the historical Jesus. He is the ultimate norm of Christian living, and that norm is not open to further criticism or analysis.

The problem posed in the meditation on the two standards is not that of choosing between what is obviously good and what is obviously evil. That problem is presumably resolved in the First Week. The real problem now is choosing between what seems to be good and what is really good, between what is good in the realm of abstract intention and what is good in the realm of concrete living. It would seem that wealth and honor can be good in themselves and also used for good. But are they a real, possible option from the standpoint of discipleship?

Here Loyola has a deep insight which is fully in accord with the historical Jesus. As we noted in the early chapters of this book, the gospel accounts of Jesus' temptation (Mark 1:12f.; Matt. 4:1–11; Luke 4:1–13) describe a basic problem that confronted Jesus throughout his life. He had to choose between two very different ways of working for the kingdom of God. The basic question was: What sort of power really helps to usher in the kingdom? One possibility was messianic power, which would lead to some sort of religious or political organization. The other possibility was the power of love fleshed out in suffering and the cross. At bottom it was the problem of God himself and his authentic mediation in history. Is he merely a God of power or is he a God of love?

Ignatius saw the same problem. He had to unmask the most basic temptation facing the Christian. It was not the temptation to elect sinfulness. It was the temptation to assume that one could use such seemingly good things as wealth, honor, and power to follow Jesus. This is obviously a complicated issue that we cannot explore in depth here. But Loyola's main point is very much the one we saw earlier in connection with Jesus himself. There are indeed many penultimate words in following Jesus, even as there were in the life of Jesus himself: e.g., his miracles. But the ultimate word spoken by Jesus is that of service rendered out of love. That is what helps to usher in the kingdom and that is the ultimate word for discipleship. Hence Ignatius wants to make it clear that even such seemingly good things as wealth and honor cannot serve as the vehicle for the ultimate word on discipleship, which is love. And since discipleship based on love operates in a structure filled with contradiction, it must be fleshed out in poverty rather than in wealth, in opprobrium rather than honor. They are the ultimate historical mediations of love, and hence of discipleship.

Another point is very much worth noting. When Ignatius describes the two contradictory lifestyles, he does not enumerate a list of concrete virtues or vices. Instead he refers to structured modes of living. Instead of discussing cases, he goes to the roots of the matter, contrasting a whole structured lifestyle based on "humility" with one based on "haughty pride." And what interests him most is not the end to be attained but the stages in the process of attaining it.

Ignatius thereby gets beyond any idealistic conception of discipleship that would suggest that one can arrive at a state of humility by mere acts of intent. He reacts sharply against any sort of spirituality based on "good will" or "purity of intention," concretizing and historicizing the process involved in arriving at a state of true humility. His spirituality, like that of the historical Jesus, is thoroughly historical. Ignatius is also very conscious of the danger of spiritualizing the life of discipleship, so he lays great stress on the stages involved in the process; those stages are verifiable. Those who usually move in the realm of wealth and honor cannot arrive at humility. Those who wish to be formed after Jesus and his humility must go through the historical stages of poverty and opprobrium.

Ignatius does not offer a structural analysis of the consequences of these two contradictory attitudes for society and social life. He does not say explicitly that wealth not only dehumanizes the rich but also oppresses the poor. He does not say that the honor enjoyed by the rich is bought at the expense of the poor's domination. In this respect Loyola's analysis must be filled out and completed by the view of current liberation theology and by the structural conception of God's kingdom to be found in the Bible. Yet Ignatius does clearly bring out one point about Christian life and discipleship, though he does it more in terms of the individual person. He makes it quite clear that Christian life and discipleship must be fleshed out in real life and history in accordance with the law of poverty: opprobrium. Submitting to that law, one can arrive at the habitual state of discipleship that Ignatius describes as "humility and all the virtues."

This vision of Christian existence is ultimately rooted in a Christology based on the historical Jesus, as is evident in his meditation on the three ways of humility. As I noted at the start of this chapter, Ignatius did make a distinction between what was commanded and what was counselled in his view of morality. The same distinction appears in his treatment of the three stages of humility when he sets up a contrast between sinning and imitating Jesus. Be that as it may, it is clear that Ignatius sees the concrete life of Jesus as the ultimate motivation for Christian living. It does not lie in commandments or in conclusions about wealth and poverty deriving from socio-economic analyses. As Ignatius puts it: "In order to imitate and be in reality more like Christ our Lord, I desire and choose poverty with Christ poor, rather than riches; insults with Christ loaded with them, rather than honors; I desire to be accounted as worthless and a fool for Christ, rather than to be esteemed as wise and prudent in the world" (n. 167).

His spirituality, however, is one of discipleship rather than of suffering. He does not proclaim some mystique of the cross, suggesting that Jesus' suffering must be imitated for its own sake as suffering. Suffering is simply a consequence of discipleship. Jesus did not take on suffering primarily so that he might shoulder the human condition with its metaphysical limitations. That is not why he ended up on the cross. Jesus took upon himself a conflict-ridden historical situation in which love succumbed to the onslaught of oppressive power. That is why and how he suffered and died on the cross. If we link Loyola's three ways of humility with his two standards, then we can see that the "imitation of Christ" is not the mere repetition of Jesus' own traits. Rather, it means situating one-self·in a concrete situation even as Jesus did. That gives rise to suffering, poverty, opprobrium, and the reputation of being a fool. By virtue of its own situational dynamism discipleship will cause one to imitate many of the traits, risks, and dangers that appeared in Jesus' life.

THE CONCEPTION OF "GOD" IN THE EXERCISES

If the Christ of the Ignatian Exercises is indeed the historical Jesus, if it is that Jesus who gives us access to the total Christ, then we cannot overlook one important feature in the life of Jesus himself. As the book has sought to show, Jesus did not preach about himself. In the last analysis he did not proclaim that people should have faith in him. Jesus preached about God and he worked for the arrival of God's kingdom. This means that a Christology based on the historical Jesus cannot bypass the problem of God. If it did, it would turn into a Jesusology. Since Jesus lived in and for the Father, since his life was a relational one, Christology cannot ignore this fundamental relational dimension in the historical Jesus. So we are led to ask: What conception of God do we find in the Ignatian Exercises? Is it consistent with the view of Jesus to be found in them?

Posing the questions in those terms, we are immediately faced with a serious difficulty regarding the Ignatian Exercises. According to the Gospels, God is the one who is coming. There can be no definitive conception of God until the kingdom is ushered into its full reality. After the resurrection of Jesus, however, Christian faith came to see that the kingdom had already dawned in Jesus and in the real-life discipleship of Christians. The figure of Jesus thus became the concrete mediation of God; apart from that figure one could not come to know God or to gain access to him. In short, the figure of Jesus moves to center stage in the Christian view of our possibility of knowing and approaching God. The logical structure of the Ignatian Exercises, however, does not seem to correspond with that view. It begins with God as the principle and foundation, moves on to consider the life of Jesus, and then ends with God again and with contemplation to attain love of God. Thus the theological scheme of the Ignatian Exercises seems to be God—Christ—God. Is the figure of Jesus really decisive for this scheme, or does Jesus simply illustrate a point that was already brought out in the first meditations on God as the principle and foundation?

If the Christology of the Ignatian Exercises is grounded on the historical Jesus, then I think we would do well to focus on this seeming inconsistency for a moment. We should try to see what it might mean. We should explore the role played by the initial meditation on God as the Principle and Foundation. This may lead us to conclude that the deepest underlying conception of God in the Exercises is not to be found in that initial meditation but elsewhere.

A Different Socio-Cultural Conception

In the initial meditation on God as the Principle and Foundation we find a formulated view of God that could well be called philosophical. In principle it is a view accessible to human reason. Moreover, the figure of Jesus is not needed to formulate the elements that are explicitly treated there: God as Creator, the human being as creature, the end of human beings, the meaning of things, etc. This of course does not mean that the meditation was a product of philosophical musing on Loyola's part. In all probability his conviction about these realities was forged in his concrete Christian, and perhaps even mystical, experience of God. The point of interest to us here is that the text, as it has come down to us, does prescind methodologically from Jesus. It presumably is quite logical and intelligible without having to appeal to Jesus.

Now if that initial meditation on God as Principle and Foundation is logically, if not psychologically, a rational reflection on God, then we must ask ourselves what its significance was in the context of the Exercises as a whole, and what meaning it might have for us today. First of all, we must realize that Ignatius lived in an age when God was taken for granted as part of society and culture. It was a sacral culture and age, though the Enlightenment and its secularizing thrust had already appeared on the horizon. God did not represent a problem, and so Ignatius could appeal to the notion of "God" when he asked people to change their lives or restructure them. Even if he did not mention Jesus explicitly, people could still picture God as a reality in whose presence they could and should find meaningfulness for their own lives.

Today the situation has changed tremendously. Our culture is largely profane rather than sacral. Even in the case of Christians we cannot presume that God is taken for granted as a part of socio-cultural life. The notion of God is not self-evident at any level of life—be it morality, conscious knowledge, politics, or social intercourse. On the socio-cultural level the meaning of life is often bound up with other ideals: e.g., progress, revolution, socialism, democracy, liberty, and so forth. On all these levels God is at least problematical if not superfluous. To the extent that cultural secularization makes headway, there is more and more difficulty in starting off from the concept of "God" when we try to reflect on changing our lives.

A Different Theological Conception of God

Even theologically speaking, we can say that the present-day conception of God seems to differ from Ignatius's explicit conception. (We shall see later that Loyola's underlying conception of God is to be found in the tacit implications of his thought rather than in his explicit affirmations.) When we read his initial meditation on God as the Principle and Foundation, it strikes us as rather theistic. The conception of God to be found there seems to have little to do with the biblical and Christian conception of God. (Once again I am referring to the text of the Ignatian Exercises, not to Ignatius's own personal experience of God.) It seems to present a God who operates as the creator, who is the author of nature. This God has a plan for humanity from the very start, which is quite clear in its demands though their execution may be costly; and he has placed creatures in a hierarchy so that they might help human beings to carry out God's plan. It seems to imply a dualistic vision of the world, since the purpose of human life is the salvation of the human soul in the world beyond. Life here on earth is simply a test through which the soul must pass if it is to achieve salvation. The God of this initial meditation is an omnipotent God, and here omnipotence seems to refer to some abstract power over everything. He also seems to be related more specifically to individuals as such. The basic task of human individuals is to save their own souls, and everything else takes second place to that. Human beings experience God as someone who regulates, orders, and integrates all the data of reality.

Paul's view is wholly opposed to the one just described. In Rom. 1:18–32 he proclaims the total failure of any such natural theology. Though human beings could have attained knowledge of God in that way, indeed though they did come to some sort of divine knowledge that way, the journey to God by that route has ended in total failure. The human heart became darkened, and people distorted the authentic reality of God. Correct knowledge and understanding of reality and created things, which Loyola's initial meditation seems to assume as a possibility, had become an impossibility in history according to Paul: "The wrath of God is being revealed from heaven against the irreligious and perverse spirit of men who, in this perversity of theirs, hinder the truth" (Rom. 1:18). In Paul's eyes it is not enough to argue with the aid of some vague conception of "God." For when "God" is understood apart from the gospel message, it becomes possible for man to use that concept to divinize created reality.

We can see, therefore, that the Ignatian meditation on God as the Principle and Foundation is full of cultural and theological ambiguity. We are prompted to ask what meaning and value it might have, what purpose it serves within the Exercises. We might also wonder if Loyola had another conception of God that goes beyond the one found in his initial meditation.

The Significance of the Initial Meditation on God

To begin with, we must note that the initial meditation on God as Principle and Foundation is not the basis of the Christian's experience of God. If it were, then the later meditations on Christ would logically be superfluous. Even worse, they would degrade Jesus to the level of a mere example showing us concretely how to do something which we already knew in theory from the initial meditation.

The whole meditation on God as Principle and Foundation is rather a preliminary supposition underlying the Spiritual Exercises as a whole. Ignatius does not begin with the God of Jesus but with a consideration of the uttermost roots of human existence, and hence of Christian existence. In the context of Loyola's own time and culture, the most adequate and satisfactory way to discuss the roots of human existence was to view humanity in terms of the deity. Thus the basic logical structure of the Ignatian Exercises is not "the God of Jesus—Jesus—the God of Jesus" but rather "the deity —Jesus—the God of Jesus."

The anthropological premise for undertaking the Ignatian Exercises is that one takes human life seriously. This presupposes some unconditional structural element underlying reality and human life, some absolute correlate other than humanity, on the basis of which we can comprehend who we are and what life is. It might be called "God" or "the deity." We must relate to that absolute element and raise questions about our life accordingly, for we find our life threatened by anxiety, sinfulness, injustice. In short, we must seek self-understanding in and through something radically different from ourselves.

In the overall theological structure of the Ignatian Exercises, then, the initial meditation on God as Principle and Foundation serves to bring out a basic presupposition underlying human life. But it itself is not the basic foundation of human or Christian living. The latter is not grounded on this initial conception of God because the God of Jesus is a different God who can be known only through Jesus. By the same token, however, Christians cannot begin to understand the God of Jesus unless they take human life seriously at the start. To bring out this point, to show that life is to be taken seriously, Ignatius uses a framework and a terminology that derives from his own age and socio-cultural milieu. He talks about God and man, creator and creature, trying to show that human life is conditional and bound up with some outside reality, that it must relate to some absolute pole outside itself. If we want to take our life seriously, then we must relate to that outside pole through concrete attitudes and actions. We must personally establish a relationship with the absolute, unconditioned pole of reality.

It is in that sense that the meditation on God as Principle and Foundation remains fundamental. We must go through that basic meditation if we want to start our journey toward the God of Jesus Christ who is described in the later Exercises. Of course that does not mean that the initial meditation could not be translated into other terms. It should be, when that is necessary. Today, for example, we might present it in terms of the absolute necessity of liberating the oppressed masses. The basic point is that we must take human life and its meaning seriously if we want to go through the Exercises that make up the following weeks.

The Idea of God in the Ignatian Exercises

Leaving aside the whole question of the value, import, and possible reinterpretation of the initial Ignatian Exercise, we must still try to see what its underlying conception of God is. I do not think it finds adequate expression in the initial meditation. Indeed I do not think we will find it stated explicitly by Ignatius, just as his view of Christ is not to be found in explicit statements. We must read between the lines, examining his fundamental insights and trying to detect his notion of God within them.

Another point is also worth noting. Since Ignatius was inclined to focus on praxis, on discipleship, we are not likely to find his view of God in any explicit statements about God in himself. Instead his view of God is to be found in his remarks about the correct way of drawing near to God. Ignatius is more concerned to tell people how they can go to God than to tell them who God is in himself.

First of all, Ignatius makes a basic statement about God insofar as he focuses on the historical Jesus and discipleship as the proper approach to him. To put it in operational terms, we approach the God of Jesus by following Jesus himself. In the initial meditation on God as Principle and Foundation, it is right use of creatures that provides access to God. That "right use" is concretized and christianized in his meditations on the eternal king, the two standards, and the three modes of humility. The road to God is now marked out by the concrete path of Jesus rather than by natural reason. Whatever Loyola's own explicit theological notion of God may have been, the notion implicit in the *Spiritual Exercises* is that discipleship is the way to gain access to the true God.

Apart from these implicit indications of Loyola's notion of God, there are other positive elements in the Exercises that enable us to discern what Ignatius thought about God. Right at the start we find a phrase that will occur again and again in the Exercises. Ignatius wants to help people with the task "of seeking and finding the will of God" (n. 1). Consistent with his practical outlook, he talks about the will of God rather than simply about God. Implied in this statement, however, is a view of God that accords with that of the Bible and Jesus rather than with any purely rational view. For the implication is that the work of gaining access to God is framed in history. Though God is indeed the creator of all things from the very beginning (a philosophical view), we do not arrive at him by going back to the very beginning. We must listen for him here and now, looking for some action in history that will show us who he is (the biblical view). In Loyola's terms, we must wait for him to show us his will.

This view of the search for God is the typical Ignatian and the typical Christian view. In the Old Testament God is a nameless God, and human beings are forbidden to fashion images of him. God is the God of the promise; and when he shows himself, he always proves to be different from what human beings had imagined. In the New Testament God is the God who is greater; or, in Jesus' view, he is the God who is still coming, who is not yet here. Despite all his actual or possible visions, illuminations, and mystical experiences, Ignatius talked about seeking the will of God throughout his life. His view is akin to the Bible's view of God, therefore. God is a God whom we can never wholly possess. We must keep looking for him further. We cannot lay hold of him once and for all in cultic worship, in orthodoxy, or even in mystical experiences. We must allow God to remain greater than us or our conceptions; we must allow God to remain God.

This constant, ongoing search for God does not simply embody our metaphysical restlessness. It is not simply a translation of Augustine's famous line: "Our hearts are restless . . . until they rest in Thee." Our search has its path marked out for itself in the following of Jesus. As Miranda puts it, it is not simply a matter of looking for God; it is matter of looking for God there where he himself told us he is to be found. Ignatius is very much concerned to make sure that this quest is not idealized. To make sure it remains down-to-earth, he instinctively turns to the historical Jesus. It is Jesus who offers a concrete road for all those who really want to look for God.

Ignatius's basic insight here is that God ever remains greater. Eventually he would describe Christian life as effort expended "for the greater glory of God." Expressed in anthropological terms, letting God be God means that God cannot be manipulated, that the desire to manipulate God is the basic theological temptation. At one point in his Exercises, Ignatius analyzes this point in very concrete terms. He does not just present a test to determine how deeply rooted and solid a person's decision for God is. He also offers a profound view of the whole problem of our relationship with God.

The whole issue is symbolized in the "ten thousand ducats," which represents "the sum acquired" (n. 153). The injuriousness of this sum does not lie simply in the fact that it can be used to break some commandment. The real problem is that it can be used as a tool to manipulate God. As Ignatius puts it, "God is to come to what they desire" (n. 154). The problem is not presented in essentialist terms concerning the true inner essence of God; it is presented in operational terms, depicting human temptation to try to manipulate a God who cannot be manipulated.

This approach corresponds with that of the historical Jesus. He, too, had little to say about God in himself, but he often spoke about human efforts to manipulate God through things already acquired. In one classic example he talks about past tradition as a means of manipulating God (Mark 7:8–13). He stresses the non-manipulability of God by talking about him as the God of the future, as the God who is not yet here but who calls for radical trust. We must break away from all the supports we have erected for ourselves through things already acquired. Ignatius brings out the same point by saying that human beings must "go to God" (n. 154).

Ignatius, then, does picture God as the one who cannot be manipulated. The radical temptation is the temptation to try to manipulate God. Here we have, at least in principle, a demythologization of reality. Everything can be converted into something acquired, but nothing is God. The importance of Loyola's work here is not in that bare assertion of course. It lies in his profound grasp of this issue and its seriousness. It is not just that the ten thousand ducats should be given up because they were acquired "not entirely as they should have been" (n. 150). It is that they may become something definitive, thus displacing God. The point is that anything might be converted into something acquired of that sort, and the danger is greatest in the case of things that might seem good in themselves. They force God to come to what we desire. Combatting this tendency, Ignatius insists that we must go out to meet God where God really is. Once again he attacks a spirituality based solely on good intentions. He does not try to resolve the problem by trying to purify our emotional attachment to acquired things; instead he insists that we must give them up if that is what the quest for God demands.

The underlying conception here is that God is absolutely greater than everything else. Rahner sees this as the characteristic feature of Jesuit spirituality, but it is not to be restricted to Jesuits. It should be the spirituality of every Christian. As Rahner puts it, the authentic and basic Christian attitude is that "God ever remains greater than everything else, including culture, scholarly knowledge, the church, the pope, and every institutional reality. We cannot give up God for any of them. Hence the Jesuit must first and foremost maintain a critical attitude towards his past . . . and remain ever open to the new, because he can never absolutize them."

Finally, let us consider the Ignatian view of God in the "Contemplation to attain Love of God." After insightfully presenting the true traits of the Christian God just noted, Ignatius comes to the ultimate and definitive Christian intuition about God, i.e., that God is love. Here again he ponders the matter in operational rather than essentialist terms. How is God's love manifested historically? What should be our response to this loving God?

Ignatius's concrete analysis here treats the historicity of God's love in naturalist terms rather than in the terms presented by the Old and New Testaments. Yet the basic intuition is that God's love expresses itself in some concrete action. He has given us our life and our senses: "God works and labors for me in all creatures" (n. 236). How then are we to respond to this God? In the simplest language Ignatius directs us back to the historical Jesus for an answer to this question. He does not exclude an emotional love for God, but he stresses that the main thing is for us to make ourselves available to God (n. 234). Love must be historicized: "Love ought to manifest itself in deeds rather than in words" (n. 230). The true lover "gives and shares . . . what he has or is able to give" (n. 231).

Thus the aim of this meditation is not to attain contemplative love but to contemplate in order to attain authentic love. By pondering the authentic nature of love, one is led to practice it. For in essence love means service performed out of love. Here the implicit structure of Loyola's thought is akin to that of the Johannine writings in the New Testament. These proclaim that God loved us first (1 John 4:11). We know this, thanks to God's action in history rather than to any abstract reflection on the essence of love (John 3:16; 1 John 4:9f.). We respond to this love with love in return (1 John 4:11). Ignatius follows this same line of thought though he does not concretize it in the same way that the Johannine writings did. The essential point in both is that we must move from an awareness of being loved by God to an active response in works of service.

Here again we find the same conception of God that was entertained by the historical Jesus. According to Jesus we respond by putting all our confidence in God who is drawing near. According to Ignatius, we must offer ourselves up to God (see the famous oblation, "Take, Lord, and receive . . . "). According to Jesus, we respond by engaging actively in service to the kingdom of God through discipleship. According to Ignatius, we must adopt an attitude of giving and accept discipleship (see the Second Week).

All this should prove what I suggested earlier about the basic structure of the Exercises. They do not begin with the God of Jesus Christ, move on to the historical Jesus himself, and then return to the God of Jesus Christ. Instead they begin with the radical seriousness of human life, move on to Jesus as the best embodiment and response to this serious issue, and then end with the God whom we can now comprehend because of Jesus and his pattern of discipleship.

CONCLUSIONS

To end this chapter, we might sum up our consideration of the Ignatian Exercises in terms of several major points.

In exploring the Christ of the Ignatian Exercises we must take cognizance of the limitations imposed by the mentality of

Loyola's own age. We must carefully distinguish between his explicit theological affirmations and his implicit ones, for his most authentic intuitions are often to be found in the latter. My purpose in this chapter was to bring out once again the authentically Christian elements in the Ignatian Exercises and their potential value in our changed situation today.

Even granting the limitations of time and place, we can say that Ignatius does appeal to the figure of the historical Jesus when he wants to help people undertake a radical change in the way of living. This does not suggest any depreciation of the whole Christ, who can and should be approached in prayer and the liturgy. But Loyola's basic stance is that the historical Jesus is the one and only way to the total Christ (see the meditations of the Second Week). Furthermore, consideration of the historical Jesus does not focus on his person as such but on his summons to discipleship. Thus the Christology of the Exercises is a Christology of the historical Jesus that triggers a concrete form of discipleship structured after the activity of Jesus himself.

The conception of God in the Exercises seems to be a bit more ambiguous. Due to the cultural and theological situation of his day, Ignatius did not feel any great need to reflect explicitly on God as such. When he does, moreover, his formulations are more bound up with a philosophical conception of God than a biblical one, with a natural view of God than with a historical one. But this does not mean that his own personal experience of God was not Christian from the start.

For all that, we can find an underlying notion of God in the Ignatian Exercises that is truly Christian, if we pose the question in operational rather than essentialist terms: How do we gain access to the Christian God? The Exercises tell us that we must maintain an ongoing search for God, that the Christian God is not identical with the God of origins depicted by other religions and by Greek philosophy. We should not try to force God to come to us. We must go out to God. God cannot be manipulated. We cannot fashion any images of him, nor can we rightly identify him with anything else, however good it might seem to be. Ignatius makes it clear that the radical temptation facing us is the tendency not to let God be God. There are all sorts of subtle ways in which we give in to that temptation. We may give up our affection for something without giving up the thing itself, pretending that we are thereby doing the will of God. All forms of idolatry are possible. The real way to respond to God is to perform acts of loving service. For God himself is love, and he has manifested this love for us in history.

Ignatius summed up his view of Christian existence as the life of a "contemplative in action." In the light of the Exercises, there can be no doubt about the meaning of this term. It is not a matter of christianizing some action through our contemplation, as is presumed all too often. It is a matter of determining what sort of action will leave room for real contemplation in it. Not every action will do that, and the Exercises present them in terms of contradictory alternatives (e.g., the two standards).

Loyola's aim is to point out the one and only locale where room is left for contemplation in action. It is to be found nowhere else except in the following of Jesus. Within the framework of discipleship we can contemplate history as God's history; we cannot do that anywhere else. Discipleship is the authentic locale of contemplation. It is there that we can see what sin and injustice and what love and hope really are. It is there we can find out who exactly the Son of Man is, the one who preceded us on the same road. Finally, it is there we can find out who exactly is this God who keeps opening out history until he eventually becomes all in all (1 Cor. 15:28).

NOTES

1. All citations from the Ignatian Exercises are taken from the English-language edition translated by Louis J. Puhl, *The Spiritual Exercises of St. Ignatius* (Westminster, Md.: Newman Press, 1954).

INDEX

Ambrose, Saint, 192
Anselm, Saint, notion of God of, 192–93, 202
Apocalypticism, 15 n.10, 75 n.8; see also Theodicy
  and hope, 242
  and understanding of Jesus' Resurrection, 242–43
Aquinas, Saint Thomas, 80, 192
Assmann, H., 2, 10–11, 40 n.41, 139 n.9, 140 n.16, 343 n.4
Athanasius, Saint, 296
Augustine, Saint, 73, 191, 336

Bacon, Francis, 29
Balthasar, Hans Urs von, 86, 139 n.3
Barth, Karl, 31, 308 n.9
Beauchamp, P., 177 n.1
Belo, F., 178 n.11
Benoit, Pierre, 177 ns. 6,7
Bergson, Henri, 178 n.24
Bloch, Ernst, 29, 308 n.6
Boff, Leonardo, xi, 16 n.25, 76 n.9, 140 n.12, 141 n.28, 272 n.12, 344 n.8
  and Christ the Liberator, 33
  and eschatology, 64, 355
  and hope, 230
  and Jesus' faith, 139
  and kingdom of God, 44
  and love, 233
  and the Resurrection, 239
Boismard, M.E., 170, 177 ns. 6,7
Bonhoeffer, Dietrich, 197, 308 n.9
  and access to God, 221
  and grace, 263
  and the historical Jesus, 274
  and reconciliation, 262

Bornkamm, Günther, 177 n.2, n.10
Borrat, H., 16 n.25
Braun, Herbert, 168–69, 177 n.10
Brotherhood, 45, 104, 121–23
Bultmann, Rudolf, 7, 9, 77 n.15, 78 n.23
  and Christ of faith, 273
  and cultic liturgy, 300–301
  and Resurrection of Jesus, 229, 237, 247, 262
  and theory of Christ's death, 211
  and theory of eschatology, 63, 355
  and theory of history, 247
  and the "way," 288
van Buren, Paul, 330, 344 n.9

Cardedal, O.G.de, 344 n.9
Chalcedon, Council of, 3–5, 22, 81, 104, 105, 202
  and doxological statement about Christ, 231
  formula of, 4, 81, 328, 330–32 340–42, 386–88
Christianity,
  and church-state relationship, 294–96
  and Roman Empire, 294, 369
Christology, see also Dogma, Incarnation, Latin America, Moltmann, J., Natural Theology, Pannenberg, W., Paul, Saint, Rahner, K., Theodicy, Theology
  approaches to
    biblical, 5, 82
    dogmatic, 3–5, 81
    experiential, 6, 82–83
    kerygmatic, 7, 353

425

Christology *(continued)*
    from Resurrection, 6, 82
    soteriological, 8, 353
    of ascent and descent, 337
    changes in, 104
    and Christian morality, 108ff., 121
    clues for framing one's own, 17–18
    dangers of, with regard to histori-
        cal Jesus, 83–84
    and Epistle to the Hebrews, 302
    and hermeneutics, 349
    and the historical Jesus, 85
    and Jesus' faith, 104–5
Clement of Alexandria, Saint, 290
Comblin, José, 16 n.25
Constantine, Emperor, 295–96
Conversion, 122–23, 125–26
    defined, 56 ff.
Cross of Jesus, 193, 204, 209, 214 ff.,
        369–74; *see also* God, Incarna-
        tion, Moltmann, J., Natural
        Theology, Reconciliation,
        Spirituality, Theodicy, Theol-
        ogy, Transcendence, Trinity
    early Christian explanation of, 189
    and Greek philosophy, 195–99,
        373–74
    as historical consequence of life,
        202–4
    and new concept of God, 179
    and Resurrection, 231, 233–34
    and salvation, 227
    as "scandal," 185, 190ff., 371ff.
    as symbol, 234–35
Cullmann, Oscar, 77 n.16, 78 n.29
    eschatology of, 63
    and Zealotism, 212
Cyril of Alexandria, Saint, 191, 328

Didache, 159–160
Discernment, 145 n.47; *see also*
        Morality
    of Jesus, 129
    necessity of, 129, 136
Discipleship, 57–59, 92, 93, 126–29,
        132–33, 212; *see also* Kingdom
        of God

and cultic worship, 275, 279ff.,
        299ff.
    defined, 69, 115, 116, 256, 394
    demands of, 115, 116, 360–62
    and discernment, 129
    and Ignatian Exercises, 405–12
    and power, 297
    radical, 127–29
    and Resurrection, 244–45
Docetism, 284
Dodd, C.H., 62
Dogma
    and Christology, 311, 337–39
    christological formulas of, 326–32
    historical development of notion
        of, 312–16
    interpretation of, 316–21
    and Justin Martyr, 330
    necessity of, 325–26
    and Nestorius of Constantinople,
        328
    and Philip Neri, 314
    positive value of, 321ff.
    and Vincent of Lerins, 313
Duns Scotus, John, 141 n.24, 336
Duquoc, Christian, 139 n.3, 344 n.8
Dussell, Enrique, 196

Ebeling, G., 139 n.3
Ecclesiology, shift to from Christol-
        ogy, 287
Egenter, R., 143 n.39
Ellacuría, Ignacio, 11, 40 n.42, 77
        n.17, 141 n.28
Enlightenment, 27
    defined, 19
    and liberation, 348
Epicurus, 195
Ernst, J., 75 n.4
Eschatology, *see also* Pannenberg,
        W., Theology
    defined, 62
    and God, 66
    and God's transcendence, 219–20
    and the kingdom of God, 354–55
    and the Resurrection of Jesus, 236,
        271

theories of
Boff, 64–65
Bultmann, 63
Cullman, 63
Dodd, 62–63
Jesus, 65–66
Moltmann, 64, 355
Schweitzer, 62, 63, 355
Eusebius of Caesaria, 191, 295

Faith (Christian)
in absence of God's reign, 57
in Christ, 269
in Christian existence, 231–32, 393
in cultic worship, 302
as distinguished from religion, 275
formulation of, 317
in the kingdom, 51
and morality, 136–38
origin of, 184
post-Resurrection, 182 84
in Resurrection, 237–40
tensions of, 275, 287–88
as trust in God, 361
Faith of Jesus, 79, 85–87, 95ff., 366; *see
also* Kingdom of God
characteristics of, 91, 102–3
history of, 91ff., 104
and Jesus' temptations, 96–100
Latin American approach to, 86
in New Testament, 86–91
Father of Jesus
and abandonment on the Cross,
184–85, 191–92, 218–19,
225–26, 231
and the Cross, 208–9
and early Christian experiences of,
267ff.
and Jesus' relationship to, 70–72,
101–2, 141 n.22, 269, 335–37,
386–87
and mission of, for Jesus, 70, 91,
as object of Jesus' activity, 155
in prayer of Jesus, 165–66, 174
and self-awareness of Jesus, 363,
366
will of, and Jesus, 156–57

Faynel, P., 344 n.9
Flick, M., 343 n.4
Frankfurt School, 29
Freedom
Jesus and, 46, 47
and sin, 49
Freud, Sigmund, 30
Fuchs, E., 139 n.3

Galerius, Emperor, 295
Galilea, Segundo, 16 n.25
Garaudy, Roger, 308 n.6
Gardavsky, V., 308 n.6
Gnilka, J., 177 n.1
Gnosticism, 284
God, *see also* Eschatology, Transcendence of God
access to, 206
as basis of Jesus' prayer, 158
and Cross of Jesus, 217–19, 224–25
as grace, 163–64
and Jesus' abandonment, 225
Jesus' relationship with, 173–74
as love, 166, 214, 225
and love for humanity, 226
and power, 209ff.
silence of, 188
sovereignty of, 163
and traditions of prayer, 160–161
Gonzalez Fauss, J.I., 344 n.9
Grace
defined, 262–63
and the impossible, 164
and Jesus' notion of God, 163,
208–9
and kingdom of God, 46, 51, 208,
213, 355, 357
Grillmeier, A., 344 n.8
Gutiérrez, Gustavo, xii, 11, 38 n.2,
140 n.10

Hadrossek, P., 143 n.39
Hahn, F., 75 n.2, 78 n.29
Häring, Bernard, 142 n.35
Harnack, von, Adolph, 15 n.12, 61,
354

Hegel, Georg,
  and the absolute, 223
  and death of Jesus, 196
  and influence on Rahner, 23
  and "person," 73, 141 n.24, 336,
    364
Hermeneutics, 291–92; *see also*
  Christology, Moltmann, J.,
  Pannenberg, W., Rahner, K.
Historical method, 247–49
History, *see also* Moltmann, J., Pannenberg, W.
  existentialist concept of, 249–50
  one-sided concept of, 250–51
  positivistic concept of, 248–49
  in terms of promise and mission,
    251–53
Hope (Christian), 230–31, 232–33,
  241ff., 361, 393; *see also*
  Apocalypticism, Bloch, E.,
  Rahner, K.,
Hubris, 221

Ignatius of Antioch, Saint, 288
Ignatius of Loyola, Saint, 143 n. 38,
  263; *see also* Rahner, K., Exercises of, 396ff.
Incarnation
  and the cross, 215
  defined, 207, 268
  as principle of Christology, 124

Jeremias, J., 9, 78 n.32, 177 ns.1, 3, 6,
  8, 9, 10; 273, 308, n.3
Jesus, *see also* Cross of Jesus, Discernment, Discipleship, Eschatology, Faith of Jesus,
  Father of Jesus, God, Kingdom of God, Liberation
  Theology, Mission of Jesus,
  Oppression, Pacifism, St.
  Paul, Pharisees, Prayer of
  Jesus, Resurrection of Jesus,
  Sin, Sinners, Zealots
  actions of, 357–58
  biblical approach to, 5
  brotherliness of, 106–7

  and Christians, 106–7, 226–27
  crisis in life of, 93–95
  death of, 180, 204, 213, 369
  defined, 3
  divinity of, 107
  dogmatic approach to, 3
  eschatology of, *see* Eschatology
  experiential approach to, 6
  external conflicts of, 367ff.
  and forgiveness of sins, 49–50
  historical focus on, 3, 9–13, 84, 397
  ignorance of sonship of, 100–101
  and justice, 121–23
  and miracles, 48, 76 n.13
  and morality, 133, 136ff.
  necessity of reflection upon, 1
  notion of God of, 174–75, 177 n.10,
    206, 208
  and pacifism, 122
  personal oneness of, with God, 336
  and politics, 209–13
  poverty of, 124
  and power, 53–54, 203, 209ff.,
    358–59
  self-awareness of, 67–70, 73,
    362–66
  sonship of, 106–7
  temptations of, 96–100, 129
  tensions between historical view
    of, and faith view of, 278ff.,
    381–84
  titles of, 267–71, 284–86, 378–79
  and universal love, 214
  as way to the Father, 340
  words of, 356–57
Johannine theology, *see* Theology,
  Johannine
Judaism, 299
Justice, *see also* Reconciliation
  personal, 119ff.
  social, 120ff., 133
Justin Martyr, Saint, 290, 330

Kähler, M., 7, 273
Kant, Immanuel
  and influence on Karl Rahner, 23
  and liberation of reason, 348

and Moltmann, 29
and Pannenberg, 26
Käsemann, Ernst, 9, 75 n.4, 205, 206
  and cross of Christ, 309 n.16
  and historical Jesus, 273, 280, 287
Kasper, W., 10, 315
Kautsky, K., 308 n.6
Kerygma, 159–60
Kingdom of God, 75 n.2, 104; *see also*
    Grace
  and Christian morality, 113–14
  and consciousness of Jesus, 67–69,
    363
  and conversion, 55–56
  defined, 42–46, 119, 209–10
  and discipleship, 361
  and faith of Jesus, 91–92, 94, 103
  and forgiveness of sins, 49–50
  Jesus' relationship to, 173, 210, 213
  and miracles, 48–49
  and the political realm, 210
  in preaching of Jesus, 41, 141 n.22,
    209
  realization of, 121, 122, 124, 125,
    134
  and sin, 50–52, 203
Klappert, B., 271 n.1
Kunneth, W., 14 n.9

Lactantius, 295
Latin America, *see also* Liberation
    Theology
  Christology of, 33–46
  cross in tradition of, 180
  oppression in, 35
Liberation, 116, 395; *see also* En-
    lightenment
  and the cross, 180
  and the Spirit, 226
Liberation theology, 10, 79, 195–96,
    224
  in Latin America, 34–35, 87, 274,
    353
  and Marx, 348
Logos, 287, 291
Love
  and access to God, 300

of Christian, 233, 263, 394
  as effective action, 135–36, 214
  and Jesus' prayer, 165–66, 173
  of neighbor, 168ff.
  and power, 136, 213, 298
  and Resurrection, 255
  as suffering, 126, 135–36
  as supreme value in life, 126
Loyola, Ignatius of, *see* Ignatius of
    Loyola, Saint
Lyonnet, Stanislas, 144 n.42

Machovec, M., 308 n.6
Marx, Karl, 20, 27, 30, 348
Marxism, and the historical Jesus,
    274
Marxsen, Willi, 9, 238
Melito of Sardis, 295
Miracles, 48, 76 n.13
Miranda, J.P., 16 n.25, 75 n.2, 144
    n.44, 220, 232, 419
Mission of Jesus, 91ff.
  failure of, 93
  and Jesus' temptations, 96
  and Resurrection, 254
Moltmann, Jürgen, 15 ns. 10,13; 21,
    22, 64, 75 n.8, 78 n.25, 199,
    228–29, 235 n.1, 257 n.10, 308
    n.9, 309 n.16, 355, 401
  and Bacon, 29
  and Barth, 31
  and Bloch, 29
  Christology of, 28–32
  and concept of history, 251–52
  and cross of Jesus, 15 ns.10,13, 182,
    234, 308 ns. 9, 16, 22
  and Feuerbach, 30
  and Frankfurt School, 29
  and Freud, 30
  and God's love, 197
  and Jesus' abandonment by the
    Father, 218, 219, 228–29
  and Kant, 29
  and Marx, 30
  and Pannenberg, 29, 140 n.11
  and Resurrection, 245, 253, 254,
    256

Moltmann *(continued)*
  and the state and deity, 293
  and theology, 326
Morality, *see also* Jesus, Kingdom of
    God
  absolute character of, 127ff.
  and conversion, 125–126
  defined, 109ff.
  foundation of, 137
  goal of, 119
  and historical Christology, 108ff.
  historically situated, 133–34, 137
  and justice, 121–22
  and need for discernment, 128, 136
  "ought" in, 110–13, 143 ns.38,39
Myth, 271 n.5

Natural theology, 222
  and Christology, 349–50
  and the cross, 222, 370
  defined, 221
Neri, St. Philip, *see* Philip Neri, Saint
Nestorius of Constantinople, 328
Niederwimmer, K., 178 n.10
Nietzsche, Friedrich W., 180

Oppression, 35, 223
  and God's love, 166, 173
  and Jesus, 47, 49
  use of power and relationship to,
    53–54
Origen, 191, 295
Orthodoxy, 389–91
  Jewish, 59–60
Orthopraxis, 2, 56, 59–60

Pacifism, 122
Pannenberg, W., 21, 22, 75 n.3, 76
    n.14, 78 n.28, 102, 140 n.11,
    141 ns.21,22, 142 n.33, 177
    n.10, 271 n.5, 343 n.4, 344 n.6,
    345 ns.16,18,21
  Christology of, 25
  concept of history of, 250
  and eschatology, 355
  hermeneutics of, 27
  and Marx, 27

and Resurrection, 238–39, 247
and surrender of Jesus to the
    Father, 336–37
Paul, Saint, 399
  and "Christ Jesus," 285
  concept of revelation of, 289
  and false theology of Resurrection,
    280–81, 381
  and Jesus' pre-existence, 268
  and knowledge of God of, 415
  letter to Hebrews of, 89–90, 302,
    366, 383–84
  and "the Lord," 267
  and Resurrection, 255
  and risen Jesus, 143 n.38, 270, 279
  and "the Son of God," 267–68
  and speech in Areopagus, 288–89
Perrin, Norman, 178 n.10
Person, 364, 387
  and Augustine, Saint, 73, 336
  and Duns Scotus, 336
  Greek notion of, 72–73
  and Hegel, 141 n.24
  philosophical meaning of, 336
  and Richard of St. Victor, 336
  theological meaning of, 336
Pflammatter, J., 257 n.1
Pharisees, 205–6, 208, 211
Philip Neri, Saint, 314
Plato, 195
Politics, 209–11; *see also* Kingdom of
    God
Poverty, 124
Prayer
  apocalyptic tradition of, 161
  and God as love, 159
  and God's transcendence, 159, 173
  locale for, 176
  of petition, 148–49
  and praxis, 149
  prophetic tradition of, 160–61
  sapiential tradition of, 161
  and silence of God, 161
  vitiation of, 147–148, 149, 150
Prayer of Jesus, 73; *see also* Love
  content of, 152–54, 175
  in crises, 155–57

decisional, 152
to the Father, 157, 160ff.
and Jesus' notion of God, 158,
160–61, 163–64, 165–66, 173–74
Jewish religious, 152
locale of, 175
personal, habitual, 152–53
of thanksgiving, 154–55

Rahner, Karl, 14 n.3, 21, 22, 38
ns.4,5,10, 140 n.16, 141
ns.30,31, 177 n.1, 178 n.10, 272
n.12, 343 ns.4,5, 344 n.9, 345
n.15; *see also* Hegel, Kant,
Teilhard de Chardin
and Chalcedon, Council of, 23
Christology of, 22–25
and faith in Resurrection, 106
and hope, 257 n.6
and hypostatic union, 333
and Jesuit spirituality, 145 n. 47,
347, 421
Reconciliation, 120
and the cross, 262
as justice, 120–21
Old Testament ideas of, 209–10
Resurrection of Jesus, 229, 231,
233–34, 236, 241ff.; *see also*
Hermeneutics, Love, Mission
of Jesus, Moltmann, Pannenberg, Paul, St., Rahner
christological meaning of, 264
historicity of, 246ff., 374ff.
soteriological meaning of, 262–64
theological meaning of, 260–62,
376–77
Richard of St. Victor, 336
Robinson, James M., 38 n.13
Roman Empire, 294–96
Ruckstuhl, E., 257 n.1

Salvation, *see* Cross of Jesus
Sartre, Jean-Paul, 20, 28
Schenke, L., 177 n.11
Schierse, F.J., 272 n.11
Schillebeeckx, Edward, 343 n.4, 344
n.6

Schlink, E., 344 n.6
Schnackenburg, Rudolf, 77 n.18, 143
ns.37,40, 144 n.43, 145 n.48,
272 n.9
Schneider, G., 177 n.6
Schoonenberg, P., 139 ns.3,5, 343
n.4, 344 n.9
Schüller, B., 142 n.36
Schupp, F., 343 n.4
Schweitzer, A., 355
and eschatology, 62
Schwiezer, Eduard, 283
Sin
attitude of Jesus toward, 50–52, 53,
92, 95, 120–21, 203
collective, 54, 120
defined, 52
in Ignatian Exercises, 402–4
personal, 51–53, 54
relation of, to power, 54–55
social aspect of, 52
universality of, 54
Sinners
anathemas against, 53
defined, 53
Smulders, P., 344 n.8
Soteriology, *see* Christology, Resur-
rection of Jesus
Spirit of Jesus, 137–39, 279
Spirit, Holy, 226, 269; *see also*
Liberation
Spirituality (Christian)
and the cross, 215–16
defined, 215
Stockmeier, P., 310 n.27
Strauss, S.F., 67
Suffering, 224
Suffering Servant, 186, 270

Teilhard de Chardin, Pierre, 23, 272
n.12
Tertullian, 192
Theodicy, 223–24
and apocalypticism, 243
and Christology, 349–50
and the cross, 371
and liberation theology, 224

Theodosius, Emperor, Edict of, 296
Theology, *see also* Latin America, Liberation theology, Moltmann, Natural theology, Resurrection of Jesus
  and the cross, 225
  and eschatology, 355
  Johannine, 77 n.12, 227–28, 268, 270, 362
  tension between, and faith, 286–92
  tensions of, 292ff.
Therrien, G., 145 n.46
Thomas Aquinas, Saint, 80, 192
Thüsing, W., 139 n.3, 177 n.1
  and faith of Jesus, 86
Transcendence of God, 163–65
  based on cross, 222, 370

New Testament perspectives of, 220–21
Old Testament perspectives of, 219–20
Trinity
  evolvement of doctrine of, 269
  in light of cross, 226

Vidales, Raul, 14 n.2, 16 n.25
Vincent of Lerins, 313, 314

Weiss, J., 62, 355
Wiederkehr, D., 139 n.5, 344 n.9
Wulf, F., 177 n.1

Zahrnt, H., 15 n.12
Zealots, 211–12

OTHER ORBIS TITLES

THE COMING
OF THE THIRD CHURCH:
An Analysis of the Present and Future of the Church

Walbert Buhlmann

"Not a systematic treatment of contemporary ecclesiology but a popular narrative analogous to Alvin Toffler's Future Shock." America

ISBN 0-88344-069-5 CIP   *Cloth $12.95*

ISBN 0-88344-070-9   *Paper $6.95*

FREEDOM MADE FLESH
Ignacio Ellacuria

"Ellacuria's main thesis is that God's saving message and revelation are historical, that is, that the proclamation of the gospel message must possess the same historical character that revelation and salvation history do and that, for this reason, it must be carried out in history and in a historical way." Cross and Crown

ISBN 0-88344-140-3   *Cloth $8.95*

ISBN 0-88344-141-1   *Paper $4.95*

CHRISTIAN POLITICAL THEOLOGY
A MARXIAN GUIDE
Joseph Petulla

"Petulla presents a fresh look at Marxian thought for the benefit of Catholic theologians in the light of the interest in this subject which was spurred by Vatican II which saw the need for new relationships with men of all political positions." Journal of Economic Literature

ISBN 0-88344-060-1   *Paper $4.95*

CHRISTIANS AND SOCIALISM
Documentation of the Christians for
Socialism Movement in Latin America
edited by John Eagleson

"Compelling in its clear presentation of the issue of Christian commitment in a revolutionary world." The Review of Books and Religion

ISBN 0-88344-058-X *Paper $4.95*

THE CHURCH AND
THIRD WORLD REVOLUTION
Pierre Bigo

"Heavily documented, provocative yet reasonable, this is a testament, demanding but impressive." Publishers Weekly

ISBN 0-88344-071-7 CIP *Cloth $8.95*

ISBN 0-88344-072-5 *Paper $4.95*

CHRISTIANS, POLITICS
AND VIOLENT REVOLUTION
J.G. Davies

"Davies argues that violence and revolution are on the agenda the world presents to the Church and that consequently the Church must reflect on such problems. This is a first-rate presentation, with Davies examining the question from every conceivable angle." National Catholic News Service

ISBN 0-88344-061-X *Paper $4.95*

THEOLOGY FOR A NOMAD CHURCH
Hugo Assmann

"A new challenge to contemporary theology which attempts to show that the theology of liberation is not just a fad, but a new political dimension which touches every aspect of Christian existence." Publisher's Weekly

ISBN 0-88344-493-3 *Cloth $7.95*

ISBN 0-88344-494-1 *Paper $4.95*

THE GOSPEL IN SOLENTINAME
Ernesto Cardenal

"Upon reading this book, I want to do so many things—burn all my other books which at best seem like hay, soggy with mildew. I now know who (not what) is the church and how to celebrate church in the eucharist. The dialogues are intense, profound, radical. The Gospel in Solentiname calls us home." Carroll Stuhlmueller, National Catholic Reporter

ISBN 0-88344-168-3 CIP   *Cloth $6.95*

THE CHURCH AND POWER IN BRAZIL
Charles Antoine

"This is a book which should serve as a basis of discussion and further study by all who are interested in the relationship of the Church to contemporary governments, and all who believe that the Church has a vital role to play in the quest for social justice." Worldmission

ISBN 0-88344-062-8   *Paper $4.95*

HISTORY AND
THE THEOLOGY OF LIBERATION
Enrique Dussel

"The book is easy reading. It is a brilliant study of what may well be or should be the future course of theological methodology." Religious Media Today

ISBN 0-88344-179-9   *Cloth $8.95*
ISBN 0-88344-180-2   *Paper $4.95*

LOVE AND STRUGGLE
IN MAO'S THOUGHT
Raymond L. Whitehead

"Mao's thoughts have forced Whitehead to reassess his own philosophy and to find himself more fully as a Christian. His well documented and meticulously expounded philosophy of Mao's love and struggle-thought might do as much for many a searching reader." Prairie Messenger

ISBN 0-88344-289-2 CIP   *Cloth $8.95*
ISBN 0-88344-290-6   *Paper $3.95*

WATERBUFFALO THEOLOGY

Kosuke Koyama

"This book with its vivid metaphors, fresh imagination and creative symbolism is a 'must' for anyone desiring to gain a glimpse into the Asian mind."
Evangelical Missions Quarterly

ISBN 0-88344-702-9   *Paper $4.95*

ASIAN VOICES
IN CHRISTIAN THEOLOGY

Edited by Gerald H. Anderson

"A basic sourcebook for anyone interested in the state of Protestant theology in Asia today. I am aware of no other book in English that treats this matter more completely." National Catholic Reporter

ISBN 0-88344-017-2   *Cloth $15.00*

ISBN 0-88344-016-4   *Paper $7.95*

THE PRAYERS
OF AFRICAN RELIGION

John S. Mbiti

"We owe a debt of gratitude to Mbiti for this excellent anthology which so well illuminates African traditional religious life and illustrates so beautifully man as the one who prays." Sisters Today

ISBN 0-88344-394-5 CIP   *Cloth $7.95*

POLYGAMY RECONSIDERED

Eugene Hillman

"This is by all odds the most careful consideration of polygamy and the attitude of Christian Churches toward it which it has been my privilege to see." Missiology

ISBN 0-88344-391-0   *Cloth $15.00*

ISBN 0-88344-392-2   *Paper $7.95*